Introduction to
Urban Studies

Fourth Edition

Roberta Steinbacher | Virginia O. Benson

Maxine Goodman Levin College of Urban Affairs Cleveland State University

Kendall Hunt
publishing company

Cover image © Shutterstock, Inc.

Image on pages 1, 113, 225, and 313 courtesy of Sanda Kaufman

Kendall Hunt
publishing company

www.kendallhunt.com
Send all inquiries to:
4050 Westmark Drive
Dubuque, IA 52004-1840

Printed in the United States of America
10 9 8 7 6 5 4 3 2 1

CONTENTS

PROLOGUE

Introduction to Urban Studies provides students of the city with a textbook that mirrors the rich complexity of the city itself. *Introduction* is a holistic text in the largest sense, meaning that the **whole city** is presented in the pages of this text. The city is studied from many angles, from the lenses of several disciplines. This "multiple perspectives" approach combines to produce one of the sharpest and most rewarding depictions of the modern city ever presented in an introductory textbook on urban studies. This combination of disciplines and perspectives allows, for example, students interested primarily in geography or psychology to anchor their study of the city in chapters connected to their own majors or specific fields of study, and also to enrich that understanding with the methodology and viewpoints of other disciplines and fields making up the interdisciplinary field of urban studies.

The unique strength of *Introduction to Urban Studies* is the large number of academic disciplines and professional fields embraced in the text. A second key strength of the book is that it succeeds in explaining the theoretical perspectives of a number of different disciplines and how practitioners actually apply these academic theories daily in the practical world of urban policymaking and administration.

Professors Virginia Benson and Roberta Steinbacher have drawn on their own disciplinary backgrounds and training in urban geography and urban psychology, and on their combined experience teaching introductory urban studies students to produce a text as complex, rich, and varied as the modern city itself. This is a text that admirably succeeds in introducing the city to the student, and the student to the numerous disciplines that comprise urban studies. Students who take the time and effort to read this text carefully will come away with a clear understanding of what urban scholars mean when they refer to the "urban tapestry" or the "metropolitan mosaic." Benson and Steinbacher have succeeded admirably in crafting this *Introduction to Urban Studies,* and in providing a foundation for understanding both the theory and practice of contemporary urban studies.

Robert J. Waste, Professor, Emeritus
Department of Public Policy and
Administration
California State University, Sacramento

ACKNOWLEDGEMENTS

We are deeply grateful to Winifred Weizer and Melissa Sikon without whose generous assistance this fourth edition of *Introduction to Urban Studies* would not have been possible.

We also wish to thank Lisa Thomas, Mary Beckenbach, Caryn Eucker, Melanie Hmada, Philip Leiter, and Doreen Swetkis for their support and invaluable contributions.

Roberta Steinbacher
Virginia O. Benson

CONTRIBUTORS

Virginia O. Benson
 Cleveland State University

Thomas F. Campbell

Mittie Davis Jones
 Cleveland State University

Ashok K. Dutt
 The University of Akron

Claire L. Felbinger

Faith D. Gilroy
 Loyola University in Maryland

Sanda Kaufman
 Cleveland State University

W. Dennis Keating
 Cleveland State University

Jun Koo
 Korea University

Gerald M. Neumark
 Georgia State University

Harvey K. Newman
 Georgia State University

Anindita Parai

Wornie L. Reed
 Virginia Tech

Dorothy Remy

Claudette A. Robey
 Cleveland State University

James E. Robey
 Mohr Partner

Stephanie Ryberg
 Cleveland State Unversity

J. Peter Shannon Jr.

Roberta Steinbacher
 Cleveland State University

David C. Sweet

Michael J. Tevesz
 Cleveland State University

Rajiv R. Thakur

Robert J. Waste
 California State University,
 Sacramento

Winifred Weizer
 Cleveland State University

Lesley Wells
 Judge, United States District
 Court
 Northern District of Ohio

PART I
Urban Places

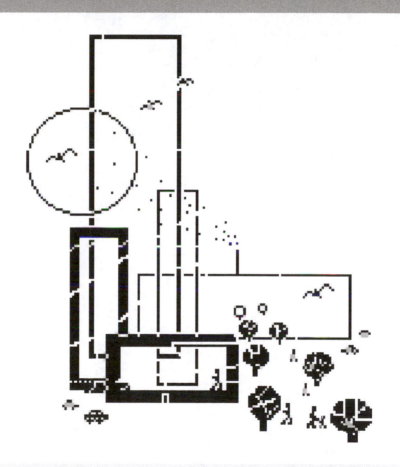

The City Evolves
(History)
Thomas F. Campbell

In 1991, Americans were pointedly reminded of modern society's dependence on certain basic commodities when the nation went to war in the Persian Gulf to protect its greatest source of energy—oil. It would be as hard to conceive of a modern city's functioning without oil and its byproducts as without electricity. In ancient times, things were not all that different. The inhabitants of early cities needed ample supplies of food and water, along with the security afforded by their location and fortifications. These same basic considerations have continued through the centuries to be seen as essential to the survival and prosperity of cities.

Images of the City

Lopez (1966) recounts that in early Egyptian handwriting the ideogram representing the word **city** consisted of a cross enclosed in a circle. (See Figure 1.1.) The cross represented the convergence of roads which bring in and redistribute people, merchandise, and ideas. The circle indicated a wall or moat. He argues that even today no other definition of a city is more fitting, for technological innovation and economic development were bound to come about at the intellectual crossroads of such an environment.

There are other thought-provoking ideas about the essence of a city. Henri Pirenne (1937), the noted Belgian historian, believed that a market was the essential center of a city. Islamic scholars defined a city as a place with a mosque, a bazaar, and a public bathhouse. Western thought has tended toward legal definitions. In the United States, a city is a municipal corporation, defined by the size of its population, but rarely reaching the prominence of the much smaller cities of the Italian Renaissance, such as Florence and Venice.

Social thinkers as disparate as Karl Marx and Thomas Jefferson looked with disfavor on the rise of cities. Marx believed cities were parasitic in nature, and his followers in the twentieth century tried unsuccessfully to limit their growth. Jefferson regarded them as "sores on the body politic," antithetical to democratic ideals, although he grudgingly came to the view that they were necessary evils. His disapproval of urban life influenced Americans' discomfort with cities, an attitude which persists to this day.

Figure 1.1
Symbol of the city in early Egyptian hieroglyphics.

Nevertheless, American cities are still very young when set against the history of cities stretching back more than 5,000 years. Urban centers in the Fertile Crescent and Egypt set the pattern for the future. In their early years, these cities had much in common. All had theocratic government located in the central part of the city, surrounded by the principal civil and religious buildings. Further from the center were the homes of the servants, while just inside the city walls lived the craftsmen and their workers. Outside the enclosure lived the hewers of wood and the drawers of water.

As trade developed, so did the population of these ancient cities, where craftsmen of different ethnic and religious backgrounds made their homes. Foreigners skilled in gold, silver, pottery, and other crafts were welcomed, and soon there were streets or blocks peopled by those of a single ethnic group. Such development was characteristic of pre-industrial cities. For example, London's Lombard Street, the banking and financial center of the city, evolved from the street where Italian goldsmiths from Lombard settled during the seventeenth century.

Migrants from the countryside and immigrants from abroad brought not only their skills, but also new ideas and inventions. The newcomers were valued for their contributions, whatever their beliefs or lack of them. The old German proverb "city air makes men free" reflected the freedom from encumbering tradition and the receptiveness to new ideas. In the bustle of the marketplace there were new challenges to existing religious philosophy, science, and political thought that demanded flexibility and ingenuity.

The Growth of Cities

As cities grew in size, strength, wealth, and confidence, they spread beyond their walls into their hinterlands and became wealthy imperial powers. The name of the sixth century Persian King Croesus was synonymous with enormous wealth. The rush to empire building was contagious as cities grew and multiplied in the Middle East, India, and China.

Along the shores of the Mediterranean Sea, the Phoenicians, skilled traders and warriors and masters of mercantile ship construction, spread both urban life and imperial controls as far as the European mainland. Later, the Greek city-states grew in power and wealth, and in time they too expanded along the northern shore of the Mediterranean from Spain to Asia Minor. The achievements of these early imperial city builders set the pattern for western European powers.

The Roman Empire

The Roman Empire, which had stretched from Asia Minor along the northern shores of Africa and much of Europe, reached its farthest western frontier when Julius Caesar invaded England in the first century B.C. The Empire built cities in order to hold its vast region together and was the single most important generator of European urbanization. Rome needed to construct an administrative apparatus to exploit the natural resources of conquered lands for the benefit of the state. The Romans built scores of cities to house their armies and administrators, but they simply did not have enough citizens to staff these operations; they then trained subject peoples to perform administrative tasks.

Ironically, in so doing, the Roman Empire sowed the seeds of its own destruction. In time, the "barbarians" rejected their subservient status and used their newly acquired skills and knowledge to destroy their Roman masters. Ultimately, the imperial system fell into sharp decline, and the city of Rome was reduced to a mere skeleton of its former glory. In the wake of the fall of Greco-Rome, the Parthenon of Athens, where once the famous lawgivers and orators held sway, lay in ruins, peopled only by shepherds and their flocks.

The conventional wisdom holds that in the period between the fall of Rome and the rise of Italian city-states such as Venice and Florence, Western Europe fell into the Dark Ages. In reality, many other Roman cities remained vigorous provincial capitals where Roman Catholic bishops and local medieval princes replaced the former Roman Proconsuls.

The most important legacy of earlier urban civilizations was literacy. The invention of writing made it possible to transmit to succeeding generations the political institutions, technology, ideas, and customs of the cities of the past. Sjoberg (1960) notes that the knowledge of many fields of learning, such as medicine and astronomy, survived in Western Europe's smaller cities and in the Eastern Roman Empire. It was the later Byzantine and Arab Empires that not only transmitted the fuller heritage of Rome and Greece but also added their own improvements to that body of knowledge. The famed Arab traders expedited the flow of knowledge, including the concept of zero and the decimal system of numerals, which they learned from the Hindus. During the middle ages, the learning of the Arabs, particularly their knowledge of medical practice, was far superior to that of their contemporaries in Europe.

Europe

Pirenne (1939) argues that Europe's long isolation ended with the eleventh and twelfth century invasions of Asia Minor and Egypt by Christian crusaders. The invaders were amazed by the wealth and splendor of the Byzantine and Arab cities such as Constantinople, Damascus, Cairo, and Baghdad. Their stories about the riches of the East excited great curiosity and envy. With the Mediterranean Sea now in control of Christian Europe, trade in spices, jewelry, and fine cloth began to flourish, particularly among the Italian and Greek residents of city-states such as Venice, Genoa, and Florence. Germans came over the Alps, and English and Flemish merchant fleets sailed to the Mediterranean to secure these goods. This trade became a major factor in stimulating town development in Western Europe.

This new commercial activity stimulated local trade and new markets in the inland cities. New trade routes opened up and old towns and sea and river ports were revitalized. Great international fairs held at important trade junctures in Europe attracted merchants from all parts of the continent.

The extensive commercialization in the Italian city-states led to the invention of new business practices: double-entry bookkeeping, maritime insurance policies, and the replacement of trade with currency or credit arrangements to meet the needs of more complicated trade exchange. Commercial banks opened and flourished.

As urban centers of commerce prospered, they became a magnet attracting the young and adventurous. Both old and new cities witnessed the rise of an affluent middle class who worked to shape their communities. Trade guilds sprang into existence to protect and regulate their members' business interests and eventually were able to act in unison to influence municipal policies. Great merchant princes such as the Fugger family of Germany were wealthy enough to loan money to kings in return for protection against lawless feudal barons who threatened the security of the highways. As the nation states evolved, wealthy merchants used their influence and money to exert political power in the newly unified countries of France and England.

The strong sense of nationalism fostered by these political struggles became a kind of secular religion best exemplified by Shakespeare's Henry V speaking to his common English soldiers on the morning of the battle of Agincourt. Appealing to their sense of national duty and patriotism, the young hero-king reminds them that it is the feast day of St. Crispin:

> *He that outlives this day and comes home safe will stand a tiptoe when this day is named. . . . We few, we happy few, we band of brothers (Henry V).*

While trade and nationalism were of great significance in creating a new order, the European Renaissance (fourteenth to sixteenth centuries) turned people's thoughts from a heaven-centered universe to one dominated by thoughts of this world. The renewal of interest in the scientific discoveries of the past and a deeper appreciation of Arabian scientific contributions to mathematics, medicine, and astronomy enriched European scholarship. Even in such a mundane matter as cleanliness, the Arab cities, with their municipal water systems and public baths, had much to teach the westerners.

As a result of this explosion of scientific knowledge and interest, great strides were made in the field of geography and in the techniques of mapmaking, shipbuilding, and the construction of navigational tools. With the invention of the printing press, this knowledge could be quickly disseminated throughout the known world.

In European cities, these developments were reflected in a new sense of anticipation and excitement about the future. Stories from travelers such as Marco Polo, along with the missionary zeal and scientific exploration of Prince Henry of Portugal, stimulated further exploration along the coast of Africa. The dream of finding new sea routes to the Far East eventually drove explorers such as Columbus into a search for new lands to conquer, both for gold and for "the glory of God."

By the mid sixteenth century, Spain, engorged with shiploads of imported gold and silver from the New World, was the richest country in Europe; but its treasures and blood were spent in acts of conspicuous consumption and unprofitable wars in Europe and against its much hated Protestant rival, England. England, for its part, established firmly planted colonies on the North American shore in the early seventeenth century with English adventurers and families who, for various reasons, wanted to build a new life in a new world. The expansion of these settlements marked the beginning of the most successful and influential empire in history. Like Rome, the British imperialists found it necessary to create colonial urban centers for purposes of administration.

Behind the English success in establishing its overseas empire lay a number of important geographic, economic, intellectual, and institutional factors. As an island, England was somewhat isolated from the endless European wars and did not have to bear the expense of large standing armies. Her chief defense was a merchant navy that could double as a naval force when necessary. As a seafaring island, England was ideally located for both European and overseas expansion.

Internally, sixteenth century England had witnessed great social, economic, and religious upheavals that increased the power of the throne and of the merchant capitalist class, who had established joint stock-trading companies, such as the East India Company. These successful enterprises lent money to the reigning monarch, financed freebooting sea captains, (e.g., Sir Francis Drake), supported colonization, and above all earned tremendous profits.

By the late seventeenth century, these merchant capitalists and their landed allies in the aristocracy controlled Parliament. Nowhere was this more evident than in the enactment of the navigation laws that ensured that England should profit from colonial expansion by becoming the workshop, market, and administrative center for all these far-flung enterprises. In return, the colonies would benefit from the increased strength of the empire and be defended from rapacious powers such as France, Holland, and Spain.

By the time of the major English colonization in the New World, the Protestant Reformation was firmly established; but there were some English, Scots, and Scotch-Irish who, differing in religious philosophy and practice from the established Anglican church, were eager to start a new life in the North American colonies. This group of immigrants was well educated and industrious. Many came from the more urbanized areas of the British Isles.

During the same period in England, the Enclosure Acts, passed to enable more extensive sheep grazing in support of the wool industry, were displacing thousands of families from the land on which they had worked for centuries. These "sturdy beggars" flocked to the towns to form the nucleus of the new urban labor force.

By the latter part of the seventeenth century, ebullient and self-confident merchants and manufacturers were enriching themselves and the country by the manufacture and export of cloth, coal, and metal wares. Old market towns were revitalized and new towns blossomed forth in the north, midlands, and west of England. The great shipping and trading port of London reached a population of 75,000 by the mid seventeenth century to become the greatest **entrepot** in the world.

Even as the urban merchants and landed classes prospered, most of the masses lived in extreme poverty, often homeless and with no visible means of support. Bindoff (1958)

Figure 1.2
Example of a Hogarth satirical print.
(© Burstein Collection/CORBIS.)

points out that it was London city officials who first analyzed the whole ensuing complex of distress and sought remedial action in the form of homes for children, hospitals for the sick, outdoor relief for the aged, workhouses for the willing, and houses of correction for the idle.

Despite these palliative measures, the poor remained wretched, relieved only by escape to cheap gin. "Drunk for a penny, dead drunk for twopence, clean straw for nothing" was a familiar saying of the day. The satirical prints of Hogarth (See Figure 1.2) immortalized the lives of London's poor. The larger provincial cities were worse than London with less social order, less charity, and more disease. Such urban conditions left an indelible impression on Thomas Jefferson when he visited England in the 1780s. He believed that large urban centers in the United States would prevent the growth and development of democracy.

North America

It is not surprising—given such social tensions, rising population pressures, and increasing religious dissension—that many middle class Englishmen and women sought social, economic, and religious salvation in the New World of North America. The first permanent English colony took root on Virginian soil in 1607. For protection against the Indians, the ill-prepared settlers erected a stockade village, which in time became the town of Jamestown. After suffering many tribulations, they were able to survive through the cultivation of successful cash crops of tobacco. Later settlers were successful in cultivating rice and cotton.

Geographic, social, and economic factors worked together to keep the South from establishing cities on the northern scale. The profitable returns on major crops made agriculture the dominant feature of the society until after World War II. The river-indented southern coastline provided easy access to the inland plantation warehouses, obviating the need for seaport cities. The planter class that rose to power invested its earnings into the purchase of more land and slaves. Their social ethos inhibited them from engaging in haggling over money like "common tradespeople." Even when they were freed from the restrictive features of the English navigation laws, southerners believed that operating mills and factories was not the work of gentlemen.

The second significant English settlement took place in 1629. Puritan clerics had challenged King James I's religious dogmas in 1603 and were forced to flee to Holland. By 1640, this group and their followers, over 20,000 Puritans, had settled in the Massachusetts Bay Colony.

From the beginning, the Puritans were very different from their southern compatriots. Their leaders were upper middle class, well educated, and deeply religious. They believed in a learned, instructive ministry. Most of their clergy were university graduates who placed great emphasis on education. The General Court of the colony established Harvard University only a few years after the arrival of the Puritans.

The Puritans sought to emulate the sophisticated urban society from which they came, coupled with a sense of religious righteousness. Their leader, Governor John Winthrop, said on board the Arbella: "Wee shall be as a Citty upon a Hill." Historian Darrett B. Rutman (1982) saw these words as distilling the essence of Winthrop's thinking about the kind of society the Puritans were going to establish in the New World. The 700 passengers would live in a single centralized city with their place of worship, government buildings, and homes and gardens surrounded by small farms—a spiritual and temporal fortress against their enemies. It was to be a city of men doing God's work on earth, far removed from what they saw as the immorality of England. Winthrop believed the Puritans had a covenant with God to build a city on a hill that would be a Christian model for the world to behold and emulate.

Early Cities in the United States

Boston, founded in 1630 as the primary city of the Massachusetts Bay Colony, was built according to a plan that was to become typical in New England. The two focal points were Dock Square along the river and the Common, the center of the community where an open market, the church, municipal buildings, and houses were located. As the city grew, the Colony laid out additional towns, which numbered twenty by the 1640s.

New Haven was a good example of how towns began in America. The founders petitioned the General Court for a charter. The town plan consisted of a grid of nine squares. The center square became the common, while the other squares were later subdivided by new streets. These frontier towns were to serve as a fortress against foreign rivals and Indians, to provide a governmental center for supervision, control, and the exchange of ideas, and to furnish a marketplace for the exchange of goods and farm products.

Like the Puritans, other religious groups and social reformers viewed the town as essential for civilized living and the maintenance of social order in the midst of the vast untamed frontier. These early settlers feared social disintegration in a new society without strict traditional controls. Even the religious rebel Roger Williams, forced to flee Boston, established another city, which he named Providence.

New York and Philadelphia, two other seaport cities founded in the seventeenth century, were to play significant roles in the development of early America. New York originated as a Dutch trading port at the mouth of the Hudson River. This river, reaching back into the interior of the mid-Atlantic region, was destined to become a great highway of commerce and communication. When, many years later, it was linked to the Great Lakes by the Erie Canal, it became a major instrument for the development of the Old Northwest.

From the beginning, New Amsterdam, as the Dutch named it, became a port of entry for a wide variety of nationals from diverse cultures and religions. The English conquered the Dutch possession in 1664, renamed its principal city New York, and within a few years controlled the American seaboard from Maine to Virginia. New York City became a major export and import center for the British Empire.

Philadelphia, like Boston, was conceived by religious reformers. The Quaker William Penn, who was granted the charter to what is now called Pennsylvania, had a well developed plan to help relieve the economic and spiritual distress that plagued Europe and the British Isles. He believed that encouraging immigration would enable the poor to improve their status in life. As a result of his vision, thousands of German, Welsh, English, and Irish settled in the new colony.

Penn told his agents that he wanted to build a city on a spot that was healthy, dry, and suitable for navigation. His great town was to combine town and country living. While he favored warehouses near the Delaware River docks, commercial expansion was not stressed. His surveyor, Thomas Holme, laid out instead a city along the lines of a British military encampment with open squares set at intervals in a modified grid system. Although the result was not the semi-rural town that Penn had hoped to build, he retained a good deal of control over its development, managing to prevent the overcrowding of multiple subdivisions until after the American Revolution when the new State of Pennsylvania came into power.

The Puritans of Massachusetts, like the Quakers of Pennsylvania, proved unable to maintain the primacy of religion and a shared sense of community in the face of the availability of cheap land and the opportunity for amassing private wealth. The aftermath of the American Revolution saw the arrival of a large number of immigrants who were not committed to the ideals of the early settlers but sought to improve their own lives. Economic and community development were expected to follow along lines similar to Adam Smith's economic theory of the invisible hand. Smith believed that as individuals prospered, the community as a whole would eventually benefit from their well-being. The social planning and controls of Winthrop and Penn began to give way to the exigencies of the free market. The loss of a shared sense of community was to have a great impact on the development of cities in America.

Although the new nation that came into existence in 1783 was primarily rural, scores of cities dotted the Eastern shoreline. Three of them, Boston, New York, and Philadelphia, had played major roles in the revolutionary break from England. The gentlemen of the rural South joined forces with the northerners to give leadership in the struggle, but it was the urban masses, inspired by the oratory of Thomas Paine of Philadelphia and led by men such as Sam Adams of Boston, that formed the vanguard of Yankee militancy.

Yet it was the urban centers that suffered the most as an economic consequence of the revolution. Americans had gained their political freedom, but economic independence was yet to be achieved. Now separated from the British Empire, they lost the lucrative trade with England and its West Indian colonies. Soon the great hinterland to the west excited people's imaginations, and the urban entrepreneurs turned their attention to the exploitation of the newly acquired Northwest Territory. Ambitious merchants from the cities increased their penetration of the upstate hinterland while the more adventuresome Scotch-Irish pushed forward into the Ohio Country, helping to establish the town of Cincinnati.

Located on the Ohio River, Cincinnati was primarily a military fort to protect the incoming settlers from hostile Indians. Its position on the great Ohio waterway, and its ambitious citizenry, transformed it within a few years into a thriving manufacturing and trading center. By the 1860s, with a population of over 160,000, it was known as the Queen City of the West. Envious southerners complained that it manufactured every need of its inhabitants from swaddling clothes to coffin nails.

In the northeastern corner of Ohio lay the Western Reserve of Connecticut, a speculative venture of the Connecticut Land Company, that had to wait to develop it until the defeat of the Indians in 1794. Two years later, Moses Cleaveland surveyed the land at the mouth of the Cuyahoga River at Lake Erie to establish the hamlet that carries his name today. The river/lake location was strategic for its development, but it was not until the completion of the Erie and Ohio-Erie canals in the 1820s that extensive urban growth occurred.

What happened in Ohio was repeated in the remaining states carved out of the Northwest Territory. Great cities were built along the southern shores of the Great Lakes. Nowhere was there such spectacular growth as in Chicago. Founded as a city in 1837, it soon surpassed Cincinnati by becoming the nation's chief grain center after the railroad network spread west across the country. It, too, profited from the Civil War and became the nation's meat packing center, "hog butcher to the world," as Carl Sandburg (1916) wrote. Fifty years after Chicago's birth, its population passed one million. In the rest of the world, it had taken most cities thousands of years to reach that number.

Many men and women helped create this great metropolis, but as Daniel Boorstin (1965) wrote, it was the businessmen in their capacity as ardent city boosters who "made" instant cities out of cornfields. He cites William B. Ogden of Chicago, Dr. Daniel Drake of Cincinnati, and General William Larimer of Denver as examples of such men. All expressed complete confidence in their adopted cities, which they believed would become important and prosperous urban settlements. They invested in real estate, promoted and built canals, railroads, streets, parks, bridges, and even historical societies in towns that had no historical past. Each was determined that his city would have a great future.

Not everyone shared the boosters' enthusiasm for rapid urbanization. Many intellectuals, Protestant clerics, and writers such as Emerson, Thoreau, Hawthorne, Melville, and Henry James echoed Jefferson's fear that democracy and public morality would be destroyed by the metropolis. It was not until Walter Whitman and Carl Sandburg that there were a few voices in praise of the vitality and strength of the city. Much more recently, Jane Jacobs (1961) asserted the role urban neighborhoods played in maintaining a sense of community within the larger city.

Well into the twentieth century, protestant clergy and church women were convinced that the great cities were dens of iniquity filled with superstitious papists and other outcasts of Europe. Countless sermons, novelettes, and melodramatic plays conveyed this message which was declared in the title of Samuel Paynter Wilson's (1910) little volume, *Chicago and Its Cess-Pools.* The attitude persists today, as reflected in a New York Times (1986) poll which revealed that the majority of Americans believed that the rural way of life was most satisfying.

At the turn of the century, average Americans gloried in the vitality and promise of their cities, where they marveled at the tall buildings scraping the skyline and enjoyed the entertainment and bustle of downtown shopping streets. In 1893, 28 million visitors to the Chicago World Fair were inspired by the ordered convenience and beauty of the "White City" built on the shores of Lake Michigan.

For the immigrant masses, the streets of America might not have been paved with gold, but they offered opportunities far beyond the horizons of the wretched European hovels or the southern cotton fields from which these masses had come. Despite the squalor of the cities, middle-class Americans found a stimulating environment in which to settle and carve out professional or business careers. A leading Progressive lawyer, Newton D. Baker, commented that perhaps the clouds of black industrial pollution were the price society had to pay for progress (Campbell, 1966).

In fact, the urban population almost doubled between 1880 and 1910 to reach 42 million, while the rural population increased by only one third. By 1910, the major cities of the United States were in place and continued to grow along with the suburban development around their rims. Miami, with its tourist attractions, and Tulsa, Houston, and Dallas, which were built by oil wealth, were the only metropolitan centers to develop into major cities in the twentieth century.

Much of this enormous increase in urban settlement in the nineteenth century took place in the West as a result of the expansionist policies of Congress, which passed the Homestead Act and provided federal support for transcontinental railroads during the Civil War. These two measures, plus the post-war support for more federal troops to protect settlers against Indian attacks, peopled the West and extended urbanization to the Pacific coast towns of San Francisco, Los Angeles, and Seattle, as well as to inland communities such as Kansas City, St. Paul, and Fort Worth.

The rise of Los Angeles was spectacular, even in an age of overnight cities. First developed as a result of a speculative boom in the 1860s, it experienced an explosion in growth in the 1880s after the railroad reached the coast and sponsored cheap excursion fares. A dollar ride from Kansas City to Los Angeles was bound to secure new residents. Such tours were extensively advertised in local newspapers and served a purpose similar to contemporary free trips to Florida designed to sell time-share condominiums or retirement homes. During the summer of 1887, over ten million dollars worth of property lots were sold in Los Angeles, and similar promotions in other cities resulted in the state's becoming the sixth largest in the nation by 1900. Los Angeles's expansion never stopped.

By 1940, its population was 1.5 million. Just thirty years later, it had become the second largest city in the nation with a population of nearly seven million people.

In the South, most cities were of modest size and fell into economic decline after the Civil War; but New Orleans benefited by increased traffic on the Mississippi River, while Atlanta, Louisville, and Dallas were revived and developed by the coming of the railroad in the 1880s. A cornfield in the 1870s before iron ore was discovered in its hinterland, Birmingham grew into a little industrial giant overnight. Capital from the North, the railroad's arrival, and sharp real estate promotion combined to turn it into a city of 132,000 by 1910.

Yet the growth of southern cities was modest compared to that in other sections of the country until after World War II, when the needs of the Cold War combined with shrewd political maneuvering to bring a pork barrel of "fair share" national defense and space projects to the South. It was said of one Louisiana Congressman that if his district got one more defense plant, it would sink into the Gulf of Mexico.

There was one American city whose development was unique: the capital of the United States. Congress located it on the Potomac River in the midst of a ten square mile area called the District of Columbia, and President Washington accepted the offer of a young French architect named Pierre L'Enfant to draw up plans for the new city. The capital was to be dominated by public buildings connected by broad avenues arranged to create fine vistas and landscaped open spaces. It was a magnificent plan that took many years to complete.

When Lincoln became President, the capitol dome was as yet unfinished, and the great hole for its unfinished dome was symbolic of the condition of the city. Thousands of civil servants and soldiers flocked to Washington during the Civil War, and their presence finally created a building boom that brought the population to over 100,000 by 1865. It was President Lincoln, ever mindful of symbolism, who encouraged the completion of the capitol's great dome.

After the Civil War, the growth of Washington D.C. kept pace with the growth of the federal government, which expanded greatly during two world wars and the great depression. During the nineteenth century and the first half of the twentieth, the city was linked to the rest of the country by an extensive railroad network. After World War II, the link was strengthened by a massive highway building program and the advent of a national aviation network.

The Egyptians' ancient epigram, a cross surrounded by a circle, representing the convergence of roads which bring in and redistribute people, merchandise, and ideas, remains a fitting symbol for the role of cities in the development of the United States. In the early years, two immense oceans created the relative isolation that is represented by the circle. Yet the circle's perimeter remained permeable so that the greatest migration of people in the history of mankind entered the crossroads to contribute their ideas and skills and aspirations to the building of a new society out of a wilderness.

More than 300 years have passed since the founder of the first city on the Atlantic seaboard aspired to build "a city upon a hill." Winthrop's dream of creating a more perfect society has been a lodestar for the city builders of succeeding generations that must search anew for the ways to make the city meet the needs of increasingly complex societies.

Name _____

The City Evolves (History)

1-1. What were the major reasons for the establishment of the world's first human settlements?

1-2. Plot these settlements on the map on the next page.

1-3. Along what rivers were these settlements established?

1-4. Compare and contrast the role of transportation in early American cities with today's American cities.

1-5. Utilizing your own definition of family, write a seven to ten page paper tracing your family's origins and migrations to your present urban residence.

1-6. Why is your central city located where it is? (What were the factors and resources that led to its location?)

The City Relies on Its Foundations
(Geology)

Michael J. Tevesz and Winifred Weizer

Introduction

Unless faced with some imminent disaster, people in cities usually are unconcerned about the structure and dynamics of the earth beneath them. This benign neglect is often costly, because geological materials and processes directly contribute to both building up and tearing down the visible structure and underpinnings of a city. Thus, a thorough awareness and understanding of the geological infrastructure of a city is essential to the successful structuring and maintenance of the urban framework and the health and well-being of its inhabitants.

The crust of the earth, that outer rind of the planet which supports all life, is mainly rock, a solid material composed of minerals. Every major feature of the crust, its covering of water, sediment, and living matter, is somehow related to this rock. Liquid water covers about 75% of the crust and is contained in basins and channels made out of rock or its weathering product, sediment. Water is also an infiltrator of sediment and rock, insinuating itself in fissures and pore spaces as groundwater, like liquid in a wet sponge.

Sediment, which appears as a granular or muddy bottom coating in water-filled basins and as soil on the land's surface, is generated when its parent rock is physically disintegrated and chemically decomposed. Primordial crustal rock that is parent to sediment and soil via weathering was igneous in origin because the entire outer layer of the planet was at one time molten. Subsequent rocks are derived from this original supply through a process geologists describe as the rock cycle, in which the three types of rock composing the crust (**sedimentary, igneous,** and **metamorphic**) are interconverted by physical and chemical conditions of their environment.

All living organisms are dependent upon rock, sediment, soil, and water. For example, soils supporting green plants (and thereby almost all land–based ecosystems) are produced by the weathering of rock and are given their life-sustaining properties by the presence of humus, which is derived from once living organisms and their products. Living organisms, generally composed of over 90% water, must absorb this substance from the environment. On land, the water needed to sustain life is contained in or on both rock and soil, while in the oceans and lakes it envelops organisms and is enriched in important nutrients by materials eroding off the land.

Rock, sediment, and water are enveloped in and often impregnated by discrete volumes of the ocean of gases called the atmosphere. The atmosphere imparts a dynamism to these crustal components through the transfer of energy from the sun and energy derived from phase changes in water, coupled with the effects of gravity and the rotational motions of the earth. This atmospheric energy empowers wind and water with the ability to rearrange features of the earth's surface, including human-fashioned structures such as cities.

Thus, these few dynamic components—rock, sediment, air, and water—contain, constitute, and constrain every physical aspect of the city and its environment. The description provided in this chapter of the relationship between geology and cities is framed within this context.

Building Up

Whenever a person is perceived as having a superficial view of a subject, that individual is open to criticism. This person is "shallow," and "beauty is only skin deep" are typical admonishments. The critics are telling the person to look below the surface because there, apparently, reside qualities that are solid, real, and useful, and after all, "you cannot tell a book by its cover." While the social and philosophical merits of this advice are arguable, there is no doubt that it is geologically interesting information. Buildings are only as solid and useful as the ground that they are built on. This is because a substantial portion of most buildings, their foundations, are contained within the ground and must bear the considerable force of gravity acting on the mass of the buildings, i.e., the weight. Events in the surrounding rock and sediment affect foundations and produce changes that are often translated to the visible portion of the buildings that rest on them. If the rock and sediment move a little, so do the buildings. In addition, any movement in foundations, small or otherwise, could result in changes in appearance and function of buildings. These changes may include structural cracking that reaches exposed surfaces and realignments that cause windows and doors to bind and stick. Additional movement may produce anything from inconvenience to catastrophe. Utility lines may break, shutting off water and possibly causing fires difficult or impossible to extinguish without water; or, in a burst of media-ready images, the building may deform to the point of disuse, or collapse.

Demolition experts are aware of the importance of foundations. Often when a building is taken down, a few well-placed charges in the foundation accomplish the task of demolition dramatically and quickly. Thus new buildings must be designed and old buildings first must be evaluated from the ground down.

One of the best known examples of a "basement problem" is that of the almost 15,000 metric ton bell tower (campanile) of the cathedral of Pisa, often called "the Leaning Tower of Pisa." The upper level protrudes almost fifteen feet over the base on the south side. The tower has subsided vertically about ten feet, which is like adding a basement to a house via the original ground floor. The campanile is composed of many different varieties of building stones and was under construction and repair over a period of centuries, dating to 1173. The overall result was to make the structure somewhat "banana shaped," due to corrections attempted during the long construction period. Unfortunately, this work did not begin to address problems caused by the building being sited on unstable soil. Ground failure due to compression caused by the structure's weight caused the tower to rotate on its base to its present leaning position. It did, however, provide an ideal platform for Galileo to test his theories of falling bodies from the bell tower of his own church.

Over the years, the tower has been reinforced in many different ways, employing cables and bands, and including a counterweight consisting of 600 tons of lead ingots added to the north side. Today, the spider's web of cables is gone, the counterweight removed, and the tower stabilized through proper engineering around its base. The lesson here? Perform a thorough, professional geological analysis first, design in light of nature's realities, and save your city loads of time and money. Poor geological analysis and engineering only rarely create an international tourist attraction.

Slopes and Slope Stability

A number of geological factors need to be considered when buildings are sited. First, and perhaps most apparently, there is the **slope.** A slope is a surface inclined at some angle away from the horizontal. Because few parts of the earth's surface are perfectly flat, most portions of it have some measurable slope. Because of this slope, objects resting on or in it (rocks, soil, buildings) are pulled downward unevenly by gravity relative to their weight and shear strengths. Thus, the earth's surface is normally unstable in this respect to varying degrees.

When rocks or soil move down slope to more stable positions as a result of gravitational pull, the resulting phenomenon is termed **mass wasting.** The speed of mass wasting is one factor used to classify it. A slow form of mass wasting, **creep,** is a downhill deformation of the soil layer often triggered and aided by frost heaving. Its effects are recognized in the form of bent trees, reclining fence posts, and exposed, bent strata. Because creep is so slow, it is not a directly observed process. Even so, creep accounts for the greatest overall volume of earth movement via mass wasting. The accompanying

Leaning tower. View of the bell tower of the cathedral at Pisa, through a Roman arch. (Photo by Anthony Zaccardelli, 2004.)

illustration shows that creep has damaged a bench as movement of the hillside has resulted in cracking and separation of the stone work.

Slumping is much more rapid than creep. It is a rotational movement of soil mass that leaves an exposed, non-vegetated scar at its upper edge. A spoon shaped depression is a signature landform produced by this mass wasting process. Other, more rapid, motions include **falls, slides,** and **flows** that displace rock, soil, vegetation and, sometimes, built structures.

The best way of minimizing damage from mass wasting is prevention by the regulation of land use before building takes place. Effective regulation includes land use-controls, drainage and runoff controls, and regulation of grading. Every system has a natural angle of repose determined by the strength, sizes, and shapes of the materials making up the slope. Humans can easily change the natural slope, but nature usually has its way in the end. Implementing effective land use planning to mitigate the effects of mass wasting involves cooperation among geologists, engineers, architects, planners, and the public, not always an easy set of tasks to accomplish.

Because mass wasting occurs as a natural consequence of an area's climate and geology, these characteristics need to be thoroughly understood in order to recognize potential hazards to consider in proper planning. More specific factors such as the shear strength and depth of soil and rock, moisture content, annual rainfall amounts, percolation rates, and vegetative cover must be assessed, as should all evidence of active mass wasting process, including any accumulation of soil and rock at the foot of a slope.

Drastic remedies often are required to correct problems resulting from insufficient or poor planning. These remedies must be carefully planned and carried out. Slope stability can be improved by reducing slope angle (as close as possible to the natural angle of repose of the material), reinforcing the bottom of the slope with additional materials or retaining structures, and removing uphill overburden. Additionally, plantings of stabilizing vegetation

Weathered bench. This bench is part of the Garfield Memorial, Cleveland, Ohio. It has separated because of the ground failure due to creep. (Photo by John Fleshin, copyright 2004.)

can help hold exposed soil. Because the lubricating effects of water aid soil and rock movements, improving drainage often improves slope stability.

Adding to naturally occurring factors, many human activities decrease slope stability. Excavation to provide habitation sites often results in the oversteepening of slopes. Also, slopes may be destabilized by the removal of trees, the adding to the weight of overburden in the form of buildings and roads, and the injection of water from sprinkling, sewer, and septic systems. Still other activities that contribute to mass wasting include slope undercutting through excavating highway road cuts, quarrying and mining operations, and the digging of ponds and reservoirs.

Finally, consideration needs to be given to the potential effects on slopes from wind-driven waves and earthquakes.

Expansive Soils and Subsidence

A second set of factors relating to the stability of foundations and buildings are **expansive soils.** These soils swell or shrink due to changes in moisture content. The materials which give rise to these soils include volcanic materials (rock, glass, and ash) and shales that decompose to form various kinds of clays. Shale is a sedimentary rock composed of smaller than sand size particles, which are termed "clay-" and "silt sized," and these particles may not be strongly cemented together. The clays swell when they absorb water and shrink when they are de-watered.

When it is impossible to avoid building on expansive soils, there are several (expensive) ways of minimizing damage. One process removes the expansive soil and replaces it with non-expansive soil, at least to a depth to provide an **overburden** sufficient to prevent expansion of underlying material. In fact, the emplacement of any heavy load, such as a large building, may suffice. Another solution is to limit and control water access to the soil. Installation of ditches and pipes redirects surface water, and mixing in sand and gravel may prevent capillary flow. The compaction of commercial gravels is, for example, very small and is known for particular types. Therefore, the response of these gravels under load can be predicted. Still other measures include pre-wetting the soil during construction, adding stabilizing chemicals, and adding impermeable materials.

Subsidence, the lowering or collapse of the land surface, has a number of natural and human-made causes. Natural causes include subterranean dissolution of limestone terrains, earthquake activity, and volcanic activity. Limestone dissolves in ground water made acidic by the incorporation of carbon dioxide gas. This process forms weak carbonic acid. Gasses added to the atmosphere through human activities, particularly those containing sulfur, may result in precipitation that is more acidic (lower pH) than natural rainfall. As the rock decomposes by reacting chemically with this acid, large caverns may be formed. When these voids get large enough near the surface, the land above may then collapse, sometimes quite dramatically, to form a **sinkhole.** This sinkhole formation process is the same one that produces limestone caverns with stalactites and stalagmites, deep, spring-fed pools, and a hummocky terrain called **karst topography** (named after the Moravian Kras region). It causes considerable damage when it occurs in urban areas. Individual sinkholes may be over thirty meters deep and over 100 meters wide.

Although this kind of sinkhole formation is quite often a natural process, it may be triggered when water drawn from wells no longer supports the rock that contained it, and thereby promotes a more rapid collapse. Other human-induced subsidence may be caused by the withdrawal of resources such as oil or gas that permeate the substructure, emptying inter-granular pore spaces and allowing the rock and sediment to physically consolidate. When this occurs along coastal terrain, it moves the land surface closer to sea level and makes it more susceptible to flooding by tidal movements of water and storm surges. Additionally, the over pumping of large volumes of fresh groundwater near the ocean sometimes results in the incursion of salty water into wells. Wells are basically holes drilled into the water table, which defines the upper limits of the zone of saturation of ground water. Because this ground water is often a critically important source of drinking water in coastal areas, the loss of wells due to seawater incursion is a very serious issue. Subsurface erosion due to excessive rainfall also can cause sinkholes to form, as can damaged, leaking water supply pipes that may collapse road surfaces.

Underground mining also may result in subsidence. Although collapse of a mine roof is a gripping catastrophe which may occur while a mine is active, and all-too-frequent news stories tell of the dangers and ultimate human cost of mining, the location of abandoned mine tunnels are commonly forgotten and later built over. These tunnels remain susceptible to collapse, forming human-engineered sinkholes. This kind of subsidence becomes an important problem when urbanization overspreads formerly mined areas. Much of Paris, France, for instance, is built over the limestone quarries that formerly provided its building stone.

Geological and geophysical information is important in identifying urban areas where subsidence is a potential problem. **Remote sensing** techniques, geology's answer to X-ray imaging and MRI, can detect caverns, cavities, and mine tunnels. If the potential for subsidence is detected, then appropriate zoning regulations need to be implemented. Responsible land uses for areas where there is a potential for subsidence might include golf courses and parks, though the use of the word "hazard" might carry more than one meaning on the back nine.

The effects of subsidence in urban areas may sometimes be ameliorated through injection of water into sediments to replace removed fluids, or by filling in mines with compacted mine waste. Other industrial wastes may be stored in this way if harmful substances in them have been removed, neutralized, or contained so they do not threaten contamination of ground water.

Stone Roots, Stone Bark, Stone Foliage

The preceding sections described a relationship between buildings and ground similar to the relationship between trees and soil. Buildings, like trees, have their foundations deeply dug into and in intimate contact with soil and rock, linking the fate of buildings to the nature and dynamics of their substratum. Similarly, it is normally necessary to cut back a freshly transplanted tree so that its top matches its cut back root system as the top must ideally match its support system. Nevertheless, people tend to take a superficial view of buildings, much as they do trees, by focusing attention on the parts easily seen. This is not to say that the above-ground portion of buildings is not important. Because the "fiber", "bark", and "foliage" of buildings normally command so much attention, this chapter would be incomplete if they were not discussed.

Building Materials

Most building materials come from rock and sediment, either directly, as with limestone and gravel and their derivative products, or indirectly, from organisms dependent on the soil (e.g., trees manufacture wood). Building materials are the largest "crop" that people harvest. These materials may be used "as is" except for possible cutting and shaping, or they may be modified by melting, firing, or chemical treatment. Examples of the former category include building stone, crushed rock, gravel, and sand. Examples of the latter include clay, limestone, and metallic ores which may be fashioned into bricks, cement, plaster and metals.

Building stone was formerly one of the most common main weight-bearing structural components of many urban buildings, such as cathedrals, palaces, and most construction in general. Its use in this way has dramatically declined over the years, and now it is principally employed as a facade or covering for decorative purposes. Other contemporary uses might include slate for roofs, sandstone for sidewalks, curbstones, and tombstones, and marble for tile and tabletops. Granite, sandstone, gneiss and limestone are all important building stones today, often serving a decorative role.

These stones—how they are used and how they react to conditions in which they are placed—provide excellent lessons in urban geology. Because cities in the U.S. are comparatively young compared to many cities in Europe, Africa, and Asia, much of the building stone is used superficially, as described above, and there are many American buildings, particularly homes, made out of wood. While many Europeans think that it is curious that so many American houses are made from wood, this choice of building material in the U.S. compared to Europe reflects the fact that wood is relatively scarce and expensive there. This is because many of the European forests were cut down long ago and older wooden homes have been destroyed by fire (the Great Fire of London in 1666 is just one instructive example). As a result of similar disasters, cities such as Paris have enacted codes that require buildings to be made of stone or prepared rock products. French builders also are required to provide a warranty for a home's structural integrity for ten years.

Crushed rock finds its way into or near modern buildings as an aggregate for concrete and as support and drainage material for roadbeds and foundations. **Sand** and **gravel** have similar uses. They accumulate as stream deposits and represent the weathered, eroded, and sorted fragments of diverse preexisting rocks. City dwellers' use of these products is so great that there are local shortages of these "mundane" materials. Where supplies are low, people have resorted to dredging ancient, submerged Ice Age valleys on the drowned margin of continents. After the ice melted and the sea levels rose, these former valleys were covered by the ocean. In many tropical areas where sand and gravel deposits are scarce, crushed seashells (e.g., oyster shells) serve in their place.

Cement is the principal prepared rock product used today for construction in cities. Mixed with sand or gravel aggregates, it becomes **concrete**, a kind of "instant rock" that is easy to manufacture, transport, and mold into practically any shape to serve the needs of construction. Cement begins its existence as limestone crushed in mills, mixed with clay, heated, crushed again, eventually mixed with water and aggregate to form a substance that will set into solid "rock" (concrete), in air or subaqueously. Because the setting is a chemical reaction, concrete can actually "dry" under water. The "drying" of concrete is in actuality a misnomer as people who work with it take many steps to see that sufficient water is retained in the mix to allow it to chemically set into the artificial stone. Its ease of use and relatively low production cost has made concrete the preeminent "building stone" of cities.

Bricks and other **ceramic** products, including tiles and drainpipes, begin their existence as clay mixed with water that is then shaped, often covered with a glaze to add strength, and fired. Clay may form when a chemical weathering process called hydrolysis dissolves rock. Clay is very stable at the earth's surface, where weathering takes place, much more so than the rocks that gave rise to it. Thus products made from clay have some further natural resistance to weathering. One of the oldest forms of "artificial stone" is brick, and in many places bricks are still made by hand, although when manufactured in this way, they are not as structurally sound as those made in modern factories. Handmade bricks, a staple construction material of ancient cities, are very labor intensive to produce. They require mixing, molding, cutting, sun drying, stacking, and finally, firing, often in a wood fire. That said, serviceable and low-tech bricks of this sort could be made practically anywhere.

Glass is made by melting rock or sediment (often a silica-rich sand derived from sandstone). This liquid is then quickly cooled, causing it to solidify before crystals have opportunity to form. With the advent of metal frameworks that bear the weight of most large modern buildings, glass has become a widely used construction material that, along with stone, has become a decorative covering of metal frameworks. The famed large areas of stained glass windows of Notre Dame de Paris and other gothic cathedrals were made possible because much of the support of the building walls was moved outside by flying buttresses, which translate the load on the walls to the ground using the impressive compressive strength of natural stone materials.

Metals today are used as the skeletal framework for many buildings and as reinforcement for concrete. Metals are extracted from **ores,** which are unusually concentrated pockets of metal-bearing minerals that may be mined for a profit. Although **aluminum** is the most abundant metal on earth and is found in detectable levels in virtually all

Bricks oven. Sun dried but unfired bricks in central Mexico are stacked by hand in a sort of pyramid that is fired by wood inserted in the lower sections. (Photo by John Fleshin, copyright 2004.)

crustal rocks, it was at one time in a class with precious metals because of its scarcity in its pure form. For example, royal families had their best eating utensils and even crowns crafted from the "rare," silvery, highly malleable metal. Moreover, the aluminum top for the Washington Monument was displayed, before its installation, at Tiffany's in New York. Today, aluminum is valued because of its desirable low weight-to-strength ratio. Because of its scrap value, much aluminum is recycled. The old aluminum siding on a house may easily be worth hundreds of dollars to a scrap dealer, who will gladly collect it from the work site. The scrap value of a commercially sized aluminum window can easily be one hundred dollars.

Iron is the second most abundant metal in the earth's crust and by far the most extensively used, especially in the form of steel. Many other metals used in construction, such as manganese, magnesium, chromium, and nickel, are alloyed with iron in the productions of various kinds of steel. Iron is much simpler to smelt or free from its ore than aluminum and its use pre-dates classical antiquity. In fact, the beginning of its usage provided the name for a comparatively advanced "age" in human history.

Plaster is made by crushing and heating the mineral gypsum. The name "Plaster of Paris" comes from productive gypsum quarries located in the north part of that city, under its highest point, MontMartre, upon which the Roman-Byzantine basilica of the sacred heart, Sacre Coeur, was built. Plaster is similar to cement because it recrystallizes or sets after being mixed with water. It is used by itself, mixed with sand, or applied to paper or board backings as ubiquitous, ever-ready, prefabricated plaster board, a hallmark and perhaps metaphor for the present age. However, unlike most woods, it does provide some firewall protection.

Plastics and other **petrochemical synthetic compounds** have become common construction materials within the past fifty years. They are fashioned mainly from **hydrocarbons.** The principal source of these hydrocarbons is petroleum, which represents the unoxidized remains of microscopic sea creatures such as **phytoplankton.** Most petroleum formed tens of millions of years ago within the sediments of ancient oceans and today is found mainly within the pore spaces of marine-deposited sandstones and limestones, particularly fossil reefs.

Forces That Tear Down

Change and Decay: Weathering

A close look at the world reveals that everything is crumbling into dust. Decay and change are everywhere. Paint oxidizes, cracks, and peels away from wood. Wood is turned into powder by bacteria, fungi, and insects. Building stone pits and cracks, its surface begrimed and etched. Metal corrodes, weakening and turning dull. Road surfaces heave and develop pockmarks and scars. Because the materials from which cities are fashioned are either pristine or processed rocks and sediments, they are subject to the same destructive forces that affect the parent materials. Deceptively solid, rocks are ground into dust at the ambient earth surface temperatures and atmospheric pressures in a process called **weathering.** During weathering, rocks are subject to both physical disintegration and chemical decomposition. Chemical decomposition yields new combinations of the atoms of the original material while physical disintegration for the most part yields smaller pieces of the original materials.

Cemetery. The headstone to the left is made of marble, which is primarily calcium carbonate, a substance which is readily dissolved by water made acidic by the atmospheric gasses, including pollutants. The stone to the right is granite, which is much more resistant to this form of weathering. (Photo by John Fleshin, copyright 2004.)

Relation of Weathering, Erosional Processes, and Cities

Weathering loosens materials and makes them susceptible to movement caused by agents such as gravity, running water, ice, wind, waves, and currents. Weathering sets the pathway for **erosion.**

Erosion-related processes affect human-made structures by directly wearing them down (wind abrasion, for instance), physically carrying them away (flood events, shore erosion) or depositing unwanted material (dune migration, for example, burying buildings and property). Materials eroded by any medium are transported generally downhill to be deposited in new locations when the energy responsible for the transporting process diminishes and the medium slows. This means that the materials that compose, underpin, and surround the urban area are constantly in motion. The geological phenomena responsible for this dynamism are a mixed blessing for a city and its inhabitants. On one hand, for example, the close proximity of a city to a large supply of running water is an indispensable resource for drinking, washing, disposal, transportation, and manufacturing. On the other hand, the excessive amount of water that appears when a river floods can spell disaster for an urban area.

In the succeeding sections, the love/hate relationship between cities and geological processes will be explored. It will be useful to keep in mind that these processes have been active long before cities were built. These processes are neither good nor bad. Rather, they are sometimes beneficial and sometimes harmful, all relative to human values.

Coastal Processes

Cities were originally situated along the shores of the ocean, lakes, or rivers because the adjacent water provided transportation and a nearby food source. Moreover, coastal regions typically have large areas of low elevation, with gently sloping terrain that may be easy to build on and adapt for agriculture. Today, in addition to retaining these traditional usages, coastal areas are valuable aesthetically and as resources for tourism and recreation.

Shore areas are extremely changeable. The same agents of weathering and erosion—gravity, water, and wind—that shape and continually modify the rest of the landscape, affect them. In addition, they are affected by waves, currents, and sediments that are perennially in motion, having a profound effect on people and buildings.

Surface Waves are mostly wind-derived energy transmitted through water. Waves have three basic interrelated characteristics: **velocity, wave length,** and **frequency** in addition to **amplitude** or **wave height.** All are important in determining the effect of a wave on the shore. Velocity is the speed of the wave in a given direction. Frequency is the number of waves passing a point in a given time. Wave height is the vertical distance between the wave crest and trough. More energy generally means higher waves and greater hydraulic impact on the shoreline. Wave length is the distance between successive wave crests. A wave is able to affect objects below the surface of the water to a depth that is roughly equal to one-half of its wave length. It follows that large wavelength waves can affect the bottom of the basin to greater water depths than small waves.

The geometry of the ocean or lake bottom is important to coastal cities in determining how waves will interact with the shore and features constructed along it. A long stretch of shallow bottom in front of a beach tends to dissipate wave energy because of frictional interaction with the water moved by the wave. Alternatively, if the bottom rises abruptly toward the beach, then more energy from the waves will be transmitted more directly against the shore. Depending on the angle of approach, waves and wind also generate **longshore currents** and **littoral (beach) drift,** which move sediments parallel to the shoreline. These cause a continual flow of sediments both into and out of coastal areas.

Beaches are accumulations of sediment at the interface between land and water. They develop from sediment deposited by streams, material from the basin bottom, or particles eroded from the land behind them. Particles reaching a beach continue to move along it because of longshore currents and beach drift. Beaches are, therefore, inherently unstable structures; the material composing them is continually being moved in and then carried away. Like rivers, they look deceptively the same from day to day while they are actually a conduit, not a repository, for what is in them. While storm energy can reduce or destroy beaches overnight, periods of calm climate are inducements for beach growth. Historically, people tended to avoid siting permanent structures on or near beaches. Today, because of their recreational appeal, beaches are heavily built up. In some cases, this is a spectacular example of a lack of good sense.

Shore erosion is potentially the greatest daily threat to structures built along coasts. Protecting shorelines from erosion is an expensive endeavor and one that is not always successful. **Breakwaters,** structures installed in the water parallel to the shoreline to dissipate wave energy offshore, are more common than the related strategy of dumping fill in the water and grading the bottom to produce a greater friction-producing surface approaching the beach.

Armoring the shoreline with **seawall, gabion baskets** (wire baskets filled with rock), and **riprap** (irregular chunks of rock or concrete) helps to keep it from being removed by waves. Less formal strategies include dumping fill and various forms of refuse, often from construction sites. While the more formal methods may be effective in retarding erosion, they may lock sediments into the bluffs behind beaches that are an important source of sand for beach nourishment. Thus, protecting the bluffs may mean destroying the beaches. The less formal methods have additional disadvantages. They not only result in an aesthetically unpleasant shoreline, but they also may be a source of toxic contaminants unless the fill material used is carefully examined prior to its dumping along the shore.

Groins and **jetties** are structures built perpendicular to the shoreline that extend out into the water. They provide a barrier to slow and trap the longshore flow of sediment on their up-drift side. Their chief disadvantage is that they may cause the starvation of sediments on their down-drift side. Thus, the beach growth they help initiate in one area could be countered by accelerated erosion in another.

The land behind the beach is subject to other factors besides wave energy that contribute to shore erosion. Poorly engineered or undercut slope may fail and deliver large chunks of land to the beach where it is carried away by waves and currents. Poor drainage also contributes to this instability through lubrication of the shoreline material, which facilitates its movement. As was previously pointed out within the context of mass wasting, **grading** and improving **drainage** are ways of stabilizing slopes, and, when applied to slopes associated with shorelines, help protect them from erosion.

Coastal erosion will remain a problem as long as people continue to build and maintain structures close to shorelines. Structures situated close to shorelines may require continual maintenance and repair. It is a common sight in summertime, for instance, to see tugs, barges, and cranes maintaining breakwaters and sea walls that protect harbor facilities. Also, harbor mouths must be dredged periodically in order to remove unwanted sediments. These sediments, often contaminated with toxic material, pose additional problems for safe disposal. People in resort areas may spend large sums, often fruitlessly, in order to protect their beach or their structures. Some of these expensive "remedies" cause additional problems. For instance, the vast quantities of sand which were dumped in the surf zone to enhance the beach at Waikiki, Hawaii, caused the death of many marine organisms by suffocation.

The long-term outlook for coastal areas of oceans is grim. Many resorts are situated on barrier islands that are actively eroding and migrating. These barrier islands also often represent a barrier to hurricanes that very well may scour them entirely. There is evidence that the sea level might be rising world wide because of global warming and the subsequent ice cap melting. If this is true, increased coastal erosion, even inundation, is likely. Along the shores of lakes, water levels rise and fall in response to precipitation in the watershed. Depending on climate cycles, lake levels may be well above or below average for a decade or more; therefore siting buildings close to the shore can be a risky and expensive business.

People sometimes blame nature for problems they cause themselves. This is never more typical than in the case of coastal erosion. Coastal erosion is a geological process that becomes a human problem only when actions are in ignorance or defiance of the natural system. The best solutions are education and the design and enforcement of scientifically realistic zoning regulations concerning the development and use of shore areas.

The following is a proposed five-point policy for the uses and protection of the coastal zone of the Great Lakes (Tevesz & Savin, 1987). This proposal was made in order to address severe erosion problems affecting many heavily built-up areas along the shores of the Great Lakes (they are large enough to contain 20% of the fresh water on the earth's surface). With some modification, they are probably adaptable to all coastal areas. They are as follows:

1. The shoreline should be zoned off-limits for *new* construction for a distance from the lake equal to the expected retreat of the shoreline during an extended period of time, ideally, the next two hundred years. The distance varies locally, but is typically between 200 and 800 feet.
2. To the extent possible, state and local governments should convert the coastal zone into park land. Erosion should be allowed to take its course in those parks, thereby providing sand to nourish the beaches.
3. Legislation should require that, when real estate in coastal zones is transferred, properties be surveyed for erosion risks. Buyers should be provided with the results of such surveys prior to purchase.
4. The government should not build breakwaters or other structures to protect private property, but should continue to provide information about the effects of and remedies for erosion.
5. Protective measures should be permitted, although not encouraged, for property on which improvements now exist. No protective measures should be permitted for property which is not now improved or from which improvements are removed in the future.

Streams, Rivers, Falls, Rapids, and Location of Cities

Streams are the natural channels that gather rain, melt, and ground waters. They erode the land, carry sediment and nutrients, and disperse them within their discharge basin. Next to oxygen, clean fresh water is the most important resource for people. It is fundamental for survival and useful for transportation, waste disposal, and power generation. The fertility of stream floodplains helps provide an abundant food supply for cities everywhere, dating back to some of the earliest large urban centers in Mesopotamia, along the upper Nile, and along the Huang Ho River. Most great cities depend on waters of great rivers.

Streams have been avenues of discovery, migration routes, and the umbilical cord to sources of supplies, as discussed in Chapter 1. Towns and villages arose and evolved to utilize and augment these linkages. A strategic fortification along a stream often represented the first step in the development of a city. Fort Cadillac, for instance, later became Detroit. The town site of Shannopin at the confluence of the Allegheny and Monongahela Rivers became Fort Duquesne, then Fort Pitt, then Pittsburgh.

St. Louis, Missouri, St. Paul and Minneapolis, Minnesota, Kansas City, Kansas, and Independence, Missouri are additional examples of large American cities that developed along or near the confluence of major streams. Despite hinterland locations, all can be linked to deep water ports accessible to an ocean. Columbus, Ohio, also located at the confluence of two streams but lacking a deep water link to the Ohio River, found itself limited as a manufacturing center until the development of major highways made it an important crossroads. The Welland Canal provides such a deep water link to many Great

Lakes cities via the St. Lawrence Seaway. New York City owed its early greatness in large part to transportation to the interior provided by the Erie Canal.

Early water power sources derived from falls and rapids became focal points of urban development (Twin Falls, Idaho; Great Falls, Montana (along the Missouri River); Grand Rapids, Michigan, (along the Grand River); and Louisville, Kentucky, (along the Falls of the Ohio). Rochester, New York, located near Lake Ontario shipping lanes, expanded along the Genesee River. Waterfalls provided power needed for gristmills to grind grain into flour. Great eastern American cities such as Philadelphia (Pennsylvania), Wilmington (Delaware), Trenton (New Jersey), Baltimore (Maryland), Washington (D.C.), and Richmond (Virginia), are not located along the outer (Atlantic) coastline but along the Fall Line of the ancestral Appalachian Mountains, where streams falling through rapids provide sources of power, including hydroelectric power, which are important to urban growth. The location of some of these cities at the edges of the tidal estuaries of the Susquehanna and Delaware Rivers, allowing port access to the Atlantic, has been helpful as well.

Numerous cities developed along the shorelines of riverine bays and coastal indentations and in estuaries, sometimes well upstream but directly connected to and well within the tidal influence of the sea. Marseilles (France), Stockholm (Sweden), Naples and Venice (Italy), Quebec and Montreal (Canada), Alexandria (Egypt), London (England), Bremenhofen (Germany), Lisbon (Portugal), Istanbul (Turkey), and Shanghai (China), to name only a few, became major trade ports forming vital links between their countries and other parts of the world. The midwestern U.S. cities of Chicago, Toledo, Duluth, and other Great Lakes ports enjoy both onshore (river) and offshore (lake water) resources.

Streams often serve as political boundaries, sometimes international, but often between states or provinces within countries. Territorial arguments break out over fishing rights, water use, and pollution while natural meandering and cutoffs carve slices of real estate into variable jurisdictions. The Rio Grande altered its course near El Paso, Texas, temporarily giving the United States more territory, but eventually its political (although not geological) return to Mexico occurred during the presidency of Lyndon Johnson. Cutoffs along the Mississippi River, a major interstate boundary, sometimes cause confusion in deciding which counties and states are entitled to citizens' tax payments. The United States Army Corps of Engineers spends a great deal of effort to keep the Mississippi in its present channel.

How People Affect Streams

Streams are greatly affected by urbanization. Common modifications of streams include containment and flood control, as well as those that use the stream for irrigation, disposal, storage, electrical power generation, and recreation. Cities benefit from some of these adjustments by ensuring predictable use of floodplain lands and reliable water supplies and power. Nevertheless, dams and channelization of streams are meant to affect their natural flow, and do.

Urbanization, with its attendant surface development of abundant concrete and asphalt, seals off water access to soil, channeling runoff from rooftops, parking lots, and street pavements eventually into streams, thereby increasing the chance of flooding. Increased industrial use and the walling off of floodplains for the siting of habitations alters natural stream flow and cuts off the natural supply of **alluvium** (stream transported sediments), often resulting in the destruction of the natural floodplain environment.

Another consequence of urbanization, encouraged until the mid-1980s was the filling in of **wetlands.** This resulted in the destruction of entire ecosystems. Wetlands provide a natural means of flood control, improve water quality, recharge ground water, establish habitat for plants and animals, enhance fisheries, and, along coasts, help control the erosion of shorelines. Stringent environmental laws now govern the use of streams and wetlands, and international protocols have been developed for improving coastal wetlands.

Floods and Their Impact

No natural hazard affects cities located along rivers as frequently as do floods. **Floods** cause aptly named **floodplains** to receive fresh deposits of water and alluvium. Sometimes these inundated floodplains get cut off from their generative streams and are temporarily turned into lakes. Many cities have grown up expecting, then fighting back, recurrent floods. This repetitive hardship is endured because the presence of home, commerce, and the indispensability of stream water outweigh the potential harm. Inertia is also a potent political and social force.

Abundant quantities of public funds have been spent for flood control in order to protect cities through upstream construction of flood containment dams, often at a considerable distance from the city itself. Also, where **natural levees** exist, they may be topped with concrete walls, effectively cutting them off from the very supplies of alluvium that created them during times of flood. These concrete walls raise flood-stage levels and confine rivers within their new, higher, artificial banks. Cities such as Cincinnati, Ohio, and St. Louis, Missouri, depend on these constructions to help protect them from floods.

Other flood control measures include straightening meandering sections of a stream by excavation and filling. This shortening of the channel allows water to pass through an area more quickly, although it is now recognized that this can do great ecological harm by altering the natural cycles of bank overflow that maintain floodplains.

Where natural levees are not present, earthen levees are sometimes constructed to prevent flooding. Nevertheless, as was evidenced in 1993 by the severe flooding of the upper Mississippi and Missouri valleys, these kinds of artificial structures are easily breached even when reinforced with sandbags. The ineffectiveness of these levees allowed powerful flood waters to cover vast areas with useless sand.

Storms, Streams, and Flash Floods

Heavy rains sometimes deliver so much water to a drainage basin that the capacity for groundwater storage and the ability of streams to drain away surface waters is exceeded, causing a flood. History contains myriad examples of devastating floods, including ones that occurred along the Huang Ho River in China resulting in hundreds of thousands of deaths, and additional disasters caused by the water-borne legacy of disease and starvation.

The millennium record floods of central Europe in 2002 caused incredible damage. For example, the Viltava River in Prague, Czech Republic, rose nearly thirty feet above normal levels, destroyed many buildings, and threatened centuries-old landmarks such

Flood damaged building. This flood damage is on a corner within fifty feet of the Krizikova subway station, which was one of many completely flooded. (Photo by John Fleshin, copyright 2004.)

as the Charles Bridge. The low-lying Karlin district witnessed the collapse of apartment buildings with the damage not entirely repaired years later. It then seemed odd that the same region suffered killing heat and drought the following year, followed by a moderately cool summer in 2004 with moderate un-summer like temperatures until August. The long-term unpredictability of weather, as exemplified here, makes planning and preparedness for urban flooding both necessary and important. Nevertheless, the many years that may occur between disastrous floods tend to blunt cities' resolve for such preparations.

Tropical storms, hurricanes, and monsoons frequently produce deluges both from rains and **storm surges.** Storm surges, where ocean waters rise under a storm's low-pressure zone, are "giant bubbles" of high water that inundate land. Extensive loss of life has resulted from the landward penetration of such storm surges from the Bay of Bengal along the low lying coast of Bangladesh, where hurricanes have taken human tolls in the hundreds of thousands. Many coastal cities lying in tropical storm tracks are repeatedly threatened. Large, water-born storms can last long enough to travel great distances in-land dumping considerable water, even though this path leads them away from the source of their energy (warm ocean water) and towards eventual dissipation.

When Hurricane Agnes moved northward in 1972 over Virginia, Maryland, and Pennsylvania, it stalled for six days, poured immense volumes of water on already seasonally wet grounds. The resulting flooding of the upper Susequehanna River devastated the Wilkes-Barre, Scranton, and Harrisburg, Pennsylvania areas. Flood control installations proved to be of little use as this "flood of the century" demonstrated that people could not protect everything and might have to concede a future similar event.

Tragically, this proved to be the case in 2005 when Hurricane Katrina came ashore in Louisiana, producing a storm surge that breached levees protecting New Orleans from the waters of Lake Pontchartrain. The combined effects of the storm (wind, rain, storm surge, and failed levees) resulted in the flooding of most of the city and necessitated a complete evacuation. Other areas along the Gulf coast, particularly coastal regions of

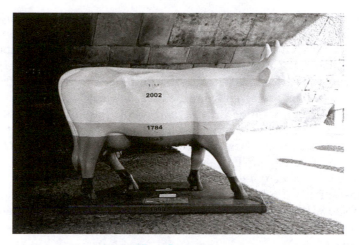

Flood cow. This a representative of the "Cow Parade" urban art exhibit of 2004 in Prague. This one is in the Kampa area, the "Venice" of Prague, and graphically represents the relative height of historic floods. Had it been situated at this spot in August, 2002, it would have been submerged under about thirty feet of fast moving water of the Viltava. (Photo by John Fleshin, copyright 2004.)

Mississippi and Alabama, also were devastated by the storm. The damage caused by Hurricane Katrina has likely made it the costliest natural disaster in United States history.

Flash flooding occurs anywhere short-term storms break over local areas, overloading watershed capacities for **infiltration** (the percolation of water into the soil) and normal dispersal via stream channels. Flash flooding in the Big Thompson River in 1976 near Estes Park, Colorado, killed 140 people.

In August 2002, the people of Dresden, Germany, learned that engineering efforts around waterways might have very unfortunate consequences. Land freed up by the construction of a canal was dramatically reclaimed for several weeks by the Weisseritz, a tributary of the Elbe. Dresden's misfortune was compounded not only by days of locally heavy rain, but also by the fact that the city was downstream from several flooded tributaries in other countries.

Environmental Consequences to Cities Caused by Dam Building on Streams

Lakes, whether natural or artificial, are temporarily dammed streams. As such, they are eventually destroyed by draining or by filling with sediments and vegetation. Dams are human-made barriers designed to trap waters for flood control, irrigation, or hydropower generation. As with any human-made structure, the useful longevity of dams is limited. Reservoirs behind dams inevitably fill with water-deposited silt, thereby limiting the usefulness of the contained but ever-diminishing volumes of water.

Another effect of artificial lakes is to alter stream flow that normally provides adequate water and sediment dispersal. The Aswan Dam of Egypt serves as a modern example of just such a change. Once described by Herodotus (430 B.C.) as the "Gift of the Nile," the annual flooding of the river, with its attendant deposition of fertile alluvium and delta replenishment, has largely been eliminated by the dam. Expansion of the reservoir behind the dam has inundated valuable records of ancient civilizations, forced the relocation of towns, increased evaporation rates, extended filtration of waters into porous rocks adjacent to the impoundment, and increased the area of infection of the serious snail-borne parasitic disease, **schistosomiasis.** Downstream, fresh and increasingly energetic waters, now relieved from the labor of carrying sediment, erode and alter dispersal channels and undermine bridges and roads. Loss of nutrients has altered biological balances and diminished the fishing industry. Loss of sediment to the delta areas marginal to the Mediterranean Sea has increased river bank erosion and poses a threat to the city of Alexandria, Egypt. This environmental havoc is the trade-off for providing hydroelectric power to serve the growing population of Cairo.

Water released from the bottom of dams is very cold, held to just above freezing by the pressure of the water above. It is an interesting but peculiar property of water that its maximum density is at four degrees Celsius, which also explains why ice floats and freezing water expands.

Dams can present even more direct threats to communities. Most public dams, either earthen or concrete, are masterful engineering enterprises designed to (and do) withstand great forces. Failure, when it happens, usually occurs at the margins of the structure, perhaps due in part to poor or incomplete grouting or because of geologically unsuitable conditions not fully studied or possibly ignored.

Failure of the California St. Francis Dam in 1928, caused by an earthquake, killed 450 people. The Baldwin Hills Reservoir collapse of December, 1963 caused millions of dollars in damages to Santa Monica, California properties, as surging flood waters destroyed 200 homes, flooded about 1500 others, ripped apart large apartment complexes, lifted roof fragments onto trees, and leveled businesses. Fortunately, early warning limited the loss of human life to six. Before the collapse of the reservoir, fluids from an oil recovery operation may have lubricated a small fault, helping trigger the events.

Along the Paive River Valley draining eastward off the mountainous spine of Italy into the Adriatic Sea, the 1963 Vajont Reservoir disaster attracted the attention of the world. The last and largest of six reservoirs constructed for the generation of hydroelectric power, the magnificent 266 meter high concrete arc structure stood majestically spanning the narrow valley. It was, however, unfortunately located in the shadow of a major rockslide zone on the side of steep Mt. Toc. A potential slide block of nearly 300 million cubic meters had little support at its base. Moreover, it was known that rising reservoir levels would raise the water table, allowing water to seep into a basal weak zone of the rock and elevate hydrostatic pressures. After the scare of the French Malpasset disaster, several **piezometric wells** were drilled into the rock to monitor it for motion. Despite increasing rates of tell-tale signs of cracks and heaves in roads at the top of the incline, tilted trees, and a very wet summer season that added much ground water weight to the porous rock, the prevailing interest was not in the possibility for geological disaster but in the dam's huge capacity for generating power.

In the late evening of October 9, 1963, the 300 million cubic meter slide block of fractured, water-laden debris came down the flank of Mt. Toc at an estimated rate of sixty kilometers per hour. It buried perhaps 150 people, displaced 50 million cubic meters of water, and generated an explosive wave 200 meters high. Part of the wave washed up the opposite valley side, inundating five villages more than twenty-five meters above reservoir level. Water penetrated the chambers of the dam, killing all the attendants. A wall of water exploded over the dam crest, cascaded downstream, and set off huge shakings and loud claps of noise from compressed air shocks and violent winds. These shocks collapsed houses and people's lungs before the water hit. The town of Longarone and 1450 of its inhabitants were wiped out. Further downstream, 450 people from three smaller villages were drowned. A five meter high wave passed through the town of Belluno, sixteen kilometers downstream from Longarone. Through this calamitous event, the dam, which should never have been built in that location, held.

Cities and Violent Geological Forces

Earthquakes

Earthquakes are instantaneous, largely unpredictable, sometimes catastrophic events. Fortunately, most are small and rarely felt. Perhaps more than a million minor recordable shocks occur annually. Results from small quakes may be only minor local disturbances and cause no more damage than cracked foundations, toppled chimneys, and broken dishes. Earthquakes are one consequence of a tectonically active planet.

During a major earthquake, an entire city or at least several neighborhoods may be laid to waste within a minute or two. Destruction occurs by the collapse of buildings and the triggering of landslides that transport and bury homes, block roads, and break utility lines. These broken electrical, gas, and water lines also cause fires and remove an effective means of putting them out. Casualties from earthquakes can reach into the tens or even hundreds of thousands. In the past, major earthquakes also triggered the onset of disease and starvation. Financial costs may be staggering as well.

Earthquakes are measured either on a scale of intensity of destructive effects or the calculated magnitude of the energy released at the focus of the earthquake. The modified **Mercalli Intensity Scale** categorizes observational events on a twelve-level system. However, it is flawed because descriptions provided by witnesses often vary and cannot be easily compared. Since the development of the ten-point **Richter Scale** in the 1930s, magnitudes have been calculated based on the varying amplitude of ground oscillations recorded by a **seismograph,** which means literally "shaky writer."

Richter scale magnitudes of micro-earthquakes are generally "two" or less; damage-causing earthquakes may start in the "five" to "six" range. Major quakes occur in the "seven" range; great quakes are at magnitude "eight" or higher. The energy released by a great earthquake is comparable to that of a very large nuclear blast. Such an event occurs on average once a year. Because the Richter scale is a geometric (logarithmic) scale, a whole number increase in magnitude represents a ten-fold increase at the underground point of energy release or **focus.** Thus an earthquake of magnitude "seven" is 100 times more powerful than an earthquake of magnitude "five." Large quakes, for example the 1906 "San Francisco Quake," are often named for cities or regions located on or near the epicenter, which is always the point located above the focus.

Causes of Earthquakes

The outermost part of the earth, the crust, is essentially solid rock that is broken into a mosaic of interlocking pieces, somewhat like a puzzle or a cracked shell of an egg. These pieces are called **plates** because they are rigid and are capable of adjusting themselves along their boundaries in the same way a person could shuffle some closely spaced dinner plates on a table. The plates can adjust to each other because they float on a denser material, capable of flow, located below them and termed the **mantle.** Because of this moveable foundation, plates may pull apart, be pushed together, or slide past each other. These border areas are termed "plate boundaries" and are weak zones in the earth's crust where most earthquakes occur.

Where Earthquakes Occur

There are three large areas where earthquake activity is concentrated. The first area is a 45,000 kilometer-long mountainous realm located mainly in the centers of ocean basins and appropriately called **mid-ocean ridges.** The second area is located around the margins of the Pacific Ocean is termed the **Circum-Pacific belt.** The third area covers an east-west trending region extending from the eastern Mediterranean Sea to the Himalaya Mountains and from that area southward into Indonesia.

The mid-ocean ridges are the most benign of these three areas. These earthquakes are mostly generated when the ocean floor in pulled apart (tensional movement) and the new empty space is flooded with lava which hardens to form new ocean floor. Generally this happens with relatively steady motion that does not produce large earthquakes. In addition, the mid-ocean ridges are mostly submerged, making them remote from cities. Geologically active Iceland is a notable exception, as it represents a section of oceanic ridge that was forced to the surface by a mantle plume, breaking the ocean's surface and forming land, the only place where one can stand on the North American Plate and the Eurasian Plate at the same time with dry feet.

Real threats to cities occur particularly in the Circum-Pacific belt and the Mediterranean-Himalaya-Indonesia areas. Compressional motions in these regions cause great expanses of rock to fracture, with the denser rocks sliding under the less dense ones at plate boundaries. Continental plates never subduct (slide under another plate), so when they collide, significant activity results. All convergent boundaries involve intense compressional energy.

The energy generated by compressive motions may be released as deep focus earthquakes when an oceanic plate slides beneath a continental plate, causing great damage to cities. For example, parts of western South America have experienced damaging earthquakes of magnitude 7.5 or greater. Earthquakes over the last fifty years have killed tens of thousands of people in South American countries such as Ecuador, Peru, Columbia, and Chile. Many of these occur because the relatively dense Pacific sea floor is diving below and is being over-ridden by the relatively light and westwardly moving South American Plate. The further inland, the deeper the quakes' focus, as they follow their oceanic plates' downwardly inclined path. The quakes decline and eventually cease when crustal material loses its rigidity as it is eventually incorporated into the mantle.

In North America, one of the most spectacular earthquakes on record occurred on Good Friday in 1964 in Anchorage, Alaska. It, too, was spawned by compressional motions. The underlying cause in this case was the North American Plate overriding the Pacific Plate.

In the cradle of Western civilization, Mediterranean and mid-Eastern earthquakes have been long documented. They are caused by the pushing together of the African,

Anatolian, and Euro-Asian continental blocks. Recent reminders of this are the magnitude 7.7 earthquakes in Armenia in 1988 and northwest Iran in 1990 that killed approximately 25,000 and 40,000 people respectively. Probably the most famous earthquake in the region occurred on All Saints Day, 1755, in Lisbon, Portugal. It killed over 30,000 people and prompted much discussion of cause and effect among European clerics and philosophers.

The consequences of sliding motions of continental plates passing each other in a transform motion are perhaps well exemplified along the west coast of the United States, particularly within the San Andreas, Hayward, and other fault systems. These motions reflect adjustments of the Pacific plate moving northward with respect to the North American Plate. North of San Francisco, this sliding plate boundary changes into a spreading center in the ocean floor. Part of it moves toward the western United States; it plunges wet ocean floor materials mixed with crustally derived sediments beneath the North American plate, partially melting large quantities of lower density rock which then punches upward to form the plutons and volcanoes of the Cascade Range. A pluton is a rising mass of magma that does not reach the surface, forming large, deep intrusive structures, primarily of granite, that may form the base of uplifts or mountains perhaps later to be exposed by erosion. The devastation caused by the eruptions of Mount St. Helens in the 1980s and, perhaps soon enough in the 21st century, are a reminder of this continuing motion.

Intra-plate earthquakes also may occur, sometimes near large cities. These earthquakes result from the deep-seated adjustments of ancient structures within continents. Examples of these kinds of earthquakes have been reported in the magnitude 5–6 range in Boston, Massachusetts (1755), Charleston, Missouri (1895), and Anna, Ohio (1937). Occasional large earthquakes of this sort have also occurred, such as those exceeding magnitude 8 in New Madrid, Missouri (1812, 1813) and Charleston, South Carolina (1886). The New Madrid quake rang church bells in Washington, D.C. and temporally reversed the flow of the Mississippi River, easily putting it in the category of a major quake, perhaps even the largest in North America.

Damage to Cities Caused by Earthquakes

The damaging effects of earthquakes to cities include landslides, liquefaction of soils, deformation and cracking of the land surface, and collapse of buildings. Fires caused by ruptured utility lines are often the greatest source of damage in urban areas.

Improperly designed large commercial buildings may be hazardous if earthquakes occur at times of heavy occupancy, such as the work day. Many buildings are not designed to withstand horizontal ground shaking. Many high-rise buildings, although structurally strong with respect to vertically directed stresses, have open spaces at ground level. This can be extremely dangerous because when the lower columns break, the building may "pancake" downward, as if purposefully imploded. Despite new stricter codes governing construction in earthquake-prone areas such as parts of California, decades of pre-code construction have produced a hodge-podge of designs of varying but all too often minimal resistance to earthquake energies.

Landslides set in motion by earthquakes often cause considerable property damage. Unless people are buried in debris, they generally survive this type of event. Roads blocked by landslides make rescue difficult and are a hindrance to building repairs.

The liquefaction of soils results from the reorganization of sediments and water after the soil has been shocked with energy from an earthquake. For example, sand saturated by water normally behaves as a solid, but when shocked, it behaves as a liquid (e.g. quicksand). Buildings situated on these kinds of soils may then sink, crack, or even collapse. Horizontally moving sands may flow through building foundations and disrupt underground utility lines. Pressurized sand boils may erupt from the ground like small volcanoes, piercing road pavements, foundations, and embankments. Muds similarly fail, often relocating entire housing tracts to lower elevations. Because water saturated soils are found in many urban areas, they commonly contribute to earthquake-related damage. For example, significant soil movement occurred in the Charleston, South Carolina, earthquake in 1886, in San Francisco, California, in 1906, and more recently, in the Loma Prieta, California, earthquake in 1989.

Seismic Sea Waves Caused by Earthquakes

Earthquakes also may trigger **tsunamis** or **seismic sea waves** that are a threat to coastal cities and sometimes to entire islands. The former name for these events, "tidal" waves, has largely been abandoned due to the fact that they are entirely unrelated to tides. The effect of the earthquake on the ocean is similar to that of a person jumping into a bathtub or swimming pool. Earthquakes, shocking the ocean floor, generate circular sets of waves which radiate outward from the source at very high speeds, often several hundred miles per hour. It has been said that an earthquake occurring in California could generate a tsunami that could outrace someone in a passenger jet flying across the Pacific. Tsunamis can and do cross large expanses of water, losing little energy in the process. In coastal areas, this energy is translated into very high waves, focused and pushed upward by shallowly covered sea floor. By the time the wave reaches shore, it is slower (20–30 mph) and higher (20–25 feet). It then crashes as a wall of water into low-lying areas, including costal cities. Successive waves of varying height often follow.

Because no preventive measures are possible, the best defense against tsunamis is good communication, allowing news of undersea quakes and potential tsunami danger to be broadcast soon after the earthquake occurs. Ships can then put out into deeper water away from the high wave front and coastal areas can be evacuated. A passing tsunami in the open ocean may raise a surface ship only a few meters.

The need for the establishment of an effective communication system was dramatically and tragically exemplified on December 26, 2004, when catastrophically deadly tsunamis devastated coastal regions of the Indian Ocean. These were set in motion by a magnitude 9.0 earthquake which occurred that day approximately 160 miles off the coast of the island of Sumatra in Indonesia. The tsunamis moved at speeds of around 500 mph in the open ocean and, when they came ashore, killed more than 200,000 people in coastal areas, mostly in Indonesia and Sri Lanka, but also in Malaysia, Thailand, Myanmar (Burma), Bangladesh, India, the Maldives, Somalia, Kenya, and Tanzania. The cause of the earthquake was sudden and violent motion within the subduction zone on the Indian Ocean floor where the Indian Plate dives beneath the Burmese Plate. The interaction of these plates resulted in a 600-mile length of seafloor rupturing, rising upward, and displacing millions of tons of water, which, as it reached the ocean's surface, moved laterally as enormous waves. As these waves approached shallow water, they began to encounter the sea floor, which pushed them upward and resulted in the waves cresting and toppling forward onto the shore, or flooding the coast as a "plateau" of water. The tsunamis crashed inland along the shoreline and then caused additional devastation as they rapidly drained back, dragging buildings, vehicles, and people into the ocean in a giant riptide.

The 9.0 earthquake that occurred off the coast of Japan in March of 2011 highlighted the need to use care and caution when building in susceptible zones. This earthquake occurred in a known subduction zone and generated a tsunami with waves of 37.88 meters (over 124 feet). The initial impact of the tsunami resulted in the death of over 20,000 people and the displacement of over 130,000 more. The failure of the backup generators, caused by the tsunami, for the cooling units at the three Fukushima nuclear power plants resulted in what many consider the worst nuclear disaster since Chernobyl. Explosions, fires and ultimately release of radioactive gases occurred. This has made the areas around the plants uninhabitable and resulted in the displacement of 90,000 more residents. The release included both cesium and strontium 90 which are considered hazardous to human health. Cesium levels continued to be monitored and spiked in some areas around Fukushima over a year later in early 2012. Higher levels of cesium have been found in areas usually used for rice cultivation within the area and in the Pacific Ocean area immediately around the damaged plants. Strontium 90 was also found in elevated levels in Tokyo. Although these earthquakes and tsunamis are somewhat rare, the lessons learned from Fukushima remind us to be mindful of the geology of any area where we might wish to site nuclear power plants.

Earthquake Prediction and Prevention

Despite considerable ongoing research, it is still not possible to accurately predict within a framework of hours or days when an earthquake is likely to occur, The best preventatives of earthquake damage are education and legislation. Stricter building codes may be helpful, as well as research and implementation of improved building designs. Restructuring and reinforcement of older, pre-code buildings would be helpful as well. Many buildings in Oakland, California had walls reinforced with steel beams before occupation permits were issued in the aftermath of the very damaging "World Series" quake of the late 1980s. Some elevated freeways in Oakland were converted to boulevards rather than rebuilt as they were, because it was discovered that their collapse was facilitated by their construction on consolidated materials.

As long as there is continuing economic pressure to design housing on unstable (often, human-made) hillsides because of the view or because of scarcity of more suitable land to build on, there is little to do but concede that disaster might occur. Economic loss due to lack of adequate insurance, unpaid claims, and even the withdrawal of insurers from handling earthquake-related claims all are likely possibilities. There are no easy solutions to the threat that earthquakes pose to cities.

Volcanoes

Volcanoes are any place molten materials called **magmas** reach the surface and quite often are conical shapes normally easily spotted either from aerial or ground level perspectives. They are produced from repeated local flows and explosively driven ejections of hot, molten materials called **lavas,** which are magmas that spill onto the earth's surface.

Magmas originate from sources within the earth's lower crust and upper mantle, and, occasionally, deep seated hot spots within the mantle. The best leakage zones for this material occur at the boundary of the great plates that compose the crust and upper mantle. Thus there exists a close relationship between the location of volcanos and earthquake activity.

Most volcanoes occurring on continents are associated with plate boundaries that experience compressive movement. Thus, they circle the Pacific Ocean forming a pattern known as the "Rim of Fire." Other concentrations of volcanoes occur in the Mediterranean Sea, along the Indonesian island chain, and in the Lesser Antilles. Tensional plate boundaries also spawn volcanoes, but as the earthquakes associated with these boundary types, they are mostly submerged. In addition, mantle hotspots may also spawn intra-plate volcanoes, perhaps the most famous examples of which are those that formed and are continuing to form the Hawaiian Islands and Iceland and those that underlie Yellowstone National Park.

The high, beautifully symmetrical **composite cones** associated with compressive plate boundaries are the volcanoes that pose the greatest threat to urban areas. They contain lavas rich in silica, making them viscous to the point where they can potentially trap large quantities of explosive volcanic gas. Lavas with lower levels of silica are more fluid and tend to erupt less violently because they are capable of containing less trapped gas. They produce the broad and generally non-explosive **shield volcanoes** such as those that characterize the Hawaiian Islands. Lava from these volcanos may occasionally slowly overrun land and buildings, but this process usually is not associated with loss of human lives, because people generally have sufficient time to remove themselves from harm's way.

Composite cones often make pre-eruption rumblings (like an upset stomach) warning people in the immediate vicinity of trouble. Sometimes, however, the volcanos explode unexpectedly. Fragments called **pyroclasts,** (literally "broken by fire") some as big as houses (**volcanic blocks** and **bombs**) but most the size of sand and dust (**volcanic ash**), are blown out. The large clasts drop quickly, but the finer material can be blown upward and outward for miles. A related phenomenon, a **nuee ardente,** or pyroclastic flow, is a rapidly moving and potentially deadly mixture of incandescent gasses, water, and pyroclasts. Such a nuee ardente instantly incinerated the city of St. Pierre on Martinique in 1902, killing nearly 30,000 people. Ash and mud flows generated by Mt. Vesuvius in 79 A.D. were responsible for the destruction of the Roman cities of Pompeii and Herculeum. Downwind drift of the ash can bury nearby buildings and shower a veneer of glass shards that disable machinery. Large areas and populations may be affected for a considerable time by reduced sunlight, atmospheric cooling, and colorful sunsets as the emitted gasses and particles influence the atmosphere's reception of solar energy.

Dealing with Volcanic Hazards

As prevention of volcanic eruptions is beyond the scope of present or foreseeable technology, eruption prediction is the key for survival in cities threatened by volcanoes. On the whole, the prediction of volcanic events is more reliable than that for major earthquakes for two reasons. First, the location of the potential hazard is precisely known because volcanos are quite normally highly visible. Second, volcanoes may give obvious signals prior to eruption, such as smoking, rumbling, and low magnitude earthquakes. These signals may precede the eruption by days, months, or even years. There is usually sufficient time for scientists to set up monitoring devices such as tilt meters (to detect the upward movement of magma) and volcanic gas analyzers. Sometimes permanent monitoring stations are set up close to major cities at risk. Based on new and historical data, hazard maps can be prepared to predict the extent of possible damage, and then evacuation routes and plans may be formulated.

There is immense pressure on scientists to deliver accurate and timely information as to when a volcanic eruption will occur which will affect people and their property. It is imperative to accurately know when the life and business activity of a city must be disrupted, often at potential danger and great cost, in order to begin an adequate evacuation. Despite elaborate studies and reasonable predictions, the eruption of Mount St. Helens in 1980 still killed about fifty people. On the other hand, although the evacuation of nearly 16,000 Clark Air Force Base personnel, family members, and local villagers prior to the eruption of the Philippines' Mt. Pinatubo in 1992 took days, all those in harm's way escaped in time.

Sometimes what is obvious to some is not obvious to others. When the Space Needle was built in Seattle, there were two entire mountains easily visible from the structure to the east. Now, however, there remains only one, because approximately one-third of the other—Mt. St. Helens—disappeared in moments in 1980. Mt. Rainier remains a beautiful view, but it is part of the same volcanic mountain chain—the Cascades.

In 1943, when the emergent Paricutin turned a cornfield in Michoacan in central Mexico into a new volcano, many people said they were surprised because they thought there were no volcanoes in the area. Nevertheless, a quick local geological survey reveals that many of the hills there are extinct or dormant volcanoes, and a common local building stone is lava-produced vesicular basalt. The closest and largest city in the area is Uruapan, where the curbs, city square, and many streets are paved with this basalt. Many residents of the area were simply unaware in the 1940s of the origin of the building

Mt. Rainier, Cascade Range, Oregon. (Photo by Zuzana Sadkova. Copyright 2004.)

Paricutin. The volcano Paricutin displays a classic cinder cone shape. The volcano produced regular lava flows for almost ten years. It still gives off smoke via fumaroles, and the area remains seismically active. (Photo by John Fleshin, copyright 2004.)

materials they were using and the origin of many of the hills in the surrounding countryside. By the time it had finished that episode of activity years later, Paricutin had built its cinder cone to a height of 424 meters, covered twenty-five square kilometers with lava (including two villages), and covered outlying areas with enough ash to kill the forests. Robert L. Ripley of "Ripley's Believe it or Not" fame offered to buy the volcano, giving three reasons: 1) as a boy he had always wanted a volcano; 2) it might fill a spiritual void; and 3) it might prove a good investment. Unfortunately, or fortunately, depending upon one's point of view, the owner of the property, Dionisio Pulido, was difficult to find, and the Mexican government has complicated laws governing the ownership of land by foreigners. Ripley did publish one of his syndicated columns and cartoons stating, "I want to buy a volcano" (**Time,** January 29, 1945, page 44).

An ocean away, the Italian government is offering to buy the homes of people in the most hazardous areas near Mt. Vesuvius around Pompeii, but the fact remains that many people refuse to move, and they, like millions worldwide, live in the shadow of volcanic disaster.

As the foregoing overview indicates, the discipline of geology provides not only important, even potentially life-saving information to at-risk populations of cities, but it also provides information that is critically important to planners and all those entrusted with the care of the environment, as they make critical decisions on land use.

Name _____

The City Relies on Its Foundations (Geology)

2-1. What are major hazards posed by earthquakes? What can be done to minimize them?

2-2. If an area is historically known to be prone to earthquakes, why might it not have earthquakes for many years?

2-3. How might volcanoes affect global climate?

2-4. Devise strategies for flood control. How does the process of urbanization affect the potential for flooding and flooding destructiveness?

2-5. Evaluate the multipoint strategy for coastal zone management presented in this chapter. What are the advantages of each point?

2-6. How can you recognize an area that is prone to mass wasting? How can you recognize potentially expansive soils?

The City Organizes Its Space
(Geography)
Virginia O. Benson

Urban geographers study the organization and evolution of urban space. Although some features of the models described below may be applied to command economies in other countries, the underlying concept of economic optimization is basic to the spatial analysis of American cities. For the American urban geographer, an important question is: "How does the city develop spatially in a free market economy?"

The scientific method, commonly used by urban scholars, begins with the observation that the city is a variegated landscape which can be classified in a number of ways. Among the models used by geographers to classify, measure, and analyze urban space, the following are the most common: **location** models, **migration** typologies, and **transportation** concepts. Although models may be called theories, the word "theory" will be avoided for most of the examples used here due to the controversial interpretations of the word. Where appropriate, the word "concept," which indicates that the idea has not been formally and rigorously tested but simply offers a clue to a predictable response, will be used. It should be emphasized, however, that many of the concepts described in this chapter have had a great influence on planners, economists, and other students of the city. Applications of these models appear elsewhere in this book. Professional practitioners, such as real estate developers in American cities, also rely on an understanding of these principles. They often propose that the three most important things in real estate are location, location and location.

Location Theories

Location theories are static concepts; they identify a pattern on the landscape rather than an ongoing process such as migration. For this reason they are easier to classify, measure, and predict than are migration models, which offer a constantly moving target.

The spatial pattern of American city locations is produced through a process that is generally attributed to economic forces. Although other forces can be added to the models, the basic framework is an economic one. The following section describes three models that explain city formation: the **external** factors that lead to the location of a city. The next section explores three models that describe the city itself: the **internal** factors that explain the structure of the city.

External Factors

von Thunen's Model

The earliest model was produced by Johann Heinrich von Thunen (1826) in Germany. He conceptualized the location of agricultural land uses in relation to the marketplace where the farm products were sold.

In von Thunen's concept, the value of agricultural land was directly related to its distance from the market. The objective of minimizing transportation costs was extremely important in an era before modern transportation methods. As a component of the total cost of the products, the transportation cost of hauling by oxcart was very high. Although transportation costs are much lower today, public concerns about air pollution, oil shortages, and traffic congestion still lead to a demand to minimize transport costs (and fuel usage) in the modern city.

Basic to von Thunen's model is the economic geographic idea of the **bid rent curve.** Figure 3.1 illustrates the concept.

The model is an abstraction from reality; it is intended to simplify a complex situation and to present a few controlled variables, which are thought to be good predictors. In the case of von Thunen's simple model, the variables tested are: the cost of land, the choice of crop, and the distance from the marketplace. As Figure 3.1 shows, the crops raised by the farmer are dependent on distance from the market and price of the crop. Because the transportation costs are less when the fields are closer to the market, the land is more expensive and the crop must attract a larger price. The greater the distance from the marketplace, the lower the land value and the lower the crop price, by weight.

If the idea were tested today, certain crops would be expected to appear as one travels from the city center to a rural area. Immediately surrounding the city, such high-value crops as garden vegetables would be found. Traveling farther away from the center, corn would be followed by wheat, and, at the fringe of the agricultural area, open grazing of

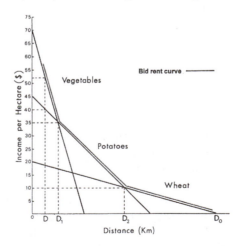

Figure 3.1
Three-crop base showing bid-rent curve.
Source: From *The Economic Landscape* by J. B. Foust and A. R. DeSouza. Copyright © 1978 by Brady Foust. Reprinted by permission.

livestock. As with any model, exceptions are to be expected, but the general pattern holds around most American cities even today. In fact, an urban-rural fringe of land, which is no longer farmed but which is lying idle in anticipation of sale as housing tracts or shopping centers, surrounds many cities.

The same concept might be applied to the value of land inside the city. The closer to the center, whether the central business district or the shopping center in the suburb, the higher the land values. This is due to the cheaper transportation cost of reaching the center where desirable activity takes place (such as employment). This phenomenon has been described as a rent gradient, a variation on the bid rent curve.

Weber's Model

Many towns and cities across America began as farm communities, centers where agricultural products were sold. These towns rapidly expanded with the introduction of manufacturing in the latter part of the nineteenth century. Those cities with the location advantages for minimizing transportation costs for raw materials achieved the greatest size. Alfred Weber (1929) published his model of industrial location, which explained the relation of raw materials to factory location and to the marketplace. Since raw materials are not evenly distributed across the landscape, the cost of transporting those raw materials to the factory to be processed and from there to the marketplace in the form of the finished product has resulted in the establishment of cities around certain kinds of industrial production.

Basic to Weber's model is the **classification** of raw materials. Table 3.1 describes the classes of raw materials. During the manufacturing process, some materials lose a great

TABLE 3.1

Solutions to Weber's Locational Problems

Material Classes	Location
Ubiquities only	Market
Localized and pure	
One pure	Anywhere between source of raw material and market
One pure and ubiquities	Market
More than one pure	Market
More than one pure and ubiquities	Market
Localized and weight losing (gross)	
One weight losing	Source
One weight losing and ubiquities	Source or market depending on relative size of input
More than one weight losing	Indeterminate (mathematical solution)
More than one weight losing and ubiquities	Indeterminate (mathematical solution)

Source: Foust, B. J., DeSouza, A. R., The Economic Landscape: A Theoretical Introduction, 1978, p. 131.

deal of their weight. Forest products are an example. Since most of the tree is left behind when lumber is produced, the sawmill is normally located in the forest area.

Other raw materials are ubiquitous, or almost so. An example is water. Where the major component of the final product is water, such as beer or soft drinks, one expects to find the bottling plant or brewery near the market in the city. Some raw materials lose no weight in processing; those products may be manufactured at any point between the raw material extraction and the marketplace because the transportation cost for the raw material and the finished product is the same.

Figure 3.2 illustrates the cost of moving the raw material (RM) to the factory and the cost of moving the finished product (FP) to the marketplace. When the costs are added together, the result is the total transportation cost (TTC). For the economically rational decision maker who wishes to minimize transport costs, the logical location for a factory is where the TTC line is the lowest. Figures 3.3, 3.4, 3.5 and 3.6 are further examples using the variations brought about by combinations of raw materials.

Although Weber's model is affected by modern transportation technology, many cities owe their current location to his concept. An example is the location of industrial cities along the Great Lakes where the raw materials for steel, iron ore and coal were available and resulted in the growth industry that spawned automobile production and a host of related products. The past location of cities such as Chicago, Cleveland, and Pittsburgh can be explained by Weber's model. Here another concept, that of **inertia** (the tendency of a body to resist motion), helps to explain why those cities have continued to grow after that initial decision was no longer as relevant.

Christaller's Central Place Model

A third factor in city location, following the agricultural market model and the manufacturing model, is the provision of goods and services to a population. Where the other two roles may be regarded as **basic** in terms of providing income to a city, the provision of

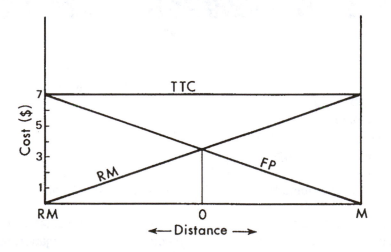

Figure 3.2
Weber's model: one pure localized raw material.
Source: From *The Economic Landscape* by J. B. Foust and A. R. DeSouza. Copyright © 1978 by Brady Foust. Reprinted by permission.

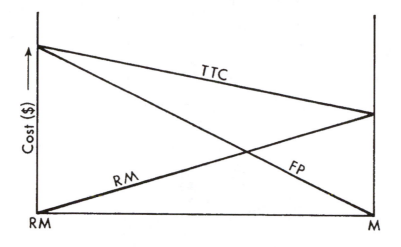

Figure 3.3
Weber's model: One localized weight loosing raw material.
Source: From *The Economic Landscape* by J. B. Foust and A. R. DeSouza. Copyright © 1978 by Brady Foust. Reprinted by permission.

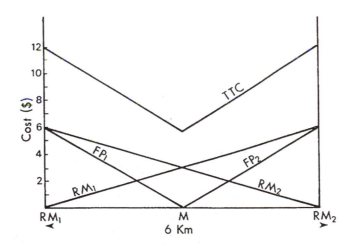

Figure 3.4
Weber's model: two pure localized raw materials.
Source: From *The Economic Landscape* by J. B. Foust and A. R. DeSouza. Copyright © 1978 by Brady Foust. Reprinted by permission.

goods and services is a **nonbasic** function in that it circulates the income that is already in the metropolitan area. Cities that have this activity as a chief role are referred to as distribution centers. Walter Christaller called them "central places."

Christaller identified city size variations in terms of their service role. His theory was described in the book, *The Central Places of Southern Germany* (Christaller, trans.

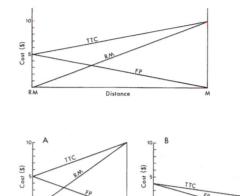

Figure 3.5
Weber's model: one localized, weight losing raw material plus ubiquities (A) Optimum
location at raw material source; (B) Optimum location at market.
Source: From *The Economic Landscape* by J. B. Foust and A. R. DeSouza. Copyright © 1978 by Brady
Foust. Reprinted by permission.

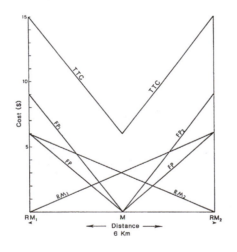

Figure 3.6
Weber's model: several pure, localized raw materials plus ubiquities.
Source: From *The Economic Landscape* by J. B. Foust and A. R. DeSouza. Copyright © 1978 by Brady
Foust. Reprinted by permission.

by Baskin, 1966). A central place is a settlement that forms as a result of trade with its
surrounding area or hinterland.

The Central Place concept is an economic geographic model based on the idea of the
economic advantages of clustering. The model is particularly focused on retailing services.
It has an immensely practical value to those who might wish to enter business, to those
who are buying a house and to those whose income is dependent on the marketplace.

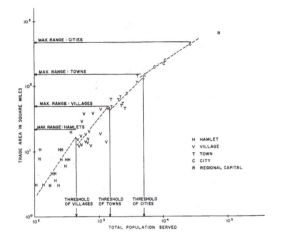

Figure 3.7
Range and threshold graph.
Source: From *Canadian Geographer,* 1967 vol XI, p. 154. Copyright 1967 by Canadian Association of Geographers. Reprinted by permission.

Two concepts that are basic to Christaller's model are "threshold" and "range of a good." The threshold is the minimum amount of sales required for a center to offer a good. (See Figure 3.7.) It may also be expressed as the "minimum level of demand" or the "minimum number of people" but the idea is the same. If a center or city or town offers a particular product or service, there must be a sufficient demand for it within the market area. The concept of a demand threshold underlies all effective retail market studies.

The range of a good is the distance that the consumer will travel to obtain a product or service. The rational economic consumer will not travel more than a logical distance to obtain a low value good, such as a loaf of bread. He or she will travel much farther to obtain a fur coat or a new car. The distance traveled is directly related to the value of the product.

When the concepts of threshold and range are combined, they create a spatial pattern of central places, which forms a nest of hexagonal shapes on the landscape. (See Figure 3.8.) This pattern represents a hierarchy of central places from the small hamlet, which offers convenience functions such as a gas station or small grocery, to a large city, which offers every possible good or service desired. (See Figure 3.9.)

The pattern described above may relate to a system of cities, as represented in Figure 3.9, or, within one city, a system of centers. Most American cities have a central business district surrounded by a series of large regional shopping malls. These would be considered A-level centers. The B-level would be smaller community centers that are found in greater numbers while the C-level would represent the more convenient retailing of the nearby strip mall. The D-level would be the corner convenience store. This pattern was demonstrated in the 1950s in the work of geographer Brian Berry (1958). He associated the various level centers with their corresponding land values and showed how land values are affected by accessibility to the market center. The currently popular concept of "critical mass" refers to the amount of goods and services offered by the market center described in Christaller's model.

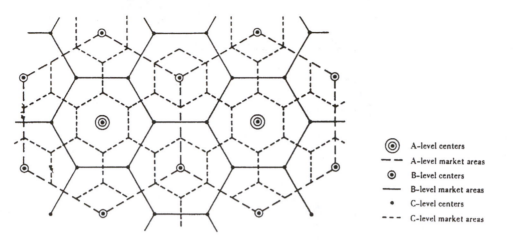

Figure 3.8
A hierarchal spatial arrangement of central places according to Christaller's k = 3 principle.
Source: From *The Economic Landscape* by J. B. Foust and A. R. DeSouza. Copyright © 1978 by Brady Foust. Reprinted by permission.

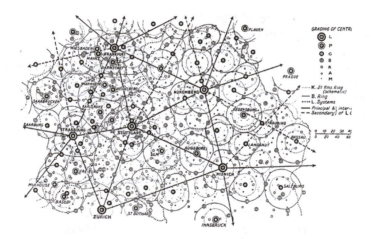

Figure 3.9
The central place system of southern Germany.
Source: From *Central Places in Southern Germany,* by W. Christaller, translated by C. W. Baskin. Copyright 1966 by C. W. Baskin. Published by Prentice Hall, 1966. Reprinted by permission.

Internal Factors

Growth Models

Just as the preceding location theories provide a framework for studying the external economic factors that lead to a city's formation, the following growth models help explain the factors leading to the internal expansion of cities. They describe the pattern of residential population growth and its resulting spatial configuration. The first of these models appeared in the work of a sociologist of the University of Chicago, Ernest Burgess (1925).

Burgess' Concentric Zone Model

In the 1920s, Ernest Burgess and others from the so-called "Chicago School" envisioned city growth as a pattern of concentric circles moving out from the center. The initial ring surrounding the central business district (CBD) was called the "zone in transition." (See Figure 3.10.) As indicated in the diagram, this was surrounded by the "zone of working-men's homes," the "zone of better residences" and the "commuters' zone." The model reflected the transportation of that day when laborers walked to their jobs and streetcars were the major public transit. At that time, all major shopping, restaurants and offices were located in the central business district.

As growth took place, each zone tended to expand its area and the occupants would invade the next zone. Although the pattern is highly generalized, it formed the basis for much of the thinking about city form that followed.

Hoyt's Sector Model

In the 1930s, Homer Hoyt (1939) produced the sector model by adding the factor of the transportation routes to the Burgess concentric growth concept. Important streets and avenues that attracted specific kinds of land uses were identified in Hoyt's model, which emphasized the role of perception (rich sectors versus poor sectors) in the growth and development of the city. (See Figure 3.11.)

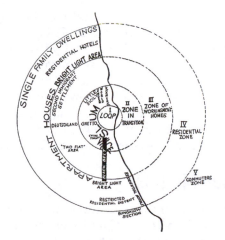

Figure 3.10
The schema of Burgess's theory of the growth of the city applied to Chicago.
Source: From *The City* by R. E. Park, E. Burgess, and R. D. McKenzie. Copyright 1925. Published by the University of Chicago Press, 1925. Reprinted by permission.

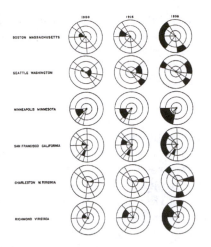

Figure 3.11
Shifts in location of fashionable residential areas in six American cities 1900–1936.
Source: Federal Housing Administration, Division of Economics and Statistics, 1939.
(*Source:* Hoyt, H., *The Structure and Growth of Residential Neighborhoods in American Cities,* 1939, p. 115).

Hoyt described, in great detail, the various high rent districts, which he found through studying sixty-four cities. These patterns still persist in sectors located along lines of fastest transportation, along waterfronts, and at high elevations where residents may escape the smoke and fumes of industry.

Edward Ullmann's Multiple Nuclei Model

In the 1940s, Ullmann's model acknowledged the impact of transportation improvements by anticipating the decentralization of residential population and development of new outlying commercial centers to service it (Ullmann, 1941).

As the city expanded, movement from high density to lower density areas where residents have more space and land costs are lower characterized the process; commercial activities soon followed their residential market, as did expanding industries seeking one-story factory space. (See Figure 3.12.) Each new node formed its own concentric rings around commercial centers. However, suburban development often occurs in a linear pattern along highways. Clusters may form at highway interchanges, once again illustrating the rent gradient as values decline with distance from the interchange.

Summary of Location Models

Each of these models focuses attention on different variables. Central place theory, von Thunen's agricultural location concept, and Weber's industrial location model are called location theories because they attempt to explain why things are located where they are. They are relevant to cities because they explain urbanization patterns (why **cities** are located where they are). The final three models, Burgess, Hoyt and Ullmann,

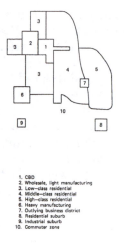

1. CBD
2. Wholesale, light manufacturing
3. Low–class residential
4. Middle–class residential
5. High–class residential
6. Heavy manufacturing
7. Outlying business district
8. Residential suburb
9. Industrial suburb
10. Commuter zone

Figure 3.12
The multi nuclei concept.
Source: From *Annals of the American Academy of Political and Social Science,* Vol. 242, p. 14.
Copyright by the American Academy of Political and Social Science. Reprinted by permission.

interpret the intra-urban patterns of city growth, particularly focused on residential development. It is apparent that the strong influence of changes in transportation technology, as they occurred in each historical period, had a great impact on each model builder.

What is the practical value of each of these models? Remembering that the only real value of science lies in its ability to enable people to predict and therefore to have more control over their lives, what does central place theory help to predict?

The central place model and von Thumen's concepts allow prediction of land values; the central place idea indicates that land at the center of the city is the highest in value while land at the fringes is the lowest. Purchase of land to build a house or a business place requires an interest in investing in property that would give the greatest return on the investment. Even though the house is a shelter, the homeowner is still concerned about its resale value. The location of a business place may mean the difference between success and failure in the venture.

The Burgess, Hoyt, and Ullmann models explain the growth of the city. Understanding city growth patterns enables prediction not only of the values of the land but also the location of needed goods and services. If the city is growing in concentric rings, (Burgess) and each ring contains a certain type of land use, or the population moves farther out from the center with each generation, one might expect that land at the fringe will grow in value. The market for goods and services will also grow. A good illustration can be seen in the suburban shopping mall expansion. Shopping facilities normally follow residential growth.

If the city is growing in sectors, those who live in a sector that is low in value might wish to move to a higher value sector. If the sectors are determined by the extension of traffic arteries, growth could be expected when a new highway is announced. Heavy traffic, on the other hand, may cause a drop in property values as intersections become congested and noise or air pollution increases. Residents may even decide to organize opposition to transportation plans if they are seen to depress the value of their housing.

In Hoyt's model, the sectors developed in a radial pattern away from the center and, if the sector began with high-value land uses, such as offices, the residential uses would be expected to be high as well. On the other hand, if low-value uses were located near the center of the city, that sector would continue the low-value residential pattern. Some cities have famous streets that are known for their high value (Park Avenue in New York, Rodeo Drive in Los Angeles). Other cities have streets that denote decay (Seattle's Skid Road, which became a generic term for "down-and-out" i.e., Skid Row).

Ullmann introduced his concept of multiple nuclei in the 1940s, when traffic arteries were extended into the hinterland and the suburbs were born. The new nuclei were commercial centers and the city was no longer centered on the downtown; in many urban areas, the suburban mall took the place of the downtown.

Much discussion has been devoted to whether the downtown still has a *raison d'etre* in light of the growth of suburban culture. The vaunted "back to the city" movement remains a dream in many cases. Someone, however, will predict the future of the cityscape for the next twenty years and will enrich him/herself by the value of the knowledge. The ability to predict is the ability to control.

For example, if the city becomes increasingly multi-nuclear, described as a number of smaller centers revolving around the main center, or if an urban landscape of "Edge Cities" (Garreau, 1988) with no central city focus should develop, certain goods and services would be in demand at these outlying centers. To start a retail business venture, one would certainly have to take these location concepts into consideration in order to succeed.

Migration Concepts

Another opportunity to predict is set forth in models of migration that are used by geographers to plan for growth or decline in population. These models address demographics in spatial terms. Demography is the study of population characteristics and can be useful in anticipating where various population groups will reside, work, shop, or carry on recreational activities. Planners of any of these activities need such predictive ability.

Scale

Initially, its scale can classify migration. The longest migrations are usually **international** in scale. The cities of the northeastern United States grew rapidly during the great international migrations from Europe in the 1800s and early decades of the 1900s. This rapid growth led to passage of many laws in cities to control the expansion of living quarters and the zoning of urban areas.

At a smaller scale, **interregional** migration has been apparent in American history as early settlers first moved to Western states; that movement was followed by a great migration from the South to the North after the Civil War. Recent decades have produced movement to the southern and western United States, the so-called Sunbelt, where the attractions have been employment opportunities and climate amenities.

Urbanization is generally considered as the migration from rural areas to the city. At an even more local scale, movement can be classified as **intra-urban** when it takes place within the metropolitan area itself. The most obvious example is the recent flow to the suburbs from the central city.

Life Cycle Stages

An example of a migration concept was produced by Peter Rossi (1955) in his book called *Why Families Move*. In this study, the author presented a "stages" approach to the question in his book title. He postulated that everyone in the United States goes through life cycle stages that may result in moving his or her residence from one place to another. Following is a list of possible situations in which a change of residence is required:

> Birth (hospital to home)
> Added family members (apartment to house)
> Graduation from high school (home to college)
> Graduation from college (college to work place)
> Marriage ("bachelor pad" to apartment with spouse)
> Divorce (house back to "bachelor pad")
> Job changes (one city to another)
> Retirement (north to Sunbelt)
> Aging (condo to nursing home)
> Final move (cemetery)

For the urban geographer, it is important to communicate to planners the understanding of the age structure of the city population in order to anticipate such movement.

Push-Pull Factors

Another way of thinking about migration is through factors that impel movement (Lee, 1966). Factors may be negative at the origin or positive at the destination. Negative factors at the origin push the resident out of his or her present location; positive factors at the destination pull the resident into the new environment.

Examples of push-pull factors are:

Negative at the **Origin:**	Positive at the **Destination:**
High costs	Attractive appearance
Unpleasant neighbors	Nice neighborhood
Expanding family needs space	Good schools
Housing condition neglected	Perception of safety
Landlord raises the rent	Convenience to work
Fire damage	Good shopping
Crime	More space, inside or out
Inconvenient to workplace	

It becomes apparent that these factors are interrelated in the sense that the negative factor at the origin may also be the positive factor at the destination. Intervening obstacles also may impede movement from the origin to the destination. Such obstacles as racial discrimination, social class distinctions, family obligations and employment situations may stop movement from taking place. (See Figure 3.13.) However, it has been estimated that one American in five changes residence every year. Between the periods of census taking, which occur every ten years, the average United States resident has moved twice. One can readily see the difficulty of planning facilities for such a mobile population.

Brian Berry (1976) described other factors involved in the American desire to move. He characterized American society as having seven traits that encourage mobility:

1. A love of newness;
2. A desire to be close to nature;
3. Freedom to move;
4. Individualism, avoiding central decision-making;
5. A melting-pot tradition;
6. Violence for control of turf; and
7. A sense of destiny.

Summary of Migration Concepts

Migration has become increasingly important as a factor in planning for business, government, and all institutions in American society. The spatial arrangements studied by the geographer are dynamic and reflect the mobility of today's citizens. Urban landscapes are in a constant state of evolution, and the ability to predict future patterns gives the student of the city a great advantage over those who cannot.

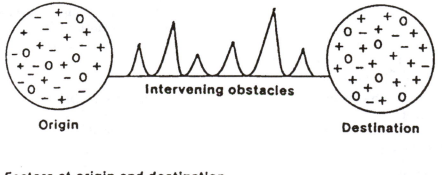

Figure 3.13
Origin and destination factors and intervening obstacles in migration.
Source: From A Theory of Migration," *Demography #3 by E. S. Lee. Copyright 1966 by the Population Association of America. Reprinted by permission.*

Transportation Concepts

It has become apparent that the spatial view of the city is very dependent on two concepts; location and movement. All movement involves costs; these costs may be in the form of time or money, but they are critical in explaining location patterns in cities.

Transportation costs are an intrinsic component of all of the models mentioned in the previous sections. Central place theory, von Thunen's agricultural location model, Weber's industrial location model, Burgess' concentric zone idea, Hoyt's sector theory and Ullmann's multiple nuclei model include the cost of movement as a basic condition.

This section demonstrates how transportation cost factors are relevant to the common experience of urban life. It may appear that, with the lowering of transportation costs over time, this factor would be less important in explaining locations than it has been in the past. This may be true with present-day location decisions. However, much of what we see in cities today is a result of historic location decisions very dependent on transportation costs. Those historic decisions have created a setting in which it is likely that settlement will continue. Some examples are:

1. The steel industry, in times past, was located on the Great Lakes in cities such as Chicago, Cleveland, and Pittsburgh. Iron ore from the Mesabi Range in Minnesota was transported by water, the least expensive way, to coal regions in Illinois, Ohio, and Pennsylvania, where it could be manufactured into steel. Although steel is no longer the dominant industry, these cities have remained in the same location and have become important diversified economies in the Midwest.

2. Manufacturing which took place in port cities on the east and west coasts was based on shipping raw materials and finished goods for many decades because it was the cheapest form of transportation. Japan moved into this market and has built much of its own economy on water transportation, since it lacks local raw materials, and has moved into the production of goods that were formerly exported by cities in the United States. However, cities on the east and west coasts have continued to grow based on a shift to the service sector.

3. Rail transportation was responsible for the location of many cities in the United States. Chicago was the rail hub of the Midwest. In spite of the decline in rail transport and the shift to trucking, Chicago remains the dominant city in its region based on other economic activities.

The following section will describe a number of factors that affect transportation costs and thereby reinforce settlement patterns even today (Foust & DeSouza, 1978).

Properties of Transportation Costs

Transportation costs are a linear function of distance in the simplest model form (Figure 3.14). Having abstracted reality to this simple relationship, further variables that affect total transportation costs may be added.

Initially, the actual transportation costs must be considered in two parts: terminal and line-haul costs. Several types of transportation modes are addressed in this discussion: ship, rail and truck. The terminal costs, which vary from mode to mode, are those accumulated before the vehicle (ship, train or truck) is out on the water, rail or road (Figure 3.15).

The concept of terminal and line-haul costs is not unlike the idea of capital costs and operating costs. Such terms are used for any building project where the structure is built

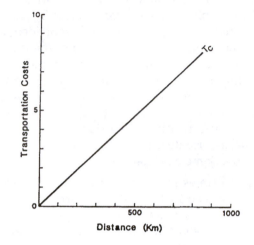

Figure 3.14
Linear transportation costs as a function of distance.
Source: From *The Economic Landscape* by B. J. Foust and A. R. DeSouza. Copyright 1978 by Brady Foust. Originally published by Charles E. Merrill Publishing, 1978. Reprinted by permission of the author.

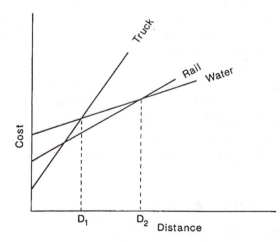

Figure 3.15
Variations in terminal and line-haul cost among different transport media.
Source: From *The Economic Landscape* by B. J. Foust and A. R. DeSouza. Copyright 1978 by Brady Foust. Originally published by Charles E. Merrill Publishing, 1978. Reprinted by permission of the author.

with capital (fixed costs) and operated by variable costs. The building at a state university is paid for by the state's capital budget (fixed costs). The operation of the building is paid for by taxes, which support the variable costs and account for the fact that some buildings are built and not occupied until tax revenue is raised.

In the case of transportation, the fixed cost consists of the following components: the purchase price of the vehicle, the tax paid on it, the insurance plus the structure in which it is stored, and the cost of maintenance. These costs continue whether the vehicle is taken out "on the road" or not. The operating cost consists of: gasoline or other fuel, road taxes, tolls, and any other cost incurred in the actual use of the vehicle.

Different modes of transportation have variations in the relationships between terminal and line-haul costs, as shown in Figure 3.15 The ship is the most costly in terms of terminal costs but least costly when it is on the water. These low costs for water transportation explain much about the locations of large cities on water bodies. Rail has lower terminal costs than shipping but has higher costs per mile when leaving the terminal. Trucking is the lowest terminal cost but given the high cost of fuel and in spite of the government subsidy of highways, trucking has the highest operating cost. Of course, trucking has the advantage of great convenience since there are many more roads than navigable waterways.

Given the simple model of transportation costs shown in Figures 3.14 and 3.15, other factors can be added to see how these affect the model. For example, because of economies of the long haul (the farther the travel the cheaper the rate per mile), transportation costs are actually a **curvilinear** function of distance. (See Figure 3.16.) For this reason, charges are not the same rate per mile when flying to a nearby city as when flying across the continent.

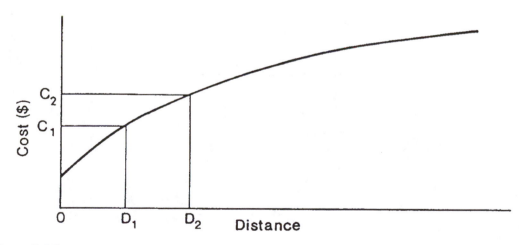

Figure 3.16
Curvilinear line-haul costs.
Source: From *The Economic Landscape* by B. J. Foust and A. R. DeSouza. Copyright 1978 by Brady Foust. Originally published by Charles E. Merrill Publishing, 1978. Reprinted by permission of the author.

Other variations in transportation costs are the following:

- Commodity variations—loading and packaging costs vary depending on bulkiness, "knocked down" over "set up" packages, special crating and packaging; damage and risk costs vary when commodities are easily damaged and require more insurance; shipment size differences result in cost variations due to economies of scale; and regularity of movement year around saves transportation costs over seasonal shipping.
- Carrier and route variations—when competition between carriers occurs, savings on transportation costs can be expected; routes that have high demand, such as between East Coast cities, produce transportation savings; backhauling produces savings when trucks are not returned empty but carry a return cargo.

Each of these factors affects the location of industries and therefore the location of cities. Break-of-bulk points, where cargo is transferred from one mode of transportation to another, such as occurs at seaports, creates a node of activity that is city-reinforcing.

Other variations in transportation rates cause advantages for certain city locations and help to reinforce the urban places on the landscape. However, to offset the favorable treatment received by the inhabitants of cities, many transportation costs in the United States are socialized. If this were not true, goods would be unavailable to people living in remote areas. Figure 3.17 demonstrates the concept. The pricing of CIF (Cost, Insurance and Freight) affects the FOB (Freight On Board) boundaries. Those who live at the marketplace actually subsidize, by higher prices for products, those who live at a great distance from the city in rural areas. This subsidy is reflected throughout the American market system. For example, if one buys oranges in California, he or she is likely to pay the same price as those who buy them in New York.

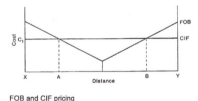

FOB and CIF pricing

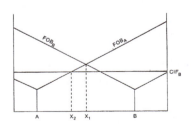

Figure 3.17
The effect of CIF pricing on market area boundaries.
Source: Foust, B. J., DeSouza A. R. *The Economic Landscape: A Theoretical Introduction,* 1978, p. 212.

Several Transportation Modes. (Photo by Philip C. Leiter, copyright 2005.)

Summary of Transportation Concepts

Since transportation costs determine many of the location decisions made in today's society, directly or indirectly, an understanding of the components and the ability to anticipate outcomes of those decisions is enhanced by the work of urban geographers such as those discussed in this chapter. In this era of changes in transportation technology, the search for new fuels, the concern over transportation infrastructure (highways, bridges, mass transit, etc.) and the environmental implications of these decisions, it is critical to integrate our understanding of the contribution that transportation makes to the smooth operation of urban society.

In addition to the economic, demographic and transportation models that provide opportunities for prediction, geographers also study the city as a setting that magnifies the spatial implications of public policies. Such important legislation as federal home loan programs, highway construction, urban renewal, bussing for integration and numerous other government policies, have had dramatic implications for the city in the final decades of the twentieth century. Such policies have affected out-migration of the affluent and, in some cases, have exacerbated the poverty problems of the remaining city residents. All these public policies are circumscribed in space; as the migration models have indicated, Americans are free to move and often vote with their feet. Many of these spatial issues will be touched upon in other chapters of this book. However, it is useful to understand that urban public policies apply to particular precincts and that effectiveness of the programs often depends upon clear comprehension of the geographic variables.

Geographic Information and Global Positioning Systems

Because geography deals with spatial variables, mapping data has long been the geographer's tool of analysis. Since the 1960s, such mapping has moved into the Information

Technology Era with two remarkable innovations: Geographic Information Systems (GIS) and Global Positioning Systems (GPS). These computer-based technologies have numerous applications to urban spatial planning. The location models described earlier in this chapter can be tested and updated quickly using GIS/GPS analyses, thereby enabling better prediction and consequently better planning.

Both GIS and GPS require digital mapping so the variables that were once confined to paper can now be computerized. GPS depends on more than twenty-four satellites, the first launched in 1978 for military purposes. Since then, civilian applications are multiplying. GPS may be used as a primary source of data for GIS. GPS data are three-dimensional, making the 3-D map possible. In the urban area, the new roads, houses, utilities, and other spatial characteristics can be quickly manipulated for up-to-date analyses.

A geographer's skills in analysis of spatial organization of cities have been enhanced by the information technology of GIS and GPS. Together with the increasing connectivity of global forces, such as trade and migration, cities will become subjects of spatial research and planning. City governments are expected to deliver a variety of services to the public. These services are scattered throughout the metropolitan areas. GIS and GPS may assist city planners in their effort to locate, maintain, and project future needs for facilities that serve the public, such as schools, parks, playgrounds, fire protection, and police services. Spatial configurations of crime statistics, of public health variables, of school populations, of property taxes and various other issues enhance the ability of city governments to plan their service programs. It is expected that one day all cell phones will be equipped with GPS so that anyone can be located in case of emergency. GPS is of critical value for police and fire dispatchers.

In addition to the service applications mentioned, geographers have found their map-making skills to be particularly interesting politically. Since most urban areas are found within counties and states, political representation is a major geographical or spatial issue. The elections have turned on state characterizations (red states, blue states) and urban constituents with particular points of view may find that they are underrepresented.

Based on the underlying geographic concepts outlined in this chapter, the business community also may use GIS and GPS in their market research to locate stores, offices, manufacturing plants, transportation networks, and real estate developments. Both public and private sectors may exchange spatial data and work together to provide improved quality of city life. It also offers considerable opportunity for creative manipulation of spatial databases. Because of the ease of mapping with GIS, it is important for its users to be familiar with the nature of geographic models described above to avoid misleading conclusions.

An example of a practical use of GIS is demonstrated in Figure 3.18. A citizen survey was conducted and the data were mapped using GIS. The map shows the zip code locations of those who stated that they would be interested in living in the Cuyahoga River Flats in Cleveland. This information is important to the public officials as well as developers who would construct housing in that downtown location for the purpose of targeting their markets and demonstrating the demand for downtown housing in Cleveland.

Application of geographic data might include finding factors that coincide in space and drawing the conclusion of causal relationships. For example, in the city, such mapping might depict occurrence of environmental problems related to demographic variables such as income. Low-income persons might be expected to live where the air or

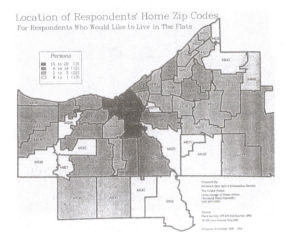

Figure 3.18
An example of a GIS map.
Source: Northern Ohio Data & Information Service, 1992.

water quality is not desirable. A public policy could be produced and implemented by planners to offset this eventuality.

Geographic information systems have many applications for city officials, city planners and others who work in various disciplines in the city. They can be used for activities as diverse as scheduling maintenance of municipal services, analyzing land use patterns, measuring the spread of diseases, or locating school children.

As the city grows and becomes more complex, and as technologies multiply and as society requires new techniques for addressing urban problems, the urban geographer will play an increasingly responsible role. Spatial analysis of geographic variables is particularly useful in the city, where spatial policy decisions are being made that have important consequences for large populations.

Geographies of the Future

All of the models described above are contingent upon location factors that were particularly relevant to the development of twentieth century American cities. Since the advent of the Internet and other telecommunications technologies, the location variables inevitably will change.

In his book *City of Bits,* author William J. Mitchell suggests some of the changes that have taken place in his discussion of space, place, and the Infobahn. Some American cities are expected to experience transformation faster than others but all are affected by new programmable architectures and unexpected spatial freedoms offered by dynamic urbanism.

The underlying theories of centrifugal and centripetal forces will be applied in new ways to the cities of the future. The student of the city will be constantly challenged to make these adjustments to the existing theories and to produce new theoretical frameworks for predicting the urban future. Further discussion of these aspects of twenty-first century urban life is found in this book's final chapter.

Name _____

The City Organizes Its Space (Geography)

3-1. Using the census map on the next page, which growth model best describes the present pattern of this urban area? Defend your answer.

3-2. Suppose you are selling a house. Apply a concept from each of the models in this chapter that would help in selling it.

3-3. Survey several people, asking them how far they are willing to travel to buy a loaf of bread, a new coat, and a new car.

Total Population for Cuyahoga County by Census Tract, 2000

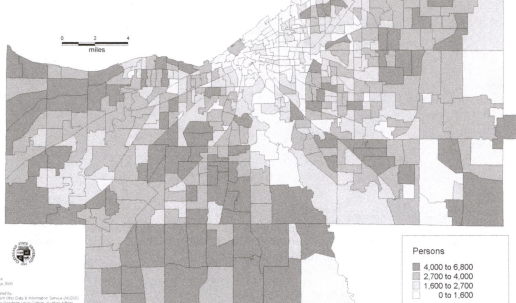

Persons

■ 4,000 to 6,800
■ 2,700 to 4,000
□ 1,600 to 2,700
□ 0 to 1,600

Source
Census 2000

Prepared by
Northern Ohio Data & Information Service (NODIS)
Maxine Goodman Levin College of Urban Affairs
Cleveland State University
October 15, 2005

The City Builds
(Architecture)

J. Peter Shannon Jr.

Architecture, the built environment of the human species, is fundamentally ecological and cultural. It is ecological because people, like all living things, interact with their environment. Through the interaction they adopt the environment as a habitat and adapt it to their needs. Therefore, human lives and the built environment fit together. Taking physical and emotional possession, people identify with their built environment. Thus architecture is cultural because, unlike other living things, humans think and make constant choices and decisions about their interaction with and adaptation to the places in which they dwell. Therefore, architectural forms of these built adaptations reflect those choices, whether conscious or intuitive.

The student of architecture must consider the **interrelatedness** of nature and of human nature within the specific cultural and environmental contexts of the human lives. Furthermore, to understand the variety of architectural forms, the student must learn to appreciate the adaptive choices of the builders of these habitats. For this is a cultural legacy documented in stone. The reasoning behind the builders' decisions, as well as the forms that resulted, affect how they build (and adapt) today.

The Ecological and Cultural Contexts of Architecture

The built environment is "the direct translation into physical form of a culture . . . it is the world view writ small . . . expressed in buildings and settlements" (Rapoport, 1969, p. 2). The sweeping scope of the study of human culture requires the subject to be divided into more manageable areas. A culture's **ecology** is the result of its peoples' interaction with their physical **environment.** It is the collection of their strategies for surviving in nature, the tools or technologies developed to utilize the resources of the environment, and the economies that result. This is reflected in architecture at its elemental level. Buildings act as environmental filters that balance the occupants' perceived physiological and psychological needs, with the climatic and geologic effects of nature. In this sense, buildings are simply large tools given form through technologies that utilize materials from the environment. In this way, the **form** of buildings is influenced by the place in which they are built. This is similar to the ways in which the climatic and geological characteristics of a location interact, resulting in different ecosystems (various mixes of plants, animals, water, soils, and rocks). Natural interactions provide the repertory of resources humans can use to build in a particular place. But what humans choose to use is another matter. Their decision rests on what the builders *perceive* as important to their lives in that place.

Human concerns are not limited to these direct ecological relationships of environment, economic survival, and technology. Being social, humans develop ways of coping with their life challenges in interaction with others around them. *Culture* refers to a people's **way of life:** their shared activities and behaviors in response to their social and physical environments. People's ways of living include habits, customs, rituals, traditions, and social institutions that form social contracts and lifestyles. Individuals are expected to accept these social contracts and lifestyles in order to sustain the group and their identity with it. *Buildings* are containers or settings for the activities and behaviors of people in a place, at the time when they are built. *Architecture* accommodates people's lifestyle through its form and spatial organization. Therefore, it reflects the patterns of their lives and the choices they have made about how to live together in a specific place.

However, neither the pragmatic adaptation to environmental forces, through economy and technology, nor the utilitarian adoption of the people's needs as a "usual" way of life are adequate to understand a culture or its architecture. It is also necessary to understand **why** people do what they do. This curious need to understand the world and explain one's place in it is part of being human. The choices people make to adopt a lifestyle and an environment for it, and to adapt them to their needs, are based on how they view their world: how they think, what they believe to be true, what they value as important—in other words, their perception of their lives in the world around them, or their **world view.** The realm of the human mind, of cognitive and symbolic thought, is the world of ideas and ideals whose reality is in its communication of meaning to others. The language, philosophy, art, science, and religion of a people combine in their world view. In turn, the world view is reflected in people's daily lives through the choices they make, whether ecological, social, or intellectual. The interaction of values, beliefs, perceptions, and ideas frame and guide human thought and decision.

A *world view* is a conceptual thought-ordering process by which people structure the patterns of their perception of human experience, in order to make sense of their world in all its ambiguity. It is "a basic process of the human mind to give the world meaning . . . by imposing order on it. Therefore built environments—buildings, settlements, and landscapes—are one way of ordering the world by making these [thought] ordering systems visible" (Rapoport, 1979, p. 8–9). Since the "unconscious activity of the mind consists in imposing forms upon content" (Levi-Strauss, 1963, p. 21), buildings are one class of ordering devices that give concrete form to the meaning of people's lives in this place.

Defining Architecture

Nearly 1,700 years after Vitruvius defined architecture as firmitas, utilitas, venustas, Sir Henry Wotton paraphrased this definition for Renaissance England. In *The Elements of Architecture,* he declared that "well-building hath three conditions: commoditie, firmness, and delight" (Roth, 1993, p. 9). It is a definition in English, but not much more understandable today than the Latin one. Twentieth century versions of Vitruvius translate the three elements of architecture as strength, utility, and either beauty or grace (Roth,

1993). The terms which will be used here—**filter environment, accommodate use** and **symbolize meaning**—have been abstracted from contemporary definitions which list four or five essential elements of architecture (Broadbent, 1975), relating the Vitruvian definitions to the current world view of architecture and culture. Although the functions of buildings have not changed much since Roman times, people seem to feel compelled to subdivide the definition of architecture into increasingly specialized compartments of thought and responsibility. That may be because such compartments are useful for managing the study of a subject. Each is a facet of the lens that focuses one's understanding of a complex activity. However, one challenge encountered when studying complex phenomena is the human tendency to simplify, by viewing the world through the one facet of a lens they know best, and believing they see all the answers in that way. That is how culture gets reduced to economy, or architecture to utility.

As one can see from the definitions listed in Table 4.1, the categories used in each definition correspond to those used in the others, despite linguistic differences over time. Linguistic expression, like architectural form, changes in time in response to what is relevant in the lives of the people at that time—how they view their world.

Architectural **style** is the result of people's consistent choices—of materials, of methods of construction, of spatial organization, and of geometric form—based on a shared vision of the relative importance of these various functions. Changes in style over time reflect changes in the perspective of a culture regarding its architectural priorities. The same is true of style in other forms of expression, whether visual arts, music, or literature.

The term for these categories has been synonymously referred to in various writings as the conditions, qualities, properties, elements or aspects of architecture. They are the **functions** of architecture—what it unavoidably does for people whether it performs well or ill. The reason for this long list of terms is a search for a substantive label for that concept since the word "function" was appropriated by early twentieth century modernist architects. They restricted its meaning to only utilitarian concerns, effectively pre-empting its use in its full and proper context. This was achieved by calling themselves functionalists and insisting on a strictly technological approach to building design based on the precepts of scientific objectivity. By co-opting the word, they implied that any other view of architecture was dysfunctional, irrational, and old-fashioned—out of step with the

Table 4.1
Definitions of Architectural Functions

Source	Era	Terms		
Vitruvius	25 B.C.	Firmitas	Utilitas	Venustas
Wotton	A.D. 1624	Firmness	Commoditie	Delight
Translators	20th Century	Strength	Utility	Beauty/Grace
Broadbent	A.D. 1975	Filter Environment	Accommodate Use	Symbolize Meaning
Cultural	21st Century	Ecology	Way of Life	World View

progressive technological advancement of society through the industrial revolution. However, their buildings all too often looked more efficient and utilitarian than they actually were in fulfilling their intended functions. Ultimately, the lasting legacy of **modernism** is the change it caused in the vocabulary of architectural form to express the technological methods and materials of industrial culture (i.e., its subjective meaning in response to its times). Ironically then, it was inescapably symbolic of the thought and values of early twentieth century modernist architects.

Since the 1960s, architecture has been attempting to reestablish a full and complete understanding of its function in lieu of this limited utilitarian definition. Even the dictionary tells us that "architecture is the art or science of building" (Merriam-Webster,1996). This either/or attitude reflects the modernist contention that scientific objectivity is sufficient to generate buildings as "machines for living in" (Le Corbusier, 1927) without considering the subjective content of their form. They considered that to be the province of art. Even they could not avoid the symbolic meaning of their buildings by ignoring it. The people who inhabit buildings invest them with meaning. That is how they make sense of their environment, by imposing their mental order on the perceived content of their world.

Therefore, architecture is the art **and** science of building (Hellman, 1988). People do not think either objectively and analytically or subjectively and intuitively but both, and at the same time. According to anthropologist Levi-Strauss (1963), people "think savagely" by totalizing their experience and learning into a complete view of the world upon which they base the choices of their daily lives. In this way "man has always been thinking equally well; the improvement lies not in an alleged progress of man's mind [scientific thought] but in the discovery of new areas to which it may apply its unchanged and unchanging powers" (Levi-Strauss, 1963, p. 230).

Speaking Architecture

This view of human thought allows architecture to communicate across continents and centuries, since contemporary people think no differently from those in any other time or place. The forms of buildings from pre-history to recent history are embedded with the life stories of their builders: how they thought, felt, and lived. If putting aside only for the moment a preoccupation with those "new areas" to which people now apply their "unchanging powers," they could read a common experience linking their lives with predecessors: it is their cultural heritage.

This commonality, a building's communal nature, can be illustrated by looking at the city pictured above. Three tall buildings dominate the skyline from left to right; these buildings were constructed in the 1990s, 1980s, and 1930s. They establish an immediate connection, then, between people today and their parents and their grandparents. But beyond that time frame they also relate to the ancient cultures of Egypt, Babylon, and Greece, across two to five thousand years of history. The tops of these buildings reflect the basic forms of an Egyptian stepped pyramid, a Babylonian Ziggurat, and a Greek circular temple. They have been interpreted and reinterpreted by western cultures from Rome through the Renaissance to the present time. The same objective forms have been stylized, rendered in different materials, and put to new uses in different environments to evoke new meanings relevant to the particular people building them.

Today's built city: historic roots in contemporary space. (Photo by Philip Leiter.)

The Egyptian pharaoh, Zoser, viewing the tower on the left, would see his tomb, its stones now clad in white, set as the Benben Stone atop an immense obelisk. He would be very satisfied with his architect, Imhotep, because his pyramid had served its purpose well. It had preserved his "Ka" (his vital force and, therefore, also that of the land and people of Egypt) through nearly 5000 floodings of the Nile and countless daily cycles of the chariot of the sun god, Ra, in which he had been riding since entombment (Norberg-Schulz, 1975). But his tomb, as the Benben Stone of an obelisk, would really please him. This pyramidal capstone symbolized the land of Egypt, rising from the waters of the Nile, to be brought to life by the radiant touch of Ra (Norberg-Schulz, 1975). For him this would be proof of objective reality, since this creation myth is also literally true. The very existence of Egyptian civilization depended on the ceaseless cycles of fertile land left by and rising from the receding waters of the Nile's annual flood to be brought to life agriculturally by the sun's rays.

Romans of Vitruvius' time would also see this building as an obelisk. To them it would mean the universal order of the Roman empire throughout the known world. Having conquered Egypt and its people, all things Egyptian were now Roman. These monumental monoliths symbolized the objective fact that the law of Rome applied everywhere to everyone. Obelisks were erected as victory columns to commemorate Roman events that extended and secured the logic of that universal reality.

Sixteen hundred years later, a citizen in the streets of Renaissance Rome could literally gaze at new horizons across its seven hills through recently opened avenues cut through that Eternal City by Pope Sixtus V. These wide straight boulevards connected the eight major churches of Rome with the new St. Peter's Basilica. This diagonal network of streets intersected at obelisks in the center of plazas in front of each of the basilicas. These monuments visually marked and interrelated those places down long vistas well before the church or its plaza was visible. To the people of the Renaissance, the obelisk, like all the classical forms of Greece and Rome, symbolized the revival of human civilization after a thousand years of Dark Ages and a new rational harmony uniting humanity, nature, and God.

The tower in the picture does all of this today. It visually marks from a distance the center of the city at the public square unseen in front of it. It symbolizes, together with the classical forms of the tower on the right, the extension and rebirth of Greek and Roman civilization—this time through the conquest of the human mind. Together with the forms of the classical world the founding fathers of American culture adopted and adapted their eternal values: Greek democratic ideas and Roman universal laws. But ultimately the building pictured (the headquarters of a banking corporation) relies on ancient Egyptian values to express its use. Its contemporary form still evokes the sense of permanence and stability through the pyramid, and of continuity, despite cycles of change, that is inherent in the obelisk. What better image could a bank project to its customers?

Historical Eras

In each of the historical eras of this example, the objective purpose, (the use which the built form serves), has differed as has its specific subjective meaning to the people of that time. These functions remained stable over long periods of time: 3,000 years in Egypt, 1,000 years in Rome, and a few hundred years in the Renaissance. This reflects the stability of those traditional views of the world, shared and accepted by the people. Yet these traditions changed over time at an ever increasing rate. In fact between eras of similar views, such as Rome and its Renaissance, there were equally long periods when that rationale had little meaning and architectural forms changed significantly reflecting this. The architectural styles of these cycles in history have been classified as either **classical** or **romantic** (Hellman, 1988).

Table 4.2
Architectural Styles of Historical Eras

Era	Objective (Classical)	Subjective (Romantic)
Classical (ca. 700 B.C.–300 A.D.)	Greek Roman	
Medieval (ca. 300–1420)		Byzantine Early Christian Romanesque Gothic
Renaissance (ca. 1420–1600)	Renaissance Mannerist	
Baroque (ca. 1600–1720)		Baroque Rococo
Enlightenment (ca. 1720–1840)	Neo-Classical	Revival

These categories reflect the nature of the thought-ordering process in the predominant world view of these eras as either objective (classical) or subjective (romantic). Objective, rational, logical, analytic, ordered, and linear thought is often viewed as scientific, while subjective, emotional, analogical, intuitive, mosaic, and spatial thinking is viewed as artistic. However, architecture encompasses both views: "there is no pure classicism or romanticism . . . the one always contains aspects of the other" (Hellman, 1988). Hellman prefers to characterize these two modes of architecture in terms of their builders' world view.

"Classical (is) man imposing order on nature (while) Romantic (is) man integrating with nature" (Hellman, 1988). The forms of classically designed buildings express with clarity the human hand and its order. Materials are refined, polished, and machined. The geometry is simple, uniform, harmonious, and static. In comparison to the romantic, classical buildings appear pragmatic, utilitarian, and rational.

The romantic approach to design results in buildings that are more ambiguous and unique in appearance. Construction reflects the organic nature of the materials and their methods of assembly. Materials are treated naturally. Their color, texture, and joining are honestly expressed with minimal finishing. Building forms reflect the complex diversity of nature.

A romantic world view is implicitly not in touch with the objective reality of the world. (Nevertheless, during more than a thousand years it was the accepted realistic tradition.) Interestingly, nowadays many of the terms applied to these romantic styles have negative connotations. For example, in current usage, **Byzantine** means devious, surreptitious, complex intrigue; **Gothic** means uncouth, barbaric, mysterious, macabre; and, **Baroque** means irregular, twisted, grotesque (Merriam-Webster, 1996). For historical reasons, it is somewhat difficult to find examples of the romantic styles in most American cities, with the exception of churches, which were sometimes designed in the Gothic, Romanesque, or Byzantine styles.

Early twentieth century skyscrapers in New York City provide the best examples in American urban architecture. Many of these "Cathedrals of Commerce" adapted the soaring lines of the Gothic buttress and vault construction of medieval cathedrals to enhance the verticality of their form; thus the nickname.

This intellectual bias is evident in the style of the buildings of the city pictured earlier in this chapter. Of all the buildings shown, the one that is most illustrative of the romantic approach is the tall tower in the center of the picture. While the top of this building resembles a Babylonian Ziggurat, it would not be recognizable to King Urnammu as the temple of the moon god, Nammar, in his city of Ur. It lacks the typical bilateral symmetry of a flat-topped stepped pyramid which it originally resembled. The form has been interpreted and stylized rather than revived as a literal object in this twentieth century building. The tower is masonry, like the Ziggurat, and treated as such. Its form is not simple regular geometry; it is bent at an angle on its vertical axis and each layer of its facade is unique, transforming from a simple rectangle in front to its dominant four-stepped central profile. It is expressive of its historical model without the clear literal reference to that object as employed by the other two towers. Why is the Ziggurat, an ancient Middle Eastern form, used symbolically in this building? It is the corporate offices of an international oil company.

Enlightening Architecture

The alternating cycles of classical and romantic traditions in architecture come together in the **Enlightenment.** The *roots* of modern architecture are here, if not the form of its *foliage.* It starts here, because the foundations of contemporary culture were laid in that era. The eighteenth century is also called the **Age of Reason,** but it was equally the **Age of Revolution** in all aspects of human life. Here the effects of the infant **Industrial Revolution** further aggravated and accelerated the displacement of a largely agrarian labor force towards urban centers and colonial emigration (see Chapter 1). The resulting social upheaval in the traditional ways of life caused a rethinking of the very nature of human nature and the social-political contract. By the end of the century, this rethinking resulted in the American and French revolutions.

Architecturally, the effects were not nearly so revolutionary. The preceding Baroque Era was seen as a perversion of the Renaissance ideals of a rational harmonious re-establishment of classical architectural thought and form. Baroque had taken these same idealized classical forms and literally twisted them into an ambiguous complex where wall, column, and ceiling were nearly indistinguishable. There was no place where one could stand and see with simple clarity the nature of the building. Wandering in and around the entire building produced a different feeling of what the reality of the building was. The building existed to delight the senses for their own sake (Roth, 1993), since there seemed to be no rational basis for this artificial illusion. To "Enlightened" architects, the essential nature of humankind should be its ability to reason. Feeling and emotion were considered the "animal" side.

However, rather than simply blaming the Baroque for its excessive sensuality, Enlightened thinkers blamed Renaissance thinkers. What had been the flaw in their rationale? Where had they gone wrong in their reasoning? The Enlightened conclusion was that the Renaissance had not been authentic enough in its adaptation of Greek and Roman built-form. They had borrowed just the outward form and details and applied them to the walls of their buildings, whereas the essential nature of classical architecture was the column and beam, not the wall as an object to be decorated (Roth, 1993). The essence of architecture and of humankind was to be discovered in its closest association with nature. The human ideal became the "noble savage" of Jean-Jacques Rousseau: "Free, virtuous and happy . . . uncorrupted by society and urban ills" (Roth 1993, p. 410).

Architectural ideals, therefore, remained the classical cultures of Greece and Rome. As viewed through the "corrective" lenses of authenticity, these were the first "truly civilized" people to be in touch with nature-a *priori* (preconceived, without examination). Roman and Greek buildings were adopted in their entirety and replicated as faithfully as possible to serve the purposes for which they were built. Thomas Jefferson did this in his design for the University of Virginia. The main quadrangle is a Roman Forum (a rectangular space enclosed in a colonnade—a covered walkway supported by columns), which connects various places of gathering. At the University of Virginia these are "cottages" used as classrooms or residences for students and faculty. In a Roman forum, these were **exedra,** the marketplaces used for exchange of goods, services, and ideas. The focus of each Roman forum was a temple to one of their pantheistic (multiple) gods. At the University of Virginia, this axial focus is the library. The classical model Jefferson used for the library was the Pantheon, a Roman circular domed temple dedicated to all of the Roman gods.

It is changed in its size, proportion, and details, and Jefferson added windows to make it function for its new use. Yet it is recognizable as an authentic reproduction of its classical model. This is the epitome of **neo-classical** building design. Its significance, however, is not in its "classical" forms but in what those forms represented—the ideals and values of classical cultures in this new democratic republic.

But what of the romantic aspect of architecture in the Enlightenment? The use of classical forms reflected a romanticizing of classical history. Idealized concepts of Greek democracy and the universality of Roman law ignored their ancient realities, since neither had been particularly democratic or universal. Specifically, it was the siting of their buildings in natural settings which was inconsistent with the authenticity of their classical context. The Roman Forum of the University of Virginia was placed in isolation among the natural rolling hills outside a small town; however, the typical Roman context was a series of connected urban spaces, each interrelated through orthogonal axes representing the universal order of Roman authority.

Nowhere was this apparently incongruous connection of classical buildings to natural landscape more evident than in the English gardens of the period. Hectare after hectare of the estates of country squires were graded, dammed, flooded, planted, and pruned to achieve just the right "natural" effect. Meandering paths were carefully cut through the woods to cross stone bridges at exactly the point where a vista was open across the pond to a Greek temple nestled among the trees on the opposite shore. These were places where the English gentry could escape the toils of London business for a fortnight and get in touch with nature to rejuvenate their natural "nobility." They were in effect Disneyland 1750 style, since many of the examples of this magic kingdom were just plaster on wood frame facades meant only for the effect of being viewed from afar (Roth, 1993). How could they rationalize these ambiguities? "Enlightened man concentrated on sensation . . . the natural 'true' image in science and art. Rationalism and Romanticism are therefore two different manifestations of the same basic attitude" (Norberg-Schulz, 1975, p. 185). To them there was no inconsistency. In fact, the contrast was complementary. They simply compartmentalized their thought, as long as each was internally coherent and the effect was pleasing.

Diversifying Architecture

Throughout the nineteenth century, these two design traditions developed a myriad of styles in a frantic search for both a form and an approach that could respond to the ever-accelerating changes brought about by the industrialization and democratization of western nations. It affected every aspect of architecture. New materials and methods of construction (especially in the structural technologies of iron, then steel and reinforced concrete) were not easily incorporated into the traditional building forms. New buildings were needed to accommodate new uses for which there were no appropriate historical models or adequate design methodologies to develop them. How is a railroad station, a public library or museum designed for the first time? Also, a need was felt to establish new national identities through architectural style. This reflected the changed political context which made previously shared historical styles less acceptable. How does an American style develop separately from English colonial traditions?

The first change was to broaden the vocabulary of neo-classical historicism to include the romantic styles. This new academic **eclecticism** eventually utilized every preexisting historical form in a **revival** style. Romanesque revival in the United States and Gothic revival in England and America gained some popularity, but it was the classical revival of Renaissance and Baroque styles fostered by the Ecole des Beaux-Arts that dominated the Eclectic approach. The answer to the new structural technologies was to conceal them behind brick or stone facades and plaster ceilings. The tall tower at the right in the picture of the cityscape shown earlier is a twentieth century example indicating how popular this style remains.

In England, midway through the nineteenth century, another approach to the industrial technologies was proposed: do not let mass-produced standardization dictate building form. This was the **Arts and Crafts** movement championed by William Morris and John Ruskin. They proposed that all buildings be designed the way most buildings had always been built anyway—in the **vernacular.** Formal styles had always been the architecture of the rich and famous, accounting for a highly visible but very small percentage of total construction (Jencks, 1971). They saw industrialization in all sectors of production, including architecture, as cheapening the quality of products and, therefore, the quality of people's lives. They proposed that buildings be designed as ordinary people had always built. Natural and local materials should be used at all times with simple, honest, conventional building techniques. Buildings should be planned from the inside out for their convenience of use, not for some preconceived exterior form (as was required in the Beaux-Arts method), or dictated by an arbitrarily imposed industrial standard. The site should be treated as naturally as possible so that the building was in harmony with nature. The romantic view of the English country landscape was still a strong influence (Hellman, 1988).

In America, this design philosophy was adapted by Frank Lloyd Wright before the turn of the century and incorporated into his principles of **Organic Architecture** or **Folk Vernacular** (Hellman, 1988). Wright legitimized vernacular as a design approach, raising it to an art form on a par with the Beaux-Arts or modernist styles of the time; however, he was anti-city and his few urban buildings fit uncomfortably. His major impact on cities was the influence of his endorsement of suburban development. When he proposed his **Broadacre City** in the 1930s, he was in tune with the American middle class who had already started an exodus from the city after World War I (Hellman, 1988).

In the photo of the city earlier in this chapter, no particular vernacular building stands out. There is no distinct formal expression uniting it as a style in the usual sense. Almost all of the foreground buildings across the sweep of the lakeshore can be considered vernacular. Such buildings are the fabric and texture, the background context of every city, town, and village.

These two design approaches, the eclectic and the vernacular, dominated American architecture in the early decades of the twentieth century. Eclecticism was usually the Beaux-Arts classicism, while vernacular, in its highest expression, was usually organically more romantic. It was into this context that two European approaches were introduced in the 1920s and 30s, although neither had a visible impact in this country until after World War II.

The first was functionalist **modernism,** previously discussed here. Its main proponents in the United States were Ludwig Mies Van Der Rohe and Walter Gropius, who had founded and taught at the **Bauhaus School of Design** in Germany before the war.

Van Der Rohe's version of glass and steel skyscraper design reshaped the American skyline from the 1950s on. In the city photo, all of the mid-height office buildings to the left of the Beaux Arts tower owe much of their form to his influence. Typically they are rectangular boxes with continuous ribbons of glass alternating with lightweight industrialized panels to form a **curtain wall** enclosing the structural steel frame, as if it is a "skin over bones" as Gropius described it.

Modernist forms are classically contemporary: clear, simple geometry with plain machined surfaces. They look logical and efficient and this explains their popularity. That look fit American industry's post-war image of frugal management and efficient operation as well as expressing the scientific technologies of industrial production. Despite the social objectives of modernism, that it could engineer better lives for people, its image is far from humane. Because of its refusal to provide any symbolic references, traditional or otherwise, it has created a mass produced neutral backdrop against which people are left to find some existential meaning through their own lives and actions—creating a modern epic of alienation.

The second approach to design is the most obviously romantic-**expressionism.** It evolved in Germany in the 1920s, along with the Bauhaus, through the work of Erich Mendelssohn. However, its roots are also back in the Enlightenment in the ideas of Etienne-Louis Boullee, which he called L' Architecture Parlent—**"Speaking Architecture."** He proposed that the essential forms of the building itself evoke a sense of the building's use: "to communicate its purpose directly to the observer" (Roth, 1993, p. 407). It was to do this without traditional historic references or conventional technology, so it seems, since Boulee's buildings were technically unbuildable in his time. Mendelssohn, however, using sculpted brick and concrete rather than glass and steel, designed and built buildings that evoked the symbolic side of technology: the streamlined speed of machine power (Hellman, 1988, p. 106).

Perhaps the best known expressionist of the twentieth century is the American architect, Eero Saarinen. Working extensively in reinforced concrete because of its plastic ability to be molded into any form, his airport terminals for TWA at JFK Airport in New York and Dulles International in Washington D.C. sculpturally evoke a sense of aerodynamics and flight. Even Le Corbusier, one of the founders of modernism, largely because of his love for concrete, eventually evolved his style towards expressionism. His chapel at Ronchamp, France is one of the most dramatic and emotionally evocative buildings of the century. The expressive forms of these buildings require a higher degree of structural sophistication than do the technological-appearing designs of steel and glass Modernism. This points out again, this time in reverse, the inseparability of objective and subjective thought in architecture. The more expressive the form, the more complex its technology. Architectural thought is truly "both/and," not "either/or."

The four modes of architectural thought at the beginning of the twentieth century (Eclecticism, Functional Modernism, Expressionism and Vernacular) are still competing and recombining as the twenty-first century begins. Paraphrasing Mark Twain, the report of modernism's death has been greatly exaggerated. After all, modernists had made similar pronouncements about Beaux-Arts eclecticism earlier in the century. Both are still around in thought as well as form, which has been only slightly modified in the city pictured earlier in this chapter. The bank tower on the left has traits of both modernist and eclectic form.

The purpose of this chapter has been to focus on the thought behind the forms of buildings so that the student of architecture might understand and appreciate the multiplicity and diversity of a city's buildings, especially the complexity of post-modern reintegrations as these design approaches interact. The strength of a city, as of any natural ecosystem, is in the flexible adaptability which diversity sustains. As long as building forms continue to express the diversity of the four approaches to architectural thought, it may be a good indication of its healthy diversity on economic, social and cultural levels also. Cultural strength is in its melting pot composition, not in its homogenization. The excitement and opportunity of the city is in its diversity; shouldn't that be reflected, as it always has been, in its buildings?

Name _____

CHAPTER 4
The City Builds (Architecture)

4-1. Use the city picture in Chapter 4 of the text to survey several people. Ask:
A. Which building they like best and which least.

B. Which building looks most natural, most useful and most meaningful?

C. Rank the following in order of importance in choosing where to live:
(1) Quality of environment

(2) Convenience for the way they live

(3) Fits the way they think about life: their values and ideals

4-2. Discuss the survey taken in 4.1.

A. Is there a correlation between what is important to people (c) and their opinions of the buildings (a)? (assume that the three parts of questions (b) and (c) are analogous)

B. How many buildings in survey question (a) were on both the best and worst lists? How can this ambiguity be explained? How can this be a good thing?

C. Answer the survey yourself. Analyze your opinions in terms of where you grew up (urban, suburban, small town, rural).

The City Plans
(Urban Planning)
W. Dennis Keating

Cities of ancient and recent origin must look to the future. For much of American history, cities in the United States were unplanned. Washington, D.C., the nation's capital, was one of the few exceptions. It was only during the Progressive era early in the twentieth century that city planning emerged as a profession in the United States.

Origins and Evolution of City Planning

The explosive growth of American cities in the late nineteenth century, described in Chapter 1, was characterized by mass immigration from Europe, industrialization, and expanding slum districts. Social upheaval and widespread poverty led to fears of urban crime and political corruption which resulted from the dominance of immigrant-based political machines. Reformers, concerned about poverty and slums, conducted surveys of these conditions. For example, the Pittsburgh Survey begun in 1907 exposed slum conditions; housing reformers in New York City, such as Jacob Riis, sought to improve the lives of the poor immigrants. The settlement house movement was led by Jane Addams who founded Hull House in Chicago.

The early city planning movement sought to transform the physical landscape, converting ugly, crowded, and dangerous industrial cities into more livable and beautiful communities. Urban parks were created in the cities of Chicago, New York, and San Francisco. Landscape architect Frederick Law Olmsted, Jr. became the most prominent designer of urban parks. Boston, Cleveland, and Kansas City led the way in creating metropolitan park systems. The urban planning movement became known as the City Beautiful Movement.

The Louisiana Purchase Exposition of 1904 inspired civic activists to promote a city plan for St. Louis in 1907. Its concerns were primarily directed at beautifying the city through urban design, land use regulation, and physical improvements. These became the hallmarks of city planning in its early phase. The Chicago Plan of 1909, developed by architect Daniel Burnham, epitomized the goals of the City Beautiful Movement. Burnham was inspired by the Columbian Exposition of 1893. A European-like "White City" was created on the shores of Lake Michigan. It featured classical architecture, broad boulevards, and parks. Burnham's plan incorporated these elements in a vision to redevelop the heart of Chicago, the nation's second city. The impetus for a city plan came from leaders of Chicago's civic and business

Cleveland Metroparks: The Emerald Necklace in Winter. (Photo by Sanda Kaufman, 2005.)

establishments. They also sought to make the city function more efficiently through coordinated transportation planning to relieve congestion in the downtown business district. Transportation became a hallmark of early city planning.

The Chicago Plan represented a plan of the civic elite mostly addressing the downtown (the "Loop") and the lakefront, while showing little concern for the problems of the poor and working classes living in Chicago's slums. However, the plan's influential supporters effectively promoted it among the ordinary citizenry. Walter Moody, who translated the plan into a popular manual, had it adopted as a required elementary public school text. Over the next two decades, many of the recommendations in Burnham's plans became reality, financed through municipal bond issues. Burnham spread the gospel of the City Beautiful Movement, planning monumental civic centers in cities like Cleveland and San Francisco. He is best remembered for his credo: "Make no little plans."

Other cities emulated Chicago. In New York City, instead of a long-range comprehensive plan emphasizing urban design such as Burnham's, planning was directed at land use regulation. Manhattan commercial interests, concerned about unregulated businesses in the garment and warehouse districts spreading into the most exclusive retail districts, successfully promoted the adoption of the first citywide zoning plan in 1916. Zoning, borrowed from Germany, is a technique used to segregate cities into designated zones (commercial, industrial, residential and mixed) to prevent incompatible uses and to preserve land values. Thus zoning, more than comprehensive planning, became a central focus of American city planning. Zoning was also an important tool in the post-World War II development of American suburbs.

The year 1909 is regarded as the real birthdate of American city planning. It was marked by the Chicago Plan, the first national conference on city planning (held in Washington, D.C.), and the first course on city planning which was offered at Harvard University.

In addition to central cities, planners expanded their focus to regional issues. In 1922, the Los Angeles County Regional Planning Commission became the first agency of its kind, formed to address issues in the Los Angeles basin. In 1929, a Regional Plan Association was formed to promote regional planning to address urban growth in the New York

City region. Regional concerns were addressed in many early "city" plans (e.g., Burnham's Chicago Plan of 1909).

The Organization and Administration of Municipal Planning

The early city planning movement was fostered by architects, lawyers, and engineers who were supported by local civic and business leaders concerned about urban problems. The first plans were produced by consultants. Soon, however, cities established planning departments. Planning commissions were appointed by mayors, city managers, and city councils to oversee the development and implementation of comprehensive plans, zoning, and land use controls. In 1914, Newark, New Jersey was the first city to hire a professional planner, the famous consultant Harland Bartholomew. In 1925, Cincinnati became the first large city to adopt a comprehensive plan for long-range capital improvements.

Municipal planning was organized so that a citizen-led advisory commission oversaw the work of a professional staff in the development of plans. Usually plans and zoning have to be enacted as ordinances by the city council to be binding, rather than advisory. A zoning officer was charged with the implementation of the municipal zoning ordinance, including the issuance of building permits. A separate zoning board of appeals, appointed by the city government, heard the appeals of landowners for exceptions (variances) to zoning. Its decision is subject to review by the city planning commission and the city council and can be appealed to the courts. This organization still characterizes municipal planning.

A longstanding debate in the planning profession is whether planning departments and commissions should be independent of the mayor and city manager or whether they should be part of their staff. In his 1941 classic entitled *The Planning Function in Local Government,* Robert Walker argued for the latter position. He believed that planning should be under the direction of the chief executive and be centralized. However, many planning agencies remain autonomous from operating departments. In either case, typically planners have not actually had control over municipal budgets or programs. Their role is advisory only. Urban renewal agencies, which were created after 1949 to carry out federally-funded urban redevelopment, were the exception to this pattern. Remaining independent from municipal government, these powerful agencies often combined the planning and implementation roles.

The Legal Basis for Planning

The authority for urban governments to plan and regulate land use and development derives from their "police power," which is their sovereign right to govern for the general welfare. In the case of urban governments, their authority is derived from the states. Thus, states began to enact enabling legislation to allow city governments to add planning to their authority. This was given impetus in 1924 when then the United States Secretary of Commerce (and later President) Herbert Hoover issued a standard state zoning enabling act. This become a much-copied model. Hoover's chief advisor was New York City attorney Edward Bassett, author of that city's 1916 zoning law and regarded by many as the father of zoning.

Another important figure was Cincinnati lawyer Alfred Bettman, who spearheaded Cincinnati's early planning efforts. In 1924, a federal judge ruled that a comprehensive zoning plan (modeled after the New York City ordinance) adopted by the village of Euclid, Ohio, adjacent to Cleveland, was unconstitutional. In 1926, Bettman was credited with persuading a very conservative United States Supreme Court to overturn this decision by a 6-3 vote and uphold the right of state and local governments to regulate private property for the common good.

Between 1929 and 1974, the Supreme Court left the issue of the legality of planning and zoning, as implemented, in the hands of the state courts for the most part. They heard thousands of cases, mostly brought by property owners, challenging decisions which limited their rights to use their land and buildings in accordance with general planning and zoning ordinances. Typically these legal disputes involved claims that the public agency acted arbitrarily.

Other zoning cases involve challenges brought under the Constitution. The most frequently invoked clauses are the First Amendment (free speech and association) and the Fifth and Fourteenth Amendments (the **takings** clause, **due process** and **equal protection**). First amendment zoning cases have covered such issues as the location of adult entertainment stores and churches, sign regulation (including billboards), and group homes in single-family residential zones.

Landowners have frequently invoked due process and equal protection where they believe that the government is treating the same class of owners differently. A recurring contemporary issue is the exclusion of locally unwanted land uses ("LULUs") in both urban and suburban areas. Another phenomenon, known as "NIMBY" (not in my backyard), is a negative citizen reaction to various unpopular development proposals. Both governmental agencies and the courts have been asked by those promoting group homes, low-income housing, landfills, shopping centers and other projects to invalidate zoning restrictions against these uses.

In recent times, the takings issue has come to the fore. The Constitution prohibits the government from taking private property for a public purpose without just compensation. In many instances, while the government has not used private property directly, it has been alleged that regulation (e.g., development controls to promote such goals as historic landmark preservation, open space, beach access, and preservation of wetlands) amounts to a taking because landowners' rights have been restricted without any compensatory payment. The courts have not yet ruled definitively on this issue, but the government has been limited in its application of regulatory planning.

Regulatory planning includes two recent policies designed to deal with rapid growth, mostly in the suburbs. Some suburban communities have instituted growth controls to limit or phase in new development. This is a reaction to the unpopular symptoms of this growth, such as traffic congestion and overcrowded schools, requiring property tax increases to meet increased demand. Many communities have charged development impact fees to offset such increased costs.

While setting limits on how these policies may be implemented, the courts have upheld the right of local government to use these planning tools, in conjunction with more traditional site planning and subdivision regulations. In 1981, San Francisco pioneered impact fees from office developers to offset the negative effects of downtown commercial development on the housing supply and mass transit. It became the first major American city to limit downtown development, beginning with its 1985 downtown plan. San Francisco became even more restrictive through a 1986 growth restriction initiative sponsored

Famous Urban Planners

Daniel Burnham (1846–1912), a Chicago architect, was inspired by the Columbian Exposition of 1893. He gained fame as the creator of the Chicago Plan of 1909, a centerpiece of the City Beautiful. Burnham also proposed monumental civic center plans for Cleveland and San Francisco (which were only partially realized).

Edward Bassett (1863–1948), a Brooklyn attorney, was prominent in the drafting and adoption of New York City's 1916 zoning ordinance, the first of its kind.

Alfred Bettman (1873–1945), a Cincinnati lawyer, led the planning movement in Ohio and the United States. He is generally credited with persuading the U.S. Supreme Court to uphold the constitutionality of zoning in the landmark *Euclid v. Ambler* (1926) case.

Robert Moses (1888–1981) was a municipal political reformer who became the redevelopment czar of New York City and New York State for decades. He was famous for building bridges, dams, highways, housing projects, and parks. He abhorred planners. He was portrayed as an autocratic empire-builder in Robert Caro's *The Power Broker*.

Rexford Tugwell (1891–1979) was an advisor to President Franklin Delano Roosevelt. He espoused planning by the federal government and headed the ill-fated Greenbelt experiment. He later became governor of Puerto Rico and promoted planned economic development.

Lewis Mumford (1895–1990) criticized modern planning. He advocated decentralization, small scale technology, growth restrictions, and the protection of the natural environment. He wrote numerous books and articles on the city and city life.

Catherine Bauer Wurster (1905–1964), as a writer, was a leading proponent of public housing in the 1930s. While a leader in planning education, she became disillusioned with the failure of the public housing and urban redevelopment programs.

Jane Jacobs (1916–) was an iconoclastic critic of urban renewal and highway clearance policies. She authored the landmark *The Death and Life of Great American Cities*. Jacobs excoriated what she deemed inhuman planning epitomized by modern highrises and advocated urban diversity, small scale redevelopment, and preservation of older urban buildings and neighborhoods.

by opponents of burgeoning downtown highrise office buildings and overdevelopment of the city's waterfront.

Ballot Box Zoning

Normally, planning decisions are made by appointed boards (e.g., planning commissions) and local elected officials, served by professional planning staffs.

However, many citizens' groups opposed to planning decisions have used the power of the initiative and referendum to force a public vote for final approval. Since most are a reaction to official actions approving zoning and planning requests, this phenomenon has been associated with NIMBY. Opposition ranges from adult bookstores to residential subdivisions to big box stores to projects aiding the poor and disadvantaged. Absent evidence of discrimination, the courts have sanctioned this form of democracy where it is authorized. Developers have fought back with a legal tactic known as SLAPPS (Strategic Lawsuits Against Public Participation) in an effort to intimidate those who organize campaigns against their projects. Whether planning approval should be subject to a popular vote is much debated.

Eminent Domain for Redevelopment

A key to the urban renewal program to redevelop blighted areas was the power of eminent domain in the event that holdout owners refused to sell their property or demanded exorbitant prices. While the urban renewal program was eliminated in 1974, cities still use the power of eminent domain, although usually for much smaller scale projects. An exception was the destruction of Detroit's Poletown neighborhood in the 1980s for a General Motors auto plant. Legal challenges and protests by some residents failed to stop this large scale clearance project. Increasingly, older suburbs with little or no vacant land for redevelopment have begun to invoke this power in order to substitute denser projects, often with the purpose of increasing their tax base. Just as in the past, residents, usually homeowners, and small businesses have challenged these redevelopment projects, arguing that the power of eminent domain is being abused primarily for the benefit of private developers who will obtain the condemned properties at subsidized prices. These disputes have landed in the courts, which have to decide if the planners' justifications are reasonable. The U.S. Supreme Court ruled that this use of eminent domain is legal in *Kelo v. New London,* 2005 which is covered in detail in Chapter 12.

Urban Plans, the Planning Process, and Plan Implementation

Urban planning is designed to deal with the future. The future can be short term (a few years) or long range (5–20 years). Plans often analyze issues and then pose alternative solutions to problems that are identified. Plans are written documents, usually accompanied by maps and other graphic illustrations in the case of physical development plans. Increasingly, planning has used such technological innovations as GIS (geographic information systems), CAD (computer-assisted design), simulation models, and advanced forecasting techniques.

Planning has been based on a rational model, which assumes that reasoned analysis can lead to rational solutions. The rational model has been criticized as incomplete or unrealistic. Political and fiscal considerations often affect the making of plans and their implementation. Large-scale urban renewal plans sometimes suffered this fate. For example, the plan of the San Francisco Redevelopment Agency to level Skid Row (South of Market), displacing thousands of low-income residents, to build a convention center, hotels, and office buildings ran into major resistance (Hartman, 1974). Political opposition and lawsuits eventually halted its progress until an alternate plan was agreed upon. Mounting costs also changed the plan. Eventually, the Moscone Convention Center was built, but so was replacement housing in the same South of Market area of San Francisco.

In the United States there has often been resistance to planning, especially centralized governmental planning. As a result, much of American urban planning has been incremental and pragmatic. In an era of federal government deregulation and local government privatization of public services, some planners have become increasingly entrepreneurial in their outlook. Long-term planning has been hampered by this factor. Rather than lengthy blueprints, many contemporary "plans" are **strategic** plans. Strategic planning seeks to identify issues and prioritize approaches (but not necessarily provide elaborate solutions).

The public planning process includes required public hearings at which citizens and community organizations can present their views on planning issues and proposed plans. In some cities (e.g., Cincinnati and St. Paul), neighborhood organizations play a role in the city's review of capital improvement plans and budgets. In New York City, appointed community planning boards must be consulted before any significant development project receives final project approval. These boards do not have veto power.

In many states, planning decisions are not only open to citizen participation but are also the subject of citizen initiatives and referenda. Many controversial development projects have been subjected to ballot box approval. This process has often pitted developers against neighborhood and environmental groups.

The centerpiece of early American planning was the comprehensive city plan. Most cities have comprehensive plans, generally addressing land use issues. While these comprehensive plans are supposed to be consistent with zoning, often this is not the case. These general plans have been criticized as being overly vague in their prescriptions for future planning and as being quickly outdated. Many major cities have not updated these plans for decades. Others have substituted capital improvement plans in order to plan for and budget major public facilities.

Another traditional form of planning is district or neighborhood planning, regardless of whether an up-to-date citywide plan exists. District plans date back to the concept of an identifiable neighborhood popularized by Clarence Perry in the 1920s. District plans are typically comprehensive but short term for a small area (one or more neighborhoods). In the era of federally-sponsored urban renewal (1949–1973), local urban renewal agencies prepared redevelopment plans for thousands of urban neighborhoods. These plans usually involved the clearance of slum uses and the redevelopment of the cleared land. Urban renewal became a primary tool for the redevelopment of the central business districts of older central cities. After urban renewal was incorporated into the Community Development Block Grant (CDBG) program in 1974, much of neighborhood planning devolved into nonprofit community development corporations. These grew in number and importance in the following decades. With a goal of improving impoverished and neglected urban neighborhoods, many of them developed their own neighborhood plans focused on affordable housing and other physical improvements, employment, and economic development (Erickson, 2009).

An even more limited type of plan is the site or project plan. This plan is for the development of a particular physical site, involving new or rehabilitated buildings. While conforming to zoning and development regulations, this type of plan may be implemented without any relationship to a citywide or district plan.

Other Planning Entities

Although most planning takes place at the city level, there are four other types of planning agencies in the United States: regional, Council of Governments, state, and federal. While regional planning has long been a concern, there are few powerful regional planning agencies in existence. Exceptions include the Depression-era Tennessee Valley Authority (TVA) and special conservation agencies (e.g., the San Francisco Bay Conservation and Development Commission). While there are COGs (Councils of Government) in most metropolitan areas, these intergovernmental agencies cooperate on such issues as planning but do not exercise direct control over metropolitan land use and development issues. In the 1970s, the federal government actively supported regional planning agencies, but that support has since waned.

Most state planning agencies do not have any great influence over local governments. Exceptions include such states as Hawaii, Oregon and Vermont, which have strong statewide land use planning authority. A few other states (e.g., California, and New Jersey) have extensive involvement in local government planning, even though municipal government enjoys **home rule** authority. In these states, local planning must conform to statewide standards.

Except for the National Planning Board during World War II, the federal government has not had a separate planning agency; however, planners work for many federal agencies on planning programs and issues.

Finally, there have been only a few examples of new town plans in the United States. Most communities have been developed privately, with small scale projects leading to overall growth. During the Depression, the federal government briefly supported the building of model suburbs (**greenbelt** towns), modeled after an earlier British concept (Ebenezer Howard's "garden cities of tomorrow"). Opposition from the realtors' lobby quickly ended this experiment.

The federal government during the Depression supported the local building of public housing for low-income residents beginning in 1937. This, too, ran into tremendous opposition from the politically conservative real estate lobby opposed to governmental intervention in the private market, which succeeded in limiting it largely to central city ghetto areas. As public housing aged and became housing of last resort for many of the poor and especially single, female-headed minority households, its image worsened and public opposition grew. Except for housing for the elderly, almost all suburbs refused to build public housing.

In the mid-1960s, the federal government briefly supported a New Towns program, designed to assist in infrastructure development for large scale planned New Towns. Inspired by the privately-financed new towns of Reston, Virginia, and Columbia, Maryland, and the post-World War II British New Town program, this was intended to overcome the problems associated with suburban sprawl. In an increasingly conservative political era after 1968, this experimental program was terminated. Federally-sponsored New Towns were not financially or otherwise successful.

The state of New York, however, sponsored New Town development through a powerful Urban Development Corporation led by Ed Logue (previously director of urban renewal in New Haven and Boston), but it, too, ran into political opposition and financial woes and had a very brief life as a major development force (1968–75).

Much of planning is functional. Planners are trained and work on plans in their area of specialization. The list is long and includes such topics as the environment, economic development, health, housing, public facilities and transportation, all matters of great importance in American cities. Some planners concentrate on such general areas as land use, neighborhood development, public finance, and urban design.

Advocacy and Social Planning

Not all planning is about physical development. Rational planning is grounded on the notion that planners seek to promote the common good; however, not all agree on what the public interest is. While the public interest is hard to define, planning is often dominated by powerful private interests (e.g., banks, chambers of commerce, developers, realtors, and homeowner associations). It has been argued that planners have a special responsibility to take into account the interests of the unrepresented and under-represented, especially the poor and racial minorities.

In the 1960s, in response to such programs as urban renewal and highway construction which displaced hundreds of thousands of poor and minority urban residents, Paul Davidoff invented the notion of **advocacy planning.** He urged planners to be advocates for those who were the likely losers rather than winners from urban redevelopment. Advocate planners developed their own counterplans. Advocacy planning played an important role in reforming urban renewal and urban highway planning by requiring greater citizen participation, improved relocation guarantees, and neighborhood preservation. While not an advocate planner, the critic Jane Jacobs popularized opposition to conventional urban redevelopment planning and architecture in her book entitled *The Death and Life of Great American Cities* (1961). Jacobs favored diversity of uses, small scale development, and preservation of older urban neighborhoods. Her *bete noire* was Robert Moses, the longtime urban redevelopment czar of New York City. Davidoff, through his group called Suburban Action, became a leader in the struggle to combat exclusionary suburban zoning.

Equity Planning

Equity planning is a concept closely related to advocacy. Equity planners seek to incorporate into planning practice and social policy the concerns of those greatest in need and with the least political influence. An early example was the Cleveland Policy Plan of 1974, developed by Norman Krumholz' city planning staff. It sought to improve housing and transportation for the city's poor residents and analyzed the costs and benefits of major downtown development proposals to try to ensure that the poor and working class citizens were not further disadvantaged (Krumholz & Clavel, 1994). Often at the behest of politicians and their powerful constituents, city planners have focused on downtown rather than the neighborhoods. Planning was typically aimed at promoting growth and development. In the 1980s, planners in cities such as Boston and Chicago sought to reverse this trend in the reform administrations of Mayors Ray Flynn and Harold Washington respectively.

Smart Growth

Suburban outward movement from central cities has been a phenomenon since the appearance of the streetcar suburbs at the end of the nineteenth century. Mass suburbanization characterized by the Levittowns began after World War II. With rare exceptions, most suburban development was not planned. Efforts beginning in the late 1960s to promote planned New Towns on the British model—like Columbia, Maryland and Reston, Virginia—did not win sustained support from the federal government. Instead, it continued to fund highways and infrastructure like sewers that helped to underwrite what has become known as "urban sprawl." Likewise, most states continued to pursue similar policies. By the 2000 U.S. Census, a majority of Americans lived in metropolitan areas but outside the central cities.

Urban sprawl has brought with it increasing congestion, has increased property taxes to fund services like schools and public safety, and has resulted in the loss of farmland and wetlands at the fringes of the expanding metropolitan areas. In reaction, many newer suburban communities have embraced growth management as a policy to limit and phase in additional development. This has taken the form of voter initiatives, many of which have stopped new development projects, and planning policies to better regulate growth. Suburban communities now regularly require residential subdivision developers to pay impact fees to offset the costs of the new services whose demand results from the occupants of their projects. Some require that new development can only proceed if there is sufficient infrastructure to accommodate additional growth. Many have declared temporary building moratoriums while they have studied and developed these policies.

Over the past few decades, a number of states have enacted statewide growth management legislation mandating localities to adopt growth management policies to meet statewide goals. Most notably, since 1973, Oregon has been a model of statewide land use policy to limit urban sprawl. By requiring infill development within designated urban growth boundaries, farmland and open space has been preserved. Portland, Oregon has been seen as a model of metropolitan planning. In addition, regional agencies have been created to regulate development to preserve such environmentally-endangered areas as the San Francisco Bay, Lake Tahoe, the Columbia Gorge, the New Jersey Pinelands, and the Adirondacks. The federal government has provided support for coastal management programs, whose goals usually include planning to protect environmentally-sensitive areas from overdevelopment.

Smart growth takes different forms. The state of Maryland adopted a policy of limiting state funding of infrastructure to already developed corridors but not undeveloped areas. The state of Massachusetts has provided subsidies to localities which adopt smart growth strategies that concentrate development around existing transit systems and protect open space. The American Planning Association has promoted smart growth legislation.

All of this has provoked opposition from landowners, developers, homebuilders, and conservative political interests which oppose governmental policies that restrict private property owners' use of their land, regardless of the public policy goal. They argue that the government must pay property owners if in effect it "takes" land off the development market or reduces its value through smart growth and growth management policies. Many have been challenged in the courts and the U.S. Supreme Court has put some restrictions on these regulatory planning policies, while not going so far as to ruling that they are indeed a taking of private property that requires compensation under the federal (and state) constitution. In many states, there have been political efforts to limit growth management policies. For example, in 2000 and 2004, initiatives promoted by pro-development interests to force Oregon governments to pay compensation to landowners affected negatively by their land use control policies passed. The former was declared unconstitutional. The second went into effect in 2005, but a counter initiative passed in 2007 substantially reduced its likely negative impact on growth management policies (Walker & Hurley, 2011).

Transit-Oriented Development

In the eras of highway building, little thought was given to reducing congestion through planning of collateral areas. The auto reigned supreme. As pressure grew for more public support for mass public transit, efforts have been made to channel denser new development along the routes and close to stations on new subway and light rail systems. Transit-oriented development (TOD) is seen as a form of smart growth, concentrating new development to encourage the use of public transit while combating urban sprawl.

Waterfront Redevelopment

Many cities have long emphasized the use of their waterfronts, whether for tourism (e.g., Charleston), shipping and industry, or public use (e.g., Chicago's parks and beaches). San Antonio created its own canals while Providence uncovered its rivers from concealment under highways and roads. Many cities which have seen formerly commercial waterfronts decline have rediscovered them and used showcase waterfront redevelopment projects to stimulate downtown revitalization. They first had to overcome obstacles like polluted water, highways and railroads limiting access, and fragmented ownership patterns. Examples include James Rouse's redevelopment of Baltimore's Inner Harbor, Chicago's Navy Pier, Philadelphia's Penn Landing, New York City's Battery Park, Chattanooga's riverfront re-awakening, San Francisco tearing down the Embarcadero Freeway to open up its bayfront, and convention centers in cities like Boston, New Orleans, Pittsburgh, and San Diego. Wherever this occurs, often there is conflict between economic development versus aesthetics and public access. Planners can serve as mediators in these difficult settings.

Historic Preservation

The movement for historic preservation took off in the 1960s, inspired by those like Jane Jacobs who sought to protect older, urban neighborhoods against urban renewal clearance and those who opposed the destruction of historic buildings and sites. While a few cities like Charleston and New Orleans had long protected some of their historic districts, New York City led the way with a broad historic preservation law that eventually led to the designation of hundreds of buildings and dozens of historic districts. A legal challenge to this policy which led to rejection of an office tower over the Grand Central railroad station was unsuccessful in the U.S. Supreme Court in 1978, ensuring the viability of municipal historic preservation programs. In addition, the federal government and many states provided tax incentives for the preservation of historic buildings. As a result, the historic preservation movement has blossomed in older cities and planners have been able to assist in the preservation of many endangered buildings and areas. Adaptive re-use has often been the key to making historic preservation financially feasible. For example, in many cities, abandoned warehouse districts in central business districts have become popular areas for housing, offices, and entertainment venues. This is not to imply that all such sites have been saved. Through long-term neglect, arson, and more profitable uses, many historic buildings have been lost, especially in those cities with weak or no historic preservation laws.

The Politics of Planning

Planning can be a politically volatile issue. Controversies over such previously mentioned programs as public housing and urban renewal have led to battles in Congress, in the courts, and sometimes on the streets. Some neighborhood groups have fought to keep out public housing (often white neighborhoods fearful of an influx of poor minorities). Others try to prevent displacement through **gentrification,** a process whereby older, deteriorated urban neighborhoods occupied by the working and poorer classes (usually renters) have been reclaimed by middle and upper income newcomers, mostly owners (Brown–Saracino, 2010).

Many community organizations have used a variety of tactics to fight public plans and policies which they felt had negative consequences, from project development approvals to the granting of zoning variances. In more politically conservative communities, planning itself has been a target, as in opposition to zoning in Houston.

Most plans and planners do not address equity issues. Traditionally they focus mostly on physical development and budgetary issues rather than underlying and related social concerns. Planners, without much involvement in operating local government agencies and without their own independent constituency, tend to play an expert advisory role. Their planning is typically based on the needs and directives of elected government officials and other administrators in charge of implementing programs. With a largely advisory role, their influence on policy outcomes is limited. Nevertheless, planners can and have played an important role in political debates over planning issues. Planners also can play a significant role in shaping these debates through their presentation and analysis of information and data.

Name _____

The City Plans (Urban Planning)

5-1. Obtain a zoning map from your city hall and answer the following questions:
   A. How many zoning categories are there?

   B. What is the highest category?

   C. What is the lowest?

   D. What is the largest category in terms of area?

   E. Do you see areas on the map where controversies might occur? Describe them.

5-2. Find an example of a NIMBY controversy in your newspaper and summarize the situation. Defend one side or the other.

5-3. Choose one of the famous planners listed in this chapter and elaborate on his/her biosketch.

5-4. Relate current racial segregation patterns to federal housing programs of recent decades.

The City Designs
(Urban Design)
Stephanie Ryberg

Cities are more than just masses of individual buildings connected by a few streets. Rather, they are intricately designed places in which someone has made a decision impacting every single element of the built environment. What constitutes the "built environment" of a city? Well, everything: office buildings, stores, houses, apartment buildings, industrial complexes, streets, parks, plazas, landscapes, sidewalks, lighting fixtures, signs, railroads, highways, statues, public art, bus stations, drainage systems, and so on. Urban design, then, is a profession that focuses on the layout, organization, and relationship of all of these elements to one another. The goal of urban designers is to improve the quality of life for those residing in urban places by improving the overall quality of the city.

Inherent in this idea that urban designers can build better cities or improve existing cities are **normative values**. These are basically judgment statements about what is right or good. For urban designers, these judgments are about how we should live, what the relationship should be between daily life and our built environment, and how we should balance things deemed in the best interest of society (e.g., clean air) with individual preferences (e.g., personal automobile use). Because the field of urban design is rife with opinions, judgments, and normative arguments, it is essential to understand who gets to make decisions about the form of our built environment and how those decisions are made.

The study of urban design involves understanding the basic principles of the field, key methods in understanding urban spaces (an essential precursor to designing urban places), contemporary influences on the field, leading theories in urban design, and the tools used to implement urban design. Furthermore, a brief discussion of the field's interdisciplinary nature and history is essential.

What Is Urban Design?

Urban design is essentially an interdisciplinary endeavor to plan the physical layout, components, and function of cities. As a defined profession, urban design is a relatively young field, with practitioners drawing expertise primarily from the fields of architecture, landscape architecture, and urban planning. In many ways, urban design is the central way that these three, highly interrelated professions come together. Urban designers address the design of buildings, not so much the architectural details, but their overall layout, form, **massing**, and scale. They also think about how all of these individually designed buildings fit together into a cohesive whole that makes sense as districts, neighborhoods, or corridors. As the scope of urban design broadens to entire neighborhoods, cities, and even regions, it is imperative to have a thorough understanding of natural landscape systems—expertise held by landscape architects. Additionally, the design of public spaces, including parks of every size, is one of the top priorities of urban designers, which draws again on the work of landscape architects. Finally, while urban designers are specifically focused on physical planning and the built environment, their work clearly overlaps significantly with that of urban planners. In some ways these are very direct overlaps–both urban designers and planners are intricately involved in protecting historic areas, redeveloping waterfronts, and encouraging transit-oriented development, for instance. Additionally, though, many of the foundational drivers for contemporary urban planners are the same for urban design: equity, sustainability, and creating livable communities for all.

Urban design is an expansive profession that works to improve the built environment at many scales. Some urban design projects focus on single sites of varying sizes, while others address a single street or urban district. For instance, many designers are involved in **streetscape** projects, or efforts to improve the visual aesthetics and function of unique, identifiable districts. Streetscape projects often involve storefront or building façade renovations, installing new lighting, seating areas, trash cans, and other **street furniture**. They might involve redesigning traffic patterns, parking layouts, vacant land, and/or public plazas. Other urban design work focuses on entire neighborhoods, considering the need for housing improvements, infill development, vacant land redevelopment, traffic flow and patterns, and other character-defining details such as paving, lighting, and so on. Additionally, some design projects address the need to build entirely new communities—either in high-growth areas or on large tracts of reclaimed, formerly vacant urban land. At the city or regional scale, designers might work on the design of new light rail systems or open-space networks. These are just a few examples to illustrate the breadth and scope of activities that fall within the field of urban design.

The Roots of Urban Design

While the profession of urban design as we think of it today is fairly young (compared to architecture and even urban planning), the idea of urban design and strategically thinking about the built environment of cities has a long history. A detailed review of the history of urban form, for instance, would illustrate that ancient Greek and Roman cities were intricately designed for ceremonial, civic, and defensive purposes, among others. Even early U.S. cities were designed, although often for a variety of reasons from civic stature to commercial profit-making. For instance, in the late 1600s, William Penn developed a plan for Philadelphia that divided the colonial city into four quadrants, connected via a grid of streets, and centered by four public squares with an additional square in the middle to house the city hall. In the early 1700s James Oglethorpe devised a design for Savannah, Georgia that relied on a modular system of gridded streets and a series of small squares or parks. One of the most famous early city designs in the United States was Pierre L'Enfant's 1791 plan for the nation's new capital of Washington, DC. L'Enfant's vision was to demonstrate the power and authority of the nation's capital, with axial streets converging on the U.S. Capitol and White House. Additionally, L'Enfant included a number of public squares and civic spaces to reinforce the young nation's democratic ideals.

Across the Atlantic Ocean, Baron Haussmann was commissioned in the mid-1800s by Napoleon III to redesign Paris, France. Haussmann's plan, which was largely brought to fruition and remains the foundational structure of modern Paris, was completed between 1853 and 1870. His design called for new streets and boulevards, regulating the design of building facades, creating public parks, improving sewer and water works, constructing city facilities, and installing a series of public monuments. One of the most visible legacies of Haussmann's design are the long, straight, wide boulevards that cut through the dense, winding, and irregular pattern of streets remaining from medieval Paris.

Throughout the late 19th and early 20th centuries, U.S. cities were growing rapidly due to industrialization and overall population growth. Rampant and rapid growth caused many undesirable conditions: overcrowding, lack of coordination between land uses, and an overall undesirable living condition for many. In 1893 Chicago-based architect Daniel Burnham designed layout and buildings for the infamous World Columbian Exposition, also known as the Chicago World's Fair. Largely considered the birth of modern city planning, this effort to rethink the aesthetics of the city was also a major step forward in the realm of early urban design. Burnham's next significant project, the 1909 Plan of Chicago, further solidified design and aesthetic considerations within the heart of urban planning and development. The plan beautifully and graphically illustrated grand civic spaces, an open and accessible waterfront, and prominent boulevards.

During the 20th century, ideas about designing cities came to ever-greater prominence. In reaction to the perceived dysfunction of industrial cities and with great hopes for the promise of technology and the future, Modernist architects and planners began to drastically rethink the appropriate form of cities. The designer who epitomized the Modernist movement in urban design was a French architect by the name of Le Corbusier. His plan, known as the Ville Contemporaine (Contemporary City for Three Million Inhabitants), developed in 1922, called for high-rise, cruciform skyscrapers to replace the dense urban fabric of industrial cities. These "towers in the park" were to be connected via a transportation hub, which fully separated every mode of transit: buses from trains from highways from people.

In a counterexample, American architect Frank Lloyd Wright, most well-known for his building designs, developed a utopian, or idealized, vision for a new kind of urban form, which he named Broadacre City. This hypothetical place was actually quite anticity, more so resembling the overall form of suburbia rather than a dense urban form. Wright's vision emphasized automobile transportation and single-family, low-density housing.

Many of the contemporary ideas, theories, and principles guiding urban designers stand in stark contrast to the visions put forth by both Le Corbusier and the other Modernists, and Frank Lloyd Wright and similar low-density, suburban advocates. In many ways, contemporary practices are harkening much further back to traditional city design, gridded streets, and dense, walkable urban environments.

Kevin Lynch and the *Image of the City*

A central element in the practice of urban design is to be able to understand existing built environments. Since many designers are working to improve existing areas,—whether dense urban neighborhoods or suburban strip malls, —it is an essential first step to analyze and interpret what already exists and how people use (or do not use) places. Over time, urban designers have developed a variety of methods to carry out existing conditions analysis; the common methods are observation, photography, mapping and diagramming, and surveys. Additionally, designers often rely on direct participation, or spending time in places, using them and being an active member of them, to gain in-depth understanding of how places function.

One of the most longstanding and popular methods of urban design analysis is cognitive (or mental) mapping. This technique was developed by the prominent urban designer Kevin Lynch (1960) and widely publicized in his landmark text, *The Image of the City*. Lynch was interested in finding out how everyday people perceive places and what meaning people give to various places. The basic technique involves asking users to draw maps of a specified area from memory, labeling important elements. Designers use this method to determine users' perceptions of neighborhood and/or district boundaries, key community focal points, and areas with high imageability and legibility. **Imageability** refers to how well a place or object's qualities conjure a strong image for an individual. In other words, within a single neighborhood some streets might have certain features—a prominent church, renowned local businesses—that instantly spark a reaction from an observer. Other streets, though, might be quite unremarkable and thus not conjure a heightened reaction. Of course, the imageability of a place will be influenced by every individual's own personal experiences. For instance, if you live on a fairly unremarkable street, it will likely have a greater imageability for you than it would for an outside observer. According to Lynch, a highly imageable city is one that is well-formed, distinct, and remarkable. It has continuity between its distinct parts (i.e., neighborhoods), and the components of the city are connected well. Additionally any observer or user of the city is easily oriented. The other key concept, **legibility**, refers to the ease with which individuals recognize the distinct parts of a city and can understand how they fit together. According to Lynch, a legible city has subdistricts, landmarks and/or paths (roads, pedestrian ways) that are easy for anyone to identify and fit within a sensible overall scheme.

Out of his work with cognitive mapping, which he tested on his home city of Boston, Lynch devised a five-concept system for analyzing the built environment. These five concepts are nodes, paths, districts, landmarks, and edges. Through observation, surveys, and cognitive mapping, urban designers can use these five organizing concepts to analyze entire regions, cities, or neighborhoods. **Nodes** are the central places in a given area that serve as focal points into which users of that place can enter. Typically, they are where there is some kind of concentration of activity. Examples of nodes would include marketplaces, parks or playgrounds, even central business districts if one is studying an entire city or region. **Paths** are the routes along which people move and typically include streets, sidewalks, transit lines, and railroads. Not all paths have the same function or use level. For instance, both an interstate highway and a pedestrian trail through a city park are paths, but they have very different purposes and levels of intensity. Ideally, the paths within a region, city, or neighborhood are well-connected and fit into an overall design. **Districts** are the subareas within a region or city that have a unique, identifying character. These areas might be identified by their unique use (e.g., an entertainment district), location (e.g., a waterfront district), or other features such as a unique building type, degree of maintenance, or inhabitants (e.g., ethnic enclaves). **Landmarks** are physical focal points within a given area. They might be either local/neighborhood or city-wide, depending on the scale at which the designer is working. These clearly identifiable, prominent elements can range from a unique building to a popular store to a monument or sculpture to even a natural feature, such as a mountain visible in the distance from various points within a city. Finally, **edges** are linear elements that typically form the boundaries of a place. It is important to emphasize that, from a designer's perspective, edges are created in the built or natural landscape, irrespective of political boundaries. In other words, many cities have official neighborhood boundaries, but these are often misaligned from residents' perceptions of their neighborhood. For example, a city might define a neighborhood as including residential areas on both sides of an urban highway, but that highway creates such a physical barrier that residents or other users likely identify the two sides as unique places. Other examples of edges include shores, railroad cuts, hillsides, and walls.

Behavioral Mapping

Another key analytical tool for urban designers is the use of behavioral mapping. Here, the urban designer observes human behavior to understand how people use spaces. The designer then communicates these findings via maps, diagrams, photos, or other tabulations. He/she uses the results to make design recommendations for how to improve places so that they function better and accommodate natural human behavior. For instance, imagine there is a small neighborhood park the size of one city block with clearly laid-out paths entering from the mid-block point along each side. In the center there is a plaza with a fountain raised from the ground via a stepped platform. The benches in the park line its perimeter and face outward to the street. Now imagine that the city has noticed that this is a highly underutilized space, despite the fact that neighborhood parks should be common gathering spaces and community focal points. What is going on? The urban designer would spend time observing the space and might, for instance, notice the following: people make their own paths into the park from the corners rather than walking to the mid-block entrances; when people are in the park, they sit on the steps by the fountain and never the benches along the perimeter, but mostly people just use the park as a pass through. Based on these observations, the designer can make recommendations to improve the park's functionality and therefore (hopefully) its use by community members. These recommendations might include changing the path system to accommodate the natural tendency of people to enter from the corners, the addition or relocation of seating areas to the interior of the park, and more reasons or activities for people to stop (e.g., adding a playground if many children are present in the area).

One of the landmark studies employing behavioral mapping was William Whyte's (1980) study of urban plazas in New York City. Whyte was hired by the city to determine why some public plazas (required of office-building developers in exchange for building higher) were highly utilized, while others were stark, barren, and dysfunctional. Whyte's team of designers used direct observation and time-lapse cameras focused on a number of plazas to figure out the patterns of human behavior. Out of their study, they determined the key elements to a successful urban plaza and made recommendations to the city for a revised zoning code regulating plaza development.

Contemporary Influences on Urban Designers

The contemporary influences driving the urban design field mimic many of the common forces driving other urban-related disciplines (e.g., urban planning). Among these, the most prevalent is often the issue of sprawl and, more generally, the "placelessness" of late twentieth-century development. Urban sprawl is the general term encompassing the continued outward growth of metropolitan areas characterized by large-lot zoning, large houses, auto dependency, stark separation of uses, and rapid land consumption. The notion of "placelessness" emanates from urbanistic critiques that sprawling developments lack any unique identity or character.

Other key influences center on environmental issues. Urban designers are increasingly concerned about the relationship between the built environment and air quality, water pollution, and overall natural resource depletion. Again, many of these concerns are intricately tied to critiques of sprawl as auto dependency causes increased air pollution, and massive amounts of impervious, or paved, surfaces cause runoff and water quality problems. Furthermore, the contemporary built environment of suburbia is largely completely automobile dependent, raising concerns about oil dependency, resource consumption, and the long-term sustainability of such patterns. In recent years the discussion about the links between natural environmental conditions and the built environment have heightened as urban designers consider the impacts of climate change and rising sea levels on urban areas. In particular, many of the most densely populated metropolitan areas in the world are potentially threatened if there is massive sea level rise, thus threatening vast swaths of the global population. This is true in the United States, where over half of the nation's population now resides within 50 miles of a coast, as well as in more developing nations such as China where coastal cities have experienced rapid urbanization in just the past few decades.

Finally, urban designers play a key role in constantly rethinking the purpose, form, and design of the built environment. Recent economic conditions including foreclosures, vacant buildings, and increasingly large swaths of vacant land are driving urban designers to find innovative ideas for the 21st century city, particularly in older, formerly industrial locations such as Cleveland, Detroit, Buffalo, and Pittsburgh.

Contemporary Approaches to Urban Design:
The Generalist Perspective

Today there are a few key ideas about how to design cities. The four theories discussed below illustrate a generalist perspective and three specific ideologies about contemporary urban design. Together they provide a good introduction to designers' thought processes, the major issues they confront, and their proposed solutions or recommendations for how to go about designing urban built environments in the 21st century. We begin with a generalist perspective, using the arguments of prominent urban designer Allan Jacobs (2011) as an illustrative model.

Jacobs published *The Good City*, in which he presents observations of cities around the world and derives 13 principles of "good cities." His intention is to learn from existing cities to drive an urban design profession that continues to produce "good cities."

Jacobs is a highly regarded urban designer, the former director of the San Francisco Department of City Planning, and author of many notable works on urban design. In many ways, Jacobs's most recent work provides an updated vision originally set forth in his 1987 coauthored (with Donald Appleyard) publication, "Toward an Urban Design Manifesto." Jacobs's 13 principles illustrate a generalist approach to urban design with the intention of making existing and new cities desirable places for people to live, work, and enjoy.

According to Jacobs, cities should (1) be livable, (2) provide access to opportunity, imagination, and joy, and (3) be authentic and meaningful. Here Jacob notes the importance of basic necessities such as clean air and water and a well-managed and healthy environment. People should have access to a variety of work and housing options, as well as the ability to engage in new and exciting experiences. Furthermore, places should have clear origins and the built form of places should be understandable (or legible).

Jacobs goes on to say that good cities should (4) value conservation and preservation, (5) encourage community and public life, (6) be self-sustaining, and (7) be accessible to all. These four elements all contribute to a place's social sustainability by providing a sense of identity and promoting common heritage amongst people (preservation), by being inclusive and having open and accessible public spaces, and by providing every individual a safe and healthy environment. Additionally Jacobs believes cities must be self-sustaining in terms of such things as natural resources, food production, and waste disposal.

Well-designed cities must also have (8) livable streets and neighborhoods, (9) a minimum density of 15 units/acre, (10) integrated activities, and (11) buildings arranged to define and enclose public spaces. Here Jacobs gets more specific in the details of urban design stating that places must be designed for people, not cars, with such features as parking available behind buildings and streets designed primarily for walking (rather than driving). He advocates for small, walkable blocks and small parcels and buildings, which allow for a greater diversity of uses, owners, and activities. He provides a specific minimum density, or how many people reside within a specific geographic area. Jacobs's number of 15 units/acre translates to about 30–60 people/acre and is his minimum required for supporting mass transit and a variety of mixed uses within a neighborhood. Furthermore, all neighborhoods should be mixed-use, or "integrated," with places to live, work, shop, worship, and play all within a confined geographic area.

Finally, Jacobs advocates for places that (12) value public places and a public way system and (13) have one or more major centers of activity. Jacobs is calling for designers to place a high value on public spaces and the urban core. He states that a central value of urban life is "public-ness," or the ability to bring a variety of diverse people together. A focus on pedestrians is key since no friendly interaction takes place between people confined to their cars. Finally, Jacobs reasserts the value of a central core or focal point that includes commerce, offices, government centers, community uses, and housing.

The New Urbanism

One of the most prominent design ideologies to emerge in the late 20th century was the New Urbanism, originally referred to as Neo-traditionalism. The New Urbanists, originally founded by a group of architects disenchanted with both the built environment of late 20th century development and contemporary architecture practice, formed in the early

1980s. While many designers and design firms adhere to the principles of New Urbanism, the leading advocates include Andres Duany and Elizabeth Plater-Zyberk whose Miami-based firm opened in 1980, and Peter Calthorpe, whose Berkeley, California–based firm opened three years later.

During the 1980s, New Urbanist projects were fairly experimental and opportunistic—meaning that they occurred as tracts of land became available to them for development and that the leading thinkers within the movement were testing their ideas in actual projects. The first, and still perhaps most recognizable, of the New Urbanists' early projects was Seaside, Florida, developed on the Florida panhandle beginning in 1981 (and made famous as the location for filming the movie, *The Truman Show*). In 1986, Duany Plater-Zyberk (DPZ) completed their first urban redevelopment (rather than new development) plan for Stuart, Florida. That same year, a New Urbanist plan was developed for the redesign of Mashpee Commons, a deteriorated and underutilized shopping area. These two projects represented the New Urbanists' efforts to apply their ideas to fix existing urban areas, rather than building new towns on greenfield (i.e., suburban) sites. By the 1990s, New Urbanists were gaining traction in the professional design and planning worlds, as well as in planning and design schools. This was aided by the publication of a series of influential books including *The Geography of Nowhere* (James Howard Kunstler, 1993), *The Next American Metropolis* (Peter Calthorpe, 1993), *The New Urbanism* (Peter Katz, 1994), and finally *Suburban Nation* (Andres Duany, Elizabeth Plater-Zyberk, and Jeff Speck, 2000). Additionally, the Congress for the New Urbanism (CNU), a membership organization, was founded in 1993 and the first annual CNU conference was held that same year. Today the New Urbanists continue to hold annual conferences, have a clearly defined charter (published in 2000), principles, and mission, and offer many built examples that follow their agenda. In 2011 the CNU updated its principles with the release of the *Canons of Sustainable Architecture and Urbanism*, which integrates key concepts of sustainability into the agenda.

The mission statement of the CNU states six critiques of contemporary development practices that the New Urbanists are attempting to rectify. Generally, these are issues that planners and urban designers are broadly attempting to address—sprawl, urban disinvestment, segregation, and environmental concerns. Furthermore, the New Urbanists argue that there is an "erosion of society's built heritage," with architects focusing primarily on iconic buildings and the vast majority of development occurring without much consideration of aesthetics and place-making.

To address these issues, the New Urbanist agenda includes a number of policy, design, planning, and development recommendations espoused in the Charter of the New Urbanism, as well as four overarching principles:

1. Restore existing urban centers and towns within coherent metropolitan regions;
2. Reconfigure sprawling suburbs into communities of real neighborhoods and diverse districts;
3. Conserve natural environments; and
4. Preserve our built legacy.

To guide their work, the New Urbanists have formalized their vision for cities and design practice via the "Charter for the New Urbanism," originally published in 2000. The Charter calls for urban designers to focus on neighborhood-scale development, prioritize pedestrians (rather than cars), reassert the primacy of public spaces and institutions, and develop places in a way that recalls local context and respects environmental conditions.

The Charter goes on to outline specific design practices for regions, neighborhoods/districts/corridors, and blocks/streets/buildings. In many ways the New Urbanist agenda mimics the goals of contemporary urban planning and tries to address many of the same issues, albeit through a design perspective. For instance, they recognize that metropolitan regions are a single, functioning economic unit and that development should occur logically throughout a region, rather than in fragmented ways. They consider neighborhoods the "building blocks of the metropolis," and advocate for pedestrian-friendly, mixed-use districts. One of their key tools for neighborhood design is consideration of the "pedestrian shed," or a one-quarter mile radius around any given point. The concept, first developed by Clarence Perry (1929) in his *Regional Plan of New York and Its Environs*, envisions a built environment in which people can access daily needs (schools, libraries, retail, daily services) within a 10-minute walk, or a one-quarter mile radius from their home. Finally, the New Urbanists call for the architecture profession to reassert itself in the practice of everyday building design. Rather than focusing on iconic, standout/stand-alone buildings, they argue that all buildings should be designed with the overall urban fabric in mind. Design should be contextual and create a cohesive whole. Buildings should not be objects to view, but framing devices for streets and public space. Specifically, the New Urbanists advocate for spaces that prioritize the pedestrian above all else, calling for retail fronting sidewalks and parking—a necessity for an automobile society—to be relegated to the rear.

In recent years the New Urbanists have refined and advanced their agenda in two key ways. First, they developed the "Transect," which serves as the basis for the Smart Code, a model ordinance intended to replace traditional zoning codes. The Transect and Smart Code call for urban development that transitions from rural to urban in a logical way that is based on density (the number of units per acre), rather than land use (as is common in traditional zoning codes). The Smart Code has served as the basis for cities to develop what is known as a **form-based code** to replace traditional zoning. The first U.S. cities to adopt such ordinances are Denver, Colorado, and Miami, Florida. As a relatively new innovation in urban design, it will take time to assess how well the form-based codes work and the difference the resulting built environments make in a city. Second, in 2011 the New Urbanists released the "Canons of Sustainable Architecture and Urbanism" to address the urban design implications resulting from global climate change and energy/environmental concerns.

For the past two or three decades the New Urbanist agenda has been front and center within the urban design profession. While many of their ideas are widely embraced by people in urban-related fields, there are a number of critiques of their work. The dominant critique is that, despite advocating for concentrated development that is the antithesis of sprawl, many New Urbanist communities are built on greenfield sites in rapidly growing suburbs, thus contributing to, rather than combating sprawl. This has largely occurred opportunistically, as land has become available for New Urbanist development. On the other hand, there are excellent examples of urban infill projects as well, including the redevelopment of the Stapleton Airport site in Denver, Colorado. Stapleton was Denver's primary airport until a new facility was built further out on the fringe of the metropolitan area. With this relocation a massive tract of land became available for development within the boundaries of the city, surrounded by older, traditional, urban neighborhoods.

The project, spearheaded by prominent New Urbanist Peter Calthorpe, thus created a new in-town neighborhood of homes, shopping, recreation, and workplaces.

The other dominant critique of New Urbanism is that many such communities are extremely expensive and thus inequitable. In many cases this is true. The average American cannot likely afford a home in Seaside, the first New Urbanist town. Service employees at the local retail shops and businesses can certainly not afford to live there. The New Urbanists counter this critique in two ways. One, they argue that the high prices of homes in their developments simply demonstrate the high demand for this type of walkable, community-based living environment. Rather than being a critique, it should serve as the basis for justifying more widespread designs of this type. Second, New Urbanists have made concerted attempts to work in lower-income areas and with mixed-income housing. Most notably, many New Urbanist firms were hired to do the redesigns for public housing transformation in the 1990s under the federal HOPE VI program, which typically demolished the most distressed public housing in the country and rebuilt walkable, mixed-income communities.

Landscape Urbanism

In recent years a group of urban designers, largely emanating from the field of landscape architecture, has launched a direct critique of New Urbanism. Recall that landscape architecture is one of the three dominant fields influencing urban design (along with architecture and planning). Broadly encompassed by the term "landscape urbanists," these designers believe that New Urbanists are nostalgic and nonresponsive to 21st century ways of life. Many New Urbanist designs call for a return to traditional architectural motifs, which opens up critiques of historicism and nostalgia. The landscape urbanists, on the other hand, embrace contemporary cities and seek design techniques that are based in the current era, rather than harkening back to the past. They argue that the underlying landscape (natural features, waterways, ecosystems) of any place should drive urban design. The unique perspective that landscape architects bring to the urban design world is this focus on ecosystems. The systems approach to design actually dates to earlier urban designers, notably Ian McHarg who, in the 1970s, published *Design with Nature*. McHarg outlined a method of analysis that relied on overlaying a series of maps to determine the least harmful places to develop. In other words, for a specific geographic area, if one overlays a map of wetlands, other waterways, fragile soils, and wildlife areas, it can be seen where they overlap the most and the least. It is then in those areas of least overlap or that are totally void of any of such sensitive lands where designers should focus.

The movement of landscape urbanism is very recent, dating only to the late 1990s, when Charles Waldheim, then a professor at the University of Illinois, organized a conference on the subject. Waldheim (2006) edited the *Landscape Urbanism Reader* and three years later took a prominent position as the Chair of the Landscape Architecture Department at the Harvard Graduate School of Design. From this position, the landscape urbanists have ramped up their vocal critique of New Urbanists and are trying to shift the urban design world in a new direction. Specifically, the landscape urbanists believe and accept that the majority of Americans like living in low-density suburbs. Rather than trying to change these ingrained cultural norms, landscape urbanists are seeking means of accommodating popular preferences while still protecting the environment and underlying ecosystems.

While the landscape urbanists offer an interesting counterperspective to New Urbanism and are breathing a breath of new air into the urban design profession, it is still a very young movement. As such, there are few built examples of their work and their arguments tend towards the theoretical and abstract. Only time will tell what their impact on the design world and the built environment will be.

Sustainable Urbanism

The concept of sustainability now permeates many urban-related fields. Urban design is no exception. An early author in this area, practicing urban designer Douglas Farr (2008) published *Sustainable Urbanism: Urban Design with Nature*, outlining an approach to urban design that fully integrates sustainability. This work, and the name "sustainable urbanism," captures the 21st century trajectory of the urban design field. The definition of sustainable urbanism, according to Farr, is "walkable and transit-served urbanism integrated with high-performance buildings and high-performance infrastructure." The key critique is that "green building" cannot be done independently of overall urban design concerns. In other words, building "green buildings" in automobile-dependent, environmentally sensitive lands makes no sense. Rather, sustainable urban design pushes for development that is compact, high-density, and provides humans with a strong connection to nature and the environment.

Many components of this approach to urban design mimic those offered by the New Urbanists; for instance, focusing on neighborhood-based design, creating walkable communities, improving public transportation, and having mixed-use places. Additionally, though, sustainable urban design pushes for self-sustaining communities, wherein the responsibility for things like waste disposal occurs within the neighborhood boundaries. Imagine the increased concern about the quantity of waste we generate and what happens to it over the long run if we had to house it literally in our own backyards. Might we become more proactive in reducing waste and finding sustainable methods of living? Furthermore, sustainable urban design reconnects people with nature. This is counter to many design practices of the 20th century—particularly during the mid-century period—in which man attempted to conquer and dominate natural systems. Reconnecting people with nature allows people to benefit from natural amenities, increases appreciation for environmental lands, and generates awareness about where resources (e.g., water or food) come from. Finally, using the sustainable urban design approach integrates green buildings and high-performance infrastructure into the profession. The former includes such features as home solar power, recirculating water, energy-efficient design, and building materials with few to no harmful chemicals. The latter pushes urban designers to think of innovative ways to reduce the environmental impacts of infrastructure (roads, sewers, etc.). One idea currently being explored in Cleveland, Ohio, for example, is preserving strategically selected vacant land to create a green network throughout the region. These sites would follow natural drainage paths to reduce the burden on local storm sewer needs. The urban designers' role in a project such as this is to understand patterns of building and development within a region, ensure that a future green network also maximizes benefits to local residents, and build such green infrastructure networks into future designs for communities.

The Tools to Implement Urban Design

Urban design schemes impact cities only if they can actually come to fruition. In other words, they have to be implemented. The nature of urban space in the United States requires varying approaches to transform design ideas on paper into real-world living environments. On one hand, there are publicly owned places such as everything in the public **right-of-way** (i.e., streets and sidewalks), parks and most open space, and government facilities. For these locations, implementing urban design plans requires public commitment and investment. Since the expenditure of local funds is typically controlled by a city council, the implementation of urban design thus has a political component. As such, it is imperative for designers to not work in a closed-off bubble, but to actively engage the general public, local leaders, and other stakeholders when developing a design plan. Today, many local governments are extremely cash-strapped. As a result, many public improvements occur via **public-private partnerships**. In this model, local governments partner with private-sector businesses, investors, and/or nonprofit organizations to raise funds for a wide variety of design projects. One common technique, for example, is the use of **business improvement districts** to pay for streetscape improvements in commercial areas. The general strategy is that businesses included within the designated area decide to self-impose an additional "tax" on themselves, with that money then used specifically for improvements to the district. These might include new lighting, special paving, marketing and signage, improved transit stops, storefront renovation matching grants or low-interest loans, and so on.

When design plans focus on districts, neighborhoods, or even entire cities, they typically call for changes both to public spaces and private spaces. The latter presents complications for implementation. Whereas local governments can directly pay for and implement design improvements on public land, they need to use other means to convince private landowners to make improvements on privately owned spaces. There are a number of **regulatory tools** that cities use to make development of privately owned land conform to desired urban design goals. The basic forms of design regulation are special review districts and zoning codes. The former includes design review and historic districts. In design review districts, property owners typically present plans for new construction to an architectural or design review board for approval. These districts include clear standards for what is desired in the area and the review board will typically work with owners to achieve an optimal outcome. Historic districts are fairly similar, but focus solely on historic areas within a city where owners must gain public approval for alterations to historic fabric and for new construction (to ensure compatibility). Finally, zoning codes have a direct impact on the type of building and development that occurs on privately owned land. Traditionally, zoning regulates things such as the height, setbacks, and land use for buildings. It is imperative to have zoning regulations that match the desired design outcomes for any given area. In an effort to achieve a better and more desirable built environment, a few cities are experimenting with the new type of zoning—called **form-based codes**—promoted by the New Urbanists and modeled in the Smart Code, as discussed previously.

Name _____

CHAPTER 6
The City Designs (Urban Design)

6-1. Walk around your neighborhood and identify all those things that might have been planned by (or with the help of) an urban designer. Discuss those things that you think are well-designed and those things that you think are in need of design improvement.

6-2. What normative values do you hold about cities? What is your ideal vision of how a city should look and function? If you were an urban designer rethinking the city you live in, what changes would you make and why?

6-3. Find an example (not mentioned in the chapter) of a New Urbanist development. How does the approach and philosophy presented in this chapter translate into a real place? Describe and critique the development, including both its pros and cons.

6-4. Find a business improvement district, design review district, historic district, or other design code in your city.

   a. What elements of the built environment does the district address?

   b. What are its design goals?

   c. How does this particular district or code further the implementation of those design goals?

PART II
Urban Processes

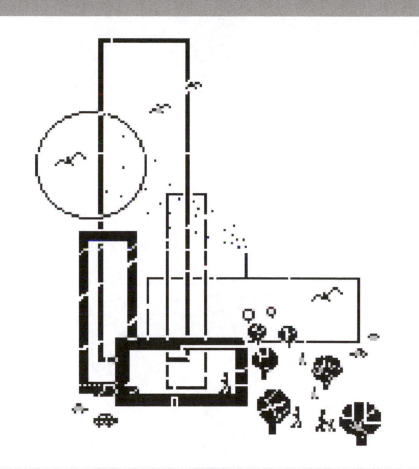

The City Governs

(Political Science)

Mittie Davis Jones

The political perspective of urban studies must address the current political environment in urban areas, as well as the history that contributes to the current political environment. An accurate backdrop for the study of urban politics requires a consideration of the early municipal governmental forms that included political machines and partisan politics, reform efforts and struggles as the established political leaders and groups were threatened by the demands of newcomers in the form of immigrants as well as racial and ethnic minorities. In the twenty-first century, a similar situation faces established political groups as the growth of racial and ethnic minorities continues in the central cities of major metropolitan areas. Several cities are now described as "majority minority" because people of color, including African-Americans, Hispanics, and Asians, exceed the white population in number. Among these cities are Los Angeles, Cleveland, Detroit, Atlanta, Houston, New York, Miami, and Washington D. C.

The discipline of political science examines the different structural arrangements that provide government in cities and how they affect current residents of urban areas. Elected and appointed officials work within these structural arrangements to provide services and meet the diverse needs of urban populations. In viewing the city from a political perspective, one must consider the conditions encountered by city residents and leaders. The structural arrangements affect the ability of cities to deal with the constantly changing urban issues faced by diverse population groups.

Political Background

Most large cities have had experience with political machines or **machine politics.** Machine politics can exist without a political machine; however, political machines practice machine politics by their very nature. Machine politics is defined as the process of exchanging favors and inducements for votes (Ross, Levine, & Stedman, 1991). The **brokerage system** associated with machine politics is the vehicle for this exchange. The political machine brokered the requests of specific persons or groups for some favor, such as a zoning variance. In return for its assistance the machine might expect financial benefits, jobs, or other compensation. Political machines were organizations that practiced machine politics using incentives to attract and direct their members (Wolfinger, 1984).

The urban political environment has always been a fertile ground for groups vying for control over resources whether, scarce or plentiful. Political machines were most prevalent during the late nineteenth century and into the early twentieth century. They arose in response to large numbers of immigrants who relocated into industrializing areas and who had basic needs, like shelter, food, and clothing, that were not being met by local government. By providing for these needs, the machines built a loyal and dedicated political base.

The leadership of the political machine and the political party of its members were often synonymous. Political machines have been run by Democrats and Republicans. They were, in many instances, indistinguishable from the official government of the city (Sorauf & Beck, 1988). The machine leaders were, in some cases, elected officials. In other cases, the machines were run by someone behind the scenes who dictated to the mayor. New York's Tammany Hall was run by several famous bosses who were not elected but who wielded political power over the mayors.

The structure of the typical political machine is pyramidal (See Figure 7.1). At the lowest level, the block captains, who were more numerous, maintained personal, door-to-door contact with area residents. They insured voter turnout for the machine and secured votes for machine candidates. The precinct captains were responsible for oversight over block captains and served as a conduit for taking their concerns to the ward leaders and conveying information back to the block captains. The ward leaders were directly accountable to the boss or his assistants. On election day, all the resources of the captains and others in the machine organization were marshaled to assist their candidates.

During the heyday of the political machines, the city governments were not well-formulated and were limited in their scope. Many activities such as transportation and utilities customarily fell out of their control. The machines inculcated loyalty in immigrants by providing social service assistance, helping them to locate homes and jobs, and functioning as a link to urban life. The political machines operated largely

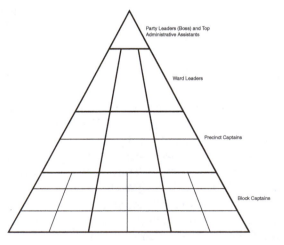

Figure 7.1
Typical Machine Organization Chart.
Source: From B. Ross, M. Levine, M. Stedman, *Urban Politics,* 4th edition, 1991, p. 110.

on a **patronage** basis, that is, as they gave assistance to individuals, their political support was expected in return. An efficiently running machine could guarantee a certain amount of political backing in return for benefits provided to individuals through jobs and/or contracts or to improvements and services to worthy communities. The immigrant nature of the machines contrasted with the political arrangement which preceded their rise as well as that which followed them. European immigrants arrived in sufficient numbers to enable their capture of local government operations from the largely Anglo-Saxon Protestant elites already in control. Among the best known machines were Tammany Hall of New York, Pendergast's in Kansas City, Frank Hague's in Jersey City, "Big Bill" Thompson's in Chicago, and James Curley's in Boston.

Political machines maintained their power through the dispensation of benefits and rewards to their supporters. Intangible benefits provided a means of inducement as well. The provision of certain city services was often contingent upon the number of votes received from a given community during an election. Machine bosses could withhold services to those who did not demonstrate such support.

The nineteenth century political machines existed in American cities where the immigrant population was small, such as Denver, Memphis, Nashville and Kansas City. However, the machines gained strength in central cities of older metropolitan areas as immigrants relocated to industrializing areas with many social and economic needs that were not met by local government. Labor unions and political parties in the Northeast and Midwest facilitated machine growth (Harrigan & Vogel, 2000).

The demise of political machines occurred as the result of two major forces—the actions of reformers seeking good government practices and the competing demands of other groups that challenged their dominance. Among the reasons for the decline of the political machine are:

1. The inability to wield the same amount of influence due to changes in election laws and public policy. Civil service protection was expanded to cover municipal jobs, requiring hiring based on merit rather than political connections.
2. Decreased numbers of patronage jobs as the result of the former. Elected officials gained the power to appoint department heads and other top policymaking types, with less emphasis on politics than ability.
3. The availability of assistance and services through government largesse, federally enacted and funded programs, which decreased reliance on the machines.
4. Lack of an ideological foundation, to galvanize supporters.
5. Unwillingness to allow for the participation for others seeking representation in local government, particularly African-Americans.

Machine-style political structures exist or existed in areas where certain elements of political machines did not or could not exist. There is a difference between political machines where a large parochial population with short-term material needs dominates and those smaller towns where one company or economic interest dominates. It may be the exercise of control through oppression in the latter case rather than material benefits and loyalties in the former case.

Another dimension of machine politics is found in the capacity of urban elected officials to circumvent obstructions to the operation of political machines. Further, legal sanctions notwithstanding, efforts to continue machine business usually form the basis for sensational headlines that connote corruption and graft. While some authors have suggested that the tenacity of these functions signals the survival of the political machine, it also supports the notion that machine-type politics have endured.

The creative hiring which results in "temporary" hirings of essentially permanent employees who then bypass civil service procedures is one example. The allocation of federal funds by municipal bodies, such as city councils, often takes on a brokering dimension reminiscent of machine political favoritism. It has been suggested that ample opportunities remain to sustain a patron-client form of politics because local governments have larger budgets, provide a complex array of services, and play an active regulatory role. A more bureaucratized government, then, may have increased the needs of citizens for intervention rather than decreasing the level of need (Sorauf & Beck, 1988).

The history of the political machines is important because of the legacy which remains present in some cities. The reforms initiated to minimize the machines have an impact on governmental operations today. Reform demands for the council-manager and commission forms of government, at-large elections, and nonpartisan elections affect current local government operations. Further, characteristics of the machines set the tone for future urban political alignments between racial and ethnic groups. The lack of an ideological foundation and the exclusion of minority group interests are major elements of machine operations that have impacts today. These issues are discussed in greater detail in the sections that follow.

Local Governance Structure

The structure and operation of local governments are related to the previous existence of political machines or the playing out of machine politics. Current urban political structures developed as a response, directly or indirectly, to aspects of machine operations that some citizens found undesirable. In some cities, the existing form of government is a direct consequence of attempts to terminate political machines and to reduce the power of ethnic politicians. The results of these reform efforts are evident in two major aspects of local government: the form of government and the means of electing city council members as discussed below (Figure 7.2).

The two major types of political structures that are commonly found in cities are the **mayor-council** form and the **council-manager** form. The council-manager form is the fastest growing type of municipal governance. (See Figure 7.3 on forms of municipal governance).

In 2003 it was reported that the largest cities, with populations over 250,000, most commonly had the mayor-council form of government (International City Management Association, 2003). In 2006, 55 percent of cities reported having the council-manager form of government compared with 34 percent reporting the mayor-council form (International City Management Association, 2008).

The council-manager form of government is found most frequently in midsized cities with populations between 25,000 and 249,999, and in Sunbelt cities such as San Diego, San Antonio, Fort Worth, Oklahoma City, and Miami. This form of governance is considered best suited to homogeneous communities with lower levels of conflict, typical of suburban communities, and a fair amount of agreement of public policies and service distribution.

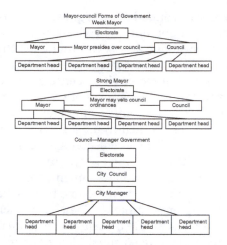

Figure 7.2
Examples of Mayor-Council and Council-Manager Forms of Government.
Source: Adapted from B. Ross, M. Levine, & M. Stedman, *Urban Politics 4th Edition,* 1991, pp. 86, 88 and 92.

Form of Government	2008	2000	1998	1996	1992	1988	1984
Council-Manager	55%	3,302 (48.3%)	3,232	2,760	2,441	2,356	2,290 (34.7%)
Mayor-Council	34%	2,988 (43.7%)	2,943	3,319	3,635	3,686	3.686 (55.8%)
Commission	<1%	143 (2.1%)	146	154	168	173	176 (2.7%)
Town Mtg.	5%	334 (4.9%)	333	365	363	369	370 (5.6%)
Rep. Town Mtg.	1% not reported 4%	65 (1.0%)	65	70	79	82	81 (1.2%)
Total	100%	*6,832 (100%)	*6,720	*6,668	*6,686	*6,664	*6,603 (100%)

*Totals for U.S. local governments represent those municipalities with populations of 2,500 and greater.
Source: The Municipal Year Books 1984–2008, published by the International City/County Management Association (ICMA), Washington D.C.

Figure 7.3
Forms of Municipal Governance.

In the largest cities the mayor-council form of government is more prevalent. The typical mayor-council city is older, larger, and nearly centered in a metropolitan area, more heterogeneous, and has more economic and social problems than council-manager cities (Frederickson and Johnson, 2001). It has been suggested that the mayor-council form is best suited for highly politically-charged environments where diverse communities have conflicting demands and expectations. This form of government is also considered more responsive to citizen demands than the council-manager form.

The original intent behind the council-manager arrangement was to diminish the political nature of local governance. The council-manager model is based upon a corporate leadership arrangement where the city council is synonymous with the board of directors. The manager is hired by the city council based upon professional qualifications rather than elected by the citizens. In reality, it is impossible to remove political concerns totally from even this type of governing environment. The city council must still win voter approval and the city manager serves at the behest of the council. Ultimately, the citizens' wishes must be addressed and the manager must please the majority of council members.

Some cities have both a manager and a mayor. In these cases, the mayor serves largely a ceremonial function, although he or she also may provide leadership to the council. The mayor, in these cases, is usually a city council member who exercises more influence than other council members.

Despite the intent of the model, politics remains part of the council-manager form of government. Although city managers may seek to be nonpolitical by staying out of political campaigns and protecting the city governance from the effects of partisan politics and patronage, they are definitely political (Harrigan, 1991). The political nature of their jobs consists of making policy proposals and trying to influence legislators and other elected officials. Given the interaction of city managers with politicians who have partisan connections, survival in their positions may depend upon alignment with the dominant local electoral coalition.

Political Reform

Evidence of political reform can be found in looking at selected American cities. The City of Detroit, for example, moved toward reform when the city adopted a city charter which in 1974 established a strong-mayor form of government. Strong mayors have wide-ranging political independence as well as the power to appoint department heads and to prepare the city budget. The Detroit city council consists of nine members elected **at-large,** that is, by all city residents. This form of governance was promoted by turn-of-the-century reformers who preferred the citywide election of council members over election from single-member districts or wards. The **ward system** remains in many large cities today. In Chicago, fifty **aldermanic** districts are represented on the city council.

The city of Cleveland has made some modest moves toward reform, first by adopting the city manager plan in 1921. In 1931, the city returned to the mayor-ward system. After abandoning a bicameral council in 1892, the number of council members was changed to 32 until 1913, when it was reduced to 26 and raised again to 33 in 1923. The number of city council positions was reduced to 21 members in July, 1981, and again to 19 in 2000.

Research has found that the at-large method of election of city officials has a negative impact on the ability of minority candidates to win elections. When voters cast their ballots based upon the race of the candidate, members of racial and ethnic minority groups are bound to lose. On the other hand, racial and ethnic minority candidates fare better when they run in districts where their group dominates. Residential racial segregation has made it easier for minority groups to elect members of their race or ethnicity in district or ward elections. The effect of the reform effort toward at-large elections has been to dilute minority voting strength. In 2006, the U.S. Department of Justice found that the city of Euclid, Ohio, diluted minority voting strength with too many at-large council seats.

City officials often find it necessary to deal with the effects of circumstances over which they have little control. In many cities, the school system is a major concern of homeseekers with children. Autonomous school boards typically have governed city school systems with neither the mayors nor city councils having direct authority over school board operations. In these circumstances, local elected officials sometimes would attempt to exert their political *influence* over these boards in order to promote the city's economic development interests.

During the 1990s, a number of major school districts came under the governance of mayors. The state legislature in Ohio turned over governance of the Cleveland public schools to then-Mayor Michael White without a vote of the people in 1998. Four years later, the citizens voted to retain mayoral governance, which allows the mayor to appoint members of the school board rather than permit the electorate to choose them. Mayors in Chicago, Boston, New York, and Detroit also have control over their school systems.

Evolution of African-American Leadership

During the late 1960s, African-American politicians began to make noticeable inroads in local politics and governance. The number of African-American elected officials has increased greatly since the passage of the Voting Rights Act in 1965. Nonetheless, the overall percentage of offices held by African-Americans nationwide is less than two percent. One of the earlier experiences corroborated the difficulty that African-Americans encountered with political machines in central cities. Congressman William Dawson was an African-American machine operative in Chicago during the early 1950s. He successfully served the machine by delivering votes from his district. Serving at the behest of the machine, Dawson and other African-American officials inside the machine retained power as long as they operated within the narrowly circumscribed boundaries of the machine's interests (Ross et al, 1991).

African-American politicians of the 1960s and later are differentiated from those of the Dawson era because they were not beholden to a political machine. In most cases, when an African-American was elected in a major central city, it was the result of a growing black electorate with demands that the official was expected to meet. In 1967, Carl Stokes was elected mayor of Cleveland and Richard Hatcher was elected mayor of Gary. They were the first African-American mayors elected of major, industrial central cities. Subsequently, black mayors were elected for the first time in Detroit, Los Angeles, Newark, and Atlanta during the 1970s. By the 1990s, black mayors had been elected in several other major cities including Chicago, New York, Houston, Seattle, and Denver.

Shortly after the election of Stokes and Hatcher, a researcher suggested that black mayors were inheriting what he called "hollow prizes" because of the conditions they encountered (Friesema, 1969). These industrial cities were losing population as white households and businesses moved to the suburbs. He predicted that as this movement occurred, the cities would lose tax revenue resulting in poor city services. This, in turn, would create a dependency on white-dominated state legislatures and the federal government. If this scenario did develop, the mayors would not really have control, because their resources to govern would be dictated by outside forces. Furthermore, the cities they led would not be as revered or have much to offer its residents.

In some cities where black mayors were elected, decline in social and economic conditions continued, as did the out-migration of whites and other middle-income households. One study found that white businesses began to leave Gary, Indiana in large numbers after the re-election of Richard Hatcher in 1971, seeing it as a sign of inevitable economic decline (Catlin, 1993). The unanswered question is whether the election of black mayors led whites to move in response to black leadership or perceived dominance; or whether the election of black mayors happened simultaneously with that decline, enabling those blacks who remained to elect more black officials.

African-American officials clearly have more influence in central decision making than during previous periods. Even where someone who is not African-American holds the mayoralty, there may be efforts in cities to achieve representative government by appointing a diverse cadre of racial and ethnic officials. Political incorporation is a term used to describe the assent of African-Americans and other minorities to political power. Incorporation occurs in varying degrees from weak mobilization to strong incorporation (Browning, Marshall, & Tabb, 1984).

The impact of incorporation is subject to varying interpretations. One generalization is that African-American incorporation in itself is not sufficient to bridge the gap between middle-income persons of all races and the substantial numbers of low-income African-Americans. Further, as the populations of Hispanics and Asians continue to grow in urban areas, the balance of political power between blacks and whites will be changed.

Incorporation has brought material benefits to African-Americans (Harrigan, 1993). Research has also shown that African-American mayors and other officials have made a difference while serving in office. Peter Eisinger (1983) found that African-American mayors were able to expand public sector opportunities for African-Americans during the 1970s largely through the aggressive use of affirmative action policies. The outcome of efforts to hire African-American employees and award contracts to African-American businesses was substantial improvement in both).

An assessment of the impact of African-American mayors suggests that they have taken advantage of opportunities to improve the condition of at least some African-Americans and other constituents. Cities with African-American mayors had significantly higher expenditures for "welfare" services and lower expenditures for parks, libraries, and fire protection. Their cities also raised more money than non-African-American cities and imported more federal aid (Karnig & Welch, 1980). With fewer federal dollars available to them, central city mayors have found it necessary to pursue alternative strategies for economic revitalization, including the aggressive pursuit of business investment.

Mayor Coleman Young of Detroit was accused of meeting the demands of the corporate community at the expense of needed improvements in the city's neighborhoods. Toward the end of his tenure, he supported the expansion of the convention center, the building of new hotel, office, and tourist complexes, and a new east side airport (Ross, et al., 1981).

Mayor Young was alternatively viewed as unfriendly to suburban and business interests, due to his strong allegiance to the African-American community. His election to five terms as mayor suggests that he maintained popularity among those persons residing in the city until his voluntary retirement from public office in 1993.

The economic benefits of black mayoral leadership to black residents have not met the expectations of some and have not followed the pattern set by the ethnic-dominated political machines in producing economic gains. Even though black mayors have made a greater impact in addressing the needs of the black community, their election has not solved the problems that disproportionately affect low-income and black communities. One explanation is that the conditions facing central cities are beyond the immediate control of elected officials. Businesses that close down operations and move them to other states or countries can have a devastating effect on urban economics. Another factor is that cities compete with each other for investment, making it difficult for one city to eliminate poverty and decline working alone. Higher levels of poverty and unemployment and poorer schools with fewer resources are among the conditions that exist in cities compared to their surrounding suburbs.

Local Government Finance

Intergovernmental revenues from states and the federal government comprise a significant amount of the money that cities use to operate and to perform functions expected by citizens. Other sources of funds include taxes, user fees, license fees, nuisance taxes, and loans. The extent to which localities rely upon these sources varies from state to state and from city to city. From state to state, different taxes and fees are permitted.

The taxes that local governments raise fall into the categories of property taxes, income taxes, and sales taxes. The majority of cities rely heavily upon local property taxes. About half of the states permit cities to levy a local sales tax. In the mid-1980s, only eleven states permitted cities to levy income taxes; only a handful of cities actually chose to levy the tax (Sharp, 1990).

The property tax is considered to be a regressive tax, because lower-income property owners pay a higher percentage of their income than higher-income households. Alternatively, higher-income households see themselves footing an unfair burden of property taxes for the rest of the citizenry. This dichotomy of public sentiment may contribute to the unpopularity of the property tax.

Property taxes are an inadequate source of revenue in cities where property values have eroded or failed to keep up with those of surrounding communities. More expensive properties tend to be located in areas where poor people do not live. Property taxes in cities that have lost population as well as commercial and industrial activities are insufficient to support necessary city services. The situation is further complicated by the fact that public schools usually are financed by property taxes. Wealthier communities are able to spend more per pupil on education than poorer ones. Efforts to reform school funding by equalizing tax expenditures have not received much public support. In 1992, the State of Michigan eliminated the property tax as the source of school funding and replaced it with a sales tax. The discussion about school financing is likely to continue across the country.

Most states allow cities to levy a sales tax in addition to the sales tax that the state levies. The sales tax is also considered regressive because lower-income persons pay a higher proportion of their income toward this tax than higher income persons. The regressive nature of the sales tax has been partially reduced by exempting groceries, prescription medicines, and some other necessities.

Cities are permitted to levy income taxes in a minority of states; however, they can represent a major source of revenue in those areas. The income tax accounts for about half of local tax collections in some communities. Persons who reside in cities that levy income taxes usually pay at a higher rate than those who work there but live elsewhere. Nonetheless, commuters typically are critical of income taxes, especially when it appears that suburban residents are subsidizing central city operations through this tax. Municipal officials, on the other hand, are likely to see income tax payments as an equitable way to cover the cost of amenities that suburban workers and residents enjoy in central cities.

Local governments have become more creative in using their taxing authority to raise needed revenues. Minor taxes and license fees include those imposed on hotel rooms, alcohol and tobacco sales, and entertainment. User fees are paid for the services rendered. They are popular because most citizens see them as a fair way to raise revenue. Surveys have found that citizens prefer user fees to raising other taxes. Accordingly, user fees often are the fastest growing source of local revenue.

Because of the differences in jurisdiction and services provided by municipalities, it is difficult to generalize about local governmental expenditures. Some variations in expenditure have been noted along the lines of resident socioeconomic status, age, and mobility. Overall, cities with larger percentages of lower socioeconomic persons spend more per capita on police protection, fire protection, water systems, housing and urban renewal, recreation, and employee retirement programs than communities with a comparatively higher socioeconomic level. Higher expenditures for health care, hospitals, employee retirement, and parks and recreation are expected with an older population (Ross, et al., 1991). Expenditure patterns and allocations are subject to revenue levels. As the tax base for central cities has declined, adjustments in hiring levels and service provision have been required. Declines in services are never received favorably by the citizenry and may lead to more residents deciding to move to other areas.

Intergovernmental Issues

One of the major issues for central cities has been the relationship between them and their surrounding suburbs. Generally, as the cities have lost population, businesses, tax base, and income, the suburbs have gained in the same categories. The disparity between the per capita incomes of city and suburban residents has increased over time.

The relationship between local units of government and the federal government is commonly labeled as **federalism.** Local units of government hold no legal relationship to the national government. The United States Constitution makes no mention of the cities. States are granted the right to create or not to create all local jurisdictions. The Constitution of the United States establishes the nature of the obligation between states and the national government. Cities are creatures of state governments and bear no constitutional obligation to the federal government. Nonetheless, direct interaction between the national and local units of government has not been precluded.

Cities receive legal powers from states in two different ways. Some establish the general powers of city government in state law in the case of **general law** cities. **Charter** cities have their powers spelled out in a charter approved by the state legislature. The charters vary in content but may describe the form, composition, powers, and limitations of city officials (Phillips & LeGates, 1981). The city charter may spell out the term of office of elected officials, the method of electing city council members, and the jurisdiction of the city over local operations such as parks. The **home rule** charter is a particular class of city charters in which the precise definition of city powers is the province of local citizens. About 75 percent of large cities in the United States operate under home rule provisions (Phillips & LeGates, 1981). The home rule charter allows voters to change from one form of local government to another without first seeking state approval.

During the 1960s, the federal government became heavily involved in urban issues. Programs emanated from Washington, D.C. as part of the Great Society era shepherded by President Lyndon B. Johnson after the assassination of President John F. Kennedy. President Kennedy initiated efforts to rectify certain urban conditions including poverty and housing discrimination. Federal spending for various programs signaled the heightened attention given to cities. Grants-in-aid increased dramatically during the Great Society era. The number of grants-in-aid increased from 132 in 1960 to 400 in 1969. The actual dollar amount of federal grants steadily rose and reached an estimated $123 billion in 1990. Federal grants-in-aid represented twelve percent of state and local revenue in 1960 and had increased to twenty-three percent by 1969. Federal aid, as a percentage of state and local expenditures, peaked at over twenty-six percent in 1978. As a percentage of state and local expenditures, federal aid fell to about eighteen percent—nearly the level it had been twenty years earlier (Press & VerBurg, 1991). Cities had to adjust to this reality in the operation of programs such as neighborhood development, and in the provision of services. Police personnel were sometimes cut, for example, in response to federal cutbacks.

The data suggest that some states more than made up for declining federal revenues while other states did not. On average, federal grants dropped by eighteen percent from 1981 to 1988, while state grants increased by sixty-eight percent, for a net increase of fifty percent. The effects of inflation, however, reduced the impact of these increases on local governments, which saw an average increase of over five percent in outside sources of revenue (Harrigan, 1993).

Cities are able to use the funds appropriated by state and local governments in different ways. In all cases, urban politics is a factor. Funds to cities from the federal government are accompanied by varying "degrees of freedom." That is, the officials responsible for program operations at the local level have some discretion over how the funds will be spent. The types of funding can be placed in three categories: **categorical** or program grants, **block** grants, and **revenue sharing.** Generally, cities are in favor of receiving the largest grants possible with the fewest strings or **mandates** possible. State and local officials often protest the imposition of mandates that accompany the receipt of federal funds. Examples of these mandates are the provision of equal employment opportunity and accessibility to handicapped persons. The objections are related to the additional cost of complying with mandatory requirements. Some objections are more substantive. For example, the requirement that low- and moderate-income housing needs must be addressed when a community accepts Community Development Block Grant funds affected the appeal of these dollars in many cities.

Beyond the issue of government finance, the ability of cities to govern themselves efficiently is impeded by the fragmentation that exists in most metropolitan areas. There are more than 85,000 local governments in the United States. The types of local governments include counties, municipalities, townships, special districts, and independent school districts. The operation, management, and well-being of a given city can be affected by all of these units of local government. As the persons elected to manage the city, mayors and city councils often are limited in their ability to control the other elements of local governance beyond their charter provisions. There is variation among cities. For example, some city governments have direct control over their public school systems, transportation systems, and public housing authorities. In other cases, these services may be provided by a regional entity or by a special district, as discussed in Chapters 7 and 10.

The following generalizations have been drawn about patterns of local public service provision and, hence, governance using data gathered by the U.S. Bureau of the Census:

1. Public education is normally provided by independent school districts, with boundaries which are usually coterminous with central city boundaries.
2. Noneducational human and social services are provided principally by county governments, though central cities play a major role in some areas.
3. Physical maintenance services are provided primarily by central city governments, but special districts have been established to provide sewerage and water supply services.
4. Traditional government services such as police and fire protection, street maintenance, and recreation are handled almost exclusively by city governments.
5. Redevelopment activities are divided chiefly between central city governments and special districts, with counties playing a very small role. (Harrigan, 1993).

Special districts are the fastest growing type of government in metropolitan areas. The number grew from 9,000 in 1940 to over 35,000 in 2002. One possible reason for the rise and apparent popularity of special districts is their ability to raise revenue for services at the same time that they maintain a low political profile and visibility (Harrigan, 1993). Many voters are confused about special districts and the distribution of the property taxes they pay. Funds for special districts generally are collected by the county. Their obscure status removes special districts from the criticism they might otherwise encounter over expenditures and service provision. Special districts often perform one function such as water or sewerage.

Metropolitan districts provide a specific public service across jurisdictional lines in a county or multi-county area. The concept behind these districts is that some services can be performed more efficiently on a regional basis. Examples of such services are water and sewerage services, parks, and transportation. One reasons that these special districts are proliferating is the resistance of city and suburban residents to general metropolitan government.

The logic and rationale for metropolitan government has far exceeded support of the scheme by voters. Harrigan discusses four types of metropolitan reorganization which have occurred with varying degrees of success when measured in terms of the goals of reformers. The four types are:

1. Central city expansion through annexation or the use of extra-territorial powers;
2. City-county consolidation;

3. Strengthening the urban county;
4. Creation of a two-tier government: one responsible for areawide functions and the second responsible for local functions (Harrigan, 1993 p. 351).

The impact of metropolitanwide government on the provision of services when compared to other areas is not well researched. Some urban scholars are cautious, therefore, in attributing improvements or difficulties in metropolitanwide areas to the governmental form. Nonetheless, it is clear that metropolitan government is no panacea for addressing problems of equal access to housing and educational opportunities. (For a thorough discussion of the types and implications, see Harrigan, 1993, pp. 348–360.) Citizen participation in governmental affairs does not increase under the metropolitan structure.

A common element of concern for city and suburban residents faced with metropolitan government decisions is whether their interests will be subverted. Central city residents have concerns about losing political power in a metropolitan structure. This is particularly true for African-Americans who have gained political clout through victories at the ballot box as they became a larger part of the city's population. The counterpoint for suburbanites is their fear of assuming the responsibility for problems associated with central cities and the cost of providing services to less financially sound communities.

The movement toward metropolitan or regional government is very slow. Places that have some form of regional government include: Jacksonville-Duval County, Florida; Miami-Dade County, Florida; Lexington-Fayette County, Kentucky; Nashville-Davidson County, Tennessee, and Indianapolis-Marion County, Indiana. Research has suggested that central cities and their surrounding suburbs would benefit from shared government but citizens and elected officials are not easily convinced (see David Rusk, 1993).

The nature of politics in the urban area is a dynamic process. Relationships between citizens within cities and those between cities in the same metropolitan area can be very contentious. It appears that the disparities between central city residents and those in surrounding communities will persist and deepen in the foreseeable future. An effective way of resolving the underlying causes of these disparities will require collaborative efforts between these communities. Some balance must be sought between the autonomy that localities have come to cherish and the reality of sustaining entire regions. The challenge faced by urban public officials to address the needs of populations that are economically, politically, racially, and ethnically diverse is not new. The history of many communities suggests that much can be learned from the past; however, new concepts are needed to face contemporary urban issues.

Name _____

CHAPTER 7
The City Governs (Political Science)

7-1. Choose an issue that concerns you. Write a sample letter to the appropriate public official about your concern:

Dear

Sincerely,

7-2. List the major cities in the United States that have African American mayors:

City	Mayor

7-3. List the major cities in the United States that have women mayors.

City	Mayor

7-4. Visit your city hall and sketch the layout of the council chambers and mayor's quarters. Describe the access to these spaces for the general public (e.g., number of seats in the council room, lobby, waiting rooms).

The City Manages

(Public/City Management)

Gerald M. Neumark

American cities cannot exist without an administrative/bureaucratic structure. **Public managers** provide the very essence of local government management. In addition, what makes a city manager's position even more significant is that the local level of government in the American federal system is the one level of government which is closest to all of us: "The activities of local government are the most important in determining the quality of a person's life" (Newman, 2010, p. 1). Local governments are the most dynamic, innovative, and organizationally diverse level of all American governments. They are also the most likely point of contact between all governments and their citizens (Cox, 2004).

Early in the history of urban America, almost anyone could have been a municipal manager. Often, the only qualification was whom you knew, especially during the era of political machines. Over the years, however, things have changed a great deal, and this is no longer the case. For the most part, urban managers are well-trained, professional public servants who are well qualified to make the important decisions incumbent on their positions. Today's city manager must undergo a rigorous course of study to understand the complexities and to fulfill the management needs of our modern urban areas.

The term "public manager" signifies an entire array of individuals from the "city and county manager" to department heads. Urban managers at all levels often have the same duties and responsibilities in their service to local governments (England, 2003). Although this chapter will focus on the specific role of the city manager, it is appropriate to generalize the roles, responsibilities, and concerns of city managers to all urban public administrative professionals. This chapter will take an in-depth look at public managers as mostly found in city manager–council forms of government. It will also investigate these managers' leadership, the politics surrounding their work, and how they are essential to the future of American cities. Once again, the reader can very well generalize from what is being written about city managers to all local forms of urban managers.

The Role of City Managers

As a group, local public managers are a rather small cadre of professionally trained administrators who serve as the chief executive officer of their departments or of the municipalities in which they serve (England, 2003). Depending on the actual position ranging from city manager to public works commissioner to the manager of a local municipal water distribution plant, the job of the public manager is very much multifaceted. Pelissero (2003) offers one generic conception of the role of public management: "Management is the dimension of city governance in which the manager establishes the resources needed to run the day-to-day affairs of city government. It includes management of human resources and budgets and acquisition of information, technology, and materials required to run the municipal corporation in a professional manner" (p. 20). More specifically, Phillips (2010) writes: "A city manager is responsible for preparing the city budget, developing policy recommendations for the council's action, and overseeing city government" (p. 437). The manager also has the power to hire and/or fire department heads.

Clearly, city managers have a great deal of responsibility, yet, at the same time they have their own set of bosses. On one hand, urban managers must deal with higher-level elected or politically appointed executives. They must also answer to the public, legislative bodies, and the courts. In spite of these constraints, successful public managers have the resources that enable them to cope with their environment (Kramer, 1981). Those with the greatest amount of expertise are the most able to fulfill all of the roles expected of the city manager. Thus, Phillips (2010) says: "The combination of professional expertise and access to and control over information gives city managers informal power beyond what is revealed in organizational charts" (p. 437).

In many ways, the role of a municipal public manager can be compared to that of a corporate manager. In fact, local governments are sometimes compared to business organizations. In Ohio and Virginia, for example, this is explicitly recognized. **Municipalities** in these states are called corporations. Indeed, one of the major goals of the public manager is to see that his or her government is run as a business: efficiently and effectively, which of course is made more difficult without a "bottom line." This, however, is what the people in a municipality expect from their executives, and a skillful local manager can be very adept at running his or her municipality as a business. To this end, it is no coincidence that the Master of Public Administration (MPA) and the Master of Business Administration (MBA) curricula are quite similar in many universities.

Of all of the possible tasks related to public management, **policy development** is certainly the most recognized. "The urban bureaucracy has a preeminent role in the consequences of policies" (Pelissero, 2003, p. 23). If policy is what a government chooses to do or not to do (Dye, 2008), it is the public manager who determines the general policies which set the direction of the municipality. It is widely understood that city councilors or county commissioners must rely on the professional advice of the full-time manager when considering policy options (Pelissero, 2003). Urban managers on all levels are the municipal, key policy-makers specifically because they possess the knowledge to address local and departmental issues. The policy role of the urban public manager is so pronounced that England (2003) refers to it as "a policy-making institution" (p. 209).

Perhaps of equal importance to the policy-making role of the local public manager is **budget development**. In a weak mayor/manager form of government, this role is almost always given to the city manager. However, even in a strong mayor municipality, department managers prepare their own budget. Although a budget is often thought of as a tool to determine public spending, it is a great deal more. For example, Robbins (1980) views a budget as an instrument for improving time, space, and resource utilization. In addition, he sees it as a method of political control. Thus, to the extent that a manager is able to have the authority to construct a budget, that manager is able to exercise political power. To the extent that managers have the confidence of the elected officials, they are more able to be allowed to do so.

The budget is also the single, most important statement of local policy. Budget calculations are never neutral: "The ways in which [budget] calculations are made affect the outcomes of the political system: who gets what and how much (Wildavsky, 1964, p. 8). Therefore, it is the most significant tool used by managers to determine the priorities of the municipality. City department managers use a variety of strategies to achieve the greatest appropriation in order to carry out their policies. They are, after all, the policy experts, and, in most cases, elected officials defer to the expertise of a skilled manager.

Ironically, it is during the budgetary process that the municipal manager on one hand, and department heads on the other can become quite oppositional. As part of their job, department managers are expected to do everything they can do to be advocates of increased appropriations to their various departments. At the same time, in an effort to trim the municipal budget, the city manager is expected to take a more global approach and allow only the most necessary appropriations, often in disagreement to what the department heads consider important. Thus, another element of good, local public management is a requirement for a great deal of negotiations among all of the professional managers.

The role of the local public manager as related to the budgetary process presents a paradox. On one hand, a government's budget is the primary statement of its priorities and policies. It is the most important tool in setting the future course of a government unit. To the extent that it is the role of the public administrator in his or her management function to develop the budget, it gives the public manager a great deal of responsibility as well as authority and independence: a part of the role to which a professional manager must give a great deal of considered thought.

Where the paradox becomes apparent is in the position of local governments within the American federal system. When considering the role of the city manager in the budgeting process, it is important to recognize the constraints put upon the contemporary American municipality. Local governments do not operate in a vacuum. They are positioned at the bottom level of the federal system: "Every policy and ordinance established and implemented by local government must be considered within the context of the rights of other municipalities as well as their own position within the state [and national government]" (Neumark, 2010, p. 14). Because of their position and the nature of American federalism, many of the expenditures in a local budget are beyond the control of department managers or the mayor/city manager. This not only includes negotiated salaries and the implementation of specific federal grants, but also of state and federal mandates. Many such mandates are unfunded by the higher levels of governments, and yet implementing such mandates are very costly to a municipality. Indeed, only four percent of local budgets come from the national government (Neumark, 2010). This obviously puts local managers in a difficult position: there are so many demands from their citizens for municipal services, but ability to fund these services is often beyond the local budget. It takes a very astute manager to remain on top of the budget-balancing act and to realize what is

2003	2010
Caucasian: 95%	84%
African American: 2%	2%
Hispanic: 2%	13%
Asian American/Native American: 1%	1%
Males: 88%	87%
(ICMA, 2003)	(ICMA, 2010)

Figure 8.1
A Demographic Comparison of City Managers Between the Years 2003 and 2010.

and what is not possible. In light of all of this, the public manager must present a budget which reflects the wishes of the citizens as well as the elected officials of the municipality.

The role of the professional local manager also includes working with diversity both within municipal departments as well as with the increasingly diverse urban population in this nation. Except in one demographic category, however, there has not been a great increase in diversity among city managers. In 2003, the vast majority of urban public mangers were white males. This still held true in 2010. The only change was a one percent increase in female city managers, and an eleven percent increase in Hispanic city managers. (See Figure 8.1 for a demographic comparison between 2003 and 2010.)

Why is diversity among city management professionals important? What is the connection between one's ethnicity, gender, or background and the role of a city manager? One's background might very well have a bearing on how a city manager interprets his or her role in judging the outputs of the position, ranging from work habits of his or her subordinates to his or her policy positions. If these numbers are accurate, a question arises concerning the ability of the city manager to govern an entire diverse population. Can a manager understand the needs of the people of those parts of the city who may have entirely different outlooks, and often with competing policy wants and desires? Of course, the true professional understands the importance of listening to all points of view; however, the more individuals of all backgrounds enter the field, the more administrators are able to rely upon their fellow managers to share how others may feel in developing sustainable public policy. Having an 11 percent increase in Hispanic city managers is a good start; however, the challenge ahead is for American cities to attract more female and minority professionals.

Before this section on the role of city managers is complete, it would be helpful to summarize the most important duties of city management. Although there are many essential roles, the following serves as a summary of the four, overall, most important duties of city managers:

- Formulate policy for the city and/or its departments
- Prepare and present, as well as administer the city or departments' budgets to the city council
- Appoint or remove department or assistant department managers

- Form extensive external relationships to help resolve local and/or departmental issues and problems (Morgan and England, 1999)

As the student reads through these duties, it is important to keep in mind how personal responsibility and politics affect each one of them.

The Public Manager as a Leader

Knowing the role of the city manager is essential in understanding how the city manages itself. As a complement to one's role is another component of successful management: leadership. Regardless of what the job description of the local public manager is, that individual must be a leader in the governing of the municipality. Indeed, public management is really all about leadership. Although there are many ways that one can define and conceptualize leadership, there is a universality regarding what one can expect from such a position: the public manager must be the focus individual of a group process. He or she must have what Northouse (2007) calls a **"leadership personality."** This leadership personality includes individual traits and characteristics, and cannot necessarily be learned. He or she must display the type of behavior that will encourage others in the municipal structure to bring about desired actions and outcomes. The public manager must not be afraid to use power and influence. That is, he or she must create a power relationship between the individual's role as a public administrator and his or her followers.

One may think it rather obvious that all city managers are leaders. That is, if you *are* a leader, you must *be* a leader. With respect to local public managers, this is not the case. Not every manager is an effective leader. What are the knowledge and abilities connected with leadership which separate the true leaders among managers from all others? Three factors of leadership point to successful public managers: awareness, understanding, and vision. More specifically, Cox (2004) outlines four important competencies that highly successful, local public administrators must demonstrate:

- Recognizing obligations to others, whether teammates, subordinates, or citizens
- Visioning and creativity
- Preventing problems
- Demonstrating leadership

Svara (2004) adds three more essential abilities:

- Local public managers must help shape the agenda of the city or county and propose policies for adoption by elected officials.
- As both individuals and representatives of their government, they must have positive interaction with people outside of government.
- They must shape the orientation of their government organization to citizens and how it facilitates citizens' participation in government affairs.

As potential local managers, it is most important that students understand how significant these abilities are. Notice that the common thread running through all of these leadership attributes is the ability to perceive, to be in charge, to guide, and to set an example for individuals both inside and outside of government.

Another way to view leadership among city managers is what Kingdon (1995) calls a **"policy entrepreneur."** These are individuals who advocate and are willing to invest their resources to promote a position: in other words, lead in the development of desired policy. He or she must have the leadership capabilities to be persistent, to recognize opportunities (open windows) when they come about, and to attach solutions to opportunities. Kingdon's view of persistence and capability as indigenous to leadership is similar to Northouse's conception of "leadership personality."

An additional important attribute that city managers must have is good, personal work habits. Managers cannot expect subordinates to serve a community to their greatest potential if the manager does not display the highest level of work habits: "Managerial work habits involve customary behaviors, such as typically showing concern for others, setting high standards or demonstrating initiative" (West & Berman, 2011, pp. 64–65). In addition, good work habits as they specifically relate to local public management include being pro-active in the face of foreseeable problems, getting along with others, being committed to a strong sense of ethics in dealing with the public as well as subordinates, and having good communication skills (West & Berman, 2011). Good work habits as displayed from those in charge serve to further the public organization's performance by helping to create a positive working environment.

Finally, no matter how one ultimately defines leadership, one attribute of a good public administrator clearly stands out: he or she must deal with people. The test of a real leader among public managers concerns how he or she is able to address political issues; regardless of which issues may arise, the leader has the ability to solve the problem, as much as possible, to everyone's satisfaction. Of course, leadership ability aside, all dealings with people are necessarily infused with politics.

Politics and the City Manager

Role and leadership ability cannot be separated from the political factors involved with city management. All city managers must understand that politics are inexorably connected to their position.

Political activity of city management begins with the conception that being a city manager is not the same as being a manager on the state or federal level. The nature of local government is very different from all other levels. Not only is city government the closest to Americans, it has the most direct effect on Americans, and is also the most accessible level of government to the people. The city level determines who gets what, where, when, why, and how (Laswell, 2008). In other words, it is the local government that determines the politics with which most Americans come into contact. To the extent that the city manager is the head of either a department or the entire municipality, it is that person who both makes and is intricately involved with these political determinations. In addition to making political decisions, the city manager often has decisions made for him or her by his or her "bosses" (the city residents, the elected officials, and in some cases, the court systems).

A majority of students of public management are familiar with the concept of **"dichotomy"**: the separation of public management and politics. Whether or not such a dichotomy in reality exists, the view of most public managers is that the concept is nothing more than a myth. City managers must deal continually with politics: "Despite the intent of the [dichotomy] model, politics remain a part of the council-manager form of government. City managers may seek to be nonpolitical . . . they are definitely political" (Harrington, 2006, p. 180). Lorch (2001) emphasizes this point when he writes that even in the decision to create a city department, politics are involved from the very beginning: "The birth of every department, division, bureau, agency and office is a political act" (p. 374).

Public managers recognized from the beginning of the discipline (when public management was still a subarea within political science) that public administrators had to concern themselves with outside forces: "As early as the 1940s, John Gause called upon political scientists to note ecological (political) factors in studying public administration. Among these factors were people, place, physical technology, social technology and ideas, catastrophe and personality" (Kramer, 1981, p. 8).

City managers must work within a **political environment**. "Local government administrators who help develop and implement policy must understand the political context in which they work. Because the best solution, idea, [or] project . . . will go nowhere without political support from the majority of elected officials, it is no longer possible to imagine separating [public] administration from politics" (Vanacour, 2004, pp. 85–86). Vanacour refers to the understanding of the political context as "political savvy." Political savvy is essential in order for city managers to not only fully appreciate why and how particular activities are undertaken through the government, but is also a necessary tool if the manager is to be able successfully to carry out his or her job.

The city manager faces a multitude of political issues coming from every aspect of his or her position; however, Dye and Sparrow (2009) believe that the most predominant pressure originates from organized interests. From the very beginning of an administrator's tenure, he or she must be concerned with **public interest groups**: "Interest groups understand that great power is lodged in the bureaucracy" (p. 451). To the extent that it is in the best interest of such organizations to establish a close relationship with the public administrator, they are very eager to do so. There are two obvious pitfalls to the establishment of such a relationship: (1) There is the very real possibility of bias in administrative actions favoring that particular organization: and (2) There can be an inability to separate such a relationship when such separation becomes necessary. Thus, instead of looking objectively at policy proposals put forth by outside groups, the city manager becomes entangled in various policy clusters. (On the federal level, this is often referred to as an "iron triangle.")

Even those city managers with a great deal of political savvy who are able to remain outside of the policy cluster must deal with powerful interest groups that have a particular stake in promoting all sorts of economic plans for a municipality. Such interest groups form alliances, often with each other, including city managers. These groups may be the most powerful of all special interest organizations. Logan and Molotch (2008) call such an alliance along with politicians and sometimes city managers the "**growth machine**." With the growth machine comes further conflict and political issues, particularly when local neighborhoods become involved in the process. "Inevitably, there are conflicts . . . that erupt among these many [growth machine] interest groups. As they all compete to support their own interests, neighborhoods often battle back if they feel that the developments being planned will change the character of their communities" (Bluestone et al., 2008, p. 14). City managers must be cognizant of the politics of the growth machine.

This is a major part of the political environment in which city managers must make their decisions. Interest groups, including neighborhoods, clearly understand the political component of the urban manager's position. A combination of professional expertise and access to and control of information gives urban managers power beyond what is revealed in any municipal organization chart (Phillips, 2010). When an organization has the public manager under its control, it might have power over the entire city. A high degree of political savvy can go a long way to prevent this from happening.

Dealing with interest groups is not the only political factor in everyday city management. In addition to interest groups and neighborhood considerations, a public manager must be able to access other levels and branches of government in order to carry out his or her policy role. The ability to do this is once again a matter of an individual's political savvy. The city manager must try to influence legislators and other elected officials. "Given the interaction of city managers with politicians with partisan connections, survival in their position might depend upon alignment with the dominant local electoral coalition" (Chandler, 2006, p. 180).

As one can see, the public manager is engaged with political desires from all directions, while at the same time he or she must be able to influence others. It is a difficult position in which to be; however, Bluestone et al. (2008) sum up this apparent paradox very well: "Politics and Power count" (p. 14).

For a public manager to be unaware of politics could spell disaster, not only for his or her department, but also for the entire city. Such awareness does not imply that a manager should necessarily take a political position, although it might be important to do this from time to time. Understanding and awareness are not the same as active participation. A manager knows when and when not to remain neutral on important political issues. At the same time, a successful city manager must be open to the views of all individual citizens and groups who may be affected by an agency's action or inaction.

Why is it that sometimes public managers are unable to see the politics surrounding what they are asked to do on a daily basis? Neumark (2011) believes this to be the result of "**cultural clash**." This model suggests that it is the differing educational training and background of public managers compared to that of traditional political scientists, who are much more oriented to the politics of policy decisions, which prevents each of the disciplines from being able to see how the other might address such decisions as they arise. The alternate orientations of the disciplines, which Neumark terms "culture clash," result in different ways of looking at how a city and issues within a municipality should be managed. Often, these differences in outlook limit the local policy decision-making process. Neumark (2011) posits a specific example to illustrate this point: this very culture clash almost stopped the largest public redevelopment project currently in the United States dead in its tracks. The clash involved a small piece of land, less than an acre, in the city of Atlanta, Georgia. The clash was so strong that it completely stopped the development of one portion of the multi-billion dollar project for two entire years. It was not until a compromise was proposed by an elected city council member, who understood the nature of the culture clash, that the project was able to be placed back on track (see Note 1). The public manager with political savvy understands and is able to work within the confines of culture clash.

A final point regarding the politics of city management concerns the increasing trend towards the **privatization** of services. Is it in the best interest of one local government to contract out a service to another local government, or even a private organization? In the end, it is the city manager who must make the decision as to whether or not to outsource a service that, heretofore, has always been delivered by the municipal government. Many in the community welcome what they consider to be a more efficient, cost-effective service-delivery model. Others oppose it as giving away what rightfully belongs to the taxpayer. The key to dealing with the politics of privatization must be flexibility. It is the ability to balance these two opposing views which can allow for privatization when appropriate and public delivery of services when it is not. As with many of the issues discussed above, this requires a great deal of skill from the city manager.

Towards the Future of Public Managers

There will always be a need for professionally trained urban public managers. Governments simply cannot function without them. They are also the leaders of the future: "Local government managers are ideally positioned to affect the future [of municipalities] . . . They help shape public events by helping policy makers decide what to do and how to do it…Making the right decisions today leads to the right things tomorrow" (Vanacour, 2004, pp. 83–84).

City managers have the awesome responsibility of determining the future. They are a part of the fastest-growing form of municipal governance in the United States today (Chandler, 2006). The growth of public managers in numbers as well as authority and political power can be traced to the advances in technology and increases in the size and complexity of society (Dye & Sparrow, 2009). There is no doubt that these two factors will continue. Only professionally trained public servants are able to supply the needed expertise for this complex society, having the ability to make important decisions even in the mundane and routine side of their work (Dye & Sparrow, 2009).

In addition to this awesome responsibility, city managers can be considered as political elites (England, 2003). They are essential in our American society. They have a "direct role in the democratic process" (Anderson & Arnold, 1983, p. 6). Indeed, it is because of the importance of their position that public managers are held to a much higher ethical and performance standard than are their counterparts in private management, and the unintended consequences of behavior are subject to more scrutiny (Felbinger, 2010).

Politics do indeed play a major role in city management, as they will in the future, but they are nothing more than part of the challenge presented by any such important occupation. The modern complex American city simply cannot manage itself without public managers.

NOTE 1: An excellent example of how culture clash between those with a political background, including political scientists as well as many neighborhood activists, involved an extremely acrimonious disagreement concerning a small, but important, piece of land in northeast Atlanta, Georgia. The surrounding neighborhoods were very much against the Atlanta BeltLine, Inc.'s (ABI) proposed high density use of the property. (ABI was the public agency in charge of implementing the entire BeltLine project). Although the property was zoned R-4, single family housing, ABI planned to sell this unneeded piece of property for the greatest amount of return because they proposed to have the land rezoned to a higher density use. While the neighborhoods saw this proposal as a politically motivated intrusion on their single-family neighborhood, and thus their entire way of life, ABI saw themselves as the stewards of public funds. Whereas the neighborhoods were concerned with their immediate surroundings, the ABI professional managers took a much more global look: how was the development of this property good for the project and the city as a whole?

This single piece of property, less than an acre, was all that stood in the way of completing the Atlanta City Council's approval for the largest urban redevelopment project in the history of the United States. Two years before, the surrounding neighborhoods, whose vote was a legislated requirement for the completion of the project, rejected the plan 200 to 0. At that point, because of the vote, further development of that segment of the BeltLine was dead. With the issue still raging as this book went to press in 2012, and the two groups still unable to go beyond the limitations presented by their differing outlooks, Councilmember Alex Wan, who has a background in both public management and politics, was able to step in and present each other's point of view to the differing parties. He was also able work out a compromise. Each side got some of what they wanted. ABI agreed to allow the property to remain R-4. The BeltLine got an understanding from the neighborhood allowing the organization to revisit the issue at some unspecified time in the future. ABI also received an affirmative vote allowing the project to continue.

The impasse might be only temporarily solved, and the issue may very well arise again. There is still a great deal of hard feelings among many neighborhood leaders. Councilmember Wan was able to diffuse the situation by breaking down the culture clash for the moment; however, whether or not the neighborhood residents understand the professional outlook of managers, and whether or not the professional managers of ABI understand Atlanta neighborhood politics, still remain to be seen.

This example does not suggest that city managers must always give ground to neighborhood organizations. They simply must understand the nature of the culture clash they might be facing and be willing to look at other points of view. Thus, Wheeland (2004) suggests that local public managers do not have to shy away from neighborhood organizations. Indeed, they can encourage citizens to form such associations and to serve as advisors to the governing body of local government organizations. If ABI could continue to work with the neighborhood on this basis, a future impasse can be avoided.

Name:_____

CHAPTER 8
The City Manages (Public/City Management)

Municipal Government

City, Village, or Township residence: _____

Form of government: _____

8-1 Executive Branch:

8-1a. Name your mayor, city manager, town administrator, or township trustee.

8-1b. When was this person first elected or appointed to office?

_____

8-1c. What is the address of City Hall?

8-1d. What is the Web address?

8-1e. List the departments within City Hall (e.g., Police, Fire, Planning).

8-1f. List the number of city employees—full and part time, if available.

8-1g. What is the total budget including General Funds and Restricted Funds?

8-2 Legislative Branch:

8-2a. How many council members represent the community?

_____

8-2b. Who is the council president or the head of the township trustees?

8-2c. How often does the council meet? When? _____

8-2d. Is citizen participation allowed at meetings of the legislative body and, if so, what is the format?

8-2e. Who is your city council representative?

8-2f. Does your local government facilitate neighborhood involvement?

Yes? _____ No? _____

8-2g. If applicable, who is your county manager or executive?

8-2h. If applicable, who is your county representative?

8-2i. Name the following members of your government:
State Representative

State Senator

Lieutenant Governor

Governor

U. S. Senators

The City Maintains Itself
(Public Works)

Claire L. Felbinger

Building cities is exciting, fun, and personally edifying. Those who design and construct them have permanent monuments of their contribution to the built environment. Others take credit for proposing and financing these accomplishments at ground breakings and again at ribbon cutting ceremonies. Still others have their legacy honored by having their names associated with buildings or landmarks—either by virtue of their dedicated public service or by purchasing the "naming rights" to a facility.

However, there is no ground breaking ceremony when a city worker patches a pothole, and there are no ribbons cut when water mains are lined to prevent leaking and infiltration. The day-to-day work of thousands of city workers involves operating and maintaining these structures over time. *The city maintains itself* primarily through actions associated with the Public Works profession. This chapter will define Public Works and its functions, operationalize city maintenance functions, and discuss the general nature of urban service delivery.

What Are Public Works?

More than two hundred years ago, Adam Smith wrote that the functions of government should be limited to providing for the national defense, affording the protection of law, and *undertaking indispensable public works*. The International City/County Management Association has offered a definition adapted from the founder of the American Public Works Association, Donald C. Stone:

> *Public works are the physical structures and facilities that are developed or acquired by public agencies to house governmental functions and provide water, power, waste disposal, transportation, and similar services, and are managed by experienced, intelligent, dedicated professionals to facilitate and ensure continuously better service to the public. (Stone 1974: 2–3).*

These "indispensable" public works are the systems and facilities which ensure the health, safety, and convenience of citizens. Oftentimes, they are referred to as urban **infrastructure** systems although the term is a little limiting. Although public works professionals are involved in the building of the public city, the majority of their work is spent in operating,

TABLE 9.1
Public Works Functions

Streets and highways	Engineering
Street cleaning	Solid-waste collections
Snow removal	Solid-waste disposal
Street lighting	Solid-waste billing
Street striping (marking)	Building inspection
Street signs	Building maintenance
Surveying	Custodial services
Traffic engineering	Construction inspection
Traffic signals	Park maintenance
Traffic signs	Cemetery operation
Water treatment	Radio system
Water distribution	Parking meter system
Water meter reading	Equipment maintenance
Water utility billing	Animal control
Water service	Computer operation
Sewage treatment	Electric power distribution
Sewage collection system	Electric power billing
Sewer utility billing	Gas power distribution
Storm sewer system	Gas billing
Storm water management	Street tree planting and maintenance
Zoning/subdivision control	Airport services

Source: Felbinger, C. L. (1994). Public Works. In J. M. Banovetz, D. A. Dolan, & J. W. Swain (Eds.), *Managing Small Cities and Towns: A Practical Guide,* p. 105

maintaining, and improving the quality of these systems. The American Public Works Association (APWA) has identified 145 different functions that are related to public works (APWA, 1990) and classifies them as municipal engineering, equipment services, transportation, water resources, solid wastes, building and grounds, administrative management, and special services. Some examples of these functions are in Table 9.1. An easy way to think about public works functions is that everything a city does outside of city hall which is not police and fire related is probably a public works function.

The people who perform public works functions are as varied as the number of those functions. Civil engineers are involved in the design, construction, and maintenance decisions of urban public works services. Laborers and skilled crafters perform functions from picking up residential solid wastes to installing telecommunication equipment. Chemists and other technicians test the quality of a city's drinking water and the treated sewage which is reintroduced into rivers and lakes. Public administrators develop plans to finance and manage these vital services. Planners oversee the ordered linking of physical systems. These are only examples of the variety of people involved in the daily delivery of public works services. For an idea on how public works agencies are organized see Exhibit 9.1.

Organization of Public Works

There is no standard or recommended organizational structure for fulfilling local government public works functions. There is not even agreement about what should be included under the label public works. Some communities, for example, place functions such as code enforcement, traffic engineering, and parkway maintenance under public works; others place such functions elsewhere (e.g., code enforcement in a building department, traffic engineering in the police department; and parkway maintenance in the parks department). Some communities place all vehicle maintenance in the public works department. Others give each operating department the responsibility for maintaining its own vehicles, or they contract out this service.

Some communities place all public works functions in a single department; others place responsibility for streets and sidewalks in a public works department but have a separate water department; sanitation department (to remove and dispose of solid waste, wastewater, or both); building and grounds department; forestry department (for street trees); and engineering department. There is no evidence to suggest that one or another organizational pattern is better; size of community, range of public works function, complexity of operations, and idiosyncratic local considerations all combine to shape the organization's structures.

The appointment of a person with a background in civil engineering as director of public works has been common practice for many years. More recently this practice has begun to give way to the employment of public works directors who have training and experience in public administration. Some communities now require their public works director to have a master of public administration (MPA) degree and work experience in a public works department. The need to use the services of consultants with highly specialized engineering knowledge and the increasing complexity of government management suggest that administrative training and experience will be increasingly demanded of public works directors in the future.

Exhibit 9.1
Source: Felbinger, C. L. (1994). Public Works. In J. M. Banovetz, D. A. Dolan, & J. W. Swain (Eds.) *Managing Small Cities and Towns: A Practical Guide,* p. 104

Issues of Infrastructure and Maintenance

Unfortunately, most people do not pay attention to public works services until they stop working. The services are taken for granted. When they turn on the tap expecting water to come out, they probably never stop to think about its purity, they merely assume it. When they flush the toilet, all of their responsibility for that waste goes away. Those who have encountered breaks in critical public works services understand how inconvenient that is. However, public works routinely work and they continue to work through systematic routine maintenance.

Deferred maintenance of public works systems was considered the prime suspect for, what was termed in the 1980s, our "crumbling urban infrastructure." Pat Choate and Susan Walter (1983) raised public consciousness of this in their book, *America in Ruins.*

As a result, in 1984 Congress established the National Council on Public Works Improvement whose mission was to prepare a report on the state of the Nation's infrastructure. Over five thousand pages of research material were prepared over a two-year period contributing to the Council's 1988 final report: *Fragile Foundations*. The graphic presentation in the report which caught the eyes of Congress and the Nation was a Report Card scoring eight public works services with grades which varied from a "B" (for water resources) to a "D" (for hazardous waste). The Council proclaimed the Nation's overall infrastructure grade to be a "C"—barely passing. Once again, the main contributor to this condition is deferred maintenance. Periodic updates to the initial Report Card document only minor improvements at the aggregate or national level.

If North Americans are so good at building the public city, why have we been so bad at maintaining it? Four contributors are: the influence of federal infrastructure policy, the hidden nature of infrastructure, the balance of financial tradeoffs at the local level, and the lack of political payoff for maintenance activities.

Federally Influenced Deferred Maintenance

Until recently, the federal government funded only the construction of new infrastructure systems or the replacement of those which had exhausted their usable life. Routine maintenance was considered both a fiscal and operational responsibility of local governments. One unintended consequence of this is that some public works managers allowed infrastructure systems to deteriorate to such a condition that they would be eligible for federal government replacement grants rather than extending the life of the systems through locally funded annual maintenance. Although this saved the citizens of those communities short-term maintenance expenditures, the ultimate impact is that all citizens bear the burden of higher cost replacement of structures with shorter usable lives. The cumulative impact of such decisions is that taxpayers are paying a higher cost to maintain the integrity of infrastructure systems. An example of this is illustrated in Exhibit 9.2.

Deferral of Maintenance of "Hidden" Systems

The second reason for deferred maintenance is that many infrastructure systems are simply hidden from view. Many are underground, such as water and wastewater systems,

---

Impact of a Federal Policy

An example of federally influenced deferred maintenance is provided by federal policy regarding the use of the federal Airport and Airway Trust Fund. The federal government will not finance maintenance through the fund, but it will replace runways that are beyond repair. Rather than spending local money to extend the life of runways, local officials are prompted to close them down (an inconvenience to citizens) and construct new runways on the same site, using federal dollars.

Exhibit 9.2
Source: Felbinger, C. L. (1994). Public Works. In J. M. Banovetz, D. A. Dolan, & J. W. Swain (Eds.), *Managing Small Cities and Towns: A Practical Guide,* p. 107

while some are even underwater, like bridge foundations. The prevailing attitude had been that if one is receiving the service (e.g., drinking water, sewage flow, access across a river), then the infrastructure must be adequate. Clearly, this is not always the case.

For example, New York City once had a policy of "maintaining" water mains by replacing ones which either collapsed by structural failure or exploded under the pressure of the gravity fed system. As long as the pipes were hidden and people were getting water, the system was considered in good condition. However, these old mains were insulated with asbestos packing. When they exploded, asbestos dust was spewn into the air, causing even more health risks for citizens and potentially debilitating liability for the city.

It has been only recently that new technologies such as remote control video machines, leak detection devices, and nondestructive testing of structures have been used to assist in inspecting these systems. Civil engineering research is working to improve these technologies for the public works profession.

Balancing Financial Tradeoffs

A third rationale for deferred maintenance is that during times of fiscal austerity, it may seem easier for a local politician to put off scheduled maintenance and use that money for other popular services (particularly ones that people can see). Once an administration gets into the habit of deferring maintenance to the future (and, maybe future administrations), it is taking a chance that the structures may fail. In essence, they are betting that threats to health, safety, and convenience will not occur during their term in office.

Of course, sometimes they lose those bets—with disastrous results. Three well-known examples include the collapse of the Mianus River Bridge near Greenwich, Connecticut, in 1983; the destruction of the Cypress Viaduct of the Nimitz Freeway during the 1989 earthquake; the Great Chicago Flood in 1992 caused by an accident exacerbating the deferred maintenance of underground tunnels. These examples indicate how rolling the dice on maintenance can potentially cost millions of dollars and many lives.

Lack of Political Payoff

Another reason advanced for the deferral of maintenance was implied at the beginning of this chapter—there does not seem to be any payoff for politicians to embrace maintenance. Politicians and other professional administrators like to be associated with activities which indicate that growth and development is occurring in the city. New programs and new structures are celebrated with events such as ground breakings and ribbon cuttings. Routine maintenance is just that—routine—and is seen as rather dull and mundane by "political" standards.

All four of these reasons advanced for the decision to defer maintenance should be seen as reinforcing each other, thereby increasing the odds that maintenance will take a back seat to other local expenditures. Even enlightened public officials may not understand the importance of maintenance, since it can be complicated or made confusing by technically trained people who cannot communicate with officials and other citizens in a way they can understand. Fortunately, the *Fragile Foundations* report raised the consciousness of the nation to the plight of our crumbling urban infrastructure. It is the job of the public works profession to keep maintenance a high priority with public officials.

Maintenance Strategies

Public works professionals organize their infrastructure maintenance strategies around the three R's: **repair, rehabilitation,** and **replacement.** Repair and rehabilitation extend the life of infrastructure systems and are usually funded by local government operating budgets. City employees from the Public Works Department often perform the work. Repair involves correcting a minor problem such as filling a pothole or patching a roof. Repair maintains the integrity of existing structures—in this case, a roadway and a building. Rehabilitation is a process by which the quality of an existing structure is improved or the structure is restored to its original condition. Rehabilitation usually means the structure is strengthened or major members are replaced. If pothole patching is repair, then an asphalt overlay on a street would be considered rehabilitation.

Replacement involves the demolition of an existing structure or facility and the construction of a new and improved one. Replacement is typically funded out of a city's capital (not operating) budget. Large scale replacement projects (like the building of a new City Hall or a four-lane commuting bridge) often outstrip the city's workforce capacity, resulting in the contracting out of various aspects of the system's replacement. (Contracting will be covered later in this chapter.)

Since one cannot infinitely extend the life of an infrastructure system, replacement is, indeed, part of the city's capital improvement program. An integrated maintenance strategy includes ongoing repair and rehabilitation and plans for eventual replacement of systems. The goal is to efficiently prolong the life of the infrastructure, which ultimately saves tax dollars.

Maintaining Human Infrastructure

If maintenance of urban infrastructure takes a back seat to other types of funding, the maintenance of its human infrastructure system is even more rarely addressed. When we speak about maintaining human infrastructure, we are referring to training and equipping those who manage, maintain, and direct the operations of infrastructure systems with the tools to most effectively do their jobs. Unfortunately, those activities most closely associated with human infrastructure improvement—attendance at training and workshop events, adoption of technological innovations, research and development—are often the first items cut in budgets during times of fiscal austerity.

The vast majority of respondents to an American Public Works Association survey indicated that a formal management degree or at least course offerings in continuing education in management (in addition to an engineering degree) are important ingredients to successful management of public works agencies in the twenty-first century. This continuing maintenance is not limited to the top management. Middle managers and supervisors often take advantage of workshops targeted to them from their professional associations such as the APWA, the Water Environment Federation, the American Water Works Association, and their affiliated state chapters.

Investments in human infrastructure also come in the form of support for research in civil engineering related materials and processes and the technology transfer activities associated with those who relate basic civil engineering research to actual practice. The ring of people involved in this enterprise is much wider than that typically considered in maintenance of our physical infrastructure and even includes those involved in management research and planning.

Delivering Local Services Effectively

Historically, the largest portions of a city's budget have gone to public works and public safety functions—those services provided outside of City Hall. Therefore, it is appropriate in a chapter on public works to discuss the nature of public services, the alternate arrangements for the delivery of those services, and the administrative issues which must be balanced regarding decisions about how urban services are delivered.

Despite the Adam Smith quote at the beginning of this chapter, we all know that cities currently are involved in more than what could be considered traditional public works and public safety services. Today, cities provide services which at one time might have been the purview of one's family, church, or charitable organization. These include social services, recreation, health care, daycare, cultural institutions and events, and many other non-traditional services. This illustrates the very nature of city services—they are not static. They evolve as cities develop and change to meet the emerging needs of citizens.

If the notion of what services a city should provide changes over time, it is reasonable that the idea of who should be in the best position to deliver services can also come into question. The answer is seldom clear cut. It can be a function of local tradition, union contracts, or even the personality of an administrator. During the 1980s, privatization of public service delivery was considered the most efficient delivery method. In the 1990s the reinventing and re-engineering experts favored having "entrepreneurial governments" arrange for service delivery. Now, the decisions on service delivery arrangements are not as clear cut. The decisions are more complex and require considerations of all delivery procedures based on the service, the history of the city, and the qualifications of the municipal labor force. Urban scholars have argued that it is the *nature* of goods and services which suggests appropriate methods of service delivery. The following sections discuss the nature of goods and services, alternate methods of service delivery (who will be involved), and managing local service delivery (how the service will be delivered).

Identifying the Nature of Goods and Services

The previous section demonstrated that service responsibility can shift over time—for example, what had been the responsibility of the family could shift to a city responsibility. Regardless, is there something constant about the basic nature of services which will assist in identifying the most logical service delivery mechanism? Most urban researchers have agreed that all services can be categorized on two continua based on their qualities of exclusion and consumption. This typology was developed by Vincent and Elinor Ostrom (1977) and further refined by E. S. Savas (1982).

A good or service is characterized as **exclusive** if a supplier can exclude someone from its access until conditions of the supplier are met. It is easy to understand exclusion if one thinks about any store purchase. The owner of the store can prohibit a customer from consuming a good until the price (the condition of sale set by the owner) is paid. If the customer chooses to try to consume the good without paying (stealing), the owner can prosecute. The continuum of exclusivity is based on how feasible it is to exclude someone from the good or service.

The characteristic of **consumption** deals with whether more than one person can use or consume the good without diminishing the quality to another person. Jointly consumed goods can be enjoyed equally by any number of individuals while individually consumed goods' qualities are denied to others by virtue of their consumption. The classic example of joint consumption involves the "consumption" of a network program on television. The "quality" of the program remains unchanged whether one or one hundred thousand people view the program. The addition of one additional viewer does not alter the quality for any of the other viewers. In the same way, when a viewer turns off the program, the quality afforded to the other viewers is neither reduced nor enhanced. On the other hand, when one "consumes" or buys a television, others are denied access to that particular television; the use of *that* television is denied to others.

The concepts of exclusion and consumption are used to define the ideal types of services a city can provide. (The definition of the term "ideal type" is the sociological one—a pure type—and not one "ideally suited" to local delivery.) **Private goods** are those which are individually consumed and for which exclusion is entirely feasible. Given the earlier "exclusion" discussions, these are functions or services which could easily be provided by market systems. In other words, the market can operate in such a way that it could extract a fee from a citizen to provide a service and exclude the citizen if payment were not made. The best examples of private urban services are solid waste collection and recreational services. In solid waste collection citizens can be charged for the pickup of wastes either by volume (number of bags) or routine (once a week) and a bill could be given to residents. In the case of recreation activities, a department could charge user fees (which may be publicly subsidized) which would allow someone to participate in their activities. If one did not pay, that citizen could be denied access to the activity. These are the sorts of activities which could be **contracted** out to firms rather than be the sole responsibility of existing departments. In other words, private goods, by their nature, are more amenable to being contracted out than other urban services since their qualities of being individually consumed and the ease with which someone can be excluded from the service fit best with provision by a private vendor—their operations are most nearly like those operative in the private market system.

Another ideal type includes services for which exclusion is feasible and for which consumption is of a joint nature. These services are called **toll goods.** The provision of cable television services, in contrast to network service, is a good example. Like network service, cable television program quality is neither enhanced nor decreased based on the number of viewers at any particular time. However, access *to the programming is limited to those who pay for the installation of the cable system and the monthly service fee.*

Another example of a toll good is a toll road. Operation of a toll road works best on limited access highways (exclusion is feasible) where agencies can extract a charge or toll for using the roadway. Presumably, motorists would be willing to pay for the convenience of driving on a higher speed roadway which had fewer turns and no traffic signals in order to reach their destination more quickly. While government typically provides a route by which any driver could reach a destination free of charge, operators of toll roads extract a convenience fee from those who wish to bypass small towns or travel on a higher speed roadway. Currently tolls are proposed on existing free highways to alleviate congestion. Variable rate tolls allow drivers the choice to bypass free lanes which might be congested. The tolls can vary by time of day and amount of congestion. Oftentimes special district governments operate these facilities; however, it is not inconceivable that other market driven private parties may provide such transportation alternatives. In both cases, the fees extracted from the tolls are used to repair, rehabilitate, and ultimately replace the roadway. Therefore, the tolls should reflect the actual cost of these activities.

The third ideal type consists of **common pool goods.** In this case, the goods are individually consumed; however, exclusion is impossible. When exclusion is impossible, then extracting a fee for service is infeasible. Rational economic actors will use up the good or service since it is essentially free. The problem for society is that this creates a situation in which the good or service can be exhausted or destroyed in the process.

The classic examples of common pool goods are natural resources. The breathable air, fish in lakes, and the beauty of wilderness areas all can be jointly consumed or enjoyed. It is infeasible to charge individuals for their enjoyment of these resources. It would simply cost too much to staff the fee collection system. Moreover, many believe that access to these resources is a right of citizenship and should not bear a cost. However, there is a role for government with respect to these services and that is regulation. Automobile emission standards and their associated penalties act to ensure the air quality. Limitations on the size and number of fish which can be caught in an area are enforced by rangers in order to safeguard the resource for future generations. Restrictions on the number of visitors in national parks or restrictions on areas they may visit regulate the use and over use of those areas. Again, a proper role for the government in the provision of common pool goods is to ensure their continued access through regulation.

The fourth and final ideal type of goods and services is that for which the consumption is joint and for which exclusion is infeasible. These are called **collective goods.** The market seldom becomes involved in the delivery of collective goods since there is no incentive to do so—one cannot exact a fee and "free riders" will use the good without paying. While some argue that collective goods cause the most problems for society (presumably since the market seldom gets involved), the more lucid argument is that it is in the delivery of collective goods that governments should be involved. In fact, they are the best, and sometimes only, reasonable providers of collective services.

National defense is the best example of a collective good provided by the government. All citizens of the United States, as well as any legal or illegal aliens residing in the country, receive the same level of national defense. Whether one agrees with defense policy or not, the government does not differentiate among its citizens with regard to defense. Moreover, it could not differentiate, since exclusion is infeasible. One cannot opt out of national defense since the consumption is joint. A pacifist receives the same level of national defense as a militarist whether they like it or not. National defense policy is justifiably debated and formed through the workings of government and collectively provided to all citizens and non-citizens alike.

At the local level, emergency preparedness and security are examples of a collective good in the public works arena. Expenditures for preparedness benefit everyone living in or driving through a city regardless if one happens to be in a flood plain, along a railroad, downtown, or in any residential area. The same amount and quality of security accrues to all in the community. It would be physically and politically infeasible for local governments to exclude citizens from this protection.

Unfortunately, not all urban services fit neatly into the four ideal type categories outlined here. As mentioned before, they may shift to and from ideal types based on society's determination regarding individual rights and the role of government in ensuring these rights. One problem with the push to privatize all services in the name of efficiency and effectiveness of private markets was the absence of an understanding of the underlying nature of goods and services which identifies appropriate roles for various sectors in providing different types of services. Having this understanding, urban service managers can propose alternate modes of service delivery in a more informed manner.

Alternate Methods of Service Delivery

E. S. Savas (1987) provides a useful distinction about various city officials' roles in the delivery of urban services: **arrangers, producers,** and **consumers.** Arrangers organize and ensure the service is delivered, producers directly supply the service, while consumers ultimately receive or use the service. Sometimes these roles are blurred; however, just as the ideal types described earlier, a focus on these roles allows easier understanding of the alternate modes of urban service delivery.

Table 9.2 displays a range of service delivery modes which range from total government involvement to no governmental involvement. None of these modes is "best," rather, in certain situations, one may be more appropriate than another based on the nature of the good or service involved.

The traditional method of urban service delivery is **governmental service.** In this mode, the government acts as both the arranger and producer of local services which are consumed by its citizens. Local policy dictates the level and frequency of service while governmental employees directly deliver the service. A city's policy to pick up residential solid waste once a week, every week, using city employees and city refuse packing trucks is an example of governmental service.

TABLE 9.2
Alternate Service Delivery Arrangements

Most government involvement

Governmental Service
Intergovernmental Agreements
Contracting
Franchising
Grants
Vouchers
Market supply
Voluntary coprovision
Self-Service

Least government involvement

When a city arranges for another unit of government to deliver services to its citizens, it is involved in an **intergovernmental agreement.** Typically, a larger unit of government provides the service for another smaller unit of government taking advantage of economies of scale. For example, many cities in Los Angeles County use the paramedic services of the county government. In these cases, each city arranges with the county to directly provide services to its citizens. The county then negotiates a fee for service with the city, the costs of which are either borne by the city (through the general fund) or shared by the city and the citizen-user of the service. In rapidly growing areas in which a private market does not exist, a new city may ask an adjoining city to collect its residential solid waste for a fee if the city is not in a position to purchase packing trucks or hire sanitation employees.

The method of service delivery most closely associated with the term "privatization" in North America is **contracting** out service delivery to a private sector firm. Given the nature of goods and services, it seems reasonable that contracting out works best with services which approximate private or toll goods. In those services, the private market has some incentive to be involved in the delivery of the service. In contracting out, the government arranges for a private (or sometimes non-profit) sector firm to deliver a specified quantity and quality of service to its citizens. Note that in contracting that the government does not relinquish all involvement with the service. It provides policy direction, oversight, and evaluation of service quality—the arrangement function—while the firm produces the service. Where contracts have supplied poor services to citizens, it is usually the fault of the government for not assuming its oversight authority and often not having performance standards specifically written in the contract. In the case of solid waste collection, a city can contract with a private firm to provide residential collection once a week, every week with a minimum of missed pickups and spills. The firm would use its own trucks and employees and would be responsible for responding to citizen complaints.

While contracting out works best with goods which approximate private or toll goods, it is also most useful for services which can be classified either as mundane and repetitive, or highly technical. Collection of solid wastes is one example of a repetitive task; data entry, road striping, and tree trimming are others. In terms of technical skills, smaller cities often contract out for engineering services, since it would be too expensive relative to the workload to have a full-time engineer on staff. Larger cities with engineering departments will often contract out large engineering projects to private design and engineering firms as the workload exceeds their capacity. In these cases, the engineering department maintains an oversight role over the conduct of the contracted engineering services.

Franchising involves the awarding of monopoly privileges to a firm to provide a service. In a franchising arrangement, the government arranges for the service but usually with strict regulation of fees and the imposition of performance standards. Most cable television and other utility operations are performed under franchise agreements, since it is infeasible for a provider of this kind of service to compete door to door for service provision due to the high capital and startup costs associated with these types of services.

Sometimes governments offer subsidies to private vendors or other authorities to provide a needed service which would not necessarily be a profitable undertaking. These subsidies are called **grants.** The most common local examples are mass transit and housing.

In the case of mass transit, the local government perceives a need for low cost transportation for all its citizens and arranges and entices (with the grant subsidy) the involvement of a contractor to provide the service. In housing, grants are often used to encourage developers to include units designated for low to moderate income citizens.

Vouchers, on the other hand, involve providing subsidies directly to the consumer, allowing them the free choice of service vendors and relatively free choice of products. The government broadly arranges the service and the consumers have the choice of vendors. The easiest example to understand is the Food Stamp program. Citizens are given stamps (vouchers) which they can use to purchase items (the variety of which is regulated by the government) at the grocery store of their choice. Once at the store, they can choose the brands or cuts of food they wish. Housing vouchers function the same way. The vendors (grocery stores, landlords) then redeem the vouchers from the government for cash.

Use of **market** structures (the private sector) to deliver local services works best when the goods and services approach private or toll types, when there is a need for a service, and when there are multiple vendors who wish to produce the product. This is also the best time for government to get out of the business of providing a service directly since the market forces will ensure that the service is delivered at a competitive price. Strategically, this is the best opportunity for local governments to "load shed" costly services.

When citizen-consumers get involved directly in the provision of a good or service, they are participating in what is referred to as **coprovision or coproduction** of services. One type of coprovision is the use of volunteer groups to augment city services. For example, a Garden Club can volunteer to beautify the grounds around City Hall or provide plants to decorate a traffic circle. Increasingly, people and groups volunteer to keep a portion of highways free of litter—Adopt a Highway programs. These voluntary efforts do not necessarily take the place of city services. For example, if a citizen fails to pick up litter on the highway, the unit of government responsible will get the phone call to clean up the mess. Voluntary service provision works best when it enhances existing city services. Its global utilization for delivering local services was overstated in many policy speeches of the 1980s.

Self-Service is a method in which citizens take responsibility for most, if not all, aspects of service delivery and usually takes one of two forms. In the first form, the government relinquishes responsibility for a service forcing citizens to arrange and provide the service. For example, if a city gets out of the business of arranging for residential solid waste collection, citizens would have to arrange and pay for a vendor to pick up their refuse or transport it themselves to a landfill.

The second form of self-service is to take private actions to reduce the need for public services. For example, using a kitchen sink garbage disposal reduces the need for solid waste collection services by reducing the volume of waste (although it increases the need for wastewater treatment). Locking the doors to one's house or car or installing alarm devices reduces the need for police services by discouraging thieves in the first place.

Any comprehensive approach to organizing the delivery of local services should take into account the nature of the goods and services involved, the variety of delivery methods available, and the needs and convenience of citizens. In some cases, citizens are willing to pay for high quality services produced by governmental employees while others would rather see the service contracted out or even dropped. There is not one good answer for every city. However, considering the nature and variety of delivery mechanisms is a good strategy for effectively providing urban services.

Managing Local Services

Examining the nature of locally delivered services and considering the range of delivery alternatives deals only with the input portion of the services. It does not estimate the impact of those deliberations on citizens. Every decision about the management of local services has both intended and unintended impacts on citizens. This section introduces some of the concepts which must be balanced in any service delivery operation.

Equality versus Equity

The concept of equality in service delivery is deceptively easy for most managers, politicians, and citizens to understand. Most would agree that services should be delivered "equally" to all citizens without regard to race, class, or power stature. However, equality is often operationalized in practice as providing equal *inputs* of service in each geographical area. City council members want equal dollars expended on each service in each ward. Equal numbers of crews should be deployed in each route. Equal numbers of squad cars should patrol each district.

While this concept of equality would be considered "fair" to all parties, it does not take into account differential needs of geographically dispersed citizens. Some neighborhoods are more densely populated, older, or have different crime rates. If one is concerned with the equality of *output* after a service has been delivered, (e.g., same condition of cleanliness of neighborhoods or similar crime rates), then *unequal inputs* may be necessary. More squad cars should be deployed, more crews dispatched, or different machinery used. The equality of the result of service is referred to as **equity.** Unfortunately, it is more difficult to measure outputs than inputs. An unintended consequence of a policy of providing equal inputs can be an inequitable service outcome—unequal service conditions. It is the job of the manager of local services to measure service outputs and convince elected officials of the need to concentrate on citizens' conditions after the service is delivered ("safe streets," "decent, safe, and sanitary housing") rather than focus on the more easily measured inputs (dollars and crews).

Efficiency versus Effectiveness

As a concept, efficiency refers to getting the most service per dollar of input. The efficiency of the private sector was often cited as the dominant rationale for contracting out urban services in the 1980s. Effectiveness concerns doing the right things correctly. Of course, effectiveness also involves performing services within budget and as efficiently as possible. However, often elected officials and managers focus so much on efficiency that they do not bother to ask questions like, "Should we really be doing this?" or "Is there something else we should be doing for citizens?" Developing service-based missions, operationalizing outcomes, and evaluating success toward achieving performance standards are the steps by which good urban managers and elected officials balance the concepts of efficiency versus effectiveness.

Ethics

Ethics takes on a major role in the delivery of urban services. Sometimes the qualities which one would value in the private sector (e.g., profit, power, privacy) are not reasonable in the public sector. In the public sector things not only have to *be* good, they have to *look* good to citizens. Managers of public sector services in urban areas are held to a much higher standard than their private sector counterparts and the unintended consequences of behavior are subject to more scrutiny. *The city maintains itself* as it maintains the integrity of its infrastructure—both physical and human—its political systems, and its ethical standards.

Name _____

The City Maintains Itself (Public Works)

9-1. Observe the route you take from your home to this class and answer the following questions:

- How many bridges did you cross? _____

- How many vacant buildings did you pass? _____

- How many parks did you see? _____

- How many new commercial construction sites were in progress? _____

- How many fast food outlets were there? _____

- How many schools were there? _____

- Sketch the route, showing the landscape features mentioned above.

9-2a. Interview the head of the Public Works Department (or the person in charge of public works) in your city and determine what percentage of the budget is spent on each of the R's.

9-2b. Also inquire of the head of the department whether the city has privatized, or intends to privatize any of its services. State which services:

9-3. Give specific examples of **exclusive** goods and **consumption** goods in your central city:

9-4. In the urban delivery system, given an example of:

an arranger

a producer

a consumer

THE CITY GROWS
(Economic Development)
Claudette A. Robey and James E. Robey

As the United States and other major countries in the world become more and more urbanized, urban expansion and development present challenges and opportunities to cities and their surrounding suburbs. To describe this diffusion of people and structures across the landscape, economists and others have coined the term "economic development." This concept often means different things to different people. For example **local economic development** cannot be equated with the **local economy**. The local economy is that bundle of activities pertaining to the production, development, and management of the material wealth of a local geographic area. It is, in essence, the process of creating wealth—and it is largely a private-sector activity. It is the role of the private sector to create wealth by producing tradable goods and services and by engaging in the exchanges of such goods.

The public sector role in this process is **economic development**. The American Economic Development Council (AEDC) defined economic development in 1984 as "the process of creating wealth through the mobilization of human, financial, capital, physical, and natural resources to generate marketable goods and services" (AEDC, 1984, p. 18). AEDC, through a merger with the Council for Urban Economic Development (CUED), became the International Economic Development Council. As urban scholars continued the study of cities from an economic perspective, the concept of economic development came to include **jobs** as well as wealth, and the **distribution** and **creation** of wealth. Thus, economic development has also been defined as the "role of the public sector in facilitating and promoting the creation of jobs and wealth by the private sector, and to ensure that it does so in a way that serves the short and long run interests of the broad population" (Bingham & Mier, 1993, p. vii adapted from Bendavid-Val, 1991, p. 21).

Recent trends in assessing the impacts of both private and public investments in economic development recognize that not all new investment will yield additional jobs. Often new investment, both in new or existing companies and in their buildings and capital stock (for example, equipment, machines, and computers), will yield more productive workers rather than increased numbers of workers. More productive workers have higher **productivity**, which is the amount of goods or services that a worker can produce in a specific period of time. Worker productivity may be increased by investments in both the tools and machines that the worker uses, as well as investments in the workers themselves. It is necessary in a global economy for workers and firms to invest in higher levels of productivity if a county or region wants to maintain a high standard of living. As companies are pressured to reduce unit costs of goods, they have turned to **offshoring** production of goods *and* services. This occurs when production is sent to lower cost/wage countries, with India and China, and increasingly Vietnam, as the current preferred choices. There is some thought that, with the rising standard of living in many of the countries that have been targets of offshoring, for the domestic North American market consumption, offshoring may be less viable than in previous periods. Local workers with higher productivity will be able to better compete in a global economy for jobs and production, and increase the potential for production occurring in the domestic market.

Local economic development activities in the United States began effectively in Mississippi in 1937 with the issuance of the first **industrial development bond (IDB)**. The emphasis of these activities has varied over time, covering four eras of changing approaches to economic development (Haider, 1989).

The first era ran from the early development of **location incentives** such as IDBs through the early 1960s. In this phase of economic development history, industrial recruitment enveloped the landscape. State and local governments attempted to attract manufacturing plants from other localities to redistribute employment. This activity is commonly referred to as **smokestack chasing**. Even the federal government participated in these activities, albeit indirectly. For example, in 1961 the Area Redevelopment Administration (precursor to the Economic Development Administration) was established in the Department of Commerce to provide technical assistance, loans, and grants to local governments for public projects, particularly those that would attract private businesses.

During the second phase of economic development, a period encompassing the early 1960s through the early 1970s, the primary goal was to improve **equity** and increase demand through **redistribution**. The federal, state, and local programs of this decade sought to provide subsidies to individuals and regions in poverty as a way both to raise income and stimulate increased economic activity by increasing consumer demand. The major emphasis of development programs of the period was on broadening economic opportunity through education, job training, social services, and community development.

During the third phase in the 1970s, government's contribution to economic development consisted of programs that attempted to stimulate economic development in depressed areas and declining city neighborhoods through a **combination** of smokestack chasing and private sector investments. Public sector interest was in the generation of employment and jobs. Much of the programmatic emphasis was on service sector employment through the development of hotels, office buildings, and other real estate–related activities.

The next stage, with beginnings extending back to about 1980, was an era of **generative** development. The controversial work of David Birch (1978) suggested that small businesses, rather than large corporations, were the real generators of new jobs. Governments thus shifted their focus to entrepreneurship and assistance to small- and medium-sized firms. Governments subscribed to the philosophy that policy should not be aimed toward creating jobs, but toward facilitating the enhancement of market mechanisms to create wealth, which in the process would create jobs.

The work of Birch, including his later work (1987), illustrates how theory can influence local development policy. In the case described above, Birch purportedly showed that most new employment was created by small businesses. Federal, state, and local governments, seeking a way out of the depths of the serious recession of the early 1980s, latched onto Birch's "theory" of employment growth and developed new programs designed to help small businesses grow. Thus, there is a practical side to theories.

In 1990, Michael Porter, a professor at the Harvard Business School, published a seminal work on national competitiveness entitled *The Competitive Advantage of Nations*. This work led to a continuing discussion about national and then regional competitiveness in the area of **industry clusters**. These clusters are groups of industries that have regional backward (sellers/suppliers) and/or forward (buyers/consumers) **linkages**. These linkages, when combined with a specialized labor pool, create efficiencies or economies that allow firms to operate with lower costs, share a unique labor pool, and create the potential for innovation. When firms compete, whether regionally, nationally or globally, they are forced to innovate in the areas of both product and process.

Current trends in economic development have focused on three parallel and sometimes concurrent areas: **regionalism**, **quality of place**, and **quality of talent**. In many ways these trends are not only parallel, but also intertwined. **Regionalism** has taken two basic forms, cooperation and consolidation. The first is when combinations of governments (usually county and/or local agencies) work with business organizations (such as chambers of commerce and local economic development groups [LDCs]) to provide a single voice in efforts to attract, expand, and retain businesses. *It is important to remember that labor markets nearly always exceed any single, local, or political jurisdiction.* Regionalism allows those groups, whether public or private, that benefit (and possibly suffer) from local business investment decisions to be involved in the decision process and to affect outcomes. For example, Team Northeast Ohio was created to facilitate economic development activities across 13 counties of northeast Ohio. This organization was created through the efforts of five chambers of commerce, the electric utility, and the local philanthropic community. The organization currently works with the state of Ohio, serves 18 counties, and interacts with more than 500 economic development entities in the region to increase jobs and investment.

A second form of regionalism is through the consolidation of municipalities in a region into a single form of government, often either as a single city or a unified city-county government. One reason cited for this consolidation is the creation of economies of scale. When Louisville, Kentucky, merged with Jefferson County in 2003, it went from the 67th to the 16th largest city in the United States. This type of consolidation allows a city to attract more federal and state funds, as well as new businesses. Indianapolis, Indiana, has a long history of a consolidated city-county government called Unigov, and the Minneapolis–St. Paul region, through the Twin Cities Fiscal Disparities Plan, has a long history of tax/revenue sharing. While these offer models with promising results and outcomes, these types of consolidations took significant amounts of time, energy, and political capital to achieve success.

The most recent form of consolidation taking place is the sharing of services, such as fire, police, and EMS dispatch services across municipal boundaries. In these cases, each jurisdiction (such as counties, cities, villages, and townships) is able to more easily achieve economies of scale for services while eliminating redundant functions. The need for fewer emergency dispatch centers across broader geographies reduces hardware, equipment, and personnel costs. Such cost savings among communities can help reduce costs to residents and businesses while making the jurisdiction more competitive.

Increasingly, much discussion in economic development is based on creating a **quality of place**. The argument is made that creating an environment that is amenable to diversity, including ethnicity and gender, is essential to attracting and retaining a quality workforce. Richard Florida has lectured extensively on the value of the "Creative Class" that seeks to capitalize on the needs of the "knowledge economy." Ann Markusen at the University of Minnesota and others have written extensively on how the arts, cultural offerings, and other amenities are essential to both attracting and retaining a qualified **talent pool or workforce**.

Economic development and **clusters** activities, in particular, have focused groups or *portfolios* of industries. Industries in the United States are identified by the *process* they use to create goods and services. This system of identification is called the North American Industrial Classification System (NAICS). This system was jointly developed by the United States, Canada, and Mexico and can be used to identify the main activity that occurs at each business establishment. The portfolio of industries that a region possesses is often referred to as its "industry mix." Current thought in economic development focuses not only on a city's or region's industry mix or portfolio of industries, but also on how the industry mix affects a region's portfolio of occupations.

The federal government has organized occupations into more than 700 classifications in a hierarchical system called the Standard Occupational Classification System (SOC). The SOC system, when coupled with NAICS data, can be combined into a table called the "industry-occupation matrix." The use of this table allows economic developers to estimate the number of workers in a region for each occupation based on the workforce in each of the region's industries. For example, research conducted at the Greater Cleveland Partnership found that, based on northeast Ohio's portfolio of industries, two out of three information technology (IT) *workers* were not employed in IT *industries*, but were employed in other industry sectors such as banking, insurance, and manufacturing.

Quality of talent continues to be an impediment to job creation across the United States, regardless of whether in an urban, suburban, or rural location or region. Current workforce needs demand that workers be able to work in a flexible environment, be team oriented, and be problem solvers. Changes in 2010 in the focus of the Cleveland/Cuyahoga Workforce Investment Board (WIB) have foreshadowed changes taking place across the country. The WIB has gone from client-focused training as a social program to one working with employers to identify current openings and then to train workers for those openings. This is referred to as "demand facing" training. Similarly, in Lake County, Ohio, employers in the manufacturing sector have banded together to form the Alliance for Working Together (AWT). AWT is nearly 100 companies working together to identify their training needs and then communicate these needs to the local community college, again a demand-facing model. A third example of this model is the Mississippi Corridor Consortium. In this example, four community-college districts share curriculum, faculty, and resources, thus eliminating redundancies. The outcome has been to attract two mega employers that are 70 miles apart—one an automobile final-assembly plant and one a steel-processing and service center.

In order to understand urban areas, one must understand theories of urban economic growth. The accumulation of knowledge consists of the process of gradual confirmation and/or modification of the theories that serve as the general premises in the explanatory scheme. For example, Birch's "theory" of the job-creating powers of small businesses has now largely been discounted (Harrison, 1994; White & Osterman, 1991).

A great deal is expected of theories. First, of course, they are expected to be accurate; that is, to explain a phenomenon as completely as possible. Theories are also expected to be both **parsimonious** and **generalizable**; however, there are tradeoffs. When the accuracy of a theory is maximized, its generality and parsimony will often be low. Finally, theories are expected to be causal. Thus, the disciples of Birch expected that the growth of small businesses would "cause" growth in the economy.

At any stage in the development of science, more than one theory could explain the same events. There is no lack of theory on urban economies and urban economic development. One source (Bingham & Mier, 1993), for example, documented over 50 theories of local development.

The task for the remainder of this chapter is twofold. First, a number of the more significant theories of urban economic growth will be presented. Second, these theories will then be linked to economic development practices.

Theories of Urban Economic Growth

Theories of development, or theories of urban economic growth, seek to explain why some areas grow while others do not. Although these theories about why some areas grow are incomplete, they still form the basis of many state and local economic development efforts.

Location theory (as discussed in Chapter 3) is the term given to models in business economics that focus on individual firm-location decisions. Location theory in urban economics evolved from simple **transportation cost minimization** models (Blair & Premus, 1993). In general, prior to 1960, studies in industrial location showed that basic cost factors were the dominant determinants of industrial location. Of primary importance was transportation: access to markets, access to materials, and access to labor.

The simplest transportation model assumes only one market and one input source (source of raw materials). Under these circumstances a profit-maximizing firm will choose a site that will minimize total transportation costs from among a set of location possibilities. Thus, if the firm's product is expensive to ship compared to the raw material, the firm will locate at the market to avoid the higher cost of shipping the product. Conversely, if the weight of the input is high compared to the cost of transporting the output, manufacturing will occur at the input site.

A site at some midpoint location might be expected if the weights of the input and output were equal; however, this is usually not the case. End point locations tend to be preferred for two reasons. First, a midpoint location entails extra unloading and loading costs. Second, the presence of long-haul economies in transportation enhances the desirability of end point locations. An exception to the tendency to avoid midpoint locations is when there is a natural break in the transportation grid. This could be, for example, due to a water port or rail terminal. Because a disruption in the shipping route occurs at these points, some manufacturers find them convenient locations for production facilities, given that unloading and loading would have to occur anyway. Cities such as Cleveland, Chicago, and St. Louis gained some of their manufacturing prominence for this reason.

In reality, of course, most firms have many input sources and manufacture a number of products with delivery all over the country or even the world. The use of locational weights can help explain where a facility will locate with multiple inputs and outputs. With today's computer capabilities, there is literally no plant operation that is too complex to model.

One of the major theories of regional economic development is economic base theory. **Economic base theory**, sometimes called "trade theory," stems from the premise that economic growth is based on the amount of goods and services produced within a geographic area that can be exported out of the region. The theory holds that firms that use local labor and materials to produce a product for export will generate wealth and jobs. ("Export" means selling the product outside of a particular region, not necessarily outside of the country.)

Economic activities of a region can be divided into two categories: those industries that produce goods or services for export to other regions (e.g., computers, tourism) and those that produce for local consumption (e.g., hamburger stands). "The economic development of a region depends on its ability to raise the volume of exports relative to consumption of locally produced goods and services. The ability of a region to sustain long-run economic development depends on its ability to continue to export goods and services" (Nelson, 1993, p. 29).

Moreover, it is argued that through the **multiplier**, every job created in export-manufacturing industries will generate several jobs elsewhere in the economy. Locally produced and consumed goods also generate a multiplier, although it is typically weaker than the multiplier of goods produced for export. It is the new money from export industries that creates increases in aggregate wealth, although reducing imports, or **leakages** from trading dollars for imports, can help keep the accumulated wealth in the region.

An input to economic base theory is the concept of **comparative advantage** or comparative cost advantage. This theory assumes that each metropolitan area is better at producing certain goods than it is at others, thus leading to regional specialization. In manufacturing, labor supply, the proximity to natural resource, transportation, power, and simple historical factors have caused industrial specialization and have given some areas an advantage over others. Pittsburgh once had such an advantage in steel, as Detroit did in producing automobiles. But how does the law of comparative advantage work?

Let us look at two cities, Birmingham and Chicago. Each city produces only two commodities—steel and computers. The hypothetical tables below show the output per hour **(productivity)** for workers in each city:

Average Worker Productivity

	Birmingham	Chicago
Steel (1,000 lbs/hr)	9	4
Computers (units/hr)	3	2

It is clear from the tables that Birmingham has an advantage in producing both goods. In both cases, Birmingham workers are more efficient than Chicago workers. Furthermore, both Birmingham and Chicago are more efficient in producing steel than computers. Shouldn't both cities then produce as much steel as they can? After all, both are more efficient at producing steel than computers. Not necessarily—and that is due to comparative cost advantage. The tables below show the units of steel and computers produced by 100 workers in each industry before the cities specialize.

	Birmingham	Chicago
Steel	900	400
Computers	300	200

Now, in Birmingham, 10 workers are shifted from computer production to steel and in Chicago 20 workers are moved from the steel mills to computer factories. The output in each city after specialization is:

	Birmingham	Chicago
Steel	990	320
Computers	270	240

Birmingham now sells 80 units of steel to Chicago and Chicago sells 30 computers to Birmingham. After this exchange, the steel and computer inventories in both cities are:

	Birmingham	Chicago
Steel	910	400
Computers	300	210

As can be seen, both cities gain from the trade. Birmingham is wealthier by 10 units of steel and Chicago is wealthier by 10 computers. Trade benefits both cities when both produce what they are most proficient at producing.

Agglomeration economies refer to benefits that accrue when firms locate in proximity to one another (Blair & Premus, 1993, p. 17). An agglomeration in this sense is a mass of business enterprises clustered together. Agglomeration attempts to explain business location through the external economies thought to be generated for all parties by proximity to each other. Agglomeration savings are most often due to one of three factors: (1) the pressure of highly specialized suppliers, (2) a deep pool of specialized labor, or (3) transaction cost savings (most often in terms of transportation and communications cost savings). The most recent iteration of this aspect was referred to as **clusters** earlier in the chapter.

Two types of agglomeration economies are most often cited and lead to the development of different types of local economies. The first is a **localized** economy of agglomeration. This occurs when factors one (specialized suppliers) and two (specialized labor pools) are present. In these urban environments **backward** and **forward linkages** are present or readily available for a specific industry. Linkages are lines of suppliers and purchasers through which a firm transacts business. As an example, suppliers of taconite (iron ore), coke, limestone, and blast furnaces are the backward linkages for the steel industry. Forward linkages (depending on the steel producer) are the automobile, and construction or aircraft industries. Included in the backward linkage is the critical input of sufficiently skilled labor. Examples of localized economies include Seattle (aircraft), Detroit (automobiles), Silicon Valley and Boston/Route 128 (semiconductors/computers), and Pittsburgh (historically steel). Included in the array of linkages are often educational institutions that specialize in training (at all levels) labor for these industries.

The second type of agglomeration economy, an **urbanized** economy, is available to all industries and is based on the size and capacity of the labor force. In this type of economy, specialized labor is available based on the sheer size of the city; larger cities are able to supply a more varied and deeper pool of labor than smaller cities and towns. While the labor is specialized (such as legal, advertising, or accounting) in this type of economy, it can be easily used in a variety of industries. In the urban economy, specialization of skilled labor (such as chemical engineer or software designer) is generally applicable to one industry or sector. Most large cities have a deep pool of labor that is able to meet the needs of diverse urban economies. Markusen, Hall, and Glasmier (1986), for example, noted the locational tendencies of a group of high-tech industries serving the U.S. military. These industries tend to cluster around military facilities specializing in product testing and those serving as the final destination for military hardware. They theorized that innovative high-tech industries cluster together in their emerging phase to take advantage of agglomeration economies—to be near sources of new information and to take advantage of specialized labor pools (particularly engineers). Later, the agglomeration grows as small business service firms spring up to provide specialized services (accounting, consulting, financial services) to the high-tech manufacturers.

In many cases, user firms of the high-tech industries' manufactured goods are also drawn to the area. Markusen et al. use the example of computer manufacturers clustering around the homes of semiconductor manufacturers in Silicon Valley. These firms in turn attract computer-software firms.

The interdependence of firms within regions has often been demonstrated using regional **input-output** models. For example, the high-output multipliers (Beyers, 1983) found in the capital goods manufacturing belt (the Midwest) indicate a clustering of industries with their semifinished goods supplies, while low-output multipliers (in rural areas) indicate a higher proportion of output accounted for by primary factor payments (e.g., forest products, food processing).

The **product life-cycle theory** of industrial location hypothesizes that industries disperse down an urban hierarchy as they progress through different phases of their product life cycle. In the early or innovative stage, firms have high costs of production and high product prices, and they rely on relatively skilled labor and outside business services. The corporate emphasis in this phase is on market share. Industries in their early state generally locate in large metropolitan areas because of the availability of skilled labor and specialized goods and services. Over time, new firms are attracted to the industry; as competition increases and profits decline, firms decentralize to more rural areas in an attempt to reduce production costs (the mature phase).

Over the past several decades, a literature has emerged concerning the **theory of wages** and the intrametropolitan location of industry. The path-breaking study of this tradition was Hoover and Vernon's (1959) analysis of industrial wage rates in the New York metropolitan area from 1899 to 1954. They found that in 1899, when industry was overwhelmingly located in the core, wage rates steadily declined from the center outward.

As industrial deconcentration began, a spike on the wage rate appeared in the inner suburban ring. By the 1950s, with dispersal complete, wage rates were found to increase with distance from the center.

This study led to discussions of labor costs and attention to the realignment of U.S. manufacturers from the core to the periphery, or the Snowbelt to the Sunbelt (Fisher, 1981; Moriarty, 1986; Norton & Rees, 1979; Rees, 1979; Wheat, 1986). Much of the industrial growth in the South has been attributed to product-cycle pressures. Rees (1979), for example, states that much of the movement from north to south occurred in industries with high labor costs during their standardization phases.

Hansen (1979) concluded that the major vehicle for industrial decentralization to the South was corporate branch plants responding to product-cycle pressure, particularly with regard to cheap labor. Other researchers studying the South came to similar conclusions. The legacy of these locations, which make sense in a product-cycle framework, includes a rural concentration of industries, relatively low incomes, relatively uneducated workers, and a large pool of female workers (Rosenfeld, Bergman, & Rubin, 1985).

Location within the **hierarchy of central places** posits that firms are perfect competitors and that they locate in such a manner as to minimize their customers' transportation costs. **Central place theory**, referred to in Chapter 3, operates through the firm's production function, or through the supply side of the product market, because it examines location based on the delivered price of the good to the customer. Location within the hierarchy of central places, however, depends more on the demand side of the market.

The hierarchy of cities posits that each central place within the urban hierarchy contains all of the economic activity of places below it and also contains qualitatively different economic functions. Those added functions are those that have low frequency of demand, which is the same as saying that demand for the function is thin. In many cases, population and income act as substitutes in the demand function (Berry, 1967; King, 1984).

The hierarchy of cities illustrated a demand-side theory of location for population-serving, or local market, industries. The hierarchy of cities also resembles a supply-side theory of location when the industry is oriented toward national market activities. In this case the hierarchy of cities also relates to agglomeration economies. This is most apparent in headquarters activities, which tend to locate in the upper reaches of the urban hierarchy. This is due to the requirement for specialized labor and the requirement to locate near highly specialized suppliers.

The national headquarters of major corporations tend to be located in major metropolitan areas. These areas will have deep human resources as well as sophisticated services and infrastructure that support global operations. They will locate other corporate activities farther down the urban hierarchy to be closer to their customers (e.g., regional claims processing offices of insurance companies) or to save on operating costs.

Government Policies and Urban Development

Nearly all levels of government are able to facilitate the development of urban and local economies. Federal, state, regional, and local entities are all able to provide assistance, either directly via economic assistance such as grants and incentives, or indirectly through information exchange and infrastructure enhancement.

Federal Policies

The federal government provides development assistance through three channels. The first is **direct assistance** in which funds are supplied to firms, often through agencies such as the Small Business Administration (SBA). As noted elsewhere in this chapter, research has suggested that small businesses are the major contributor to numerical job growth in the United States. The SBA through grants and loans has been instrumental in the promotion of small firms, as well as incubators and small-business industrial parks. **Incubators** are specialized types of industrial parks in which new firms are able to pool resources to provide necessary overhead services such as clerical, receptionist, and accounting. These types of facilities also help reduce costs by providing flexible space to accommodate the needs of each firm, as well as sharing of common areas and maintenance costs.

Another federal agency that directly supports economic development (and mentioned earlier in the chapter) is the Economic Development Administration (EDA), part of the Department of Commerce. Although regularly on the chopping block regardless of the party in charge, EDA is essential in providing grants to develop strategic-planning documents called Comprehensive Economic Development Strategies (CEDS). CEDS processes help counties and regions identify priorities for development by helping regions engage in dialogues about paths to economic development. Additionally, EDA funds are used to develop infrastructure (such as water and sewer lines), and provide funds for transportation access (such as roads and bridges), and for building facilities such as incubators.

The second contribution of the federal government is through **information sharing**. The Bureau of the Census is instrumental in collecting and maintaining databases about the population. It also provides detailed, annual surveys about businesses in County Business Patterns (CBP), as well as surveys of individual industrial sectors such as manufacturing, transportation, services, and wholesale and retail trade. Both CBP and the data on industries provide detailed and summary information about the nation, state, counties, and metropolitan areas. This census information is used by researchers and governments to track changes and trends in urban economies, and by businesses to identify customer markets and locate potential sites for firm expansions.

The third contribution of the federal government is through **indirect activities**. The first, and probably the most important, is the use of federal funds in infrastructure changes. Most notable is the use of Department of Transportation (DOT) awards to alter the structure of the built environment. The addition of new and the expansion of existing highways can substantially alter the flow of products and labor within the urban region. As the result of a long-term study of Cleveland, Ohio (Cuyahoga County), housing trends and movements, Thomas Bier (1991) suggests that changes in highway capacities have adversely affected the central city, with employment and families moving from the city (and county) out into the suburbs, often located in adjacent counties within the Primary Metropolitan Statistical Area (PMSA).

Similarly, other types of federal investments (and disinvestments) in airports, seaports, military bases, parks and recreational facilities, and federal offices can affect urban economies by providing (or reducing) demand for capital, space, labor, goods, and services. Federal trade and monetary policies, as well as the relationship the United States has with individual countries and trading blocks, can affect the competitive and comparative advantages of an urban region through international demand for local products and the supply of production inputs.

State Policies

The states, while unable to affect trade and monetary policies, are able to offer assistance similar to that of the federal government. The states often supplement federal funding and may be the oversight or contracting agency for infrastructure projects, particularly highways.

States have attempted, through the use of trade missions, to open international markets to local products. These missions often showcase products that are either critical to urban economies or are new and innovative, springing from new firms that are often unable to afford exposure and entry into international markets. It is clear that cities no longer compete only with other cities in the region for industries and employment; they also compete internationally (Porter, 1990). Detroit products (automobiles) compete with products from Seoul, Tokyo, and Stuttgart in both the United States and internationally. New York competes with London, Tokyo, Miami (Latin America), and Berlin (as the monetary center of the European Union) to control capital markets. Cleveland no longer competes with Pittsburgh and Youngstown for steel sales; the city competes with cities in Korea, Germany, Brazil, Italy, and Scandinavia to offer various types of specialty steel.

State government is able to spur development by offering financial incentives to firms to locate in the state, and often in specific areas. The most common incentive is **tax abatement**. While authorized by the state, the use of abatement is at the discretion of city governments. This incentive reduces or eliminates all or part of the property tax bill at the new or redeveloped location. The tax reduction is often based not on the total value of the property, but on the value of improvements that were necessary for the firm to locate there. While the use of incentives has mostly been used to attract business, it is becoming increasingly important for retaining firms, with local governments abating the taxes on improvements and investments that were necessary to keep the firm on site.

In some areas, city governments are funded by income taxes. One of the new methods of incentives is for cities to share income tax collected from employees with the new company, usually through a rebate. Although abatements help to attract and retain business in the city, the downside of abatements has been the effect of these tax reductions on local schools. School districts in Ohio are funded primarily by property taxes. The diminished revenue to schools from abated property taxes can have a long-term adverse effect on the community as schools are unable to provide competitive services, which in turn provide a less competitive labor force. In the end, a less competitive labor force will make the area less competitive in the global market and the city will have an increasingly difficult time in attracting new investment.

Positive aspects of abatement policies have been discussed by Bartik (1991). This research suggests that in some localities in special situations, benefits can be derived from abatements. Communities that are likely to benefit have high unemployment, undervalued land, and lower-paid workers. Bartik found that in the long term (up to eight years), disadvantaged communities might have increased wage levels, increased property values, and lower unemployment after attracting business with abatements. These benefits more than offset the costs of lost revenues to the school systems. Cities that are generally healthy do not benefit from these incentives. Since property values and wages are generally higher and unemployment lower, the persistence of the effects is not clear. Cities may be *buying* business without gaining any real benefit. As discussed previously, firms locate in a region based on other location factors and resources, not because of tax incentives. Firms appear to make **intraregional** (within the region and between cities) locational decisions based on lowest cost between viable points. It can be inferred from Bartik's work that cities in the same county, using financial incentives to attract firms, may be spending money unnecessarily, but if the incentives are used to alleviate distress in a particular community, it may provide a longer run benefit.

States may also permit cities to engage in **tax increment financing (TIF)** and set up special districts that offer additional tax (such as wage) incentives to firms in targeted locations. One of the newer methods of attraction was used by South Carolina to attract BMW. The state provided a training facility across the street from the proposed plant and paid much of the training costs for new workers at the plant. While directly deferring some of the training costs, the benefits also accrued to the workers; they also had a marketable skill that would allow them additional opportunities beyond BMW.

Finally, many states are taking a regional approach to economic development. In this case, the state is often divided into substate regions, and increasingly, coupled with a private sector–led organization to act on behalf of the state. While the state retains control and oversight of incentive offerings and grant making, the regional entities do the day-to-day work of economic development. This form of public-private partnership allows for a hybrid of responsiveness with the agility of the private sector, including the ability to hold and use confidential project information, coupled with the assets of the state and its responsibility to use public funds prudently.

County Policies

In many states, county governments are able to influence development, both indirectly and directly. The primary method of influence is through a central county-based planning agency. These agencies not only offer physical planning of the built environment, but also often have development specialists who provide direct assistance to firms that are expanding or relocating within the county. It may include help with loan (both private and government) and grant applications, aid in securing building and business permits, and assistance in the site selection process. In many areas county government is "sold" through its planning and development agencies to prospective firms and businesses.

As noted later in this chapter, some governmental services (such as highways and water and sewer services) are controlled by larger governmental units; often one of these units is the county. How a county distributes mass transit routes and highways can greatly influence where businesses and employees decide to locate.

The traditional model of the urban region suggests that the most valuable property in the region is located in the central city or central business district (CBD). As one moves away from the center, the value of property declines. The use of the property will be determined by the property costs (the value of the property) in light of the value of production (**value added** by what a firm does). Firms that are able to be the most productive (have the highest value added) will be able to pay the most for property; this is called **bid rent**, illustrated in Chapter 3. In most cases the types of businesses that are able to bid the highest (and so locate in the CBD) are those such as legal, financial, and business services (e.g., accounting and advertising) that are productive in small vertical spaces and often require face-to-face meetings. These higher value-added types of businesses usually locate in the downtown or CBD areas, and make use of vertical space (high rise buildings). Farther from the center property usage changes, as does the "highest and best use" of each parcel, which is based on the most productive (the combination of cost and value added) use of that location. Moving away from the CBD and high-density office use, one encounters retail and wholesale areas. High-density housing (apartments), manufacturing, low-density housing (single family), and agricultural land use follow.

When a county builds new roads or transportation routes, the value of the properties along those routes will generally increase. As accessibility increases, firms will be better able to use the more distant locations, which will offer some relative cost savings over urban locations. In particular, manufacturing will be most attracted to newly available **greenfields**, usually perceived to have low environmental risk.

Modern manufacturing plants have shifted their production from multistory buildings to one-story factories to one-level (horizontal) production. Horizontal manufacturing occurs in nonurban and greenfield locations where land costs are less and assembly is easier than in a highly subdivided urban area.

City Policies

It is important to note that there are two general schools of economic development, "growth" and "development." The path each city takes is, in the long run, decided by local policy makers. A strategy that pursues "growth" is one that attempts to recruit and expand the existing business base; in this case a "more is good" strategy, with more of the same type of jobs being the goal. A strategy of "development" is one in which different sectors and innovative firms are sought. A strategy of growth, while adding numerically to the number of jobs, does not substantially raise the quality of life for the city over time. As noted elsewhere in this chapter, products have life cycles and cities that do not become proactive in the upgrading and expansion of industries will see them decline; with these declines, the quality of the city suffers.

The new "development" strategy seeks to attract or develop businesses that are on the "cutting edge." These types of businesses have a longer, expected life span given their early position in the market, yield higher returns given their position in the "profit cycle" (Markusen, 1985), and will require higher levels of skilled labor, which in turn will pay higher wages, ultimately increasing the cities' standard of living.

The first of these strategies is based on the local educational system. A good school system is necessary to generate a highly skilled (as measured in a global context) labor force that can be used to attract high-tech companies. One impediment to using this strategy in many central cities is the perpetually poor academic performance of central city school districts. Since companies and their surrogates called "site selectors" often use the core city school district as the measure of academic quality, this can be a difficult impediment for economic developers to overcome when attracting new investment into the region. Most urban regions are recognized by their central city, not by the cities in their suburban ring. It may be necessary for suburban districts to help central city school districts, at least when they are underfunded and unable to provide adequate levels of technology, as well as books and materials essential for learning. This would help to create a consistent quality within the urban labor force that would permit better marketing of the city and suburbs to industry.

The second area that city development strategies can affect is the level of public services and infrastructure. A high-quality public service system (police, fire, and refuse collection) can help reduce costs to a firm. A secure environment will help lower insurance costs while reducing the need for a firm to supply its own security. People will want to work where they feel safer and more secure. In the area of infrastructure, a good system of transportation (roads, highways, intercity and intracity public transit) is essential to attracting and retaining businesses.

Although cities cannot change their natural surroundings, they can provide opportunities to utilize natural amenities such as marinas, ski slopes, parks, golf courses, and other recreational areas that capitalize on natural assets. Cities can also support cultural programs, such as museums, theaters, libraries, and playgrounds. There is a growing desire on the part of the workers in the 21st century to live in a place that provides a good quality of life. There is also speculation that firms will seek to locate where skilled workers are, while previously workers moved to sources of employment.

Special Entity Policies and Districts

Many urban regions have quasi-governmental entities that coordinate public services and planning. The boundaries of these entities exceed those of central cities and may exceed the central county, including much of the region, whether defined by the federal identifiers (e.g., Metropolitan or Micropolitan), state identifiers (e.g., economic or planning districts), or through self-defined regions. These agencies deal with regional planning, transportation, sewers, and other public works. When these agencies plan service changes, they may affect other services and amenities that each municipality offers. These decisions often make one city appear more favorable than another.

In addition to entities that exceed municipal boundaries, most cities have public-private partnerships that provide support at the neighborhood level. These agencies, usually in the form of community development corporations (CDCs), have some public and some private funding and address issues that are applicable to neighborhoods of the city. While many CDCs initially started out as economic development agencies providing job training and facilities, they have also traditionally been involved in housing issues. Some have recently entered into environmental and recycling services. Most of these agencies are tied to traditional neighborhoods and are often associated with specific boundaries such as census blocks.

With CDCs and LDCs also comes the potential for special taxing districts. These districts may levy a tax or a surcharge, or offer "zones" in which taxes are forgiven. In some cases, these taxes are directed at either retiring debt or funding specific functions. In the city of Cleveland, there is "bed" tax on hotels and motels that creates revenues, some of which are used to fund the Cleveland Convention and Visitors Bureau, as well as the Medical Mart and Convention Center. In Providence, the income and sales taxes generated by "writers, composers, and artists" is exempt within special areas as defined within the enabling legislation. In St. Louis, via a regional city and county district, the Zoo-Museum district is funded through a dedicated revenue stream from property taxes. In the same area, the Regional Arts Council is funded by taking a portion of each tax dollar collected through the hotel/motel or "bed" tax in both the city and county of St. Louis. Finally, in the Denver region, a sales and use tax of .01% that is collected across seven counties funds the Scientific and Cultural Facilities District and its more than 300 organizations.

Policy Implications

As noted elsewhere in this book, the early city was a "walking city," in which the area around the central city was mixed use, with administration, retail, manufacturing, and residences all in close proximity to each other. Innovations such as railroads, streetcars, and most important the automobile and the highway system, permitted the city to begin to expand past the walking areas into the larger city. Fixed transit corridors, based on new rail and highway locations, permitted uneven development within the city. Uneven urban development occurred along spatial lines. Being on a corridor promoted earlier development. As distance from a corridor increased, so did time of development. Economic and ethnic factors exacerbated the problem through redlining and steering of minorities. In the post–World War II period, uneven development expanded into the suburbs due to the expansion of rail and highway corridors.

Economic development policies attempt to increase the number of jobs (growth) and to improve the quality of the type of jobs (development) in the urban region, with the ultimate goal of improving the local standard of living. In general, the standard of living for most urban *areas* has been improving. But when cities, and particularly central cities, are considered, increases in the standard of living have not kept pace with the rest of the urban region.

Policies that contribute to physical development usually favor development in the suburbs and exurbs. Most notably, highway construction has permitted easier access to areas that are increasingly distant from the central city. This has facilitated the decentralization (the movement from the city to the suburbs) of both employment and population. New and relocating firms are able to develop new facilities at lower costs in the suburbs than in the central cities. Similarly, many people want to take advantage of the more private space offered in the suburbs. Access to highways reduces the commute time and makes longer distance commutes more feasible. As the affluent and the middle class move to the suburbs and exurbs, coupled with the movement of retail and wholesale trade and manufacturing, the city tax base is severely impacted. It is important to note that while some firms are relatively mobile, others are tied to a location due to rail or water access, proximity to raw materials and suppliers, and nearness to markets and other city amenities and linkages.

The attraction and retention policies of many suburbs, most notably tax abatements, have forced central cities to offer similar inducements to retain existing firms and to attract new firms. As most large urban areas have large infrastructures in place, decreasing revenues due to the migration of population and business make it difficult to afford its maintenance. When cities must give up revenues to keep their employment base, some services must be affected. In most states, school districts are funded by property taxes. Tax abatements generally reduce property taxes. The use of abatements reduces revenues to the schools, which given the migration of population and jobs, are already under fiscal stress. When school districts are under fiscal stress, not only are progressive programs such as computer labs and advanced science and mathematics courses eliminated, but the basics of education, such as teaching materials, sufficient staff, and building maintenance may be unavailable. Cities need to have the best-prepared labor force available; the low-skilled, high-wage jobs for which people migrated to the cities are no longer available. These types of jobs have moved out of the city, in many cases to rural and southern locations or to other countries. These sites often offer highly productive workers lower wages. If regions are to compete globally, they must develop *all* of the labor force, including those that are from the disadvantaged urban core. While it is clear that some urban areas need to pursue a strategy geared to growth while others pursue a strategy for development, all urban areas need to focus on *even* development of the future labor force.

Research by Bingham and Kimble (1994) indicates that the central city remains viable, and that high-paying jobs continue to be available downtown. The problem remains that high wages are tied to high skills, and many central city schools lack funding to compete in the future labor market.

There has been a trend toward the "regionalization" of economic development strategies. Firms for the most part are locating in a region because it provides advantages over other locations. The use of financial incentives merely shifts the location of the firm within the region; they do not attract business that might have located in another region. The intraregional competition merely depletes resources of cities, to the detriment of the region, while benefiting only the firm.

Cities that attract firms are not the sole beneficiaries; people commute and purchase goods and services across municipal boundaries, with many cities in the region benefiting from new growth and development. Similarly, a regionally good system of education can help employers attain high productivity and make the region, both urban and suburban, attractive to firms.

Name _____

CHAPTER 10
The City Grows (Economic Development)

10-1. Describe some of the industries that resulted from steel production.

10-2a. What is meant by the realignment of U.S. manufacturing "from the core to the periphery, or the snowbelt to the sunbelt"?

10-2b. Give specific examples of industries that have been realigned.

10-3a. What economic development policies are used in your city (e.g., tax abatement)?

10-3b. List five projects for which these policies have been used.

10-4. List the suburbs that border your central city and categorize them according to population size.

Suburb   Population

The City Sustains Itself

(Environmental Studies)

Sanda Kaufman

Looking at cities can give a special pleasure, however commonplace the sight may be. Like a piece of architecture, the city is a construction in space, but one of vast scale, a thing perceived only in the course of long spans of time. ... On different occasions and for different people, the sequences are reversed, interrupted, abandoned, cut across. It is seen in all lights and weathers. ... Every citizen has had long associations with some part of [the] city, and [the] image is soaked in memories and meanings.

Kevin Lynch, The Image of the City, 1960

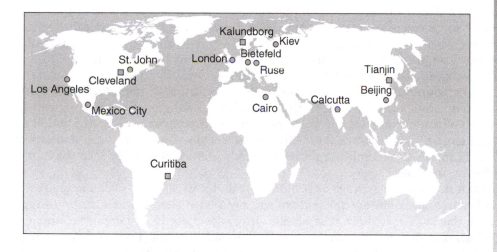

What do the cities of St. John, London, Mexico City, Bielefeld, Ruse, Cairo, Kiev, Calcutta, and Beijing have in common? It is certainly not geographic location: this list of cities spans continents. Neither is it size, culture, religion, history, economic system, degree of industrialization or level of resources: these cities are more different than alike along all their dimensions. Rather, these cities have all been at the brink (and some still are): their environmental degradation has reached near-disastrous levels during the past 30 years. But where there is understanding of the problems and the will to change, there is hope for the future of cities, and people in some of these cities have taken action to sustain them.

The Brazilian city of Curitiba is an early example of the quest for urban sustainability. It tackled its problems through a creative mix of measures including a transportation solution. Other cities around the world are also attempting to devise and implement ways of protecting residents' quality of life. For example, Denmark's Kalundborg has implemented "industrial symbiosis." Cleveland's EcoVillage has engaged in green building. China's Tianjin Eco-City has restored contaminated land and transformed it into a model for sustainable urban living. We learn from these cities that to sustain and enhance urban quality of life there is a need to act, and that there are no universal recipes; rather, each city needs to devise its own ways that take advantage of, and respond to, local conditions.

Air, water, and land problems plague cities, threatening their citizens' health and well-being in ways that challenge technology, stress resources, and strain community relations. The first section of this chapter outlines the nature of urban assets and related environmental problems. The second part identifies some characteristics of these problems that make them difficult, resistant to solutions, and even intractable at times; it discusses obstacles to the remediation of current critical environmental issues. The last part presents some of the ideas proposed by researchers and implemented by professionals to bring cities back from the brink, and to prevent them from reaching that point again.

The Urban Environment

During the 1990s, demographic forecasts placed more than half of the world's population in cities at the dawn of the 21st century (Hiss, 1992; Palen, 1992). According to the United Nations World Urbanization Prospects (2009 Revision), these forecasts came true during the first decade: more than 50% of people now live in urban areas. Recent predictions have about 69% of the world population in cities by 2050 (estimates vary depending on the boundaries considered when the midyear population of areas defined as urban in each country is reported to the United Nations). To gauge the exploding speed of growth of the urban share of world population, compare the 69% prediction to the recent and more distant past: in 2005 49% of the world's population (approximately 3.2 billion) lived in cities; in 1950 the figure was only 30%; and in 1900 less than 14% of the world lived in cities!

Urbanization, the process whereby people came to live in cities, has been long-drawn in history. It began approximately 6,000 years ago, proceeded slowly, and sometimes registered great setbacks. These days, it is accelerating especially in developing countries, and is at its fastest in Asia and Africa. Its pace is slowest in Europe, because it is already highly urbanized. In 2000, 411 cities exceeded one million, housing 39% of the world, compared with only 288 such cities in 1990. In the United States, 82% of the population lived in cities, with about 8% in nine cities with more than 1 million inhabitants by 2010.

Population growth (and the rate at which it urbanizes around the world) is rapid. A city of 5 million—8 in the world in 1950, 41 in 2000—was considered a "megacity." Only 10 years later, to be a member of the megacity club requires a population exceeding 10 million. There were 26 such cities by 2011. Tokyo, Japan, Guangzhou, China, and Seoul, South Korea, top the world list with populations surpassing 25 million. In comparison, New York is in eighth place with about 22 million. In 1950, at 12 million, New York had been the largest city in the world. Having attained 16 million by 2000, it was the largest city only in the United States, and had fallen to third place in the world.

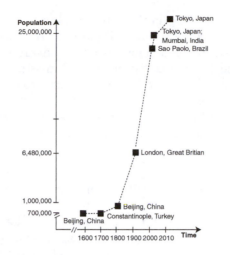

Figure 11.1
Largest cities in the world in time.

Megacities are a rather recent phenomenon. For most of the past 6,000 years, cities remained relatively small, and the scale of their physical problems kept them more or less manageable. During the 20th century, however, the confluence of rapidly growing populations (see Figure 11.1), advances in transportation and communication technologies, political changes in the world's balance of power, and the globalization of economies—as well as the cumulative effect of centuries of unwise practices—have placed the world's cities in physical jeopardy (Briscoe, 1993). Daily environmental challenges, from large-scale and daunting to small, accompany citizens of all ages in all walks of life. The cities of the 21st century are reaping the environmental problems sown by the unwise, unsustainable practices of the 20th century. They are also acting to stave them off.

A city is essentially the **physical environment** in which human activities take place. The urban environment comprises natural and built structures with the spaces surrounding them, as well as the natural and artificial processes that interact with space, structures, and living entities. City residents experience the interactions as recreation and lively entertainment opportunities, roads to work, drinking water supplied to their houses, breathing air, and interesting and sorry sights.

Together, the components of the urban environment account for the **quality of life** in cities. Although this concept eludes precise definition, people have a keen sense of which cities offer a good quality of life, and which do not. This sense, however, draws on perceptions that do not necessarily correspond to the physical reality, and on memories that are not always accurate. Pittsburgh, Pennsylvania, had its image marred by heavy air pollution from the steel industry long after the last steel mill had ceased to operate and many of its buildings had been scrubbed clean. Similarly, Cleveland, Ohio, has been unable to erase from the collective American memory an incident in 1969, when the polluted Cuyahoga River that passes through its downtown caught on fire (Opheim, 1993). Jacksonville, Florida, appeared for a long while unable to capitalize on seemingly ideal tourist amenities such as sandy beaches, historic sites, and a mild climate because of its reputation as "the city that smells bad" (Mehta & Manning, 1988). On the other hand, *Money* magazine ranked Sioux Falls, North Dakota, as the "best place to live in the US" in 1992, despite its apparent disregard for the environment at the time (Ford, 1993). By 2009, the city had dropped to 45th in the same ranking—perhaps because of increased public awareness of the contribution of the environment to the city's quality of life—but was back in the top 10, this time for number of foreclosures.

The environmental aspects described below illustrate the **scale** and **interrelatedness** of urban activities and outcomes and their connection to quality of life in cities.

Urban Physical Structures

The stock of **physical structures** constitutes an incremental story of a city's life: some paragraphs can be erased, but most make a long-term statement because each component constrains at least for a while the location and features of the facilities that follow it. So cities tell stories. A city that looks younger than its age because of frequent and extensive facelifts suggests little public value was set on its history, with its spatial wrinkles that link people to their past and contribute to their sense of belonging. Vacant lots used to tell of a lack of resources or resolve to utilize spaces deserted by vigorous suburbanization (Jackle & Wilson, 1993) or by **sprawl** into the cities' hinterland. More recently, vacant lots have been telling the story of a foreclosure epidemic that accompanied the economic crisis of 2008. The absence or disrepair of sidewalks not only speaks of insensitivity to pedestrians (London, 1991), but also reflects an urban culture that views cities as collections of activity nodes to be reached by cars as quickly as possible, at great expenditure of energy and with negative consequences for human health. Visible structural blight and rusty cars may indicate atmospheric acidity probably due to air pollution. **Brownfields** that dot the urban landscape are the legacy of industrial contamination of sites, to the point where they cannot be safely reused except with cleanup efforts requiring large investments, rare to come by especially during economically difficult times.

Notions of what is beautiful, interesting, convenient, or worthy of preservation in a city change with time. However, urbanites seem consistent in their preference for varied cityscapes, for accessible, safe facilities, and for mixed uses that bring housing in close proximity to shopping and entertainment opportunities. The sense of history preserved in older structures put to new uses adds a time dimension to space. The identity and variety of urban places is enhanced by use of local construction materials and urban design that acknowledges the climate and the underlying natural landscape configuration with its salient features (Register, 1992). For example, the buildings in Cleveland's Flats area along the Cuyahoga River let in (through orientation and design of openings) the river, its activities, and its intricate network of bridges. In contrast, Cleveland's downtown is much the poorer for having been configured in ways that obscure the important presence of Lake Erie at its edge. Cities that ignore their natural assets, or whose natural and built environments have deteriorated from neglect and pollution, lose a valuable contributor to their quality and find that restoration is costlier to their image and reality than ongoing maintenance and prevention of damage.

Regulatory devices act mostly indirectly on the quality and aesthetics of the built urban environment, which is largely the result of numerous, mostly private, often independent, decisions. At times, however, such decisions do respond to public opinion and to financial incentives created by public investment (e.g., through infrastructure or tax abatements). Therefore, an active, informed public can affect its environment, protect its history, and demand quality in design.

What are some of the cities' environmental assets, besides physical structures, that can contribute to quality of life and are therefore worth protecting and enhancing through policies, design, and wise use?

Urban Outdoors

Air is sometimes visible, can be smelled, and even felt! When that happens, it signals an extreme level of air pollution, called **smog**, that plagues cities around the world from Los Angeles to Milan, Italy, to London, England, Sao Paolo, Brazil, and to Beijing, China. The latter had to take drastic measures to mitigate the intense air pollution in order to host the 2008 Summer Olympics. In 2012, the first time in China's history, the number of people living in cities exceeded the number of rural dwellers. The poor air quality has forced repeated airport closures for lack of visibility. It has also caused unrest among citizens (Jackson, 2012). Even when invisible, air pollution threatens the health of residents, especially the vulnerable among them—the very young, the aged, and the sick.

The numerous urban air pollutants from point sources such as industrial smokestacks, area sources such as landfills and construction sites, and moving sources such as motor vehicles (see Figure 11.2) are quite difficult to identify, monitor, and control (EPA, 2011). A *National Geographic* article (Grove, 1987) reported that about 65,000 chemical compounds had entered the environment since 1950, of which only very few had been listed as hazardous; by 1995, 7,000 more had been added, with only limited testing of effects on humans and on the environment (Pope et al., 1995). Industrial processes contribute particulates of various sizes and compositions, sulfur dioxide (SO_2), and ground-level ozone (O_3), which impair the human respiratory system. Cars and trucks produce carbon monoxide (CO), nitrogen dioxide (NO_2), and lead, also noxious to humans. Some of the air-borne pollutants including particulate material (PM) damage physical structures and their appearance, and affect the health of plants and animals.

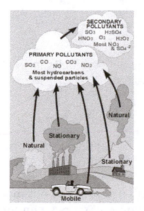

Figure 11.2
Sources of air pollution.
Source: EPA http://www.epa.gov/apti/course422/ap3.html

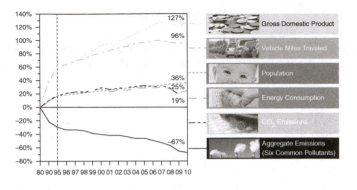

Figure 11.3

Some bad news and some good news

Comparison of growth areas and emissions, 1980–2010.

Note: CO_2 emissions estimate through 2009 (Source: 2011 US Greenhouse Gas Inventory Report)

Gross Domestic Product: Bureau of Economic Analysis

Vehicle Miles Traveled: Federal Highway Administration

Population: Census Bureau

Energy Consumption: Dept. of Energy, Energy Information Administration

Aggregate Emissions: EPA Clearinghouse for Inventories and Emissions Factors

Source: US Environmental Protection Agency: http://www.epa.gov/airtrends/aqtrends.html

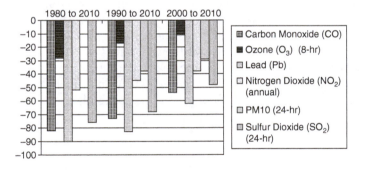

Figure 11.4

Comparison of emissions of six principal pollutants in the United States.

Source: US Environmental Protection Agency

   The Clean Air Act of 1970 and the application of the Environmental Protection Agency's National Ambient Air Quality Standards (NAAQS) have contributed considerably to the reduction of urban air pollution levels (see Figures 11.3 and 11.4).

   However, many Americans still live in areas not meeting air quality standards. Large cities still experience yearly a number of days when vulnerable residents are advised to remain indoors to avoid breathing heavily polluted air. Addressing air quality requires adequate monitoring and enforcement of regulations with respect to industrial facilities, transportation planning, gasoline formulations tailored to local conditions, as well as a

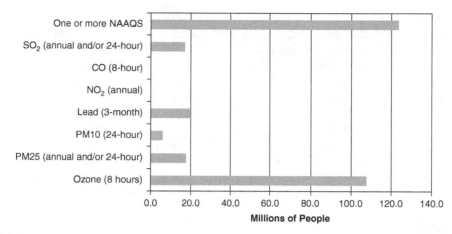

Figure 11.5

Number of people in counties with air quality concentrations above the National Ambient Air Quality Standards (NAAQS) level in 2010.

Multiple years of data are generally used to determine if an area attains the NAAQS.
The chart above is for 1 year only.

Source: U.S. Census Bureau, Population Division http://www.census.gov/popest/counties/asrh/CC-EST2009-agesex.html

host of voluntary measures that can address problems out of the regulatory reach. For example, natural gas- or electricity-powered buses, and manually or electrically powered lawn mowers instead of gas-powered ones can make a surprisingly large contribution to the reduction of urban air pollution. Transit authorities can make a difference through their choice of which public transportation vehicles they purchase, while individual city residents can benefit the environment through their choice and frequency of use of lawn mowers.

The **open spaces** of cities are key contributors to overall quality of life. Tempting to developers in times of high demand for housing and services, they are among the first casualties of crowding, which in turn correlates with residential dissatisfaction (e.g., Hur et al., 2009). Not all open spaces are desirable: vacant lots detract from a city's appearance and do not support the kinds of uses, such as recreation, which city residents associate with a good quality of life.

Which open spaces are valuable? Parks of all sizes improve the cityscape. The large ones enable residents to commune with nature through a variety of activities, while the small parks breaking the dense urban fabric accommodate a few people on a lunch break or offer a brief rest in a quiet city nook.

Small open urban spaces have fallen victim to an urban deforestation trend stemming from the pressure to build, and a decline in planting and maintenance that are among the first on any list of budget cuts in fiscally difficult times. The larger parks also have enemies: suburbanization has led to urban sprawl—built areas creeping farther and farther away from city centers—encroaching on formerly open spaces and parks and straining urban water resources. For instance, to accommodate its fast growth, its 1.9 million residents (2010) and its more than 35 million yearly visitors, Las Vegas, Nevada, has put destructive pressure on water resources, threatening the surrounding Mojave Desert which in turn will eventually affect tourism negatively. These effects are expected to be exacerbated by climate change (Report of the National Conference of State Legislatures, 2008).

Waterfronts are highly valuable urban open spaces. Even when underdeveloped they tend to hold a fascination deriving from the intersection of land and water, rich both visually and symbolically. Many American cities, however, have neglected their unique waterfront assets or let them become privatized or used for industrial purposes that could have been accommodated elsewhere. Cities have allowed raw sewage and runoff to pollute waterways, further reducing the potential of waterfronts. Such neglect is unwise in several ways: it foregoes opportunities for recreation and economic activities that can benefit city residents; and, when awareness finally leads to waterfront reclamation, the costs of cleanup are sometimes prohibitive.

Urban Indoors

In many cities, homes offer comforting shelter and threaten human health at the same time, in rather invisible and therefore treacherous ways. Lead, part of the homes' structures, and radon, embedded in their soil, are relatively common, hidden, and dangerous household contaminants.

Lead is ubiquitous in older, residential water pipes and paint. The insidious poison, which impairs the physical and mental development of children, affects city residents differentially. The Environmental Protection Agency (EPA) estimates that the number of American children with elevated-blood-lead levels has been steadily declining (see Figure 11.6). Nevertheless, poor, often minority, children in inner cities are at higher risk of lead poisoning than the general population, because they live in older, deteriorating structures whose peeling lead paint and lead-leeching pipes have not been replaced yet, as they have been in other areas.

Direct lead emissions in the air have been controlled by the gradual elimination from use of leaded gasoline. Despite other efforts, such as the EPA's project LEAP (Lead Education and Abatement Program), designed to prevent and abate home exposure in several states, lead remains a severe environmental hazard especially for urban children.

Radioactive radon, contamination of the soil around and under houses, is more evenly distributed throughout city areas than lead. Without specific tests, it cannot be detected and may cause its damage through long-term exposure. Unlike other urban pollutants, it tends to be considered a homeowner's problem. Therefore, its detection depends on residents' awareness; its elimination, which consists of removing from around and underneath homes the soil containing radon, requires financial expenses not always within reach of households.

Urban Service Systems

A city's **service systems** include transportation, waste management, and the provision of electricity, natural gas or oil for heating, and water. They all contribute to the quality of the urban environment. These systems have multiple, far-reaching effects on spaces, human health, aesthetics, and resources of cities. They involve complex technologies that are costly to implement, operate, and maintain. Partly because service systems are largely invisible until they malfunction, policy makers and managers faced with difficult choices about the allocation of limited resources tend to ignore problems until a crisis occurs.

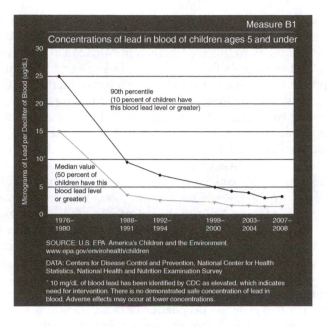

Figure 11.6
Concentrations of lead in the blood of children ages 5 and under.
Source: EPA http://www.epa.gov/ace/body_burdens/b1-graph.html

Then solutions are more difficult and expensive and some of the damage is irreversible. For example, a few incidents of widespread illness attributed to drinking water bacteria have focused attention on the quality of urban water supply, although the problem is not new. Similarly, hardly any public attention is devoted to waste disposal until a local land-fill closes down, forcing a city to hastily implement a recycling program. Until startlingly widespread and prolonged blackouts occurred throughout the country, causing inconvenience to residents and severe regional economic losses, there was little awareness of the need for (or willingness to upgrade the system of) grids delivering electricity to cities.

- **Transportation** of people, goods, and services pervades all aspects of urban life. The urban sprawl resulting from extensive, continuing American suburbanization has increased residents' commuting time and their reliance on cars (Wachs & Crawford, 1993). Trucks transporting goods to spread-out metropolitan areas travel longer, using energy from nonrenewable resources and contributing to air pollution and accidents on roads. A safe, efficient **public transportation** system can reduce the number of pollution-emitting vehicles on the roads. However, more than just a means of transportation, the automobile represents for Americans status, and symbolizes a desirable way of life. Public transportation systems have difficulty competing with its convenience and symbolism until a crisis is reached, such as the oil embargo in the early 1970s, the excessive commuting time in the Los Angeles area, or the dramatic rise in fuel prices in response to periodic supply shortages and rising demand pressures from the developing world in the first decade of the 21st century. Education and environmental awareness as well as economic disincentives may bring about a change in lifestyles that will favor investment in urban public transportation. Other solutions involve rules restricting the times and places of access for motorists, as in Tokyo, Rome, and Mexico City, adding options such as bicycle lanes, and incentives for residents to live closer to, or within, cities.

- The **management of urban waste** faces some critical difficulties. One problem is that existing, conveniently located landfills are running out of space, which should not be surprising considering the staggering volume of waste Americans produce. Another problem is that new landfills are difficult to site, since no one wants them "in their back yard". Landfills and waste-processing facilities top the list of locally unwanted land uses (LULUs). On the other hand, siting such landfills at greater distances from cities adds considerable hauling costs which residents are reluctant to pay. Moreover, in the case of toxic waste, long-range conveyance increases the likelihood of accidents and the number of people potentially exposed to resulting toxic fumes. Therefore, landfill and waste-disposal facility operators prefer brown-field sites (existing, locally unwanted land uses, or (LULUs), already contaminated by some previous facility and likely already permitted for similar uses (Kaufman & Smith, 1999). Figure 11.7 indicates encouraging trends. Despite the constant rise in tonnage of municipal waste, the amount going to landfills has dropped over the past three decades, while a growing proportion of yearly waste is handled through other means, such as recovery, and combustion with or without recovery. It is becoming necessary, however, to also reduce waste creation through judicious product and packaging designs, and through "cradle-to-grave" product design, whereby thought is given to minimizing waste during their production, use, and disposal. Cradle-to-cradle design goes even further, making it possible for obsolete products to be reused, either in energy generation or as recycled ingredients in other products.

- American society is heavily dependent on **electricity** in all aspects of daily life. Coal- and oil-burning power plants use fuels whose supply is limited and whose burning pollutes the air (through emissions), the soil (through accidental spills and disposal of by-products), and the water (through spills, leaks, and discharges of coolant at elevated temperatures that damage aquatic life). Besides, coal mining is a high-risk occupation, and it tends to leave its landscape scarred. Hydroelectric power plants, a cleaner means of electricity production, require the damming of rivers, which alters and even destroys natural ecosystems. Although nuclear power plants pose small risks of accidents, these can be devastating, affecting the health of large numbers of people and condemning large swaths of land for a long time. A vivid example of the scale and severity of such consequences is the 2011 earthquake and tsunami-triggered meltdown at the Fukushima Daiichi nuclear power plant in Japan (Makhijani, 2011). Moreover, a safe, permanent repository for spent fuel that remains radioactive for many generations has not yet been implemented, largely for NIMBY ("not in my back yard") reasons. Alternative, cleaner, and safer sources of electrical energy, such as **eolian plants** (using the wind's energy) and **solar cells**, are still struggling to compete economically with more traditional sources, though as oil prices increase they look increasingly attractive. Until the next generation of energy technologies is implemented, considerable and irreversible environmental damage will continue to occur unless city dwellers alter their lifestyles.

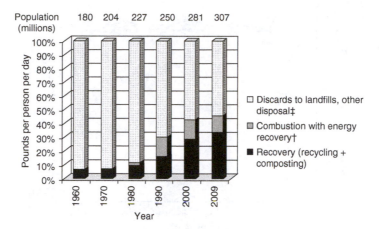

Figure 11.7
Waste materials recovery, composting, combustion with energy recovery, and discards of MSW, 1960 to 2009 (in % of total pounds per person per day generated).
Note: the population has steadily increased between 1060 and 2009, so the percentages in each category are computed from correspondingly increasing amounts in each category.
†Includes combustion of MSW in mass burn or refuse-derived fuel form, and combustion with energy recovery of source separated materials in MSW (e.g., wood pallets, tire-derived fuel).
‡ Discards after recovery minus combustion with energy recovery. Discards include combustion without energy recovery.
= Details might not add to totals due to rounding.
Source: EPA, Municipal Solid Waste in the United States: 2009 Facts and Figures. http://www.epa.gov/osw/nonhaz/municipal/pubs/msw2009-fs.pdf

- The goal of a clean **drinking water** supply for all cities has yet to be reached, despite the increasing number of regulations designed to ensure it. The drinking water of American cities used to be sometimes so inadequate that it threatened human health. By 2008, however, according to an EPA report, the drinking water quality had drastically improved, even if some problems persist (for example, in EPA region 2; see Figure 11.8). The chemicals contained in the drinking water may harm through direct use of the water, and indirectly through the food chain they penetrate, extending the damage in scale and time. Urban water supply illustrates well how remedies for one problem can cause another. For example, the chlorine used to control some contaminants poses dangers of its own, through the toxic compounds it forms in the steam people inhale when taking showers.

Bacteria and some suspension particles are amenable to purification processes widely used in urban water systems. However, some water contaminants such as heavy metals and other toxic substances cannot be removed through traditional processing once they have penetrated the water supply system. For example, poor maintenance increases urban stormwater overflow that can be heavily contaminated, sometimes by activities designed to control other urban problems (Dombrowski, 1987). The salt used to de-ice roads in winter and pesticides applied for lawn care are carried by storm water, damaging rivers and lakes, or seeping into underground water that feeds drinking reservoirs.

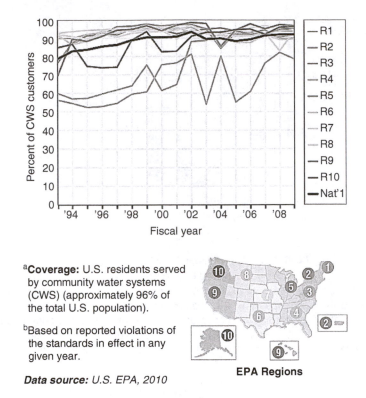

a**Coverage:** U.S. residents served by community water systems (CWS) (approximately 96% of the total U.S. population).

b Based on reported violations of the standards in effect in any given year.

Data source: U.S. EPA, 2010

EPA Regions

Figure 11.8
US population served by community water systems with no reported violations of EPA health-based standards, by EPA region, 1993–2009.[a, b]

Drinking water is vulnerable to so many sources of contamination, and requires delivery systems so timely maintained that it is not surprising to find some urban areas still failing to meet standards. While the costs of water delivery increase steadily, the willingness of urban residents to pay for this service has not kept up with needs. Awareness of difficulties is low because, with the exception of extreme cases where deficient water quality is reflected in odors, poor taste, or coloring, water *appears* adequate. Therefore, any rate increase is perceived as burdensome and meets with great public opposition, further impairing the ability of service providers to meet standards. The cost of implementing newer, more effective technologies places them out of reach of many cities.

Drinking water supply problems differ from region to region. Arid parts of the country experience fierce competition for water among agricultural, industrial, and residential uses. Cities like Denver, Colorado, face special dilemmas around drinking water supply. Growing populations, urban sprawl, and lifestyle choices such as maintaining pretty grass lawns have increased demand for treated water, which further strains facilities and supplies, especially in drought years. Solutions to this problem require public awareness, lifestyle changes, and policies that might be very unpopular especially at the outset. In areas experiencing no water shortage, such as the Great Lakes, industrial and agricultural pollution—direct, air-borne, or seeping through soil—threatens the source of drinking water for large numbers of city residents. Illegal dumping of toxic substances makes matters worse. Remedies are very costly and city dwellers are unaware of the full extent of problems; the costs of mitigation make them very reluctant to accept the necessary service rate increases.

Overall, absent a crisis, problems of service systems that protect the quality of urban environments tend to be invisible to the general public (Koines, 1988). The horizon of politicians positioned to make infrastructure decisions is limited by their time in office, which typically spans two to four years. Politicians are therefore rarely eager to devote resources to areas in which the political benefits will be reaped, at best, by their successors.

Global Urban Issues

The list of urban environmental woes is not complete without mention of **global problems** that have **local effects**, as well as local decisions whose impact can be felt at great distances.

At global levels, the same interrelatedness of human activities with their environment obtains, adding a layer of difficulty to predictions and solutions (Weiner, 1990). For instance, **transfrontier pollution** results from toxics emitted at one location and carried through air or water to another location that did not contribute to the production of the pollutants, did not reap any economical benefits from it, and can do little to stop it. Exponential population growth in some regions of the globe also has transfrontier impacts. It affects not only those regions but also the many other locations to which people migrate in search of employment and shelter, straining local resources and the ability to protect quality of life. The ozone hole and the global climate change phenomena are the cumulative global consequences of numerous individual and public choices around the world. They pit against each other countries that differ in priorities and level of resources. Following are several other examples of global interdependence that impacts urban environments.

- As a result of industrial activities in the northern United States, air pollutants travel to Canada, where they afflict urban areas in the form of **acid rain** that damages vegetation and the structure and appearance of buildings.
- Radioactive fallout from the Chernobyl nuclear accident in the Ukraine found its way to urban areas in northwest England (Allot, 1992). Some of the possibly contaminated debris from the Fukushima Daiichi nuclear accident in Japan has reached the western shores of the United States (OurAmazingPlanet 2011, Subramanian, 2011).
- The fires that burned Kuwait's oil wells during the Persian Gulf War of 1990 spread air pollutants throughout the Gulf countries.
- The Danube River, which crosses several European countries, collects and carries sewage and industrial waste through their cities. By the time it reaches the Bulgarian town of Ruse, the Danube visits upon it an accumulation of nearly intractable problems, despite Romania's and Bulgaria's mitigation efforts (Engelbrekt, 1992).
- Countries surrounding the Mediterranean Sea share it for better and worse: they enjoy scenic beaches and the tourism revenues they provide, but continue to discharge into it with little restraint industrial and household waste. One country's waste washes off on the other's beaches, and all suffer from the slow depletion of

this wondrous natural resource. These problems are compounded by past neglect, a dearth of resources, lack of control over the producers of contamination, and lack of cooperation stemming from a long history of enmity among some of the countries. This example illustrates the **"tragedy of the commons"** (Hardin, 1968). Each country chooses to profit as much as possible from the shared resource (or commons), lest others take more advantage of it, with the net result that all lose from the eventual exhaustion of this valued resource.

- The Rio Grande transfers pollution to cities in the United States from industrial facilities in Mexico, some of which are owned by American companies that moved production across the border to avoid the costs of compliance with American environmental regulations. The toxic water is suspected to have caused severe health problems, such as a higher-than-normal incidence of anencephalic newborns (who suffer from the congenital absence of part or all of the brain).

- The **hole in the ozone layer** of the Earth's atmosphere has been blamed for failure to screen ultraviolet sun radiation, which continues to cause a worldwide rise in the incidence of skin cancer. The hole, looming over Antarctica, has been produced by the presence in the air of substances such as **chlorofluorocarbons** (CFCs), used in the past refrigeration and air-conditioning units as well as in aerosol cans of hair spray or deodorants. Activities that released chlorofluorocarbons used to occur mostly in developed countries, which have made great efforts to discontinue aerosol products and devise new technologies for refrigeration. The resolve of any single country barely affects the rate of ozone depletion it is trying to stem. International agreements were needed to make a difference, but they are extremely complex, and grind slower than the increase in the size of the ozone hole. Successful negotiation of international agreements has stemmed its growth. That it still has negative health consequences illustrates the fact that it takes time both to inflict damage on global natural assets and to heal them. Therefore, by the time we notice the damage, it is sometimes too late to mitigate it; as well, we should not expect quick results of mitigation efforts, lest we give up before they materialize.

- Similar issues arise around **global climate change**. Few scientists still dispute that it is a real trend, rather than a periodic fluctuation in climatic patterns, and that it is caused by carbon dioxide–producing human activities. If that is indeed the case, a global effort is needed to curtail production of carbon dioxide. The Western world is capable and willing to change technologies, and is already working on alternatives. Some innovative remedies have been implemented, including hybrid vehicles that reduce the amount of direct burning of fossil fuels. Less developed countries have the option of taking a turn using the old fossil-fueled technologies the Western world has enjoyed for a long while, with potentially catastrophic global results. An alternative Third World countries consider inequitable is to forego the turn, which may mean a longer wait for comforts the Western world would continue to afford. Another alternative is for these countries to skip a stage and implement from the start a next generation of less polluting technologies.

Third World and some formerly Eastern Block countries lack resources, and their publics and political systems may not prioritize the consequences of urban environmental degradation over economic development (Jorgenson, 1992). For example, some East Asian cities (Bruestle, 1993) and cities of formerly communist (Eastern Block) countries

(Engelbrekt, 1992; Peterson, 1993; Zimmerman, 1990) contend with air pollution and lack of sanitation that bring illness and even death to large numbers of exposed city dwellers. By contrast, the United States is in a unique position among nations contending with urban environmental problems: it has a relatively higher level of economic resources to devote to environmental remediation than many other countries. It has also mustered, on occasion, the political will needed to allocate resources to urban environmental concerns. Most importantly, it may be able to benefit economically from the development and sale of new materials and products that are less damaging or outright environmentally friendly. The promise of economic development fueled by demand for environmentally sustainable products is an important incentive for change.

We have argued that the natural and built environment of cities matters, and we have reviewed some ways in which urban environments are threatened by local, regional, and even global activities and decisions. We ask next why containing and preventing environmental damage and enhancing urban quality of life are difficult, even when people value their environment.

The Nature of Urban Environmental Problems

Why are urban environmental problems so challenging? Solving these problems requires information—understanding phenomena and being able to predict consequences of intervention—and the ability to make collective decisions to intervene, with possibly extensive consequences for the lifestyles of individual residents of cities. This section discusses several aspects of environmental problems that make them "wicked" (Churchman, 1967) and resistant to resolution. They include the complexity of intertwined environmental issues, due to scale and the potential irreversibility of some consequences as well as their uncertainty, and the high costs of remediation of environmental damage. We also discuss some characteristics of individual and collective decision processes that render environmental policies difficult to formulate and implement.

Environmental Complexity and Interrelatedness

One reason why urban environmental problems appear daunting is that most phenomena and processes that affect the environmental quality of cities are *interrelated*, hampering people's ability to understand and predict them (Kaufman, 2011). While net gains in the environmental protection of cities can rarely be achieved, net losses accrue continuously from lack of resolve and action to change the status quo. Progress in one area often comes at the expense of another, requiring painful tradeoffs that cause decision impasses (Susskind & Cruikshank, 1987).

The problems posed by urban waste management illustrate well some of these difficulties. Advocates of reusable cloth diapers hoped to reduce the vast amount of nondegradable plastic and slowly degradable paper overwhelming urban landfills. However, reusable diapers also affect the environment, albeit indirectly. The energy used to power the washing machines that wash cloth diapers is produced from oil and coal, both nonrenewable resources. Until they were reformulated, laundry detergents had high phosphorus content. Sewage laden with phosphorus promoted excessive algae growth in lakes, "suffocating" them and reducing the biodiversity of their aquatic habitats.

This example is not to suggest that waste management practices should not be scrutinized. Cities ignore at their peril recycling options and other measures to reduce the volume of waste generated by their residents. Rather, it speaks to the need for making our choices as informed as possible, even if perfect information is not possible. Good stewardship of public resources means applying them where they can make a real and positive difference. This was not the case in the diaper example, although people renouncing the convenience of disposable diapers felt they were contributing to environmental protection. Such strategies should, however, be based on a fuller accounting of costs and benefits over the entire life cycle of products, rather than on a visible but narrow segment of it.

Phenomena involving the natural and built environments and their interactions tend to be highly *complex*. Scientists do not yet understand them at levels enabling reliable prediction and intervention. So environmental issues and their linkages tend to be shrouded in **scientific uncertainty**. As a result, it is difficult to control the environmental consequences of various policies and decisions. Acting with imperfect information has its perils. Yet not taking actions until we can be certain is a recipe for disaster we can ill afford. Therefore, to make decisions that sustain the urban environment we need to ensure access to, and understanding of, the best available information and technologies, and then act cautiously without the expectation of eliminating all uncertainty.

Technology can help us reduce some of the risks involved in making decisions with imperfect information. Widely accessible computers and software offer sophisticated storage and handling of geographic data, and means for spatial modeling and visualization of consequences of some of our decisions in the urban space. For instance, Geographic Information Systems (GIS) consist of software to store, process, and display geographic data, whose characteristics include spatial location (see examples in Figure 11.9). GIS software has become indispensable in the management of urban service systems such as transportation, sewage, and the supply of electricity, gas and water.

Computational and display tools have increased scientists' ability to model environmental phenomena such as the path and longevity of pollutants in different media, and to communicate results to decision makers and communities. For example, data collected by instruments aboard space satellites have been used to track and then predict the behavior of the ozone hole above Antarctica; visualization software has contributed to public understanding of the scale of this phenomenon, and the public's cooperation with measures to reduce its progress. Modeling the trajectory of river deposits of pollutants has enabled the use of river cleanup strategies that target specific depths and locations; costly, large-scale dredging of riverbeds was avoided, freeing resources for other remedial initiatives. However, knowledge is still incomplete about numerous phenomena, impeding effective prevention and remediation actions. The cost of expertise and information sometimes places them out of the reach of users such as policy makers and community groups. So complexity slows down the accumulation of knowledge, and makes it more difficult and costly to impart this knowledge and apply it to solve environmental problems.

The **complexity** and **interrelatedness** of urban environmental phenomena tend to defeat partial or narrow solutions, which at times can even worsen the status quo. For example, solving the solid waste disposal problem by locating landfills at large distances from population centers to avoid contamination of soil and water takes the issue away from the public eye, but spreads the environmental damage over larger areas (eventually, there will be no sites sufficiently distant from cities), and increases hazards

Current Streamflow

Drought

Flood

Past Flow/Runoff

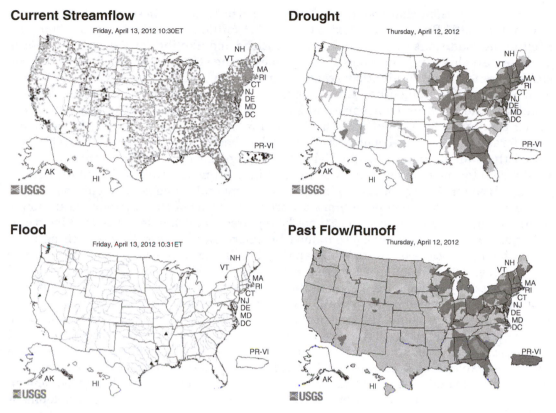

Figure 11.9
USGS maps of water issues in the United States.
Source: http://waterwatch.usgs.gov/

associated with the transportation of waste over long distances. Moreover, this partial solution disguises the costs of the current practices that are producing the waste. Instead, a comprehensive solution would reduce the volume of waste both in the production and consumption of goods whose packaging or by-products end up in landfills. But whereas the siting of a new landfill involves a rather small number of parties and decisions, the comprehensive solution that reduces the need for landfills involves considerable shifts in technology use and, more importantly, in lifestyles. The latter require the cooperation of many, and lengthy periods of time, as they involve multifaceted and costly efforts to educate consumers. An added obstacle is that benefits of such extensive efforts accrue slowly while public and political lack of patience and short attention spans demand quick results in order to justify sustaining the effort.

Scale matters in urban and environmental issues, first in terms of the problems and extent and severity of consequences, and then for the decision processes involved in solving the problems. Residents of both Mexico City, Mexico (Miller, 1993; Pearce, 1992), and Chelyabinsk, Russia (Peterson, 1993), face severe effects of prolonged exposure to air pollution. However, the difference in size between these two cities in terms of population (21.2 million in Mexico City vs. 1.1 million in Chelyabinsk in 2009) and geographic conditions suggests different solutions and likelihoods of success—*caeteris paribus* ("all else being the same")—which means the statement would hold if the two cities were identical in all other respects but size; in reality, Mexico City and Chelyabinsk also differ along other dimensions, adding further strength to this statement. Similarly, the creative transportation solutions that turned Curitiba, Brazil, into a model community (see next section: Pioneering Solutions) are unlikely to be easily transferable to Los Angeles or New York, as has been suggested (Dietsch, 1993). Nor would the Danish small town of Kalundborg, engaged in *industrial symbiosis,* be a good model for megacities such as Beijing, China, Mumbai, India, or Istanbul, Turkey.

The **irreversibility** of some kinds of environmental damage adds one more layer to the complexity of urban environmental problems. Some of the environmental components that have been harmed can at times be repaired. For example, some drinking water pollution can be filtered out or contained by chlorination. Water bodies such as Lake Erie, which came close to "death"—its capacity to self-purify and support normal aquatic life had been severely damaged by years of neglect and abuse—are being restored. Soil contaminated by leakage from a gas station storage tank can be completely dug up and replaced with clean soil; some types of soil contaminants can be eliminated using bacteria engineered to consume the noxious substances. However, cleanup efforts tend to be very costly, from diagnosis of the type and extent of contamination to solution design and implementation. Then, uncertainty about the success of cleanup efforts lingers. In some cases, the value of contaminated and neighboring properties decreases to the point of preventing sale and reuse of the land. Such properties, labeled **brownfields**, become an eyesore and impose a financial burden on their communities, preventing development and reducing tax revenues.

Other environmental consequences of human activities cannot be undone with current technology even at great expenditure of resources. Bodies of water have died, wetlands have dried up, some wildlife species have become extinct, and people have died from the consequences of exposure to toxics in all media.

Prolonged exposure of children to lead, for example, has irreversible health consequences. Currently, one in every eight American women can expect to contract breast cancer. Only about 12% of the approximately 227,000 new cases diagnosed each year in the United States are credited to hereditary factors (NCI-NIH, 2012). Environmental factors are suspected to account for the balance of the breast cancer epidemic, which contributes to making cancer the second leading cause of death (22%) among women. Health effects that stem from long-term exposure to risk, such as second-hand smoking, are irreversible even if at some point their causes are identified and eliminated.

The **uncertainty** of effects and the **irreversibility** of some damage, together with the high **cost of remediation**, have led to the realization that the best strategy for combating at least some urban environmental problems is to prevent the pollutants from entering the various media in the first place (Commoner, 1990). For example:

- Sorting and recycling waste might eliminate at least part of the need to solve landfill leakage problems.
- Eliminating lead from paints and gasoline obviates the need for medical treatment of exposed children, very likely with greater effects and at less cost.

- Treating sewage before release in water bodies is easier and more effective than after-the-fact cleanup.

Solutions to these and other problems involve a shift in responsibilities, costs and benefits, full-cost accounting, and cradle-to-grave design of products. Usually, communities bear the responsibility and the costs of various cleanup efforts while those whose activities produced the contamination reap economic benefits. In contrast, control of pollution at its source becomes the responsibility of the individuals whose activities produce pollutants, who should pay the costs containing contaminants before they damage the environment.

Theoretically, control of pollution at its source might appear to be an equitable arrangement, especially if the reader is not among producers and therefore can more easily identify with the community side. However, implementation of such strategies faces great obstacles. While in the long run producers shift some of the added production costs of their goods and services to consumers, they face considerable and unwelcome short-run expenses. These detrimental effects have increased with the globalization of economies that force environmentally responsible producers, and those subject to various regulations, to compete with others who do not face similar costs. Some have moved their product manufacturing to countries with less stringent or no environmental regulations. The effect of this flight is double-edged: it has left communities in the United States deprived of employment, while imposing environmental costs of production on their new host countries that often do not benefit from the manufactured products or the profits form their sale. In general, the remediation approach diffuses both costs and benefits of urban environmental quality; benefits are limited in scope (since some damage is irreversible), and tend to be very costly in the long run. The control-at-the-source strategy concentrates costs and diffuses benefits, but its results are far-reaching and less costly to all in the long run. Current short-run interests favor remediation approaches, but control at the source is gaining ground, sometimes because we are running out of options and resources. Both strategies are needed. Ideal remedies should be comprehensive, many-pronged, and sustained, making them costly in resources and political effort, and often disappointing in the short run.

Individual and Collective Decisions

The quality of urban environments is the outcome of numerous **individual** and **collective decisions**. Some are decisions whose consequences are detrimental to the environment. Others are deliberate decisions to protect, enhance, and sustain it.

Individuals make numerous choices about the urban environment that compound problems or contribute to their solution. When someone drives a car to work instead of car pooling or using public transportation, one more source of air pollution is active. Smog is the result of numerous such daily individual choices. When someone spends time carefully separating recyclable materials from waste, a small amount of solid waste is diverted from landfills to recovery. The sum of countless such efforts is reflected in the overall trend of Figure 11.10, showing that during the last decades there has been a slow (but meaningful) drop in the proportion of total municipal waste still sent to landfills.

What influences individual and collective decisions to respond to urban environmental challenges? Individual decisions reflect attitudes toward the environment, as well as perceptions of options, consequences and their likelihood, and perceptions of the future (Kaufman, 2011). Environmental attitudes (see Figure 11.10) emerge from the cognitive combinations of: factual as well as processed information (e.g., from the media, peer group, or community); personal priorities and preferences over outcomes (in economic, political, aesthetic, or cultural terms); and values (e.g., rooted in moral, ethical, or religious tenets). These individual combinations interact with their context, where current political, economic, and social conditions combine to make specific issues more or less salient to the public.

Individual differences in risk perceptions are at least partly the root of these attitudes toward the environment. The notion of risk combines the probability with the extent of negative consequences from decisions. It is at times rather difficult to factor in decisions. For instance, the degree of familiarity with certain substances affects individuals' perception of the risk they pose to health. Gasoline, highly toxic, exemplifies how familiarity breeds tolerance: people filling their car tanks are mostly unconcerned about inhaling its fumes or about an occasional spill when filling.

The past few decades have seen decreasing tolerance for any risk from activities over which individuals have no direct control. Thus, although the risk of accidents is relatively high, people drive cars because they feel in control. In contrast, people demand risk-free urban products and services, although risk cannot be completely eliminated from certain activities even at very high costs. Parcels of urban land become brownfield even after extensive cleanup, because no one will invest in them unless certain that all risks have been eliminated forever, which is nearly impossible to do or verify.

Occasional outbreaks of scares that occupy public attention for a while and then vanish from open debate have induced a dose of cynicism in the general public. The health

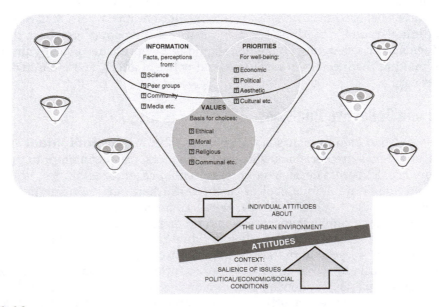

Figure 11.10
Components of Individual Attitudes Toward Urban Environmental Issues.

effects of closeness to power lines, alar on apples, bacteria in the drinking water, or dyes in foods and cosmetics have all had their brief moment at the center of public attention. Although at least some continue to warrant investigation and caution, public awareness often subsides as soon as the media deserts the issues. It is not surprising, therefore, to find that attitudes about urban environmental problems are prone to media and political manipulation (Layzer, 2006). Whatever individuals' preferences, knowledge, and attitudes toward risk, the environment has yet to become a routine component of their evaluations of the urban quality of life. Informed individual awareness of qualities and risks is a key ingredient of sound collective decisions.

No authority, public or private, is able to scrutinize each decision and monitor intentions. How, then, can the net outcome of all decisions be favorable to the environment? Are there ways to ensure this happens? The answers to these questions hinge as much on reality as on individual perceptions and collective resolve. Since the urban environment plays a role in the overall quality of life in cities, collective decision processes are needed to ensure that despite the variety of individual interests, perceptions, preferences, and behaviors, the public interest in matters of urban environmental quality is protected. But how should the public interest be identified? Ideally, all interest groups in a city would be represented in a political process that leads to consensus and action. Reality is less perfect: power, resources, access to information and technology are not equally distributed among city interests.

Some groups are rarely present at the decision table, and not surprisingly, collective decisions do not tend to reflect their interests. For example, facilities that pollute their environment (LULUs) may select locations in the proximity of poor, inner-city neighborhoods that are less able than affluent suburbs to stage an effective "not-in-my-back-yard" (NIMBY) battle. The emerging pattern of outcomes has been attributed to environmental racism, because in many cases the involuntary hosts of LULUs are minorities (Arrandale, 1992b). Cleanup efforts in such neighborhoods are also more difficult to implement for similar reasons (Thigpen, 1993). Environmental justice has emerged as an area of research and activism in response to concerns about the inequitable pattern of environmental costs and benefits in cities (e.g., Shepard et al., 2002, Elliott et al., 2004).

Other groups, such as children and future generations, are excluded from the decision process that shapes their future. As argued earlier in the chapter, some decisions can cause irreversible damage to the environment, and in many cases current knowledge does not enable accurate prediction of long-term consequences. Then it becomes important to incorporate into collective decision processes some safeguards against the prevalence of short-run thinking and action. Some obstacles to sound decisions related to individual attitudes have already been mentioned. Collective attitudes—those shared by groups who can affect the shaping of public policies—can also impede the process of protecting and improving the urban environment.

The false dichotomy that has taken root in public perception regarding economic development threatens the already weak ability to reach public consensus on environmental issues. The perception that economic development, actively pursued at local and regional levels, is inherently at odds with environmental protection is prevalent around the world (e.g., see Healy, 1993, on similar problems that the European community already faced a couple of decades ago). One reason is that a short-run, salient consequence of environmental protection measures is the need to change old ways of locating facilities and producing goods. In the long run, such changes may sustain urban environmental quality, through continued availability of resources for production and the emergence of demand for new products and technologies that lead to environment-enhancing economic development. However, the continued framing of these two issues as incompatible defeats collective resolve and thwarts efforts to identify creative solutions that serve both economic development and the environment of cities.

Another obstacle to public consensus and action is inertia: proposing and implementing changes in the status quo is difficult (Layzer, 2006) even when the benefits are obvious and accrue quickly to all segments of the urban population. The changes required to promote and protect the quality of the urban environment make a claim on already strained resources; their benefits are not obvious and do not materialize in time spans commensurable with public attention; and, in the short run, not all segments of the community benefit equally. Therefore, it appears easier to continue on the present course, especially as there is widespread disagreement over what issues are important, critical, or marginal (Susskind & Cruikshank, 1987), not least due to the complexity of the issues involved and the current scientific uncertainty over their consequences.

Public debate around environmental issues is hampered by the public's lack of trust in elected officials and bureaucrats. At times this attitude is warranted. In general, however, like any other collective perception of the moment, this one too may not be completely congruent with reality. A tendency toward sporadic and inconsistent levels of public involvement in collective decisions combines with the lack of trust in politicians to prevent focused attention and progress on environmental issues.

Lastly, there is a prevalent lack of will to spend public resources on long-term objectives, especially as a sufficient number of more immediate urban crises lay frequent claims on the scarce resources. Unfunded federal mandates, discussed in Chapter 7, require local environmental protection measures without providing the financial ability to meet standards. These mandates meet with the hostility of local public officials who have to address the added financial burdens by increasing service rates and local taxes.

The previous litany of obstacles to environmentally sound decisions and policies projects an overly pessimistic picture for the prospects of urban environmental sustainability and quality protection. There has been notable progress in several areas, mainly due to regulatory efforts, for example, improvements in air quality (see Figure 11.4). Public awareness has also increased—witness the community activism that surges in the face of siting or change in unwanted facilities. Perhaps quick results should not be expected, given the complexity and the incremental nature of changes in the factors described above, especially individual and collective attitudes.

Urban Environmental Remedies

In the face of seemingly intractable problems and collective lack of resolve, there have been calls for drastic changes, such as a return to simpler lifestyles of times past. Such idyllic solutions are quite unrealistic. Instead, complex problems such as those of modern and future cities require solutions that match them in complexity. The urban environment requires a many-pronged approach that combines the best technology has to offer with changes in human behavior brought about by educated awareness, as well as policies and regulations that create the incentives to behave in sustainable ways which enhance, rather than exhaust the environment. Effective and implementable remedies need to rely on innovative collective decision making, planning, and individual awareness and willingness to pay for environmental quality. Scientific inquiry should play a central role in decisions that affect the environment (e.g., Ozawa 2005a and 2005b).

Goals for Action

The goal of decisions that benefit the urban environment has to be specific enough to guide actions, but it also has to allow for all the variation among cities in terms of population, climate, physical and economic conditions, history, and plans for the future. **Sustainability** is a candidate goal that has garnered solid support from many quarters (e.g., Kates et al., 2005, Brown, 1994).

Sustainable development is a paradigm that can eliminate the old competition between economic and environmental interests. This goal reflects the belief that economic growth is compatible with policies that not only sustain, but actually expand the stock of environmental resources (Knight, 1993). The focus of this paradigm is not the city, but the larger region in which it is embedded, and on whose ecosystem it depends (Gappert, 1993). The strategies and tactics that serve this goal involve resources management including recycling and recovery, and renewable energy sources; rehabilitation of ecosystems, such as polluted lakes and deteriorating open spaces; changes in lifestyle that decrease the use of nonrenewable resources and reduce pollution and waste; and, education to foster public awareness and sustained participation in collective decisions.

The decision-making component of sustainability is critical; it is the device that can free and shift necessary resources without which sustainability cannot happen. This process has to reframe decisions about the urban space, moving from adversarial to cooperative terms. It requires constant nurturing of public consensus on environmental threats and priorities, through effective communication of complex, science-intensive issues. Above all, the decision processes that support sustainable development can enable individuals to think globally and act locally. Sustainable development already has champions around the world, as some of the following examples illustrate at different scales, from entire cities to neighborhoods.

Pioneering Solutions

Experimental cities—planned and implemented—are not a new idea. Early attempts at designing the "ideal" city stemmed from architects' flights of imagination, in the vein of Le Corbusier, Soleri, and Sant'Elia, whose most audacious plans, never implemented, involved a completely new start and relied on technological prowess (Pevsner, 1968). In contrast, today's innovators do not shrink from remodeling cities of the present to adapt them to a sustainable future—enduring in time through judicious use of environmental and energy resources. The range of concerns has expanded beyond technology to include organizational, economic, political, and lifestyle aspects of the future city. This broader spectrum of concerns promises to render the postmodern dream of the "ideal" city implementable. In some cases, the dream has already come true.

- **Curitiba**, Brazil, has become the symbol of what can be achieved today on the path to the "ideal" city (Canty, 1993). That a model sustainable city is located in Brazil, which is a developing country, suggests that a lack of resources is not nearly as limiting as a lack of resolve. On the other hand, having a politically astute architect as mayor (Jaime Lerner) may help to both dream and implement innovative visions (Kroll, 1999). His was, in his own words, a city that "wastes the minimum and saves the maximum" (Zelov, 1995).

About 60 miles from the Atlantic coast, and 210 miles southwest of Sao Paolo—ranked eighth in the world with a population of 20.4 million in 2011, and expected to become the fourth most populous city in the world by 2025 with a population of 22 million—lies Curitiba, capital and largest city of the state of Paraná. Its residents numbered about 1.75 million in 2012. Its masterplan, adopted in 1965, is innovative in content, but even more so in its intent to promote sustainability despite Brazil's exploding trend in urban population growth, and the high incidence of urban poverty.

Some of the physical planning tools for achieving sustainability included ample provision for—but control over location of—low-cost housing; affordable public transportation complete with well-designed shelters and automated controls that give it preference in heavy traffic; a pedestrian downtown; relegation of high density and industrial development away from the city center; and, preservation of the downtown's historic colonial structures (Herbst, 1992). Financial and service delivery arrangements such as waste recycling complement the physical features which can be found in isolation in numerous other cities, but have been combined in Curitiba to achieve a relatively high quality of life at reasonable cost. For example, in 1992 per capita spending on services stood at $156, compared with $1,279 for Detroit (Hawken et al., 2006). About 1.3 million passengers ride daily five kinds of buses that compose the Bus Rapid Transit system, whose buses are owned by 10 private companies (Goodman et al., 2006).

Curitiba is headed toward a sustainable future that does not seem to come at the expense of economic development, but rather enhances it by providing it with a desirable urban environment. Many of the amenities that now serve as models for cities around the world have been added in time. It suggests that Curitiba's continued success is due not only to creative initiatives, but also to efforts sustained in time by political will that feeds on public support. Most of Curitiba's elements can be found in many other cities around the world. Its uniqueness is the combination of planning, technological, social, and political solutions, and their continuity, which is a prerequisite of sustainability.

In Europe, the World Health Organization has tried to develop demonstration projects for healthy cities based on Leonard Duhl's vision of a city without crime, drugs, unemployment, or pollution.

- One intriguing example of European planning for sustainability is the small, Danish city of **Kalundborg**, 75 miles west of the Danish capital of Copenhagen, whose 2011 population was 16,400. There, sustainable development has been pursued since the early 1970s through industrial ecology. Reducing environmental costs through income-producing reuses of industrial waste was the idea driving the Kalundborg initiative. The solution entails voluntary exchanges among a group of key partners that include the community, a power station, an oil refinery, a plasterboard factory, and an international biotechnology company, as well as several other companies that have bilateral exchanges with some of the partners.

The arrangement, called "industrial symbiosis," consists of members reusing each other's products and waste in their own industrial processes. For example, the refinery supplies the plasterboard plant with gas. The power plant is the city's heating steam supplier. The biotech company's sludge goes to fertilize a farm in its vicinity, while the yeast, another biotech byproduct, is offered to another farm for pig feed. Fly ash from the power plant gets reused in the cement factory. Hot salt water from the power plant goes into nearby fishponds. The net effect of this net-worked exchange is to reduce industrial pollution in all media—air, soil, water—in a way that also happens to reduce the participants' production costs, providing an economic incentive for sustaining the partnership in time.

Scale, small in this case, worked well for this arrangement that relies heavily on the small distances between the facilities and on the personal neighborly relation-ships between business owners and community residents.

American examples of cities going down the path to sustainability are Denver, Colorado (Demos, 1994) and Davis, California, an early pathbreaker (Morrison, 1986) that enacted waste-recycling measures in 1972 and required citizens to dry their clothes outdoors and make use of solar energy panels. Portland, Oregon, stands out as an example of how wise planning can foster urban sustainability (e.g., Ozawa, 2004).

- More recently, Cleveland's EcoVillage has become a national model for sustainable revitalization of urban neighborhoods (Kellogg and Keating, 2011). As in Kalund-borg, the driving force here has been a partnership between a neighborhood devel-opment center, a local environmental nonprofit that promotes sustainability, local foundations, and the host community. The partners resolved to adopt "green build-ing" principles and to apply them to the development of several housing units and the redesign of a train stop in the neighborhood.

  Green building affects both the construction and the operation phases through design and choice of materials. During construction, waste is reduced through use of recycled materials and through building processes with few by-products and emis-sions. During operation, the need for heating and cooling is reduced by the building design. As well, energy-saving processes are used wherever possible. Other features of the buildings and their surroundings reduce their impact on the environment.

  As in the Kalundborg case, the challenge was to implement plans in a cost-effective manner that would make green building an economically viable alterna-tive to traditional building methods. As a result, housing units and train station are not only kind to the environment, minimizing waste and including energy-saving designs, but also economically sensible, thus providing an incentive for others to replicate this model.

- Tianjin Eco-City in China is a "wasteland-to-community experiment" (Liu & Climatewire, 2011) that emerged through cooperation between the governments of China and Singapore. It is expected to accommodate 350,000 people on a site half that of Manhattan. The intent was not only to build an ecocity but also to model how contaminated land can be brought back and sustained, using green technologies to provide inhabitants with clean (solar and wind) energy, clean water (recycled rain-water and desalinated sea water), green spaces for recreation, short commutes to employment, and a light rail transit system that will constitute 90% of the traffic. Interestingly, the planned structures are reminiscent of some of the structures proposed by the urban visionaries of the early 20th century. This should not surprise: they proposed compact buildings interconnected above and underground that required technologies now available for implementing cities of which they could only dream.

What are the tools of sustainability? The Curitiba, Kalundborg, Cleveland, and Tianjin models and other experiments around the world suggest the tool bag of sustainability can include combinations of planning, regulation, market, and policy devices and incentives, always enriched by partnerships and by public awareness, support, and participation through lifestyle changes and direct voluntary action. In these three examples, leadership provided by a sustainability champion was also key to moving from vision to implementation on the ground. Brenke (1992) argued that, in general, many of the needed adjustments in physical structures, as well as institutional arrangements and economic incentives for promoting sustainability, could be implemented without major social or economic disruptions. Some examples follow.

- **New technologies:** In the past, solutions to difficult urban problems have resulted from timely technological innovation, which also holds some of the hopes for the future. "Green building," characterized by judicious use of building materials and designs that minimize energy use has been made possible by novel technologies and materials. Product life cycle considerations have shifted design trends toward minimizing waste during production, over the expected duration of a product's usefulness, and at disposal time when as much as possible of the materials is recovered and recycled instead of being sent to landfills or polluting bodies of water. Clean energy generation from renewable sources is making great strides toward becoming a viable alternative for fossil fuels. One key virtue of the new technologies is that not only are they friendly to the environment, but they also make economic sense, saving resources during production, use, and disposal, thus providing incentives for users to adopt "green" products.

- **Physical planning:** The physical configuration of city systems can play an important role in containing urban sprawl, managing water resources, and improving air quality, as well as protecting open spaces. For example, the permaculture approach (Kennedy, 1991) proposes to discard the traditional, linear, sectoral organization of human support systems, such as water and energy management, in favor of systems that create linkages between the elements needed for each specific task. Various nontraditional configurations of land uses and other new planning strategies also promise to contribute to environmental quality while also improving some city functions. In addition, the practice of reusing central city land, replete with brownfields, can contribute both to the reduction of urban sprawl and to revitalization of economically disadvantaged areas. Instances from around the world suggest, however, that planning efforts alone cannot carry the burden of ensuring sustainable development. Partnerships between public and private sectors may improve the odds for the success of planning initiatives.

- **Regulation:** Toronto, Canada, is one of 14 members in the Urban CO2 Project that set policies promising to reduce urban carbon dioxide emissions at lesser expense than alternative methods (Harvey, 1993). The American Clean Air Act of 1990 adopted some new approaches for alleviating urban air pollution problems. Many industries find that keeping abreast of new regulations and even actively keeping a step ahead is less costly in the long run than fighting protracted court battles and paying fines for noncompliance.

- **Market devices:** Government regulators, environmentalists, and the public have come to the realization that at times better results for the environment can be achieved if private sector cooperation is secured through market incentives, rather than through adversarial means such as litigation. So economic tools have been increasingly used to foster protection of the environment among developers. Cities competing to attract businesses for their economic development are often including the quality of their environment among their assets, which typically also feature good public education systems and recreation amenities. This suggests the environment has come to be widely perceived as an integral part of the quality of urban life, a key step toward public and private resolve to invest in its maintenance.

- **Policy devices:** Mexico City and some southern California cities are on a similar policy path regarding their scarce water resources. Arid cities have switched from responding to demand by increasing the supply of treated water, to managing the demand through conservation policies that solve the scarcity problem at less public cost. In southern California, for example, water conserved through increased efficiency of use constituted the largest single source of additional water in 2010. Other urban needs can be alleviated by instituting conservation policies (Vig & Kraft, 2009). The difficulty is that in the absence of crises, such policies are difficult to enforce and easily abused by noncooperative individuals, unless accompanied by extensive education efforts.

- **Leadership and partnerships:** In the future, sustainability may become a broadly shared goal, whether because it is economically compelling or because resource scarcity will have imposed it. It will then probably be institutionalized through regulations, building codes, and permitting procedures. Until then, sustainable initiatives must still rely on vision and leadership, and must still depend on volunteer efforts and on public-private partnerships for their implementation.

In many of the cases in which such initiatives emerged, they have been driven by persons or by organizations devoted to the protection and enhancement of urban environments, broadly construed to include natural and built features. Various types of partnerships formed around implementation, but one shared characteristic is that they tend to be broad, including parties not traditionally working together, such as industry, environmental groups, community members, and politicians. These partnerships can endure when members build trust through frequent encounters and exchanges, and when their endeavors are successful and serve everyone's interests. However, they are rather vulnerable because of funding difficulties and lack of time for members to engage in voluntary activities necessary for sustaining the effort.

- **Public participation:** Efforts such as the Regional Environmental Priorities Project undertaken in four counties surrounding Cleveland, Ohio, to rank regional environmental risks (Kaufman and Snape, 1997) have been recognized for more than two decades as important, not only for the information they provide public and private sector decision makers, but also for their value in rallying the public, increasing awareness, and securing cooperation with policies that require lifestyle changes. Another early example of initiatives that enlist public participation is mega-cities (Cohen, 1993), aiming to foster the creation of socially just, environmentally sound cities for the 21st century by raising people's level of awareness regarding their contribution to environmental problems such as air pollution. While some of these projects are tinged with utopia, others have made important contributions to the debates that eventually led to public demand for, and implementation of, sustainable urban development.

- **Life styles:** Implementing lasting changes in the ways people conduct their lives is one of the more daunting challenges to a sustainable city. A small set of such changes can be imposed through laws and rules. For example, curbing the use of cars in heavily polluted cities by restricting the times and places of access, as in Mexico City, Tokyo, and Los Angeles can have only limited results and can be set back by politics (Orcutt, 1992). Self-restraint, car pools, and using public transportation impose some hardships, but, voluntary and based on increased awareness, they might be more stable in time. Waste recycling is more complex; it requires not only time invested in separation and disposal of household and office waste, but also the public willingness to provide a thriving market for recycled products. Many states have passed legislation regarding waste reduction and recycling. However, in the absence of public awareness and cooperation, the legislation may come under attack based on economic arguments. A rather extreme proposal for resolving London's severe smog problems consisted of Eco-Nuisance guerrilla-like groups that would challenge offenders until they discontinued their environmentally harmful practices (Keane, 1990). Clearly, less adversarial ways to foster lifestyle changes are preferable and their effects will be more lasting if they rely on exercise of personal responsibility rather than external enforcement.

Barring a crisis, a change in individual and collective attitudes is a slow process that requires sustained effort from several directions, targeting all age groups through information, education, activities, incentives, and voice. Elementary and high school education must include sustainability concepts and incorporate them in the study of science and citizenship. Other educational efforts have also been underway in specific areas of environmental concern. For example, water conservation strategies rely on community education. Other community channels of communication need to be tapped to reach people of various ages and occupations. Informed and motivated city residents who believe their individual attitudes and actions count can make sustainability happen.

Name _____

The City Sustains Itself (Environmental Studies)

11-1. Choose one megacity in each populated continent (except Australia). Briefly describe the cities in terms of location, population, and per capita income. Identify one environmental problem that is likely to affect each city you selected. Record your sources.

11-2. Analyze the quality of life in your city in terms used in the chapter. Identify what makes this city special for you, as well as environmental elements that detract from its quality.

11-3. Investigate the effects of specific pollutants in the urban environment;
a) carbon monoxide; b) lead from household exposure; c) chlorofluorocarbons;
d) heavy metals in water; e) a contaminant of your choice.

- search for recent articles on this subject, using the library computer search facilities;
- using the computer abstracts, select one article that interests you;
- briefly report on the topic.

11-4. This chapter discusses difficult decisions such as landfill siting and the use of disposable diapers. To explore the complexity of urban environmental problems, find one other example of a decision that is difficult because it is shrouded in scientific uncertainty, or because it requires uneasy tradeoffs.

CHAPTER 12

The City Regulates Itself
(Law)

Lesley Wells*

Introduction

Law is as fundamental to the city as its infrastructure. The dynamic legal environment in which a city exists is as determinative as is its physical environment.

The law permits with one hand and prohibits with the other hand. It can expand or restrict the implementation of visions of what the city could or should be. Law requires much from those who govern, do business in, reside, or work in a city.

It would be difficult to understand urban affairs anywhere in the world without understanding some of the ways in which law protects and punishes people, regulates public and private concerns, enforces established principles, and provides, not only for the justice system, but for the common good.

This chapter uses some real cases involving real people to examine and exemplify some of the ways in which law impacts urban America. Law is a human institution, born of human need. American democracy is rooted in the Declaration of Independence and the Constitution of the United States.

The promises in the 1776 Declaration are bold:

> We hold these Truths to be self-evident, that all Men are created equal, that they are endowed by their Creator with certain inalienable Rights, that among these are Life, Liberty, and the Pursuit of Happiness – That to secure these Rights, Governments are instituted among Men, deriving their just Power from the Consent of the Governed, that whenever any Form of Government becomes destructive of these Ends, it is the Right of the People to alter or to abolish it, and to institute new Government.
>
> *(Declaration of Independence, 1776)*

*Judge, United States District Court, Northern District of Ohio, with research assistance from Daniel Miller, Gabrielle Moses, Jennifer Miller, and Johnny Hutchinson.

The United States Constitution, full of wise restraints, is introduced with an equally powerful preamble:

> We the People of the United States, in Order to form a more perfect Union, establish Justice, insure domestic Tranquility, provide for the common defence, promote the general Welfare, and secure the Blessings of Liberty to ourselves and our Posterity, do ordain and establish this Constitution for the United States of America.

(U.S. Constitution, 1787)

The Constitution belongs to each person in America. For the first time in history, people, through a written constitution, granted power to a government they created themselves. A very brief document, the Constitution sets forth how we govern ourselves, how we provide for the common good, and protects us from our government by setting forth the rights which cannot be taken from us. The United States Constitution is our core document as Americans, our fundamental law.

States, too, have constitutions. Federal and state constitutional authority create multiple additional and overlapping networks of law. In myriad forms, federal, state, and local governments create, enforce, and administer law affecting the city. This chapter discusses a variety of examples of the statutes, ordinances, regulations and rules which can have an impact on every area of urban life. The lens that will be used to examine the city is made up of some of the fundamental rights and liberties Americans are privileged to enjoy as individuals. Looking through this lens focuses on the dynamic tension which exists between the rights each individual claims and the demands all of us together make as citizens, on our cities.

Sign Language

"It's a free country; I can say what I want." Most of us have thought, if not said, similar words. How and where we say it might make a difference.

Speech is given powerful but not absolute protection under the U.S. Constitution. The First Amendment to the United States Constitution states that "Congress shall make no law . . . abridging the freedom of speech. . . ." (First Amendment, 1791). This amendment, applicable to the states through the Fourteenth Amendment, has protected speech in most, but not every, situation. Falsely yelling "fire" in a crowded place and causing a panic or using "fighting words" inciting people to riot are examples of speech which might not be protected.

Rights do not operate in a vacuum. Often the assertion of a right by an individual collides with interests asserted by a city on behalf of the people collectively. As was discussed in Chapter 5 of this book, in the examination of land use and zoning practices, cities have interests in controlling some of the residential activities within their boundaries. Cities and states have the power to enforce their interests by passing and implementing laws designed for the health, welfare, and protection of their citizens. This authority is known as a state's "police power." Against those interests, however, a person's home and activities within it receive powerful (but not absolute) constitutional protection. As an example, consider the situation of a woman in Ladue, Missouri, who wanted to put an anti-war sign on her lawn but who discovered that her town prohibited residential signs. So she applied for a variance from the city which would give her permission to put up her residential sign. The city denied her request, but the woman put a sign up anyway in a second-floor window of her home. It was an 8 1/2 × 11-inch sign, which read: "For Peace in the Gulf."

The Ladue City Council then enacted a new ordinance, which prohibited residential signs, but set forth ten exceptions and a long list of reasons for the law:

> Proliferation of an unlimited number of signs in private, residential, commercial, industrial, and public areas of the City of Ladue would create ugliness, visual blight and clutter, tarnish the natural beauty of the landscape as well as the residential and commercial architecture, impair property values, substantially impinge upon the privacy and special ambience of the community, and may cause safety and traffic hazards to motorists, pedestrians, and children.
>
> *(Ladue v. Gilleo, 1994)*

Ms. Gilleo persisted. She sued and won in the federal trial court (*Gilleo v. Ladue,* 1991). The city appealed the decision, but the woman won in the federal court of appeals (*Gilleo v. Ladue,* 1993). Again, the City of Ladue appealed the decision to our nation's highest court, the U.S. Supreme Court. There, Ms. Gilleo won, once and for all (*Ladue v. Gilleo,* 1994). Since it could no longer appeal the judgment, the city was forced to sacrifice its interests in keeping a city free of "visual blight and clutter" for Ms. Gilleo's rights to free speech guaranteed by the First Amendment.

The Supreme Court understood that the city had the power to address problems of residential signs under its police power. In doing so, however, the Supreme Court said the city must comply with the First Amendment. Cities may make some "time, place, or manner restrictions" on speech, as distinct from content regulations, but in this case, the Supreme Court found there were no adequate alternatives available. "Displaying a sign from one's own residence often carries a message quite distinct from placing the same sign someplace else, or conveying the same text or picture by other means" (*Ladue v. Gilleo,* 1994).

The U.S. Supreme Court said: "Special respect for individual liberty in the home has long been part of our culture and our law; that principle has special resonance when the government seeks to constrain a person's ability to speak there" (*Ladue v. Gilleo,* 1994).

Actions Speak

Cities deal with all manner of public conduct: riots and rituals, parades and performances, circuses and ceremonies. Issues of maintaining social order and managing peaceful resolution of citizen conflict sometimes end up at the court house because they intertwine with issues of the protection of individual constitutional rights and civil liberties. Generally, governments are allowed to make reasonable restrictions on the time, place, and manner of speech.

A man was convicted of and sentenced for the crime of "desecrating a venerated object" after he burned a flag in front of City Hall in Dallas, Texas, during the 1984 Republican National Convention, as part of a protest of the Reagan administration's policies. The Texas Court of Criminal Appeals overturned the conviction (*Johnson v. State,* 1988), and the United States Supreme Court agreed. The reason was the First Amendment (*Texas v. Johnson,* 1989).

The U.S. Supreme Court opinion in the case explains how the First Amendment, which on its face forbids "abridging the freedom of speech" rather than conduct, nonetheless can shelter some conduct (*Texas v. Johnson,* 1989). The nonverbal conduct itself must be expressive. There are many further restrictions.

Additionally, city officials must sometimes balance the individual liberties of some of their citizens against those of other citizens. For instance, New York City allowed a group known as Rock Against Racism ("RAR") to host concerts at the Naumberg Acoustic Bandshell in Central Park for several years, and for several years, the surrounding residents complained about the noise. Also, an area a few hundred yards away (known as the "Sheep Meadow") was reserved by a decree from the mayor for the quiet, passive enjoyment of other park patrons. When RAR refused to respond to numerous requests by the city to turn their volume down at a concert (out of respect for the Sheep Meadow occupants), the city shut off power to the band shell. The audience became rather unruly, and RAR sued the city, contending that New York City had placed an unconstitutional restriction on their freedom of expression. Ultimately, the U.S. Supreme Court found that the restriction was "content-neutral" (i.e., didn't discriminate against the group because of its message) because it simply dealt with the volume of any performance done in the shell, and because the city's sound engineer was required to let performing groups' sound mixers control the sound board up to a certain volume limit (*Ward v. Rock Against Racism*).

Cities are also restricted by Federal and State constitutions and laws from restricting the commercial expression of businesses through advertising. Even in the name of preventing social ills such as gambling, the government may not regulate expression unless the regulation directly advances their interest in stifling it, and unless the regulation is not more extensive than is necessary to serve their interest. One state interest, as the next case demonstrates, is to protect the morality of its citizens, but this state interest is not unlimited. In addition to private citizens, the media, too, has constitutionally protected freedom of expression. Commercial speech (eg., advertising) is protected under this standard provided it "concerns lawful activity and is not misleading" (*Greater New Orleans Broadcast Ass'n. v. United States,* 1999).

These cases relied upon definitions of several spheres of individual rights into which city governments cannot intrude and upon the function of free expression in our society:

- The "function of free speech under our system of government is to invite dispute. It may indeed best serve its high purpose when it induces a condition of unrest, creates dissatisfaction with conditions as they are, or even stirs people to anger" (*Terminiello v. Chicago,* 1949).
- "If there is a bedrock principle underlying the First Amendment, it is that the government may not prohibit the expression of an idea simply because society finds the idea itself offensive or disagreeable" (*Terminiello v. Chicago,* 1949).
- "Even in a public forum, the government may impose reasonable restrictions on the time, place, or manner of protected speech, provided the restrictions are justified without reference to the content of the regulated speech that they are narrowly tailored to serve a significant governmental interest, and that they leave open ample alternative channels for the communication of the information" (*Ward v. Rock Against Racism,* 1989).

- "If there is a fixed star in our constitutional constellation, it is that no official, high or petty, can prescribe what shall be orthodox in politics, nationalism, religion, or other matters of opinion or force citizens to confess by word or act their faith therein" (*West Virginia Bd. of Ed. v. Barnette,* 1943).

Assault on Assault Weapons

Among individual rights recognized as fundamental is the right to bear arms. In addition to the Second Amendment to the U.S. Constitution, state constitutions also recognize the right to bear arms (Second Amendment, 1791).

"A well-regulated militia, being necessary to the security of a free State, the right of the people to keep and bear Arms, shall not be infringed" (Second Amendment, 1791).

As cities struggled to protect people from violent crime, the regulation and control of guns has become an issue of heated public debate and legislation. Finally, in 2010, the Supreme Court in *McDonald v. Chicago* held that the right of an individual to "keep and bear arms," protected by the Second Amendment, is **incorporated** by the "*due process clause*" of the Fourteenth Amendment and therefore, applies to the states. This decision came two years after the Supreme Court decision in *District of Columbia v. Heller* which had found the right of an individual to "keep and bear arms" applied in federal enclaves. These cases do not stand for the proposition, however, that cities and states can never regulate the possession and sale of firearms. The Court in McDonald made clear that a city or state can prohibit the possession of firearms in schools and government buildings, impose conditions on the commercial sale of firearms, and outlaw the possession of firearms by felons.

Despite Heller and McDonald, and a number of lower court cases interpreting these Supreme Court decisions, there remains uncertainty about the exact contours of a citizen's Second Amendment right to bear arms and what a state or city can do to restrict it. One thing is for certain: because the right of an individual to bear arms is a right guaranteed by the federal Constitution, a state's ability to control gun violence is limited.

Voting Rights

The ability of citizens to vote their representatives out of office if those representatives do not comply with voter wishes comprises a key defense of the people from the power of elected officials at all levels of American government. Historically, some elected officials have sought to destroy this defense by having voting districts drawn to disadvantage, particularly minority groups, often those most harshly affected by a particular official's policies. In an older example, the city of Tuskeegee was found to have violated the Equal Protection Clause of the Fourteenth Amendment by deliberately redrawing the city's boundaries (transforming it from roughly a square into "an uncouth twenty-eight-sided figure") because the move was so obviously targeted at disenfranchising (denying the right to vote of) local African Americans (*Gomillion v. Lightfoot,* 1960).

More recently, Hispanic voters sued the city of Watsonville, California, under the Voting Rights Act of 1965 as amended in 1982. Hispanic voters complained that the "at-large" mayoral and city council election procedures (meaning all the voters in the city vote as a group for the mayor and even those not in a particular council member's district vote to elect them) denied them full participation in the political process and the ability to elect representatives of their choice.

According to the 1980 census, 48.9% of the city's population was Hispanic and Hispanics constituted thirty-seven percent of the city's voters. Nonetheless, no Hispanic person had ever been elected mayor or to the city council (*Gomez v. Watsonville*, 1988).

Although the trial court ruled in favor of the city, the court of appeals decided that the Hispanic voters had made their required showing—they had demonstrated they were sufficiently large and cohesive enough to constitute a majority in a single-member district, were politically cohesive, and that whites engaged in "racial bloc voting." (*Gomez v. Watsonville*). Therefore, the appellate court decided that the city's at-large mayor and council election system violated the law by diluting the voting strength of Hispanics and blocking their effective participation in the political process. The U.S. Supreme Court sent the case back to the trial court to implement a new law which would comply with the Federal Voting Rights Act.

Normal redistricting efforts (required in some states to be done when the census is taken every ten years) sometimes violate the "no vote dilution" requirement articulated in Gomez by "unpacking" the concentrations of minority voters. The tension is between the certainty of election of a minority-backed candidate, which could be accomplished by concentrating minorities into a few districts and increasing the overall political influence of minorities by giving them a better chance in multiple districts. The U.S. Supreme Court, in declaring Georgia's redistricting plan invalid, held that: "[On] one hand, a smaller number of safe majority-minority districts may virtually guarantee the election of a minority group's preferred candidate in those districts . . . On the other hand, spreading out minority voters over a greater number of districts creates more districts in which minority voters may have the opportunity to elect a candidate of their choice" (*Georgia v. Ashcroft,* 2003).

Minority Set-Asides

Cities, like their inhabitants, often hire contractors to perform particular jobs. Those contractors, in turn, hire other contractors ("subcontractors") to work for them in performing specific activities to complete the job. In the past, discrimination against minorities manifested itself in many locations in the awarding of or failure to award these contracts. Many local and state governments have looked to race-conscious remedies to assist minority contracting businesses. Principled efforts by government to remedy effects of past discrimination and the right to equal treatment for all citizens are implicated. For example, the city of Richmond, Virginia, passed a racial minority "set-aside" ordinance for city construction projects requiring non-minority owned contracting companies to subcontract at least thirty percent to minority subcontractors. Minority contractors were not subject to the ordinance. Like many other cities, Richmond declared its purpose to be to encourage broader participation by minority-owned contractors and to remedy past discrimination in the field of contracting.

A contractor who was the only bidder for a particular job, but who had difficulty meeting the set-aside requirement, challenged the constitutionality of the ordinance when the city rejected his bid and rebid the project. The contractor lost his case in the federal district court and in the court of appeals.

The United States Supreme Court nullified the court of appeals' decision and sent the case back to that court for further consideration (*Richmond v. Croson,* 1986). The court of appeals then decided that the minority set-aside ordinance violated the Equal Protection Clause of the Fourteenth Amendment. "No State shall . . . deny to any person within its jurisdiction the equal protection of the laws" (Fourteenth Amendment, 1868).

The Supreme Court agreed: "The Richmond Plan denies certain citizens the opportunity to compete for a fixed percentage of public contracts based solely upon their race. The court decided that the general history of discrimination did not justify a "rigid racial quota in the awarding of public contracts," and that Richmond had "failed to demonstrate a compelling interest in apportioning public contracting opportunities on the basis of race" (*Richmond v. Croson,* 1989).

The Supreme Court's disapproval of the Richmond set-aside plan required cities to prove specific instances of past discrimination that their race-conscious remedy was designed to fix. After the *Croson* decision in 1989, the city of Denver, Colorado restructured its racial preference program. Appointing a commission to study the problem, Denver set annual goals in city contracts for minority and female-owned business participation. In compliance with *Croson,* Denver required potential minority contractors to show that their firm had either been the specific victim of past discrimination or was in the city construction industry prior to a certain date. When a local concrete firm sued the city and the county, Denver presented statistical evidence purporting to show that there had been widespread discrimination in contract awarding before the cut-off date. The court of appeals ultimately upheld Denver's position, requiring only "strong evidence from which an inference of past or present discrimination could be drawn" (*Concrete Works of Colo. v. City and County of Denver,* 2003).

Poor Joshua

Not all urban violence is in the streets. Over the last several decades, there has been a profound shift in public concern and consequent legal interventions in violence which occurs in the home. Federal, state, and local law now intervenes in family relationships on behalf of society, the community, and the alleged victims. This is a break from the traditional restraint of the law which tended to view family matters as private and, with rare exceptions, beyond its proper reach. Consequent intrusions by government into family matters remain controversial. Not only the propriety of intervention but its effectiveness and proper limits are matters of earnest debate.

One case to consider concerns a boy named Joshua. Joshua was beaten repeatedly by his father who had legal custody of him from infancy and with whom he lived. Local officials and social services workers responded in various ways to complaints—which they confirmed—that the boy was being abused by his father.

When Joshua was 2 1/2 years old, his father's second wife complained to the police that the father was "a prime case for child abuse." One year later, Joshua was admitted to a hospital with many injuries. The physician reported abuse to officials and obtained a juvenile court order putting the child in the temporary custody of the hospital (*DeShaney v. Winnebago County,* 1989).

A county team evaluated the situation; Joshua was returned to his father's custody. One month later, the emergency room reported to Joshua's caseworker that the child had again been treated for suspicious injuries. The caseworker made monthly home visits and documented suspicious injuries on the child's head, along with her suspicions that someone at home was physically abusing Joshua. The emergency room again reported treating Joshua for injuries they believed came from abuse. Although the caseworker was told on her next two home visits that the child was too sick to be seen, no action was taken by officials.

Four months later, Joshua's father beat him into a coma. Emergency brain surgery showed severe head injuries over a long period of time. Joshua lived; he is profoundly retarded and institutionalized (*DeShaney v. Winnebago County,* 1989).

Joshua and his mother sued the county and various county employees for violating his constitutional rights "by failing to intervene to protect him against a risk of violence at his father's hands of which they knew or should have known." The trial court, the court of appeals, and the U.S. Supreme Court all ruled for the county and its employees, finding a tragic situation but no constitutional violations (*DeShaney v. Winnebago County,* 1989).

The majority opinion stressed that "the harm was inflicted not by the State of Wisconsin, but by Joshua's father."

> The people of Wisconsin may well prefer a system of liability which would place upon the state and its officials the responsibility for failure to act in situations such as the present one. They may create such a system . . . with the regular lawmaking process. But they should not have it thrust upon them by this Court's expansion of the Due Process Clause of the Fourteenth Amendment.

(DeShaney v. Winnebago County, 1989)

Three U.S. Supreme Court Justices had a different view. Justice Brennan stated that he could not agree "that our Constitution is indifferent to such indifference." Justice Blackmon concluded:

> Poor Joshua! Victim of repeated attacks by an irresponsible, bullying, cowardly, and intemperate father, and abandoned by respondents who placed him in a dangerous predicament and who knew or learned what was going on, and yet did essentially nothing except, as the Court revealingly observes,

> *[ ], 'dutifully recorded these incidents in [their] files.'*

> It is a sad commentary upon American life, and constitutional principles—so full of late of patriotic fervor and proud proclamations about 'liberty and justice for all'—that this child, Joshua DeShaney, now is assigned to live out the remainder of his life profoundly retarded. Joshua and his mother, as petitioners here, deserve—but now are denied by this Court—the opportunity to have the facts of their case considered in the light of the constitutional protection that 42 U.S.C. § 1983 is meant to provide.

(DeShaney v. Winnebago County, 1989)

The fundamental principle articulated in *DeShaney*—that the government does not have a constitutional duty to protect people from harm (e.g., child abuse) by private citizens—has generally been upheld. Cases upholding this ideal often share a common bond with *DeShaney*—they usually involve tragic facts and circumstances. However, it appears that Justice Blackmon's appeal to "fundamental justice" has taken hold in some areas of the country. In a more recent case, a government-employed social worker transferred Anthony Juarez into the custody of his natural father, Christopher Vargas, and allowed him to remain there, despite the father biting the child, dunking him in a bathtub full of water, and pouring boiling water on him, which ultimately killed him. The Court decided that the social worker could be sued, even though she worked for the government: "If [the social worker] knowingly placed [Anthony] in a position of danger, they would not be shielded from liability by the decision in *DeShaney*." (*Currier v. Doran*, 2001).

In a case decided in June 2005, the U.S. Supreme Court declined to extend their "fundamental justice" thinking to a slightly different constitutional question with tragically similar facts.

In June 1999, Jessica Gonzales's three children were playing outside of their mother's Castle Rock, Colorado home in the early evening when their father, Simon, took them away. The Gonzaleses were in the process of a divorce, which included a restraining order against Mr. Gonzales that barred him from being at his ex-wife's home, but allowed him access to his children once a week for a "dinner visit." Throughout the night, Mrs. Gonzales, who discovered the children gone soon after they were taken, made frantic calls to the police to have her husband located and arrested, but, according to Mrs. Gonzales, the Castle Rock Police declined to do so. The city disputed this, and claimed that they had made multiple attempts to locate Mr. Gonzales, and that Mrs. Gonzales had assured them she didn't think the children were in any danger.

After the children were discovered dead, Mrs. Gonzales sued the city. She argued that the restraining order against her husband was a constitutional property interest that guaranteed prompt response by the police department, and that their failure to locate her husband constituted a violation of her right to due process articulated by the Fourteenth Amendment (Fourteenth Amendment, 1791). The U.S. Supreme Court found that, because police have discretion in enforcing restraining orders, they had no duty to protect the Gonzales girls if they felt that there was not probable cause to enforce the restraining order (*Castle Rock v. Gonzales,* 2005). The two dissenting Justices found that Colorado had assumed the obligation to protect the Gonzales children (found not to be present in *DeShaney*)—and that Ms. Gonzales had reasonably held her expectation of the protection embodied in the restraining order.

Although the legal issue is slightly different than in the *DeShaney* line of cases, the consequence was the same—the government could not be sued for failing to intervene in domestic disputes.

Preserving History

As American cities mature, increasing efforts are made to preserve buildings and places deemed to have particular value. Hundreds of cities have enacted historic and aesthetic preservation legislation. The goal of preservation, however, frequently clashes with the goal of new development. The buildings with which such preservation legislation is concerned have private owners whose desire may not be to preserve, but to develop their property to increase its worth. In recent years, several private owners of buildings designated "landmarks" have challenged preservation legislation under the "Takings" Clauses of the Fifth and Fourteenth Amendments (Fifth Amendment, 1791, Fourteenth Amendment, 1868). The clauses prevent the government from "taking" private property without repaying its market value to the owner. "No person shall . . . be deprived of life, liberty, or property without due process of law; nor shall private property be taken for public use without just compensation" (Fifth Amendment, 1791). "Nor shall any State deprive any person of life, liberty, or property, without due process of law" (Fourteenth Amendment, 1868). Private property owners contend in these lawsuits that by restricting their ability to use their property, the government, in effect, is "taking" it. (This concept will be more fully discussed in the section entitled "Taking Private Land").

Penn Central Transportation Co., owner of the Grand Central Station in New York City, proposed to build a fifty-story office building above the eight-story terminal. Because the Landmark Preservation Commission of New York City had designated Grand Central Terminal as a "landmark," its owner was not free to modify the exterior of the building without prior approval from the Commission.

The Commission denied Penn Central's request to build above its terminal, but Penn Central went to court and won (*Penn Central v. New York,* 1975). The Landmark Commission appealed the New York trial court decision and the Commission won in the New York appeals court, which found the restrictions on development of the terminal were necessary to promote the public purpose of protecting landmarks (*Penn Central v. New York,* 1977).

The United States Supreme Court agreed, finding that the Landmark Preservation Law of New York City did not interfere with the present use of the terminal and so did not amount to a **taking** of Penn Central's property so as to require "just compensation" (*Penn Central v. New York,* 1978). Denial of the ability to exploit commercially the airspace above the terminal building did not rise to the level of an unconstitutional taking under the Fifth and Fourteenth amendments (Fifth Amendment, 1791; Fourteenth Amendment, 1868).

The Court emphasized that an analysis of the character of the "particular governmental action" and "nature and extent of the interference with property rights" is the focus of eminent domain decisions (*Penn Central v. New York,* 1978).

Taking Private Land

As noted in the previous section, the government cannot take the property of private individuals unless it is for a public use and unless just compensation is supplied to the private owner. However, the phrase "public use" is subject to multiple interpretations. (Fifth Amendment, 1791). Recently, the U.S. Supreme Court refined the legal standard for "public use," which cities around the country must follow before they exercise their eminent domain power to reclaim private land for public purposes.

The city of New London, Connecticut, experienced a steady decline culminating in unemployment rates far above the state average, drastically reduced tax revenue, and a designation as a "distressed municipality" in 1990. To combat this problem, Connecticut authorized the city to use its eminent domain power to reclaim large tracts of privately-owned land to create an industrial park for the Pfizer pharmaceutical company

(*Kelo v. New London,* 2005). The result, the city said, would be increased tax revenues for the city, which would lead to public benefit. More controversially, New London then ceded control of the development and the construction process to a private development company. Some of the private lots and the homes occupying them belonged to Suzette Kelo and her neighbors in the Fort Trumbull area of New London. One of the citizens had lived in her house for all 87 years of her life. Although New London offered the residents just compensation, they refused and objected to New London's use of eminent domain power. Ms. Kelo and her neighbors contended that taking private property for private development could never be a "public use."

In a 5–4 decision, the U.S. Supreme Court disagreed, and authorized New London taking of the homes for the industrial park. The court majority defined "public use" broadly, holding that if the proposed taking was for "public purposes" (such as increased tax revenues), it was valid under the Fifth Amendment (*Kelo v. New London,* 2005). The Supreme Court stated: "Promoting economic development is a traditional and long accepted function of government. Clearly there is no basis for exempting economic development from our traditionally broad understanding of public purposes" (*Kelo v. New London,* 2005).

The four dissenting Justices were concerned that, after the *Kelo* decision: "Nothing is to prevent the state from replacing any Motel 6 with a Ritz-Carlton, any home with a shopping mall or any farm with a factory . . . the government now has license to transfer property from those with fewer resources to those with more . . . the founders cannot have intended this perverse result" (*Kelo v. New London,* 2005). In response, the majority noted that the plan was "carefully formulated," and that deference to New London's judgment on the matter was proper, as they were better able to assess their local needs than was the U.S. Supreme Court sitting in Washington D.C.

The Homeless

In the 1970s and 1980s, residents of some urban areas became concerned about individuals roaming the city streets during the day and sleeping in public spaces at night. (Smith, 1996). This group of people became known as the "homeless." Much as Ms. Gilleo's signs troubled the city of Ladue, the public appearance of homeless people concerned city councils in urban centers across the country. In response, cities began to pass "anti-sleeping" ordinances, criminalizing sleep in public. Fearing that a perceived connection between drugs, homelessness, and gang violence would threaten the safety of their citizens, many cities passed laws restricting access by the homeless in certain urban areas.

One such ordinance was at issue in the case of *Johnson v. Cincinnati.* The city had created certain "drug-exclusion zones," into which individuals who had been convicted of drug crimes could not go (Cincinnati Ordinance, 1996). Michael Au France, a homeless man, was arrested for possession of drug paraphernalia and was prohibited for four years from going into one of the drug exclusion zones, an area of Cincinnati called "Over-the-Rhine." Mr. Au France applied for a variance from the Cincinnati City Council to allow him to enter the area because he regularly got food, clothing, and shelter from various social services located in Over-the-Rhine, and, furthermore, because his lawyer's office was located there. His application was denied, and he filed suit (together with Patricia Johnson, a drug offender who needed to care for a grandchild living in Over-the-Rhine).

The First Amendment guarantees freedom of association, and the U.S. Supreme Court has held that a right to intrastate travel is inherent in the language of the Constitution. The federal district court held that this ordinance violated Mr. Au France's freedom of association, and that Cincinnati's interest in "enhanc[ing] the quality of life and protect[ing] the health, safety, and welfare of persons" in the drug-exclusion zones was not sufficient to override Mr. AuFrance's constitutional rights. The federal appeals court agreed (*Johnson v. City of Cincinnati,* 2002) and the U.S. Supreme Court declined to review the case, letting the appeals court decision stand.

Taking Out the Garbage

Not only are cities' interests sometimes in conflict with individuals' interests, they also occasionally conflict with *other cities'* interests.

It is the perennial task: to take out the garbage. The problem, of course, is where is "out" when garbage is concerned? Local and state governments face increasing garbage disposal challenges as more of us and our institutions and industries "take out" more. Of equal concern is what our garbage contains as the potential negative effects on our health and environment of components of waste become clear. Not only the sheer volume of liquid and solid waste, but also its condition as toxic, radioactive, contaminated, or otherwise hazardous, has become a matter of public concern accompanied by regulation, legislation, and litigation.

In 1987, a barge carrying 3100 tons of garbage traveled the Atlantic Ocean for almost six months in search of a dump for Long Island garbage which was originally en route to North Carolina for methane conversion (Gutis, 1987). North Carolina refused to allow the barge to dock. Alabama, Louisiana, and other states also refused as did several countries.

Having traveled the ocean as far south as Belize, the barge returned with its rotting cargo to anchor outside New York City. Surrounding areas rejected its unloading in areas of their jurisdiction. Ultimately, a Brooklyn judge permitted the trash to be burned in Brooklyn on condition the resulting ash would be returned to Long Island (Gutis, 1987). The garbage barge had traveled over 6000 miles, becoming "an enormous floating symbol for an ever-worsening national problem of solid-waste disposal" (Gutis, 1987).

In a different case, New Jersey, like many other areas, had effectively sealed its borders against waste from other states. A New Jersey statute prohibited bringing into the state most "solid or liquid waste which originated or was collected outside the territorial limits of the State" (New Jersey Statute, 1978). Several cities, including Philadelphia, Pennsylvania had contracts for waste disposal with operators of private landfills located in New Jersey.

A constitutional challenge to the New Jersey law was decided by the U.S. Supreme Court after the New Jersey Supreme Court had found the New Jersey statute to be constitutional (*Philadelphia v. New Jersey,* 1978). With two of the Justices dissenting, the U.S. Supreme Court reversed the New Jersey State Supreme Court under the Commerce Clause of the U.S. Constitution.

The Commerce Clause states: "the Congress shall have Power . . . To regulate commerce with foreign nations and among the several States, and with the Indian Tribes" (U.S. Constitution, 1787).

Central to the federal decision was the idea that one state not be permitted to isolate itself from a problem many states have by putting up a wall against interstate activities such as trade, communications, and transportation.

Conclusion

The impact of law on the city is continual and dynamic. Cities derive their authority from the state, not from the federal government. They are constrained, however, by the federal as well as their state constitution and by myriad federal, as well as state and local, statutes, ordinances, rules and regulations. Familiarity with how the law operates in the urban context is more important to an understanding of the city than are particular laws.

As the Declaration of Independence proclaims, government derives its power from the consent of the people and exists to secure our fundamental rights (Declaration, 1776). We are those people, every one of us. The U.S. Constitution is the supreme law in the United States and it belongs not only to those of us who are scholars, lawyers, judges, and officials, but to every one of us.

Our constitutional rights are not just high sounding principles; they are real rights for real people. The responsibility for our laws, our government, our common good, and for our cities is our own.

Name _____

The City Regulates Itself (Law)

12-1. What are the six purposes for government which the people of the United States set forth in the Preamble to the Constitution?

12-2. What does "establish justice" mean?

12-3. What does the First Amendment mean when it states that the government can make no law respecting an establishment of religion? How is this different from the statement that the government can make no law prohibiting the free exercise of religion?

12-4. What is public purpose? How do you determine when a private purpose becomes a public purpose?

12-5. If a private landfill operator in your town contracts to take all the garbage from surrounding towns and dispose of it in your neighborhood what could you do?

PART III

Urban People and Cultures

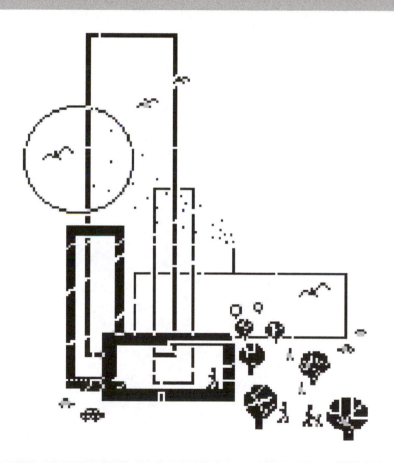

The City Worships
(Religion)
Harvey K. Newman

Religion and the Origin of Cities

Many scholars believe that religion has always played an important role in cities. In explaining how humans created the first cities, Lewis Mumford suggested that religion led humans to settle into community groups that would become cities. As he described the process, the earliest cities grew around sacred places where nomadic hunters and gatherers returned for ceremonies and rituals. Humans gradually began their settlements around these sacred landmarks. Thus, religion provided the impulse for the founding of cities.

Evidence of this process comes from archaeologists who uncovered the remains of the first cities in the Middle East. Among the ruins, archaeologists found that the main physical features of these urban places included walls, narrow streets or alleys, two and three-story houses, and the step pyramid of the ziggurat dominating the cityscape as well as smaller shrines and temples serving neighborhood residents. The "City Description of Assur," dating from around 700 B.C., mentions thirty-four of these temples and chapels. As Mumford (1961) remarked, "Every feature of the early city revealed the belief that man was created for no other purpose than to magnify and serve his gods. That was the city's ultimate reason for existence" (pp.75–6). For Mumford, it is not an exaggeration to suggest the origin of the city itself was occasioned by the needs of men and women to worship their gods.

The objective of this chapter is as follows: to consider the role of religious groups in cities. One question to consider is to what extent do the conditions of city life affect congregations of religious people? On the other hand, how do congregations themselves influence cities? These questions will provide a framework for examining how the city worships.

Immigrants, Religion, and Cities

Colonial Times to Civil War

Among the early European settlers to North America, the Puritans established their cities in the wilderness of the continent as beacons of light to show their faith. In his "Model of Christian Charity" written in 1630, Governor John Winthrop described the settlement that would become Boston.

First Iconium Baptist Church, Atlanta. The church was built by an all-white congregation and sold to First Iconium, an African American congregation, whose members are also moving to the suburbs as gentrification changes the neighborhood. (Photo by Harvey K. Newman.)

Winthrop quoted the scriptural vision of how the cities of New England would be built, "we shall be as a city upon a hill. The eyes of all people are upon us. . . ." (Winthrop, 1960).

For the next hundred years, the Puritans and those who shared their faith shaped life in the towns and cities they built in many parts of New England. Their religious institutions were the very heart of life in places like Boston. The spires of churches served as landmarks that dominated the skyline of most cities in America. As an example, on the evening of April 18, 1775, it was the steeple of the Old North Church in Boston that was used to signal a waiting group of riders on the other side of the Charles River. The two lanterns appearing in the steeple were the signal for Paul Revere and his colleagues to begin their ride to warn revolutionary leaders that British troops were leaving Boston.

The visual prominence of places of worship in cities continued long into the nineteenth century. For example, on May 1, 1846, the faithful gathered to dedicate the new building of Trinity Church on Broadway at Wall Street in New York City. The soaring spire of the church in lower Manhattan dominated the skyline of the city. For the next half century, Trinity's spire was the tallest structure on the New York skyline and served as a beacon for ships sailing into the harbor. Fast forward to the present and Trinity Church is dwarfed by the tall buildings of Wall Street that surround what appears as a tiny church in the midst of the city. Yet whether it is Trinity Church in New York, a Buddhist temple in Los Angeles, or any other places held dear by their adherents in cities throughout the U.S., these sacred landmarks remain as places of worship and important spaces for people in urban areas.

Worship has always played an important role in the life of city dwellers in America. As immigrants came to the cities, they brought their religious traditions with them. As a result, cities have always included a collection of places of worship that reflected the places of origin of those who came. This was true not only of the Puritans as they established cities in New England, but also of the Dutch as they brought their form of Protestant Christianity to New York. English Catholic settlers concentrated initially in large numbers in Baltimore and other cities in Maryland. The Anglican Church was brought by residents of the southern colonies to Jamestown, Virginia; Charleston, South Carolina; and Savannah, Georgia. The Spanish brought Roman Catholicism to the settlements they established and named in the southwest such as Los Angeles and Santa Fe. In Florida, the Spaniards founded Saint Augustine, while the French Catholics came down from Canada to the midsection of the continent, bringing their faith to settlements they named such as Saint Louis and New Orleans.

In the holds of slave ships, men and women brought elements of folklore, music, language, and religion from many different tribes as part of the African Diaspora. As Raboteau (1978) observed, "One of the most durable and adaptable constituents of the slave's culture, linking African past with American present, was religion" (p. 4). The slaves' religion was not transported to this continent in a pure form, but was continually adapted to conditions of life in the new world. One of those adaptations was to the life of slavery in the city.

While much of our image of slavery in the south is connected to rural life on plantations, city life presented challenges to slavery and the religious traditions brought from Africa. In spite of efforts to eradicate all forms of African culture as a way of maintaining control, elements of the African tradition remained strong among slaves in urban settings. Travelers to southern cities such as Frederick Law Olmsted observed the church meetings of slaves and freed blacks and commented on the fusion of Christianity with religious elements from Africa (Wade, 1964).

From whatever place they came, migrants to American cities carried their worship traditions with them, creating a pattern of religious pluralism that contributed to the separation of church and state embodied in the Bill of Rights to the U.S. Constitution. With many different faiths represented within the cities and states, it was thought best to prohibit the establishment of any one group within the new government of the United States of America. This was one of the many ways that religious groups exerted an influence upon cities and the nation from the very beginning.

Modern Period

The influence of immigrants and their religion on cities continued with the waves of migrants that have come to U.S. cities since the 1960s. With diverse points of origin ranging from all parts of Asia, Central and South America, the Caribbean, former republics in the Soviet Union, and elsewhere, these migrants are the most recent to arrive in cities across the country. Many have brought their religious traditions with them, which contributed to new patterns of diversity in the landscape of urban areas.

For example, in the Atlanta metropolitan area the percentage of foreign-born residents in 2000 was higher than at any other time in the city's history. Among the Asian immigrants were 39,114 who were born in India (Census 2000). Many of these are part of the growing Hindu community in the metropolitan area. In 1984 the group incorporated the Hindu Temple of Atlanta and erected a large building that serves as a cultural, educational, and religious center for many of the faithful who live in Atlanta. By 2010 the number of Asian Indian born residents of the 5 county Atlanta area had

The Hindu Temple of Atlanta. The subculture of Indian-American scattered throughout the Atlanta metropolitan area gather at the Hindu Temple for spiritual, cultural, and educational activities. (Photo by Harvey K. Newman.)

increased to 57,786 (Census 2010). New Hindi Temples have been built on are under construction in the Northern Suburbs. Where recent immigrants have tended to settle.

The Impact of Cities on Religious Groups: Two Views

The relationship between cities and religious organizations also runs in the opposite direction as the urban areas themselves affect congregations of religious people. Early social scientists who studied cities, such as Emile Durkheim, felt that the very conditions of urban living had profound effects on urban dwellers. Durkheim used the word *anomie* to describe the sense of alienation, isolation, and feelings of being cut off from one another as a result of the crowding and impersonal conditions of urban areas.

In the writings of another social scientist, Georg Simmel, the crowded conditions of city life were thought to cause mental stresses that affected the sanity of urban residents. In his essay, "The Metropolis and Mental Life," Simmel (1950) described how the stimuli of noise, congestion, and crowding bombarded the senses forcing those who were able to do so to flee the city for the relative tranquility of rural areas and small towns.

Louis Wirth

One of Simmel's students, American sociologist Louis Wirth, developed these concepts even further in an article, "Urbanism as a Way of Life." Wirth suggested that three aspects of cities, their size, density, and heterogeneity, exert a profound impact on the interpersonal relationships among urban dwellers. Using Durkheim's term *anomie,* Wirth said that the conditions of the urban setting cut people off from close interpersonal primary relationships. While the individual may be associated with a number of organized groups including a congregation, these organizations do not provide the social integration that comes with living in a small town or rural area. City life is characterized by secondary rather than primary social relations. Wirth described the contacts among individuals in a city as "impersonal, superficial, transitory, and segmental" (1964, p. 71).

The urban condition pictured by Wirth would have significant effects upon groups of religious folk in cities. Organizational life within the congregation would be affected by the size of a city with its dense crowds of people drawn from many different places. Religious organizations that are supposed to provide the integration needed for people to feel meaning in their lives would be challenged by the conditions of the urban environment itself. Relationships would be difficult to maintain among the people who live cut off from strong interpersonal connections with one another. The results of the urban condition for individuals are stress, estrangement, individualism, and social disorganization.

Wirth added, however, that the characteristics of the city did increase economic competition, leading to a greater number of organized groups. These groups operate within the economic climate, or as Wirth described it, "the pecuniary nexus," of the city where "the purchasability of services and things has displaced personal relations as the basis of association" (Wirth, 1964, p. 76). Thus, Wirth regarded the urban environment as having an impact upon both individuals and their congregations, which would exist in great numbers in cities, but fail to provide the close interpersonal relations characteristic of a rural area or small town.

Claude Fischer

More recent social theorists have regarded the effect of cities on religious groups in ways different from Louis Wirth and his colleagues of the Chicago School. Claude Fischer (1984) wrote that city life does not weaken the bonds that hold together social groups as Wirth and his colleagues theorized. Instead, the conditions of the city actually strengthen the bonds that hold together small collections of people he called *subcultures*. Fischer defined subcultures as culturally or ethnically distinctive groups of people who tend to interact disproportionately with one another and who manifest relatively similar beliefs and behavior. Taking an image from Robert Park of the Chicago School, Fischer described cities as "a mosaic of little worlds which touch but do not interpenetrate." In a city, it is easier to form a critical mass of individuals who comprise a subculture. Thus, the conditions of city life encourage the formation of a variety of subcultures including organizations of religious folks.

The larger the city, the more likely there are to be devotees of a particular activity with new subgroups forming as people come into contact and communication with one another. Rather than urbanism weakening social bonds, Fischer argues that the condition of the city intensifies subcultures. He adds that as the subcultures in a city come into contact with one another, the usual result is to strengthen the commitment of the individuals to their own social circle. The contacts between subgroups can cause friction between groups as they rub against and sometimes irritate one another. A common reaction is "to embrace one's own social world all the more firmly, thus contributing to further intensification" of the individual's bond to the subculture (Fischer, 1984, pp. 37–8).

Fischer's subcultural theory of urbanism would certainly account for the presence of large numbers of congregations in cities and the incredible diversity of these organizations. If religious groups are viewed as expressions of subcultures in the city, then the conditions of urban life play a role in strengthening and reinforcing the bonds that hold people together. The ties that hold people together in religious organizations are not weakened by the urban environment, but may instead be expressions of the cohesion that brings people together in urban subcultures. The larger the city, the more numerous and important subcultural groups such as religious congregations become in the lives of urban dwellers. If Fischer's ideas are correct, the conditions of cities themselves have an influence upon religious organizations, but in the opposite direction that Wirth and his predecessors would have predicted.

The Impact of Religious Groups on Cities: Two Views

What is the impact of religious groups on cities? This relationship also has been examined by scholars, who, not surprisingly, arrive at different conclusions. Some urban scholars argue that congregations promote the status quo as they function to keep conditions the way they are in cities. Others argue the opposite that religious groups act as agents of change in urban areas.

Conservers of the Status Quo

The idea that religious groups are conservers of the status quo is consistent with the view held by a diverse group ranging from Karl Marx to Clarence Stone. Marx is, of course, well known for his description of religion as "the opium of the people" (Marx, 1959, p. 263). In Marx's view, religion blunts the class consciousness of workers by keeping them from realizing the extent of their exploitation by the owners of the means of production. According to Marx, most religious groups emphasize the acceptance of the prevailing economic, social, and political order since the faithful will receive their rewards in an afterlife.

As an illustration, in a study of the role of religious organizations in late nineteenth century Atlanta, most white congregations acted in support of political and economic leaders to enforce a vision of order to keep African Americans and women in their place under the domination of white males. White church leaders supported the city's economic, political, educational, and other institutions to promote racial segregation and deny women opportunities to serve in leadership positions within congregations (Newman, 1977).

The perspective that religious organizations are conservers of the status quo is also articulated by Adolph Reed, Jr.,(1986) who describes the contemporary black church as "an intrinsically antipolitical agency" operating in a completely separate sphere from politics. Reed dismisses as "myth" the historic involvement of black religious leaders in the process of political change (p. 60 and p. 44).

In Stone's *Regime Politics* (1989), the black clergy in Atlanta are described as conservers of racial solidarity whose support of black politicians such as the city's first African American mayor, Maynard Jackson, is sometimes at odds with the needs of lower-income black residents. In contrast to Reed's description of the black church as antipolitical, Stone argues that members of the black clergy are deeply involved in city politics. African American religious leaders are "key links between black officeholders and the black public," sometimes acting like old-style precinct bosses as the clergy ask city officials for favors and considerations for parishioners (pp. 167–168).

Stone is critical of Atlanta's black clergy because they have supported the mayor on several policy issues which favored the interests of upper strata groups and disregarded or harmed the interests of lower strata groups. He cites three economically regressive policies pursued by Mayors Jackson and Young. First, unionized city workers were not able to obtain higher wages and had two strikes broken by the city. Next, Atlanta sought to attract development at any cost without providing any system of linkages to the employment needs of low-income residents, job guarantees, or affordable housing. Finally, the city enacted a regressive sales tax as a major source of local funding for its rapid transit system and as a general revenue source. Each of these policy decisions by the city's black elected officials was supported by members of the black clergy in spite of adverse impacts on low-income residents. Stone suggests that black ministers are part of the pattern of "going along to get along within the Atlanta governing regime that makes a critical stance against black political leaders unlikely" (pp. 166–168).

Agents of Change

In contrast to those who regard the church as a conserver of the status quo in cities, other scholars such as Lincoln and Mamiya (1990) challenge this view and see the church, within the African American community, as an agent of change. Lincoln and Mamiya regard the black church and its clergy as key institutions in promoting the survival of the race and as continually involved in a broad range of political and social activities. Rather than an opiate, the black church and its leadership provide the bedrock of faith, which sustains action to promote change in American cities. After conducting detailed surveys of the seven mainline black denominations representing more than eighty percent of all black Christians in the U.S., Lincoln and Mamiya conclude that the major function of black churches is to provide "mobilizing and communicative networks in local and national elections" (p. 234).

The Concerned Black Clergy of Atlanta

In 1994 a case study examined more closely the role of Atlanta's Concerned Black Clergy (CBC) in the years following Stone's description of this group as conservers of the status quo in Atlanta. Rather than playing the more limited role of precinct captains in the electoral process, this case study reinforced the conclusions of Lincoln and Mamiya that the black clergy were active in elections as well as in promoting action to change conditions in the city. In one example, the CBC mobilized its membership in support of the redevelopment of a central city hotel as transitional housing for low-income people that was strongly opposed by the city's downtown business coalition. The CBC influenced Atlanta's African American mayor to support their proposal and then convinced a local financial institution to provide a loan to fund the project (Newman, 1994).

In 1991 the CBC adopted a manifesto outlining its direction for the future and the commitment of black ministers in the city to promote change through active political participation. The manifesto begins by reaffirming the support of CBC for religion and the family. The document describes how the black clergy are committed to promoting excellence in education as the key to the future of the black community in Atlanta. The CBC resolved to participate in all phases of politics in order to influence policy decisions and to promote change. The manifesto concludes with a commitment to economic independence through job creation aimed at eliminating poverty. For the city's African American ministers, this means they will be active in local politics as the CBC members "seek out and challenge any systems and/or structures that perpetuate economic dependency" (Newman, 1994, p. 31). The manifesto of Atlanta's CBC leaves no doubt that the city's African American churches are intent on promoting change.

While the desire to promote change is strong, the ability of organizations like Atlanta's Concerned Black Clergy to exert influence on the cities in which they are located has limitations. The congregations and their coalition are most effective in rallying voters for an election or mobilizing their large membership base to influence a community decision. In Atlanta the CBC has also been effective in joining other regime participants in forming alliances that can influence local decisions. The weakness of these coalitions is that they have difficulty sustaining such partnerships over time. Stone might suggest that this is due to the absence of resources that characterize stronger participants in local politics such as business leaders organized into a Chamber of Commerce. Stone (1989) describes the informal partnerships between these private groups and public officials as an urban *regime* which makes and carries out local decisions.

Religion and Politics

The main point that needs to be emphasized is that many congregations, and not merely within African American communities, attempt to play an influential role in city politics. Religious groups are most likely to tell members about opportunities to participate in political activities such as petition campaigns or lobbying. This type of political participation takes place among 37 percent of the members of all religious organizations in the U.S. The next most frequent political activity by faith groups is providing voter education through the distribution of voter guides. This type of voter education activity is done by 27 percent of the members of congregations. The third type of political activity that many religious organizations undertake is to mobilize their members to participate in a demonstration or to march in support of or opposition to some public policy.

According to the National Congregations Study (NCS), twenty-one percent of the members of faith groups actually participate in a demonstration or march. Only twelve percent of the members of a congregation listened to a speech by an elected public official, while 6 percent had someone running for office as a visiting speaker (Chaves, 2004). When taken together these activities represent a significant level of political participation by all types of congregations. Indeed, in many cities religious organizations form the bedrock of political education and mobilization in local elections.

As noted, Stone's (1989) urban regime theory would suggest that the effectiveness of political participation by religious groups is often limited by the few resources available to most congregations. In comparison to business groups, religious organizations lack the resources to maintain their influence in local decisions. For example, in Atlanta, the political influence of the CBC is limited in comparison to the city's business community by the fragmentation of African American churches into many small groups. The median size for all congregations in the United States is seventy-five regular participants and only fifty participating adults (and an annual budget of only $56,000). These two issues of small size and limited resources affect many aspects of congregational life. The major activities of smaller churches are likely to be focused inward on worship services and religious education classes with little energy available for broader political and social service programs (Chaves, 2000). Many pastors of smaller churches manage to hold their positions in the church while working full-time jobs in order to support their families. These bi-vocational pastors are less likely to be involved in political activities than the pastors of churches with larger memberships. Occasional participation in meetings of groups like the CBC may be all that the pastors of smaller congregations can do to promote political and social causes. This makes it difficult for these organizations to maintain their focus to influence long-term urban policy issues such as employment, education, and housing.

The splintering of congregations into small groups is consistent with Fischer's subcultural theory of urbanism. Fischer's theoretical perspective suggests that the conditions of city life nurture the formation of small social groups (subcultures), such as religious groups. The larger the urban area, the greater number and diversity of these small social groups would be found. This explains the incredible diversity of types of religious organizations observable in cities. People base their religious identifications on ethnicity, race, and general interest categories which find expression in an array of urban subcultures. The existence of these religious subcultures does not necessarily mean that these groups will form based on people living near one another in city neighborhoods. Fischer observes, "The large subcultures of cities challenge people's allegiance to a group based primarily on geographic proximity" (1984, p. 119).

Congregations and Neighborhoods

Most congregations in cities were initially located to serve the needs of people living in a particular neighborhood. Polish Roman Catholics living in a neighborhood in Detroit would worship in a congregation within walking distance of most members. German Jews would build their first synagogue in a community like Summerhill in Atlanta where most members of the community lived. Faith groups such as these formed important institutions within neighborhoods where most residents shared a common ethnic background.

Even in neighborhoods where ethnicity did not define a majority of residents, congregations could form an important part of what Logan and Molotch (1987) describe as the "use value" of a neighborhood. This term refers to the attachment people feel for their home as a place of residence apart from its monetary value as a piece of property. Use value is the sentiment residents have toward a place that satisfies essential needs of life.

The concept of use value as described by Logan and Molotch has several dimensions that are important for religious groups in urban neighborhoods. Use value suggests that people develop a special relationship with a place such as a church building, synagogue, or mosque. While churches and other religious institutions do not provide the same kind of use values for their members that homes do, small congregations are typically an important part of their neighborhoods. Houses of worship provide a physical focal point and sense of place to neighborhoods.

Most individuals once lived within the neighborhood and maintained a routine that included participation in worship within a group that served the local community. This helped to develop use-value sentiments toward religious organizations that were based on a variety of events and meanings such as births, weddings, and funerals. Both the religious structures and the institutions become repositories of invaluable historical information. These histories can tell much about the institution of the congregation itself and the neighborhood as it changes over time. The members of a faith group may form part of the informal support network of people who are needed for providing important goods and services. Low-income people and the elderly often depend upon these relationships more than other groups, but the movement of an important institution such as a neighborhood congregation can disrupt these support networks.

The Hebrew Benevolent Congregation (The Temple), Atlanta. The synagogue was originally located in the Summerhill neighborhood where most of its German Jewish members lived before they relocated to the more fashionable north side of the city. The current building on Peachtree Street was bombed in 1958, an event featured in the film, "Driving Miss Daisy." (Photo by Harvey K. Newman.)

Places of worship are also social centers providing food, clothing, and other essentials such as housing and a variety of community-based activities. Membership in a faith group also provides the sense of shared social space that is needed to give residents of a neighborhood a sense of security and trust. Religious organizations can provide an important source of identity, both for members and others in a neighborhood. Neighborhood houses of worship can provide tangible links between an immigrant ethnic group and the regions and countries they left behind. As such, these congregations become symbols of the community.

Many places of worship are or contain works of art in their architectural design and features, stained glass windows, and the craftsmanship shown in their furnishings. This is an important use value for religious institutions.

Finally, there is a sense of joining together with others who share common traits of social status and background to form an organization which stands together against others. The use value sentiment that members of a neighborhood feel for a congregation can be strongest when the community joins together in the face of an external threat such as a proposed development that is unwanted in the area. Then, religious organizations and other community groups rally to protect use values in the area. On the other hand, if the congregation opposes the use values of the neighborhood, it might find itself in conflict with neighborhood residents (Newman, 1991).

This form of conflict between a congregation and its surrounding neighborhood is increasingly common in cities where over time the residents of an area who started a congregation have moved away. This echoes Fischer's (1984) comment about the decline of neighborhood religious organizations as subcultures that are no longer based on geographic proximity.

Atlanta Masjid of Al-Islam. Faithful members of the Masjid gather for prayers in their mosque that is located in a strip mall in the East Lake neighborhood of Atlanta. (Photo by Harvey K. Newmen.)

During a recent interview, one faith-based community developer in Atlanta suggested that the major challenge in revitalizing older neighborhoods is the fact that congregation members no longer live in the area. Another community leader expressed the same sentiment more bluntly when she said that none of the faith groups in her neighborhood was involved in the efforts of her community center to improve the lives of neighborhood residents.

The National Congregations Study indicates that this problem is not unique to Atlanta. Only twenty percent of the national sample of local faith groups surveyed in the study indicated that as many as a third of their members live within a 10-minute walk of the church, synagogue, or other religious institution. Most houses of worship draw at least half their membership from within a ten-minute drive, but there are many members of religious organizations who drive considerable distances to attend services. The NCS found that twenty percent of congregations have at least a quarter of their members living more than a thirty-minute drive away (Chaves, 2000).

This lack of a neighborhood-based membership makes it difficult for a congregation to understand the needs of the community surrounding its building since few live in the immediate area. For instance, the commuters who drive to worship might see the need to buy property and tear down houses for more parking as a priority for the members of the religious group. At the same time, the neighborhood might want to protect and improve housing in the area. This puts a congregation in opposition to the wishes of the surrounding neighborhood residents and can make the preservation or revitalization of the neighborhood more difficult.

A faith group might retain its building in an area where few members live for several reasons. A cemetery or historic building may serve as an anchor to members who wish to maintain a link to a particular place. In other cases, the residents of a neighborhood might have moved in response to change in the community. This change may be based on race, ethnicity, or class as the new residents to a neighborhood displace those who previously lived in the area.

In one example of this process in Atlanta, the large sanctuary and education building belonging to a white Baptist church were sold to an African American Baptist church after the original members fled to the suburbs as part of the "white flight" from the area. Currently, the African American Baptists are moving from the neighborhood to suburban DeKalb County as whites return to gentrify this area known as East Atlanta. The pastor plans for the African American church to stay in the neighborhood as long as members return to the church to take part in the activities of the congregation. Most members of this group stay in the church because of the pastor's charismatic leadership.

This pattern is typical as many people are attracted to a congregation on the basis of either the personality of the leader or the program of the organization, and they are willing to commute in order to participate. The members of this house of worship may be viewed as an urban subculture whose members live in areas that are distant from the location of the church building, but who are still committed members of the group.

This congregation tries in a variety of ways to influence change within its neighborhood. The group feeds the homeless and provides other social services to the poor. It operates a school for children in kindergarten through the eighth grade as well as an after school program. The congregation created a community development corporation as a separate nonprofit organization to aid in the redevelopment of the neighborhood. Yet this array of social services provided to the neighborhood is threatened by the gentrification of the area.

As the neighborhood attracts more affluent residents, will the community continue to need the social services provided by the congregation? This is one of the subtle effects of neighborhood change on a large, well-established religious organization. Other faith groups may be less willing or able to remain within a changing neighborhood. The smaller store-front congregations that serve the religious needs of residents in many low-income neighborhoods would be more vulnerable to displacement by gentrification.

Activities of Congregations in Cities

In many ways faith groups have a reciprocal relationship with the cities in which they are located. At many times the conditions of city life affect religious organizations, while the reverse is often true also. For example, a majority of congregations do what they can to improve the lives of people in need. These social services activities, such as providing clothing, food, housing, and education, are significant activities for some faith groups. According to the NCS, fifty-seven percent of all congregations in the U.S. offer some type of social services, but most organizations are small groups operating with limited budgets. As a consequence, providing social services has to be a peripheral activity for these smaller groups which have few resources. No more than six percent of the congregations in the NCS have a staff person who devotes at least twenty-five percent of his or her time to social service projects (Chaves, 2004).

As Livezey (2000) observed in a study of seventy-five Chicago religious organizations, "Most of the congregations principally serve their own members, with service to the wider community and advocacy for public causes relegated to small committees and discretionary portions of annual budgets . . . Programs of social service and social action account for but a fraction of the religious contribution to the quality of urban life" (p. 20).

While the social service activities of most congregations are modest, the cumulative effect on cities is important. For example, during the era of the most rapid expansion of cities as industrialization created jobs for immigrants and rural migrants to American cities, religious organizations attempted to respond to the needs of these new arrivals. Many faith leaders promoted settlement houses, "institutional churches," support for better housing conditions, child labor laws, labor organizations, and other proposals that would benefit the urban poor. These reform efforts were usually taken over by public agencies and a host of other nonprofit groups, but religious organizations continue to assist in these urban social service activities.

More recently the neighborhood renewal movement has received support from a variety of faith-based groups. In a collection of case studies from cities across the country by Von Hoffman, (2003) many of the central city revitalization success stories result from the actions of faith groups and religiously-inspired individuals. These people are attempting to rebuild urban neighborhoods house by house and block by block. Other evidence is provided by the variety of case studies from Chicago collected by Livezey (2000). These cases also indicate the extent to which congregations are engaged in transforming cities. In another locality, one of the efforts of the Maxine Goodman Levin College of Urban Affairs, Cleveland State University is to document the role of congregations in neighborhood social service delivery and economic development.

Worship and Education

In addition to social services and economic development, congregations do other things to promote change in cities. According to the NCS, congregations are almost always involved in three activities: 1. the production of worship events, 2. the transmission of religious knowledge, and 3. the facilitation of artistic activity. According to Chaves (2000), these three activities "occupy more congregations, engage more people, use more resources, and contribute more significantly to communities" than social services, political activities, or anything else (p. 14). It is the regular gathering of people to worship that Mumford suggested led to the founding of cities. For most of the time since these first gatherings, people have built places of worship in which to carry on these crucial human activities. Once assembled as worshipping congregations, attention was also paid to instructing the young in an effort to transmit religious knowledge from one generation to the next. These two aspects of congregational life in cities, worship and the transmission of religious knowledge, are widely understood.

Artistic Work

It is less well known that congregations are centers for the facilitation of artistic activity. The production and consumption of music as part of worship services is perhaps the most obvious example. For ninety-eight percent of those who attend congregations, singing is a part of the worship service, and ninety-one percent of people attending services hear performances on musical instruments of various types. People are also more likely to see dance and drama in worship services than anywhere else in society (Chaves, 2004).

The performing arts, such as music, dance, and drama are not the only ways in which faith groups produce and consume art. The visual arts are also a significant contribution to the arts by congregations. This can include using the building for exhibits of paintings, photography, and sculpture, which is a common practice among most religious organizations. A second form of visual art that is important for houses of worship is the architecture of buildings.

Constitutional Issues Involving Congregations and Cities

The First Amendment to the U.S. Constitution states that "Congress shall make no law respecting an establishment of religion, or prohibiting the free exercise thereof. . ." These two passages, known as the "establishment clause" and the "free exercise" clause, are the basis for the formal relations between religious organizations and government in the United States. While the amendment is addressed to Congress and the federal government, the passage of the Fourteenth Amendment made it applicable to states and to the cities created by the states. Often the test cases to sort out the relationships between congregations and government involve the use of land or the application of zoning regulations that take place in cities.

The Constitution's limitation on establishing any sort of religion is sometimes joined with the free exercise clause if a local ordinance is seen as giving preference to one religious group over another. Most conflict in cities comes from local government regulations that are regarded as burdensome to the free exercise of religion. For example, the town of Murfreesboro, Tennessee, denied permission for a Muslim group to build a larger mosque and a community center. Similar rezoning requests for the expansion of a Muslim worship center were denied in the Atlanta suburb of Lilburn. In both towns there was hostility to Muslims as well as the proposed mosques. The Lilburn city council twice turned down the request for rezoning, so the congregation sued the city, claiming the denials restricted their free exercise of religion. The suit claimed religious bias on the part of local officials seeking to appease members of the public who did not want a mosque in the neighborhood. Federal courts have jurisdiction in these and similar cases where the constitutional issues are clear that cities may not use their zoning laws to discriminate against religious groups seeking to build places of worship.

Muslim groups are not the only religious organizations whose plans have generated conflict with the zoning ordinances of local governments. Efforts by congregations to operate homeless shelters and food banks often run into conflict with local governments' zoning regulations. In these cases, federal courts have upheld the right of the local governments to impose zoning restrictions on religious groups if these ordinances are generally applicable and do not prevent the congregations from practicing their religion. In all of these types of cases, congregations may not claim that their free exercise of religion exempts them from local government regulations, as long as the ordinances are designed to promote the general welfare of the community and apply equally to religious groups as well as nonreligious ones (Nolan and Salkin, 2006).

The federal government's effort to protect the free exercise of religion from restriction by local governments is covered by the Religious Land Use and Institutionalized Persons Act of 2000 (RLUIPA). The act protects the First Amendment free exercise of religion by restricting local governments from zoning out congregations from their jurisdictions. When local governments in Murfreesboro, Tennessee, and Lilburn, Georgia, attempted to restrict Muslim congregations from building mosques, the federal courts protected the rights of the congregations under RLUIPA. Other religious groups also seek protection under the 2000 federal law. Churches in two Atlanta area suburbs have used this legislation as part of their defense against local zoning ordinances. In one case, the Church of Scientology wanted to expand its building by eliminating a parking garage owned by the congregation. In this instance the town of Sandy Springs was allowed to enforce its parking ordinance against the Church of Scientology, since the same parking-space requirements apply to both religious and nonreligious groups. On the other hand, the town of Marietta lost a case in which the local zoning ordinance imposed a minimum lot-size requirement of 5 acres on religious institutions, but did not make the same requirement for nonreligious organizations.

In summary, RLUIPA requires a local government to allow the religious exercise of religion, within reasonable limits, and to treat religious institutions the same as secular groups (Bowen, 2006). Given the unpopularity of some religious groups, it is reasonable to expect conflicts between local governments and congregations to continue. These conflicts will be fought out in court cases because the First Amendment and RLUIPA protect the free exercise of religion from the actions of city governments.

Conclusions

From the earliest cities to the present, sacred places for worship have been crucial features of urban areas. In the first cities, residents shared a common faith expressed in the central ziggurat, as well as smaller shrines scattered through the residential areas. Today, smaller cities and sprawling metropolises are characterized by a fragmentation of religious groups reflecting the pluralism of American urban civilization.

This mosaic of religious subcultures was once largely based in the city neighborhoods where residents lived and worshipped together. Over time, people relocate and these congregations are no longer made up primarily of neighborhood residents. Yet many of these faith groups, especially in low-income neighborhoods, continue to provide important use values to their members who not only share worship, but also share social services and economic development activities within the community.

Whether viewed in broad terms such as subcultural formation or in more subtle ways such as neighborhood change, cities influence congregations. Yet in reciprocal fashion, religious groups influence the urban areas in which they are located. Congregations can participate in local politics as coalition partners attempting to influence change or serve as key components in voter education and mobilization. They also provide social services ranging from the provision of clothing and food to helping neighborhoods organize to secure better housing and jobs. The buildings of congregations can provide important use value sentiment for neighborhood residents.

These buildings provide the space for people to come together for the central event in the lives of most congregations—worship. They also provide room for the transmission of religious knowledge in the important function of education that most congregations continue week after week and year after year. These same buildings, their windows, and their furnishings can provide visual art for the communities in which they are located. They serve as space for the performing arts produced by religious organizations as they worship. Above all, the buildings erected by faith groups need to be recognized as sacred landmarks in continuity with the places where people have worshipped in cities as long as urban areas have existed.

Name _____

CHAPTER 13

The City Worships (Religion)

13-1. Give examples of early settlers in your city and describe the influence of religion on their way of life.

13-2. List the churches, synagogues, mosques or other places of worship in your neighborhood and discuss their role in the urban community.

13-3. Compare Fischer's theory to that of Wirth. What did each predict about cities and religious subcultures?

The City Explores Its Behavior
(Psychology)

Roberta Steinbacher and Faith D. Gilroy

Human beings are social animals, gathering into groups to meet their needs. The cities around them are extensions of themselves. Systems of food delivery, energy consumption, waste disposal, memory storage, health control and infrastructure all mimic human biological systems on their most fundamental levels. Like the organic systems that sustain individual lives, these larger systems not only act, but interact in complex cycles and networks that in the end return and mold each individual in a city. The discipline of psychology contributes to the overall understanding of the individual's place in the larger system, the city, and its subsystems.

There are many specialties and sub-specialties of the discipline of psychology which offer insightful theories that are essential to an understanding of urban areas. For example, the study of punishment, which is one focus of behavioral psychology, leads to better methods of reducing crime in urban settings. To understand leadership in civic affairs, one must first know what moves people to act; this is the study of motivational psychology. Social psychology contributes to the understanding of group interaction, consensus building, and the formulation of public policy. This chapter will expose the student of the city to a variety of these psychological theories and their application to urban life.

Human Psychological Needs

If one were asked to make a list of what a human being in an urban area needed to survive, the chances are that the list would be dominated by a set of physical needs such as air, food, and water. But if one were to ask this individual urban dweller what would be needed if he or she were going to be left behind on a desert island, the person in question would undoubtedly expand the list to include certain non-essentials that would make the isolation easier to tolerate. A person is more than the sum of his or her physical needs. Families, friends, groups, institutions and cities all contribute to satisfying those needs beyond the physical, that is the psychological.

One may well ask, how important to one's survival are these psychological needs? A radio, some company and a little hope of rescue may make being stranded on an island more comfortable, but are these necessary for survival?

Studies in the 1940s indicated that infants placed in orphanages, where they were given none of the usual attention an infant at home can be expected to receive, became withdrawn and depressed even when all their physical needs were met (Goldfarb, 1945; Spitz, 1946).

In animal studies, Harlow (1958) discovered that when a baby rhesus monkey was placed in a cage with a mother monkey doll made of wire to which a mechanical feeding device was attached and a mother monkey doll made of cloth, the baby monkey would gravitate to the cloth doll even though the wire doll was its source of food. These classical studies indicate the necessity to include psychological, as well as physical needs when considering the behaviors and attitudes of city residents.

A model that takes into consideration both physical and psychological needs was proposed by the psychologist Abraham Maslow (1970). Maslow constructed a pyramid-shaped hierarchy where the more fundamental needs were at the base, and those less necessary were at the apex, as displayed in Figure 14.1. At the bottom were the most essential physical needs such as food and water. The step above the essentials were security and safety. These two physical levels were followed by three psychological needs: belongingness, esteem, and finally self actualization. Maslow proposed that one must satisfy more basic needs before progressing to those higher in the hierarchy. Although Maslow's theory has not had strong empirical validation, there have been recent studies., (eg., Dominguez & Carton, 1997) that do support some of his principles.

Maslow's theory served as the basis for the development of existence, relatedness, and growth (**ERG**) theory by Clayton Alderfer (1972). Alderfer thought that the seven needs Maslow identified actually fit into three main groups. ERG theory takes into consideration that desire for some needs is chronic in nature. This means that while an individual may seek to satisfy higher order needs, their desire for lower order needs remains. Alderfer also noted that if an individual is frustrated in achieving satisfaction of higher order needs, there is an increase in desire for those in the lower order.

Maslow's hierarchy of needs and Alderfer's ERG theory provide useful models for understanding a variety of human behaviors in cities. For example, these models assist in understanding causes for academic failure rates in urban school systems. In schools

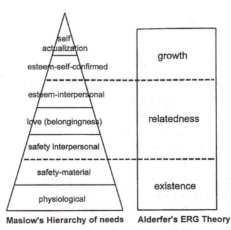

Figure 14.1
Comparison of Maslow's Hierarchy of Needs and Alderfer's ERG Theory.
(Adapted from Alderfer, C. P. 1972, p. 25).

where gang violence is prevalent, and teachers or administrators are unable to protect students from that violence, it is rather unlikely that the students will try to satisfy their need to self actualize by doing their school work, while the more fundamental need for safety is not being met.

There are signs that government policies are beginning to take into account the complexity of citizens' needs and to evaluate programs in more than measurable, physical terms. In an examination of the effects on nursing home residents of the Omnibus Budget Reconciliation Act of 1987 (OMBRA), it was argued that due to the relationship between how well the needs of the residents are met and their quality of life and survival, this legislation must also respect "an appropriate need mix" (Umoren, 1992).

Further understanding of human needs and their effects on behavior can enlighten policymakers in their efforts to improve the livability of urban centers. Indeed, those communities which offer, in addition to the bare essentials, self-actualizing services such as good schools, recreational facilities, and social services are considered by many to be the most desirable. Yet, if the city is truly an extension of its inhabitants, a well balanced approach on the part of government officials to meet the psychological needs of cities and their inhabitants, one which addresses the more fundamental issues of safety and security before moving up the hierarchy, is of paramount importance.

Crime and Punishment

Understanding the psychology of people in the urban environment provides cities with more than a means to meet their needs. By utilizing the principles of human behavior, city officials are better able to address civic problems. Crime is perceived by urban citizens as a major problem in society today. They believe that crime threatens their basic needs of security and safety. In spite of stricter laws, more diligent enforcement, and stricter punishments, crime continues to diminish the quality of life in cities. Behavioral psychology offers a theoretical perspective from which to understand the effectiveness of society's responses.

Numerous studies throughout the history of the discipline of psychology indicate that behavior can be changed by the use of **reinforcement.** Reinforcement can be both positive and negative in nature. For example, a student who has studied for a test and receives an "A" will be positively reinforced to study for other tests. Negative reinforcement occurs when an unpleasant or painful event is ended by a specific action, for example, taking an unpleasant tasting medication to relieve an upset stomach. Ending the pain is negative reinforcement. Behavior can be positively and negatively reinforced simultaneously. If the medication itself is tasteful (positive reinforcement) and the pain is relieved (negative reinforcement) it will most likely be taken again in similar circumstances. This same process contributes to an understanding of drug addiction. Taking drugs provides both positive (the immediate high) and negative (reduction of stress and ennui) reinforcement.

The Effectiveness of Punishment

The effectiveness of punishment on behavior has been a subject of discussion in psychological research for many years. Punishment may be defined as an action which is administered after a behavior occurs in order to decrease (**suppress**) it or eliminate it altogether. Pioneering psychologists such as Thorndike (1932) and Skinner (1938) voiced doubts as to whether punishment could eliminate undesirable behavior. Later studies have indicated that the way punishment is administered affects the degree to which it controls behavior. Three factors which are important for an understanding of the effectiveness of punishment are: **Intensity, generalization, and schedule.**

Intensity

One of the first systematic inquiries into the application of punishment dealt with the intensity of the **aversive** (negative) stimulus. Classic experiments conducted by Miller (1960) and Azrin (1960) concluded that punishments that grew in intensity with successive applications had less effect on behaviors than punishments that were intense in the early stages. Furthermore, given an initial intense shock, subjects later were more likely to suppress undesired behaviors with the same results using a subsequently less intense aversive stimulus (Church, 1969). In other words, if one wanted to stop an individual from doing something, the effective way would be to punish him/her severely the first time the undesirable behavior occurs. Even if the behavior recurs, one can then use a less intense punishment to achieve the same results. On the other hand, if the punishment is made worse progressively, the individual could become desensitized to it, even in its extreme form, and will continue the behavior.

Generalization

One of the problems faced in using punishment to modify behavior is to ensure that the punishment extinguishes only the undesirable behavior in question. Quite frequently, punishment is effective for not only the undesirable behavior but also for behavior that might be similar to it. In other words, the individual generalizes from one stimulus to another. The backfiring of an automobile in a crowded intersection elicits the same response as a gunshot in many of the pedestrians on nearby city streets. The issue of **generalization** was encountered in early research by the founder of the behavioralist school of psychology, J. B. Watson, in the famous Baby Albert experiment.

Generalization is a pernicious and enduring difficulty in the use of punishment. Although techniques exist to target a punishment to a specific behavior, ethical issues arise in their application to human subjects. Even the Baby Albert experiment would be considered unethical by today's behavioral psychologists.

Schedule

Another aspect of punishment and its effect is that of timing. In the early 1960s it was discovered that the longer the delay between the behavior and the punishment, the less effective the punishment was on suppressing behavior (Baron, 1965). Research has shown that the amount of times the behavior occurs before being punished will also influence the effectiveness of the punishment. An example of this phenomenon is found in an experiment by Azrin (1963). The experimenters trained pigeons to peck a button to get food. They then attempted to extinguish the behavior by applying an electric shock on a **fixed ratio** schedule. A fixed ratio schedule is one in which the punishment is applied after a fixed number of times that the behavior occurs (eg., at every third peck on the button the pigeon receives a shock). What Azrin discovered was that the subject would return to the act but at a slower rate. Consequently it may be concluded that the more often an act goes unpunished, the less likely punishment will eliminate the behavior.

The Baby Albert Experiment

In 1920 J. B. Watson, in collaboration with Rosalie Rayner, attempted to explain the fear reaction of infants in terms of classical conditioning. In classical conditioning a stimulus (unconditioned) which produces a response can be substituted for a non-response producing stimulus (conditioned) when the two stimuli occur together. This is the same principle behind the earlier experiment with Pavlov's dog, where the animal responded to the sound of a bell (conditioned stimulus) as it were meat (unconditioned stimulus) by salivating when it was rung.

Watson and Rayner (1920) hypothesized that people had a fear response, as in the case of phobias, because they had made such an association with an unpleasant stimulus. To prove their hypothesis, they took a nine-month-old child, Baby Albert, and exposed him to a white rat. At first the child showed no fear of the animal. Then a laboratory assistant struck a piece of metal producing a loud, unpleasant sound each time the child saw the rat. Baby Albert soon associated the rat with the loud noise and started to cry when he saw it, whether or not the sound was made.

Unfortunately, Watson and Rayner were more successful than they ever had imagined, because Baby Albert began to show the same fearful response to a Santa mask, a seal skin coat, and a wad of cotton balls. Although the experimenters had attempted to condition him to fear only rats, Baby Albert had generalized the association to anything white and furry.

EXHIBIT 14.1
The Baby Albert Experiment

Psychological research appears to indicate that for punishment to be effective, these conditions need to be in place: First, it must occur as close in time as possible to the commission of the act. Second, the initial punishment should be as intense as possible and should not increase as a behavior recurs. Third, there must be certainty that the act will be punished. These approaches to punishment are applicable to reactions of the criminal justice system in most urban areas. In cases where frequent acts of violence go unpunished because the offender has eluded law enforcement officials or has avoided prison for a variety of reasons, the punishment obviously does not occur immediately after the act; therefore, the criminal is not likely to stop this behavior as a result of some potential future punishment. In the criminal justice system today, the initial punishment is often lighter for first offenders, and increases with repetition of the offense, a practice unquestioned by most Americans (and the opposite of the **intensity** condition above). Finally, the condition of certainty of punishment exists in some state and federal statutes through mandatory sentencing. This punishment has raised considerable debate as to its effectiveness in eliminating repetition of the criminal behavior. In the third condition of the psychological model, certainty is essential.

Behavioral psychology offers insights on the way in which punishment works to modify behavior. How these insights are used is critical for maintaining basic needs of safety and security in cities. The human dimension must be addressed when programs are developed, so that they are tempered with a respect for civil liberties, ethical treatment, and justice. The chief concern in using psychology without this human dimension is that it might lead to what philosophers call a "slippery slope." What is acceptable to change the behavior of criminals today might well become acceptable to change the behavior of law abiding citizens tomorrow.

Perceptions of the City

In a representative democracy much civic authority is delegated to elected and appointed officials. Although a democracy expects these officials to use their judgment to decide management issues, the question that often remains first and foremost in their minds is: "How will this look to the public?" (or on a more local scale: "What will the neighbors think?"). There are few citizens who would take comfort in the knowledge that their actions would be met with public condemnation. It is for this reason that the discipline of psychology often focuses on how people make judgments and form an image of their urban surroundings.

The Subjective Witness

People make judgments that greatly influence the course of events in urban settings. The most obvious is when people vote; however, there are many other important functions they perform that involve formulating an opinion. They sit on juries that decide the guilt or innocence of their peers. They participate in social, religious, civic, and private organizations that exert political influence on their representatives as part of shared values in a democracy. The simple act of buying a product in a supermarket or watching a television program has broader implications to society, because it can give insight into what the public wants.

Much of how opinions are formed by city residents rests on what is remembered of events. Psychology examines the evolution of objective sensory perceptions as they become subjective memories. In research done by Loftus and Palmer (1974), this process was investigated in order to test the objectivity of eyewitness testimony. Subjects were shown a traffic film of a car accident and then asked to fill out a questionnaire. They were randomly divided into four groups in which a single word was altered on a question asking them to estimate the speed of a car (i.e., How fast was it moving when it "smashed," "collided," "bumped," "hit," or "contacted" the other car?). The results of the questionnaire indicated that by changing the wording used, the subjects' observational judgments were somehow changed. The "smashed" group reported a higher speed than did the "collided"; and the "collided" faster than the "bumped" group. These authors suggested that either the change in wording led the subjects to a conclusion, or that the actual memory of the event was somehow altered. In large cities, where residents are daily confronted with monumental amounts of information (written, spoken, e-mailed, texted, and all forms of social media), it is strenuous to process these inputs as well as accurately recall them.

In a second test, 150 subjects were asked to complete the same questionnaire after watching the film of the traffic accident. When a week had passed, they were asked the question: "Did you see any broken glass?" In the movie there was none, and 80% reported so. Among those who **did** report seeing broken glass, sixteen were in the "smashed" group. Loftus and Palmer (1974) concluded that the actual memory of the event had been altered by being exposed to information after the fact. This research explains the use of so-called "spin doctors" by public and private organizations who are seeking to foster support for various social causes or candidates for elective office. It also underlines the necessity, for example, to find juries that have not been exposed to opinion-shaping information that may be misleading.

Building upon these early research findings, the accuracy of eyewitness testimony continues to be studied. Several investigators (eg., Loftus, 1997; Mazzoni & Memon, 2003) have presented data indicating numerous variables that affect the accuracy of such memories, and judges now often instruct juries to evaluate such testimony very critically.

Bystander Intervention

Bystander intervention became an area of study in psychology after the tragic Kitty Genovese murder in 1964. Kitty Genovese was attacked and repeatedly stabbed as she tried to enter her apartment in New York City. Even though she cried out for help, and thirty-eight of her neighbors later admitted witnessing at least part of the crime, nobody so much as called the police to help her. Bibb Latane and John Darley (1968) were struck by lack of assistance to the victim and performed a number of experiments to attempt to determine the causes of bystander intervention or lack of it. They found that there are a series of internal decisions made by individuals in these situations.

The ambiguity of the situation (Is this a real emergency or not?) must be resolved before any action is attempted. Even if the determination of an emergency is made, an individual's action can often be influenced by the number of bystanders present. The more bystanders there are, the less likely one individual will intervene to help the victim. Bystanders also must decide what the appropriate course of action would be and if they are capable of doing it. Finally, a decision is made to intervene based on the personal, physical, and social risk involved.

More recent studies have examined the personality characteristics of those who assist victims and those who do not. Bierhoff, Klein and Kramp (1991), reviewing previous studies, identified the components of the **altruistic personality** which help to distinguish these individuals from their non-involved bystanders: They have a strong sense of internal control; they believe in a just world; they are empathetic; and they demonstrate a concern for others.

Attribution Theory

Human beings are by nature curious and involved in the events occurring in the places they live. When people observe these events, they are likely to attribute them to a cause. Rigorous methods in psychology are used to prevent this tendency from interfering with accurate conclusions, but most people must rely on less formal methods when making their judgments. One such informal methodology is described by attribution theory.

According to attribution theory, one can either blame a person or a situation for the outcome of an event. Personal or **internal** attribution bases the cause on the character of the person involved. Situational or **external** attribution bases the cause on the circumstances around the event. So if Jane is late for class, it could be attributed to traffic problems (situational) or to the perception that she is lazy (personal).

There are several factors that influence how one decides between the person or the situation. Three of these factors are **distinctiveness, consensus,** and **consistency** (Kelley, 1967). **Distinctiveness** describes the uniqueness of an event with respect to the situation. If Jane had never been late to any of her other classes, it is unlike her behavior elsewhere and is therefore very distinct. **Consensus** compares performance to others. If everyone in Jane's class was late, there is a great deal of consensus behind her behavior. Finally, **consistency** is the degree to which a behavior is repeated in similar situations. If Jane were always late to her morning class, her behavior is very consistent (Iacobucci & McGill, 1990). In passing their judgment, people weigh these three factors in their minds, and the one that is the most salient to them determines whether they attribute it to the person or the situation. For example, if distinctiveness or consensus is the highly salient factor, then one is more likely to blame the situation (Kelley, 1967).

McElroy (1991) applies performance factors to describe how people perceive the success and failure of their leaders. Once again, these factors are divided into **internal** and **external** attributions. The outcome of an event is seen as **internal** when the salient factor is either the ability or the amount of effort put forth by the person in question. **External** causes are pursued when task difficulty or uncontrollable circumstances (eg., luck) are viewed as being the most important. These factors are also broken down into either stable or variable patterns of influence. In other words, when a situation is governed by ability or task difficulty, it produces a more stable effect than effort or luck. McElroy (1991) argues that a leader's ability to control these performance factors is of greater importance to the perceived success of his or her duties than is the actual outcome of events.

> *The extent to which politicians remain in power, therefore, depends on their ability to obtain credit for positive outcomes (whether deserved or not) and avoid being blamed for failures. The ability to unseat an incumbent depends, of course, on being able to do just the opposite relative to the incumbent's record while maintaining a record of attaching themselves to successes and avoiding failures. (p. 95)*

By way of example, McElroy offers the two presidential administrations of the 1980s. Ronald Reagan was so apt at controlling his image that he was called the "Teflon President" (i.e., no "dirt" would stick to him). On the other hand, President George H. W. Bush had such difficulty avoiding criticisms about the Iran-Contra scandal that he was sometimes called the "Velcro President." Regardless of how well an elected official performs, the public can only act on what it sees and hears. If proper care and attention are not given to one's public image, that official might well be unseated regardless of his or her performance.

Heuristics

Another informal methodology people use is heuristics. Heuristics are implicit strategies for getting an answer when one is unsure of a methodology that will produce a definite result. Typically one can rely on these informal methods to produce generally accurate predictions of an event; however, problems arise when these informal methods take precedence over more appropriate strategies.

One type of heuristic bases its conclusion on stereotypical thinking, or how much a sample appears similar to a population. This is called a **representativeness heuristic** (Kahneman & Tversky, 1972). While using other heuristics based on a means-end strategy, or on working a puzzle backwards to its solution may be useful in a great number of situations, the representativeness heuristic is frequently misleading. In experiments conducted by Kahneman and Tversky (1973), subjects inappropriately tended to rely more heavily on stereotypes than they did on their knowledge of probability.

Given a room with a 100 people in it, of whom 30 were lawyers and 70 were engineers, subjects were asked the probability that one person from that group was an engineer. None of them showed any difficulty in reaching the correct answer, which was 70%. They were then given personal information on two other individuals who were also chosen at random.

> *Dick is a 30-year old man. He is married with no children. A man of high ability and high motivation, he promises to be quite successful in his field. He is well liked by his colleagues.*
>
> *Jack is a 45-year old man. He is married and has four children. He is generally conservative, careful, and ambitious. He shows no interest in political and social issues and spends his free time at home on his many hobbies, which include home carpentry, sailing, and mathematical puzzles (Kahneman & Tversky, 1973, pp. 241–242).*

The description of Dick was not intended to give the reader any information that could be useful in determining his profession. On the other hand, the description of Jack was intended to describe characteristics stereotypically favored by engineers. In deciding the probability that either Jack or Dick was an engineer chosen from the room, subjects tended to disregard the prior information in favor of the statistically irrelevant personal description. Subjects erroneously reported a 50% likelihood that either one was an engineer. City newspapers and television news report a variety of statistics and stories on crime, drugs, unemployment, homelessness, poverty, and other urban problems. This negative portrait of cities has the potential to give urban dwellers "prior information" with which to form stereotypes, as well to provide material leading to stimulus generalization. For example, a story or broadcast exposing a city official's questionable or potentially illegal conduct can evoke a response in the reader of generalizing such conduct to other elected officials—the "all politicians are crooks" notion.

A second heuristic that is frequently misleading is based on the influence recent or easily recalled events has on estimating frequency and probability. This is called the **availability heuristic.** Tversky and Kahneman (1973) had subjects read two lists of famous and non-famous names separated by gender. They were then asked to recall the names. On the average, twelve of nineteen famous names were recalled as opposed to seven of twenty non-famous names. The subjects were then asked to estimate the number of names from each list. Although each list differed by only one name, subjects tended to overestimate the number of famous names relative to non-famous names.

Another common misuse of the availability heuristic occurs when dramatic events tend to stand out in our minds. A plane crash is one such dramatic event. In spite of the fact that plane travel is safer than travel by car, people tend to be more nervous flying away from an airport than they are driving up to it, especially after a news report of a crash.

Memory research, attribution theory, and heuristics offer broad and very useful insight into the formulation of public perception and judgment. It is both a strength and a weakness that human psychology works in such a manner. Descartes realized in the seventeenth century that human senses were flawed and subject to deception. It was his belief that truth can be found only in an appeal to rational meditation. Often human beings do not have the time or resources to deliberate over every detail of their lives. They therefore rely on imperfect memories and informal methods to guide them in creating their image of the city. An understanding of how these principles are used is therefore essential not only to those whose role it is to keep the urban public informed, but also to any citizen-member of participatory government.

The City: A Crowded Place?

One of the frequently overlooked needs of living things is the need for space. Whether the living thing in question is a one-celled organism, plant, or human being, if there is inadequate room to grow, development is stunted, health is diminished, and life expectancy is cut short. In recent years as the world population has become increasingly urbanized (in the United States 250,000,000 people live in urbanized areas and share 3% of U. S. land), the effect of overcrowding is becoming an ever more controversial topic. Psychology has addressed this topic along a broad body of research.

One of the most debated and disturbing pieces of research conducted on the effects of crowding was an animal study done by J. B. Calhoun (1962). Taking a ten by fourteen foot room divided into four interconnecting pens, Calhoun assembled a population of 80 white rats. This was a population density far in excess of anything that would be found in nature. Because rats tend to be social animals, the effects of the crowded conditions were observed in the hope that it would be analogous to human behavior in similar conditions. Over the course of the experiment, the population was held constant by removing rats when there were several births, or by replacing rats as they died.

The observations made by Calhoun and his assistants were striking. Female rats' ability to make adequate nests for their young began to deteriorate until they finally quit building them all together. Their newborn pups were dropped indiscriminately around the pens, and the care and protection of the young was neglected. Dominant males would suddenly become aggressive and attack females, juveniles, and less dominant males by biting their tails. Among other aberrations such as infanticide, cannibalism, and disruption of typical instinctive behaviors, Calhoun also reported a type of rat that was completely passive and would wander around in a dazed state totally detached from social interaction.

Calhoun's study was influential in later studies conducted on the effects of density and crowding; however, caution needs to be taken in applying these conclusions to human beings in cities. Jonathan Freedman (1979) noted that the effects of density and crowding are complex and do not necessarily mean that the results are consistently negative. More recent studies have shown that coping behaviors in animals differ between species. In a study by Peter Judge and Frans B. M. de Waal (1997), rhesus monkeys responded to crowded conditions by increasing their coping behaviors, taking steps to defuse situations before fights broke out. These results by primates are the opposite of what generally occurs in studies using rodents.

Crowds and Stress

The ability to handle crowded conditions might depend on social and cognitive factors; however, once stress is encountered, there are definite physiological effects. Selye (1974) contends that there is a reaction that follows several stages of what he calls the **general adaption syndrome.** When stress is encountered, there is an initial "alarm reaction" which puts demands on the autonomic nervous system. This is the mechanism that is triggered to deal with emergency situations by increasing activity in heart rate, blood pressure, blood sugar, and respiration. If the stress continues, the subject enters the "resistance" stage. Further physiological resources are called upon to deal with the specific stressor at the expense of focusing on more positive emotions. As more of these are elicited to manage the problem, the subject is able to deal with fewer and fewer other situations until finally there is nothing left. When this is reached, the subject is in the "exhaustion" state, which can result in permanent damage or even death.

This process is influenced by cognitive appraisal of the situation according to Lazarus (1993). This means that a person's response to any given situation will be based on his or her previous experiences or knowledge of similar situations. As a person is presented with situations, he or she develops either direct or defensive coping skills which are then used to deal with other situations. This process enables an individual to avoid the extreme state noted by Selye (1974).

One of the causes of stress in individuals is crowding. Baum (1994) notes that there may be a distinction between population density and a subjective condition called crowdedness. The following explanation distinguishes between the two concepts.

> . . . *people do not feel crowded unless there are other people around and space is somewhat limited. Thus density is necessary for the judgment of crowding to be made. However, people do not always feel crowded when density increases. High density at a sporting event, concert, or political rally is necessary to generate desired levels of excitement. In such cases, although density is fairly high, most people do not feel crowded. However, the same density can become aversive and be experienced as crowding under other circumstances such as trying to get to one's car and leave the parking lot after the event is over. (p. 365)*

Baum further states that men are more negatively affected by crowding than are women. It is suggested by the author that there is something inherent in the way men are socialized that makes them more vulnerable to the negative stress of crowding. Baum also points out that there is a difference in how various cultures define "crowded," depending on their socialization processes.

Finally, Baum indicates that the goals of each individual seem to play a role. When the population density tends to interfere with the performance of a person's task, it creates a greater amount of negative stress.

Effects of Crowding

Parallels between what was observed by Calhoun and others and what can be observed as major psychological problems in the urban setting can easily be drawn. Stanley Milgram (1970), in trying to account for changes in human behavior due to the added stresses brought on by overcrowded cities, believed that urban dwellers suffer from **sensory overload:**

> *This term, drawn from systems analysis, refers to the inability of a system to process inputs from the environment because there are too many inputs for the*

system to cope with, or because successive inputs come so fast that Input A can-
not be processed when Input B is presented. When overload is present, adapta-
tions occur. The system must set priorities and make choices. Input A may be
processed first while B is kept in abeyance, or one input may be sacrificed alto-
gether. City life, as we experience it, constitutes a continuous set of encounters
with adaptations to overload. Overload characteristically deforms daily life on
several levels, impinging on role performance, evolution of social norms, cogni-
tive functioning, and the use of faculties. (p. 153)

Milgram then listed six adaptations to overload used by urbanites. The first two adaptive mechanisms are mentioned in the above paragraph: **give each input less time,** and
disregard low priority inputs. A third mechanism is to **redraw boundaries** for social
or economic transactions to shift the burden to the other party in the exchange (Milgram,
1970). An example of this shift is a taxi or bus driver (or the transportation company)
demanding that the consumer produce correct change.

The fourth mechanism is **blocking off inputs** before they enter the system. One of
the most noticeable differences between people from large cities and people from rural
areas is the boundary they place around themselves to shield themselves from strangers.
While it might be customary in the country to wave at every passer by, on a Manhattan
street it would be unusual for anyone to make eye contact with a stranger.

A fifth adaptation to overload is by **filtering inputs** so that only weak and superficial
interaction with others is allowed. According to Milgram, when people live in a densely
populated city, it might be uncommon to know the names of their barber, the person who
delivers their mail every day, or even their next door neighbors, whereas in the country,
people are likely to know them and their relatives as well.

The sixth adaptation is the **development of institutions** to absorb inputs that
would otherwise be too overwhelming for the individual to handle. In this adaptation,
Milgram referred to institutions such as human service agencies that prevent the poor
from needing to beg for a living and also attempt to keep panhandlers off the streets and
away from pedestrians.

Finally, psychogenic stress has been linked to many physical pathologies, from benign
episodes of insomnia and skin irritations to fatal heart attacks. The stress flowing from
lack of monetary resources has been highlighted in a recent review article by Gallo and
Matthews (2003). These authors conclude that socioeconomic status is highly correlated
with numerous health outcomes. They further suggest that low socioeconomic status environments, while being stressful in themselves, provide minimal resources for individuals
to manage resulting stress. City planners might be encouraged to familiarize themselves
with the current research by psychologists on hardiness (Kobasa, 1979) and resilience
(Bonanno, 2004; Kelley, 2005), so that individuals living in crowded, underprivileged
neighborhoods might be provided with the psychosocial resources necessary for their mental and physical well-being. Price and Crapo (2002) note that in many different societies,
persons living in an urban environment tend to demonstrate more competitiveness than
those in more rural settings or in small towns. One might argue that in today's American
urban scene, this tendency is accentuated by the limited availability of required resources.
When many persons are crowded into high-rise buildings and congested inner cities, such
crowding, in and of itself, is generally viewed as a source of stress and can have physical
as well as psychological consequences.

Group Behavior and Conformity

Individuals living in cities obey laws and customs, conform to standards, and are moved to act in ways dictated either directly or indirectly by other people in their environment. The discipline of psychology, specifically social psychology, has greatly contributed to the study of conformity and ways in which conforming behaviors can be expected to manifest themselves in cities.

A typical example is that of a group of pedestrians waiting at a traffic signal that is glowing "red." Given no traffic from the opposite directions, a lone pedestrian often ventures across the street on "red" only to be followed by most, if not all, of his or her fellow urban dwellers.

From a very early age, people learn to follow the behaviors of those around them. Infants will mimic the facial expressions of adults (Vinter, 1986). In a classic experiment performed by Bandura, Ross, and Ross (1963), children were exposed to films of adults who attacked a bobo doll. The children then were observed to be more aggressive in their playing behaviors, illustrating a phenomenon Bandura called **observational learning.** Studies of exposure to media violence (Black & Bevan, 1992; Huesmann & Eron, 1986; Eron, 1987; Josephson, 1987; Lore & Schultz, 1993) attest to the power of television to provide observational learning of violent behavior, particularly in children and youth in American cities. Anderson *et al* (2003) conclude that media violence does have a modest direct effect on serious forms of violent behavior, and moreover, strongly affects aggressive behaviors in general.

Solomon Asch (1956) tested the ability of individuals to resist group pressure. Taking a set of college students, the experimenter projected the image of lines on a screen. The subjects were then asked to judge which of them was the longest. All but one of the students were working with the experimenter, and would give wrong answers at specific times in the test. The one genuine test subject was then forced to either give an incorrect answer or stand in opposition to the group. The results of this experiment showed that among the genuine test subjects, one third tended to conform to the group by giving incorrect answers. Further testing showed that the size of the group had an influence on an individual's response. When test subjects stood in opposition to only one other student, she or he was less likely to give an incorrect answers; however, there seemed to be no greater influence on individuals beyond three opposing subjects. Having at least one other supporter in the group tended to negate the effects of peer pressure.

Asch (1957) then repeated a similar "line" experiment with one critical difference: participants **wrote** their answers in secret. Conformity dropped considerably. This finding sheds light on the potential difference between one's public behavior and one's private adherence to social norms and values.

Conformity permeates city life; yet urban dwellers have a strong desire to maintain their individual identity. Burger (1987) conducted several studies of this propensity for individuality. In one experiment, he separated subjects into two groups according to their desire for personal control, as measured on a previous test. They then rated cartoons according to how funny they thought they were. Some subjects rated the cartoons alone; others were in groups that had already been coached by the experimenter to rate the cartoons high on the "funny" scale. The **real** subjects who were high on the personal control variable yielded less to the accomplices' "pressure" than did those who scored low on the variable. The low scorers conformed to a greater degree (by rating the cartoons funnier than the high scorers). Of those who rated the cartoons with no one else present, there was no difference in the high and low personal control groups; both rated them as not very funny.

Even though the pressure to conform exists throughout the daily lives of urban dwellers, the desire to maintain their individuality often leads them to resist the influence of their peers and other groups in their environment.

Authority and Individual Values

When authority figures exert pressure their influence on individuals might be even greater than that exerted by a group. In a well-known experiment conducted by Stanley Milgram (1974), individual subjects were asked by the experimenter (the authority figure) to administer electric shocks to a person for incorrectly answering questions. The voltage (ranging from 15 volts to 450 volts) would be increased each time an incorrect answer was received. No shocks were actually administered, but the test subject was led to believe that they were. The elaborate electronic apparatus the subjects saw was authentic. As the experiment progressed and the voltage "administered" increased, screams came from the "victim," visible through a large glass window in the adjoining room. Toward the end of the experiment, the screams were replaced by silence. Although test subjects frequently expressed concern for their victim, almost two-thirds of them were persuaded by the experimenter to continue until the end of the test.

It should be noted that since most subjects needed to be coaxed to continue the experiment, it was not their desire to harm another person. On the other hand, one third of the participants were able to resist the pressure placed on them by the authority figure and chose not to complete the experiment. This suggests that there were some differences in the subjects' ability to act on their moral principles.

Lawrence Kohlberg (1976) theorized that individual moral behavior follows a set of developmental stages. In a series of interviews where subjects were asked their opinion of a list of moral dilemmas, Kohlberg identified six types of explanations for doing the "right" thing. In the first stage, children would only identify acts as "bad," or "against the law." Violating these codes was prohibited by external punishments. In the second stage, right and wrong were established by how they tended to benefit the parties involved; at this developmental level, fairness is goodness.

At stage three, subjects interpreted moral dilemmas in terms of what others expected of them. This is also called the "good" boy or girl stage because it reflects a concern for others' opinion. The fourth stage is represented by a concern for social order. Laws are observed as agreed upon duties and should be observed for the social good.

The final two stages are what Kohlberg refers to as the "principled" level. It is here that individuals lift themselves up from the control of the group for their moral guidance. Stage five recognizes a variety of differing but equal moral values, holding only certain principles as nonrelative in the interest of fulfilling a kind of social contract. The rule of the majority becomes the standard of right and wrong. The sixth and final stage embraces a set of universal and self-chosen ethics. The law is typically based on such ethics and therefore should be followed inasmuch as they have this base. At this stage, subjects employ the use of very abstract concepts such as "justice" and "equality."

Kohlberg's model of a developing morality follows subjects in what is referred to as a "longitudinal" study. This means that the same set of questions were asked to the same subjects at different times in their lives. Kohlberg observed that some people did not progress beyond certain stages in their moral development. If this is the case, it could offer some explanation for the differences between subjects in the Milgram experiment.

Carol Gilligan (1982) challenged Kohlberg's work on the basis that it used the male model as a standard. Prior to Gilligan's research on moral development in women, psychological studies often assumed that men and women had the same basic approach to learning, knowing, and what constitutes ethical behavior. Gilligan began to reexamine gender differences in ethical behavior by showing the complex interaction of the situation, the larger environment, and personal relationships. Her research indicated that women often rely more on an ethic of care and responsibility whereas men tend to utilize abstract laws and universal principles in making moral judgments and choices. While there have been challenges to the objectivity of her research, (eg., Pollitt, 1994; Sommers, 2004) Gilligan has been very influential in proposing that women's greater willingness to negotiate and seek consensus, rather than assert authority, might lead to lessened violence in our cities (Tiger, 1999).

Much earlier the noted anthropologist Margaret Mead (1935) had argued that masculine and feminine traits were a result of culture, not inborn characteristics. The way in which cultures (or cities) were organized and experienced led to the unique roles played by each gender. Men and women might be shaped by their urban surroundings differently; in addition, they might **shape** their environment in a distinct manner. Both, using the principles of human behavior contributed by the discipline of psychology, will be able to enrich the quality of life for themselves and for the cities in which they live.

Name _____

The City Explores Its Behavior (Psychology)

14-1. Define ways in which urban dwellers achieve a sense of belongingness.

14-2. In your city, observe and record five ways in which urban spaces are designed for protection against crime.

14-3. Compare and contrast urban/rural differences in bystander intervention.

14-4. Give an example of stimulus generalization in an urban setting (other than the example in this chapter).

14-5. Watch your local TV news each evening for four days and complete the following:

Date:

Number of Crimes reported:

Location

1.

2.

3.

4.

5.

Date:

Number of Crimes reported:

Location

1.

2.

3.

4.

5.

Date:

Number of Crimes reported:

Location

1.

2.

3.

4.

5.

Date:

Number of Crimes reported:

Location

1.

2.

3.

4.

5.

The City Confronts Social Issues

(Sociology)

Wornie Reed

In the late nineteenth and early twentieth centuries, large cities in the United States experienced their greatest growth. At the same time, sociology began to emerge as an academic discipline. As these large cities grew in population, increasing attention was paid to the concomitant social problems. Early sociologists studied these urban problems and produced a heritage of applied urban sociology. Many of these early studies were conducted by sociologists at the University of Chicago who were attempting to develop solutions to problems such as crime, delinquency, prostitution, and mental illness.

As the field of urban sociology developed, however, the problem-oriented focus was replaced with a concern for developing general theories of urban structure and process. As the studies of social deviance and crime have become specialties of their own, urban sociology has focused more on comparative urban structure. Concern with social problems has been a secondary interest in urban sociology. However, there have been recent attempts to integrate a sociological frame of reference with the analysis of the problems of cities (Wilson & Schulz, 1978).

What is the subject matter of urban sociology, especially the sociology that encompasses both the *social problems* and the *social structure* approaches? Sociological studies are based on the assumption that the experience and actions of human beings are shaped by the social arena in which they take place. In other words, the social organization influences individuals' perceptions and behaviors. *Urban Sociology* assumes, then, that the city influences behavior and social relationships and it seeks to determine and describe the processes by which this occurs.

Urban sociology overlaps with a number of other sociological subfields and traditions. For example, urban sociologists study issues in social stratification, small groups, formal organization, the family, modernization and economic development, and political sociology.

Urban influences may be "organizational (growth in social complexity), cultural (ways of thinking and behaving), and political (relationships of power and control)" (Flanagan, 1990, p. 2). Consequently, urban sociology has a variety of approaches. Flanagan (1990) has divided these approaches into two major orientations: those that study the cultural, organizational, and social psychological consequences of urban life, and those that are concerned with the wider economic and political impact of the city. Sociologists using the first orientation, **culturalists,** deal with people's experiences in cities; those using the second orientation, the **structuralists,** are concerned with the distribution of wealth and power. Culturalists address how urban life feels and how people react to the urban environment; structuralists are concerned with the urban structure—the interplay between political and economic forces, and changing spatial organizations.

The Development of Urban Sociology

Industrialization and rapid urbanization of Western societies caused concern about the condition of urban life. Scholars sought to address the issue of how social order would be maintained. Ferdinand Tonnies and Georg Simmel were two key nineteenth century scholars who influenced the development of urban sociology. Tonnies adapted the terms **Gemeinschaft** and **Gesellschaft** from the German language to draw distinctions between life in small-scale rural societies and life in growing cities (Flanagan, 1990). Gemeinschaft referred to living in intimate social integration in a single community. The individual is submersed into the whole, the group. The term Gesellschaft was used to refer to life in the public, in the wider social world without intimate ties. Gemeinschaft translates roughly to "community," and Gesellschaft translates roughly to "society." The terms came to refer respectively to rural social life and urban social life as attempts were made to distinguish between the rural and the city in the forces that draw and hold people together. The assumption, of course, was that urban life drew people apart, away from intimate social integration.

In his essay, "The Metropolis and Mental Life," Georg Simmel sought to explain how the urban experience affected the way people thought, as well as the way they behaved (Wolff, 1950). Simmel posited that urban life affected individuals' thought and acted upon them in two ways—through the intensity of the stimulation and sensation in the city and through the market's effect on urban relations. Simmel argued that big city life produced too many random stimuli. As a result, urban dwellers had no choice but to become less personal and insensitive to the events and people around them in order to protect them from the stress of city life. They needed to develop a special capacity to avoid emotional involvement in activities occurring around them.

Urban sociology in the United States grew principally out of the work of Robert Park and his colleagues at the University of Chicago in the early decades of the twentieth century. Park went to Germany in 1899 and studied with Georg Simmel. After returning to the United States and spending several years as a secretary and assistant to Booker T. Washington at Tuskegee Institute, he took a teaching position at the University of Chicago.

Sociologists associated with the University of Chicago in the 1920s and 1930s became known as the **Chicago School,** discussed in Chapter 4. They developed the ideas that served as the basis of theory and research in urban sociology for several decades. The three key scholars were Robert Park, Ernest Burgess, and Louis Wirth. Robert Park and Ernest Burgess developed an ecological approach to urban analysis; Louis Wirth, in a famous essay, characterized urbanism as a "way of life."

The **urban ecology** approach advanced by the Chicago School held that the ecology of cities was similar to the biological ecology in the physical environment, and that urban settlements and the distribution of various types of neighborhoods within cities followed a spatial division of the city that corresponded to the functional division of labor occurring within it. Park proposed that specialized areas of a city such as the **central business district,** (CBD), exclusive residential areas, industrial areas, slums, and immigrant communities were natural areas, the products of natural forces that worked to distribute the city's populations and functions.

The urban ecology approach held that cities are organized into concentric rings. In the inner ring is the inner city, consisting principally of businesses and decaying private homes. Beyond that ring were older neighborhoods, where stably employed, lower-class workers lived. Farther out were the suburbs, which housed higher-income groups. Processes of invasion and succession occurred between the rings. For example, as the inner city decayed, poor urban minorities entered the area while the previous residents fled toward the outer residential rings.

Over time, several shortcomings became apparent in the theory. On the one hand, the theory offered no consideration of conscious design and planning. On the other, the theory fit some, but certainly not all, American cities and few European cities.

The second conceptual idea from the Chicago School was Louis Wirth's characterization of urbanism as a way of life (Wirth, 1938). Wirth was concerned less with the internal differentiation of cities than the nature of urbanism as a form of social existence. He saw urbanism as life at one end of a continuum, while life at the other end of the continuum was rural or "folk" society. In Wirth's urban arena, individuals are alienated and alone in a morass of competing norms and values. Increasing size, density, and heterogeneity of cities leave people socially uprooted and politically powerless (Flanagan, 1990).

Critiques of Wirth's thesis have revealed its limitations. While many social interactions in urban areas are impersonal, many are not. Wirth's theory was developed based on several American cities; yet it was generalized to urbanism everywhere.

Current Approaches in Urban Sociology

The so-called classical tradition in urban sociology which emanated from the Chicago School in general and Louis Wirth's analysis in particular emphasized the negative aspects of urban life. It was anti-urban; it dealt with the loss of solidarity and security. In this view, individuals are powerless, alienated, and isolated from each other. Over the years since the publication of Wirth's essay in 1938, urban scholars have been describing urban areas and urban relationships that show the existence of strong senses of "community" and social solidarity. This different view has developed from urban community studies, where close ties and supportive relationships exist in some social groupings or **social network.**

One of the first such studies was William F. Whyte's *Street Corner Society* (1943). His portrayal of a working-class neighborhood varied substantially from what outsiders saw in the same area. Outsiders saw elements of disorganization and moral decay. Whyte saw such phenomena as street-corner gangs and racketeers bribing police; however, he did not see any elements of community breakdown or disorganization. Instead, his study revealed an urban area with its own sense of right and order, and social solidarity.

Since Whyte's seminal study, many scholars have demonstrated that urban residents act neighborly and have a strong sense of community. Elliot Liebow (1967) described the strong sense of solidarity in a group of black street corner men. Gerald Suttles (1968) studied a poor multi-ethnic area of Chicago and found a well-organized social order based on strong territorial relationships, strong territorial identity, and solidarity. Most of the open conflicts in the area occurred between local youth and youth from outside the area.

In *The Urban Villagers,* Herbert Gans (1962) reported on his study of a working-class Italian-American neighborhood, considered a slum by outsiders. Gans described strong social relationships between kinfolks and friends who lived near each other. He described a peer group society that had strong intra-group loyalty and strong suspicion of outsiders. More recently, Elijah Anderson (1978) has described a structure in the social relationships among black urban ghetto residents. His later work also included descriptions of strong informal social codes among black residents of communities typified by social disorganization (1990, 1999).

Each of the studies mentioned above, as well as many other similar studies, examined neighborhoods—not whole cities—in general and social networks in particular. Thus, attention was focused on social relationships of individuals in loosely defined subsets of cities—neighborhoods or communities. In this sense, community takes on the meaning of social relationships in a defined geographic area. Most importantly, however, these types of studies show that community solidarity still exists in urban areas.

In a structuralist approach, a community can be seen as a social system. A social system has both external and internal aspects—relating the system to its environment and the units of the system to each other. Another way of describing these dimensions of the community as a social system is in terms of **vertical** and **horizontal** aspects (Warren, 1972). A community's vertical pattern is the structural and functional relationships of various units to systems external to the community. On the other hand, the horizontal pattern is the structural and functional relationships of various units to each other.

Irwin Sanders (1958) presented a social system approach to the study of communities. In this approach, a community is viewed as a total system dependent upon the interaction among various subsystems. Within the community are major systems such as family, economy, and government; examples of subsystems within the major system of government are political party, bureaucracy, and police.

A higher proportion of blacks lives in metropolitan areas than do whites—87.8 percent to 79.8 percent (Horner, 2002). One-fourth of the population of central cities in the United States is African American; and in a number of major cities, the percentage is much higher. Therefore, studies of urban communities are often about African-Americans issues.

To illustrate the social system approach and the manner in which external and internal factors affect local communities, selected external and internal forces will be examined as they affect African-American families in predominantly black urban communities.

Billingsley (1968) developed a conceptual paradigm that characterized African-American families as a social subsystem mutually interacting with subsystems in the African-American community and in the wider society. He depicted black families in a schematic circle embedded within two concentric circles representing the two larger systems, the local community and wider society. Billingsley proposed that an understanding of the African-American family would, of necessity, require an understanding of the combined effects on black family functioning of external subsystems in wider society and the community as well as the family. This conceptual paradigm was developed further by Robert Hill with Andrew Billingsley and other colleagues (Hill, 1993).

Best Friends (Photo by Philip C. Leiter.)

External subsystems in the wider society include societal forces and institutional policies (eg., in economics, politics, education, health, welfare, law, religion, and the media). Subsystems in African-American communities include schools, churches, peer groups, businesses, and neighborhood associations. Internal subsystems—within families—include intra-household interactions between husbands and wives, parents and children, siblings, other relatives and non-relatives.

The focus of the discussion that follows is on the family as a community subsystem interacting with other subsystems in the community and with systems in wider society, rather than subsystems of the family.

External Factors

Social Forces

One of the primary forces that affect African-American families and their members is class structure, the ranking of individuals and groups in a stratification hierarchy on the basis of their socioeconomic resources. It is a form of institutionalized inequality, in which opportunities to achieve societal goals are related to one's position in the class hierarchy. Consequently, groups occupying disadvantaged class rankings are more likely to resort to nonconforming adaptations than groups occupying advantaged positions. African Americans are disproportionately in the lower class positions (See Figure 15.1.) and a major cause for this is racism. In racial stratification, groups are ranked on the basis of their racial-ethnic background; this ranking is directly related to their differential power, prestige, and wealth.

While there has been a decline in prejudiced attitudes and discriminatory behavior among white individuals (individual racism), institutional racism might not have decreased, but it might actually be increasing. Institutional racism refers to laws, regulations, policies, and informal practices of organizations or institutions that result in

Figure 15.1
The Social Structure of the Black Community. Solid lines denote relatively stable divisions between classes, whereas broken lines indicate that demarcations between substrata are often blurred. (Adapted from Blackwell, 1991, p. 169).

differential adverse treatment of racial and ethnic minorities (Flanagan, 1990; Hill, 1993). As Carmichael and Hamilton (1967) observed, institutional racism can be unintended as well as intended. See also Jones (1997).

Structural or unintended racial discrimination refers to societal forces or policies that have adverse effects on racial and ethnic minorities, although these actions might not be designed to be discriminatory. Society-wide trends such as recessions, inflationary spirals, the closing of plants in inner cities, automation, and the shift to high-tech industries have had unintended disparate effects on African-American families. Such structural discrimination has contributed to the persistent high rates of structural unemployment among workers in black families.

A demographic factor that has contributed significantly to the sharp increase in black female-headed households is the relative shortage of black men to black women of marriageable age. In the 1970s and 1980s, a veritable "marriage squeeze" existed for African-American women (Glick, 1986). This marriage squeeze resulted from the increase in births during the baby boom period, the late 1940s and 1950s, and the tendency for young men to be two or three years older than the women they marry. As a result, a woman born in 1947, when the birth rate had risen, tended to marry a man born in 1944, before the birth rate rose. Twenty to twenty-five years later, there would be more females than males in the prime marrying age.

While this phenomenon applied to whites as well as blacks, it affected blacks to a greater degree, because blacks have higher mortality rates than do whites, and men have higher mortality rates than do women at every age. Thus, there is a large discrepancy within cohorts between the **sex ratio** for whites and the sex ratio for blacks. In 1970, there were only eighty-two percent as many black men as black women in the prime marriageable ages—men 20 to 26, and women 18 to 24 years. The ratio improved to 89.8 in

2000 (U.S. Census Bureau, 2000). However, as the ratio improved during the 1980s the African-American marriageable pool was still below par because of the increase in unemployment and decrease in labor force participation. This economic situation made large portions of African-American men unmarriageable.

African-American workers have been disproportionately affected by recessions. One reason is the practice of seniority in many jobs, where the last hired is the first fired ("laid-off")—and African Americans are disproportionately the last hired. Another reason is the concentration of African Americans in unskilled and semi-skilled jobs, the jobs that are most vulnerable to economic slumps. The tripling in unemployment of African-American family heads in the four recessions in the 1970s and the early 1980s (1970–71, 1974–75, 1980, and 1981–82) led to alarming increases in family instability and poverty (Hill, 1993). Brenner (1973) has shown that high levels of unemployment produce devastating social consequences, including physical and mental illness, and alcoholism.

Social Policies

Employment

The four recessions during the 1970s and 1980s did not occur naturally. They were induced by federal fiscal and monetary policies. The Federal Reserve Board in its traditional approach to halting inflation adjusted the interest rates while permitting the money supply to expand more freely. Such fiscal policies induced the recessions of 1970–71 and 1974–75 (Hill, 1993).

Soaring interest rates led to another recession in 1980; subsequent tight money policies brought on the 1981–1982 recession—the most severe decline since the Great Depression. These spiraling interest rates also contributed to the disproportionate failures of African-American businesses. In general, federal fiscal and monetary policies during this period had an acute adverse impact on African-American workers, families, and businesses (Swanton, 1988).

Some public and private housing policies have had positive effects on African-American families, while others have had serious negative effects. One of the early government housing policies responsible for opening the suburbs to low-income and middle-income whites, at the same time confining African Americans—regardless of income—to central cities, was the Federal Housing Administration (FHA) mortgage program established in 1934, which insures mortgage loans made by private lenders (Hill, 1993). The policies of the FHA were expressly discriminatory from the beginning. Its handbooks dissuaded residential integration by discouraging the granting of mortgages for houses that were not in racially separate areas of the community (Blackwell, 1991).

The FHA "redlined" many neighborhoods, separating white and black residential areas from each other for the purposes of determining eligibility for FHA home mortgages. Banks, insurance companies, and private lenders collaborated in redlining and segregating residential areas, basing their refusal to invest in home mortgages for African Americans on the articulated FHA home mortgages. Since FHA procedures have promoted racial discrimination overtly and covertly, African-American families have been largely restricted to ghettos in central cities, while the "white flight" to the suburbs has been subsidized by black as well as white taxpayers. Thus, the policies of FHA and related federal agencies helped to institutionalize all forms of racial segregation in housing (Blackwell, 1991; Doob, 2004). Although practices such as **racial steering** and **blockbusting** have been declared illegal, some real estate agents continue to reinforce residential segregation through various subtle techniques.

Many government trade policies have had adverse effects on African-American workers and their families. Industries with the job losses due to imports have a higher representation of African-American workers than those industries with the largest job gains due to exports (Hill, 1993). African Americans gained 229,000 jobs through exports in 1970, and lost 287,000 jobs because of imports—for a net loss of 58,000 jobs (National Commission for Employment Policy, 1978). Private disinvestment policies related to plant closings in inner-cities can also structurally discriminate against wage earners in black families:

> *Blacks are especially hard-hit because they are increasingly concentrated within central cities and in those regions of the country where plant closings and economic dislocation have been most pronounced. Moreover, as the number of jobs grew rapidly in the South, whites moved in to take the overwhelming majority of them. How capital mobility can have a discriminatory impact, intentionally or not, is shown clearly. When a laundry located in St. Louis began to decentralize in 1964, its work force was 75% black. By 1975 after it had opened 13 suburban facilities and reduced its downtown operation, its black work force was down to five percent (Bluestone & Harrison, 1982 pp. 54–55).*

Education

After 1960 there was a definite and significant attainment of educational opportunity, a result of the desegregation movement. For almost two decades, colleges and universities were opening admission to substantial numbers of African-American and other minority students. However, in the 1980s there was a reversal: previous gains in education were eroded. Though the factors influencing this development were mostly systemic (due to demographic, social economic, and policy trends), the consequence had a differential racial impact.

After coming to near parity in 1975, the gap between the rates at which black and white students go on to college began to gradually widen. By 1982, the gap was accelerating in size, creating an ever-widening "access gap" between black and white students. Between 1975 and 1985, the high school graduation rate of black students rose from 71.6 to 79.0 percent, while the college-going rate of those graduates fell from 31.5 to 26 percent. Conversely, the high school drop-out rate decreased (U.S. Bureau of the Census, 1993). By 1999, the college-going rate of black high-school graduates had increased to 39.2 percent. However, they lagged substantially behind whites, who had a 45.3 percent college-going rate.

The decline in the rate of college enrollment of African-American youth was occurring in the face of rising college entrance test efficiency by African American students. Although the SAT (Scholastic Aptitude Test) scores for white students were decreasing slightly between 1970 and 1990, the SAT scores of African-American students were increasing. Blacks were graduating from high school in record numbers and improving their SAT scores, but proportionately fewer of them were gaining access to colleges, thus placing limitations on the social mobility of young African Americans (U.S. Bureau of the Census, 1993).

One of the primary reasons for the decrease in African-American college enrollment in the 1980s was the decreasing availability of grants (Garibaldi, 1991). The federal cuts in financial aid grants during the early 1980s adversely affected all races of students, but the impact was greatest on black students, as significantly more of them depended on financial aid. The aid programs changed from an emphasis on grants to an emphasis on loans. Since fewer African-American families could secure the loans, college attendance among the children in these families suffered.

Internal Factors: Community Forces

Unemployment among urban African Americans is a well-known societal problem. Large numbers of African-American men are not working, a situation that creates and perpetuates serious problems in African-American communities. One of these problems is the rise in black families headed by women. While the rise in black families headed by women is the result of multiple forces, data suggest that the decrease is due at least in part to the decreasing economic status of African-American men.

There is a strong correlation between the African American male unemployment rate and the increase in African-American female headed families. As the black male unemployment rate increased between the mid-1960s and the mid-1980s, and as more black males dropped out of the labor force altogether (stopped looking for work), the percent of black female-headed families rose. In 1960, 10.7 percent of African-American males were unemployed, 1.3 million were unemployed or out of the labor force, and 20.0 percent of African-American families were headed by females only. In 1980, the African-American male unemployment rate was 14.5, some 3.2 million were unemployed or out of the labor force and the black female-headed families had increased to 49 percent of all African-American families. By 1992, the black male unemployment rate was 15.3, four million were unemployed or out of the labor force, and 52.5 percent of black families were headed by females only (Center for the Study of Social Policy, 1986; Horner, 1994; Staples, 1986). By 2002, 4.8 million African American males were unemployed or out of the labor force (Horner, 2002).

Men who cannot find work have trouble maintaining a stable marital and family life, or getting married at all. When it comes to a choice between remaining single or getting married, individuals often do a cost-benefit analysis; hence, women do not often marry men who are not working. As incomes rise, so do the number of African-American men who marry. Thus, the higher the income of blacks, the more likely there is a bi-parental family. On the other hand, the majority of female-headed households are poor. For example, among middle-class families, 83 percent are married-couple families compared to 17 percent who are single parent families. Among the working-class poor 33 percent are married-couple and 67 percent are single-parent families; and among the lowest income poor, 75 percent are single-parent while only 25 percent are married-couple families (Horton & Smith, 1990).

Poverty takes a devastating toll on its victims. The poor are more likely to suffer from hunger and inadequate housing. It has been shown that high rates of unemployment are directly associated with high levels of alcoholism, wife abuse, child abuse, family breakups, mental illness, physical illness, suicides, crime, and punishment. The poor are also less likely to receive needed medical care and more likely to have high infant mortality rates.

As many major studies of crime have shown, minorities with the highest rates of unemployment also have the highest rates of crime (Hill, 1993). Consequently, blacks are overrepresented in arrests, convictions, and incarceration. While African Americans comprise twelve percent of the population of the United States, they account for over one-fourth of arrestees and one-half of the state prisoners. African Americans, especially males, are more likely to be arrested, convicted, imprisoned, and executed than are whites committing the same offenses (Blackwell, 1991; Reed, 1993).

Such disproportionate rates of arrests, convictions, and incarceration contribute to the formation of single parent families. African-American male criminal offenders are less available as marriage partners in two ways. First, they are unavailable because they are incarcerated for long periods of time. After imprisonment, they are limited in acquiring legitimate employment because of their police records (Meyers and Simms, 1988).

Second, African Americans are not only overrepresented among criminal offenders, but among the victims as well. Much of this victimization is occurring at the hands of juveniles, as increasing proportions of community crimes are committed by African-American juveniles. They are arrested for one-fourth of the property crimes and half of all the violent crimes committed by juveniles. Consequently, most inner-city black youths, especially males, are likely to have had some contact with the criminal justice system. It is estimated that over fifty percent of black male adolescents in poverty areas have arrest or "police contact" records (Hill, 1993).

Nongovernmental community support systems serve as **mediating structures** to help individuals and families cope with and counteract adverse social forces. These mediating structures include both formal organizations (such as churches, private schools, and voluntary associations) and informal subsystems (such as social clubs, neighborhood groups, peers, friends, and extended family networks). The social and economic status of members of the community is crucial to the success of such self-help.

Summary

The preceding discussion has considered the family as a community subsystem and presented several factors that affect the welfare of families in the social system of the community. Specifically, selected factors external to the community, as well as factors internal to the community, were shown to have effects on the well being of the African-American family. External factors (**vertical influences**) included both social forces and social policies. Social forces included racism, demographic trends, and national recessions; social policies included federal housing policies, fiscal and monetary policies, and educational funding policies.

Internal (**horizontal**) community factors included unemployment and poverty, crime and delinquency, and self-help organizations. Self-help organizations traditionally act as mediating structures against the effects of issues like poverty and crime. However, the more extensive the community problems, the less viable the self-help organizations. For example, if unemployment and poverty are widespread, self-help institutions and programs will be hampered in their ability to deliver needed assistance.

Name _____

The City Confronts Social Issues (Sociology)

15-1. What is institutional racism? Give several examples that might be occurring in your city.

15-2. Identify ten neighborhood organizations that serve as "mediating structures to help individuals and families" in your central city.

The City Encounters Diversity

(Anthropology)

Dorothy Remy

The study of ethnicity and race in the city is critical to the understanding of how human beings interact and strive to maintain or improve their quality of life in urban areas. The discipline of anthropology argues that both ethnicity and race are "socially constructed categories." Anthropologists believe that the meaning given to any person's ethnic or racial identity depends on the context, and the context, in turn, is shaped by interactions among people. Consequently, much of the discussion in this chapter will be focused on what might be called the **boundary edges** of ethnicity and race—the places where members of different groups come together to work, to live, to shop and to play: namely, the city.

The quality of the encounters and interactions between members of different racial and ethnic groups in urban areas is shaped both by the **structure** within which they occur and by the **action** of the individuals involved. The two, structure and individual action, are equally significant. Looking at structure alone results in a deterministic view of human life, suggesting as it does that individual lives are formed exclusively by external political and economic conditions. But concentration solely on the behavior and cultural characteristics of individuals, on the other hand, leaves them in a vacuum, untouched and unshaped by the historical period in which they live. The dynamic tension that links structure and individual action gives form and energy to urban life.

This chapter will lay out a coherent, empirically based method for understanding the changes occurring in cities today from the anthropologist's perspective. Students of the city will also find it useful to draw upon their own experience as members of families with diverse ethnic and racial heritages. Too much of the public discussion of ethnicity and race concentrates on an idealized version of cultural heritage that obscures the complex-lived reality of a culture's members.

A way of engaging in such personal reflection is to hold three questions continuously in mind:

1. How can one retain his/her own cultural identity (or identities) and still participate fully in American life?
2. How can "new" (post-1965) immigrants and established residents bridge their suspicion of each other?
3. How can one shift personal anxieties about the future away from targeted ethnic or racial groups and toward mature leadership?

A Systems Approach to Urban Ethnicity

The dramatic development in computer interconnections known as the "information highway"—which in fact is more like an enormously complicated piece of weaving than a highway—provides a powerful illustration of systems at work and offers a vivid metaphor for thinking about how life in cities works. Indeed, computers, and especially their global linking through various forms of networks, can neither be understood nor effectively used by those who retain a linear or simple causal way of thinking. They require the ability to think in terms of relationships, in terms of position within systems, and in terms of rapid, multiple adjustments to small changes in the environment. Such systems thinking is equally crucial to understanding the city.

To think about a city as a system is to grasp that individuals exist in relation to each other. Each is connected with each other such that information, action, and reaction flow in both directions. The system is in continual, often rapid, motion as even minor changes in the external environment or in any one of the elements of the system reverberate throughout the entire system. And, critically, the system, as system, persists over time with its characteristic style independently of particular actors. Individuals may come and go, but the system retains its integrity. What is important in systems thinking, then, is position within the system, not the idiosyncratic attributes of the actors.

City Life and Global Economics

Among the most powerful of the systems that shapes life in contemporary American cities is the global economic system that has arisen in the past fifty years and swallowed up most purely local economic activity. One example, drawn from the clothing industry, will illustrate how the lives of Americans living in, say, Washington, D.C., and Baltimore are intertwined with those of people living in Singapore and Bangkok.

A major apparel company, with a glossy catalogue and outlets in malls across the United States, operates from a modest red brick building in a small town near Boston. Highly skilled, well-paid designers transmit patterns for the garments via satellite to high-resolution televisions in a Singapore factory. The factory is both a distribution center and a key stop in the production process. Fabric, much of it silk produced in China, is cut by sophisticated laser machines from the electronically transmitted patterns. Once cut, the pieces are redistributed to an extensive network of small factories dispersed throughout Southeast Asia. Women, many them recent migrants from rural areas seeking waged employment for the first time, sew the final garments. Typically, these seamstresses are paid by the piece, given no medical or other benefits, and work only when there is specific demand for their labor. The completed products are reassembled in Singapore and shipped to the United States, where the labels are sewn on. The garments are now ready to be dispersed to retail outlets and catalogue distribution centers.

This composite company is typical of many manufacturing processes in the global economy (Nash & Fernandez-Kelly, 1983). Understanding it requires systems thinking. The entire process forms a single unit with many interconnected elements. Each element exists in balance with all other elements such that a shift in one (such as a breakdown in delivery of silk to the Singapore factory) has immediate implications for all other elements in the system. Second, the system as a whole has a defining style. The entire operation, regardless of the characteristics of the individual elements, promotes that style. And third, position in the system shapes behavior, rather than the culture, language, gender, or race of any of the participants in it.

The story of this factory is also the story of ethnicity and race in American cities. In the last twenty years, the structure of the United States economy has been profoundly changed by the transformation of manufacturing. Introduction of sophisticated technology, such as computer-transmitted patterns, laser cutting of garments, computer-linked and geographically dispersed manufacturing and distribution sites, has transformed the production of goods and with it urban life. A three-tier global economy provides the structural backdrop against which individual lives unfold.

The highly skilled designers, artists, and managers in the suburban headquarters of the above example are members of an international high-tech economic stratum. They are joined by the engineers, lawyers, bankers, and planners who design, produce, regulate, finance, and direct a complex, worldwide network of rapidly changing production and distribution enterprises. Membership in this stratum is highly competitive and limited to men and women with professional training beyond their college degrees.

The secretaries, accountants, food service workers, office administrators, and maintenance staff of the suburban headquarters participate in a much larger second tier of the economy. They have steady, reasonably well-paid jobs with at least some health and retirement benefits. Their work requires skill, often at least some college education, and a commitment to a structured work environment. Second-tier workers rely on other second-tier workplaces for the goods and services they require. Their consumption patterns fuel the shopping malls, restaurants, and convenience stores that proliferate in American cities.

The third tier is more fluid. The catalogue and retail sales outlets of this company could not exist without a large pool of workers able to work intensely on short notice on a seasonal basis. This sector of the economy is often called the informal sector because both the organization of work and the personal lives of those who work in it lack the structure and predictability of the other sectors. Informal sector jobs interlace with the second tier of the economy. Workers with second-tier jobs often rely on the informal sector for childcare,

Hard work within the second tier of the economy balanced by employee benefits and relatively high wages. (Photo by Jeanne Somers.)

Collecting newspapers and walking dogs for cash payments represents one hub in the network of relations which sustain the informal economy. (Photo by Jeanne Somers.)

housecleaning, lawn mowing, quick lunches from street vendors, haircuts, and even income tax preparation. Informal sector workers often buy or barter for the goods and services they require within the informal economy.

This three-tier economic structure exists in various forms throughout the world and fundamentally shapes the flow of immigrants to the industrial countries (Portes & Rumbaut, 1990). Companies in the United States, such as the suburban garment firm, are linked, as discussed previously, to Southeast Asia. The existence of that system and others like it exerts a powerful influence on many people. Farmers become pulled into the global economic system as they shift from growing food for their families to growing cash crops for export. The need for cash for food, fertilizers, and the expanding array of consumer goods stimulates a flow of farm family members to the cities, where they hope to find good factory jobs. Young women, especially, work in the factories, sending the little money they make home. Others participate in the informal economy in order to survive. The combination of a disturbed subsistence farming economy, a vastly overcrowded urban informal economy and, at times, profound political instability, coalesce into the decision to move again to seek a better life. The computer links of the manufacturing company connect even rural villages with the suburban headquarters. The path of migration, in some sense, can be seen as the human side of this abstract system. Very real people with very real aspirations move along defined pathways shaped by this global system to land in the United States.

Experience shows that movement of the United States' investment capital, either to underdeveloped, low-wage areas of the United States or elsewhere on the globe, is generally followed by migration of residents of those areas back to the developed, financially strong, high-wage areas where the investment came from.

The demographic profile of the migrants also reflects the influence of the global economic system. The United States is a major receiving country of the so-called "brain drain." That is, men and women from poor countries all over the world seek out the United States for advanced training in the most advanced technological fields. Graduate schools in the United States, especially those in the sciences, engineering, and business, are filled with international students seeking a place in the first stratum of the global economy. In addition to the students, many foreign nationals work in technologically advanced professions in the United States (Portes & Rumbaut, 1990). The adult workers in this group can be found in some first-tier jobs.

Middle-class citizens from areas of the world affected by integration in the global economy, political instability, or both also migrate to the United States. These migrants often arrive with very little money but with the middle-class skills required to run businesses and to take advantage of the educational opportunities available here for their children. They begin their life in the United States in the border economy, which links the second tier of stable firms with that part of the informal economy that serves it.

A third broad category of immigrants are illiterate or barely literate men and women from rural areas and the informal sectors of the urban economy. These immigrants travel to the United States in search of political and economic stability. They lack both money and the middle-class skills that facilitate movement through the schools, housing markets, social service agencies, and other institutions with which they must connect. This group of immigrants are positioned in the shifting space between the informal economy and the lower levels of the secondary economy.

Movement along the pathways of the global economy, however, is two-way, not only toward United States cities and other fully developed financial centers, but also in the other direction as well. Introduction of production and products in once isolated areas of this country and the world is transforming the formerly local economies of those areas into systems with many of the characteristic features of the dominant global capitalism. Not incidentally, the movement of people along the pathways of the global economy shapes urban racial and ethnic relations in the United States and elsewhere.

Pathways through the City

The creative tension of the city arises from the tension between its **structure** and the **action** of its residents. Ethnicity and race contribute to the vitality of the tension through the variety of expressions of cultural identity. The previous section focused on the global economic system, arguing that its interconnectedness created a structure which, in its broad outlines, is replicated in the many regional subsystems around the world. This section explores the human expression of the system. The movement of people through the system over time creates pathways. Much of the energy of the city arises from the movement along them. On the surface, the pathways appear to be a jumble of random lines, much like a tangled ball of strings. But the lumps of variously colored strings can be seen, on closer inspection, to be persistent centers for exchange, connection, and transformation. The pathways, the colored strings, are formed by links between kin, friends, and mentors and patrons. The concentrated clusters of various pathways are the institutions of the city, some of them formal, most of them informal.

The Path of Kinship

The most fundamental pathway through the city is kinship. All urban residents, regardless of whether they are currently in touch with relatives, are part of a family system. The term "family of origin" is used to identify the family one is born into. It also distinguishes this family from the family created by the union of two adults and their children. But "family of origin" also captures the sense of family for many immigrants to the city—the family of origin is the family of home. The connection with this family creates the pathway between present city life and the life of one's ancestors, most likely rural, in another land.

The family story of migration to the city frequently provides the core sense of self-identity as well as ethnic and racial identity. While each family has a unique story of its move to a city in the United States, all stories have in common a decision to move, an often wrenching displacement from the familiar land and from other family members, a series of stops along the way, and a final arrival in a strange city. Many family stories begin with a single person, often a young man, making a solo journey of exploration. He returns home to bring with him siblings, perhaps a wife, and children. This outpost of the family then becomes the center of connection for other kin as they follow. Over time, the thin path of the first explorer becomes a well-worn trail for a family very broadly defined.

For some families, the move to the city represents a profound distancing from the place and family of origin; in emotional terms, the distancing is never final. Grandchildren and great-grandchildren often make enormous effort to trace the connection back to home, to the land, and the relatives left behind. African Americans are eloquent about the power of this quest for a home in Africa. The same quest is pursued again and again by members of many nationalities.

Where circumstance has not created a break with home, the information flow between the new land and the country of origin animates the connections in the global economic system. Through the pathway of kinship, men and women in most remote areas of the world hear stories of another world from returning migrants or from the friends and relatives who have visited them. At the same time, new residents in cities of the United States keep well informed on the intimate details of the lives of those at home as well as of the political and economic context of those lives.

There is work to kinship, and the work, which usually is the work of women, has many dimensions (di Leonardo, 1984). At its most private and intimate, women as sisters and daughters and mothers relay the family stories along the pathway. At its most universal, these family-of-origin stories define the culture and heritage of all racial and ethnic groups. The stories often directly affect the emotional life of the family. One woman may amplify each sign of distress into a major crisis, intensifying anxiety and fear about the new and the different. Another may approach each new difficulty as a challenge to be learned from and overcome.

In a new land, the simple daily activities of making a home, feeding a family, and preserving at least a few of the old ways can be a daunting task. Women from all racial and ethnic backgrounds share the common story of searching in vain in the new environment for that one item essential for the proper dish or cure or celebration. And many women confess the daily tension between transmitting the old ways to their daughters and their pride in their daughters' ability to speak English, attend school, and dress like Americans.

A significant part of the work of kinship is the drudgery of keeping a household in operation in a strange land, without enough money, and often in another language. The physical labor of keeping a house clean is enormous when the house accommodates far more people than the designers intended, when the heat and hot water can be erratic or nonexistent, when the washing machines are in a dangerous basement or blocks away, and when everyone must work for money to pay the high rent. Frequently women become overwhelmed by the literal, physical work of kinship entailed in running a household and the social work of kinship, including offering hospitality to visiting relatives and newcomers to the city (Williams, 1988).

Families deal with the most intimate issues of assimilation and cultural heritage. The decisions about whom to invite over as friend, whom to date and, eventually, whom to marry take place within the family. In some ways, the quality of the choices made reflects the maturity of the family system. It is helpful to see the range of responses as falling along a continuum. At one end are families who seek to reinforce racial and ethnic identity by prohibiting members of other groups to enter the private space of the family and by expelling family members who seek to create close friendships outside the family system. At the other end of the continuum are families who welcome many different ethnic and racial groups into their family and who participate in family-based activities with people from racial and ethnic heritages different from their own.

Urban literature, theater, art, poetry, and music—not to mention academic history, sociology, and anthropology—are filled with the stories of families deciding to welcome in the stranger or to expel the family member who wants to "marry out." Here where two pathways of kinship intersect is where the emotional richness of city life is captured. Over time, families of origin become complex, multihued reflections of the diversity of urban life.

The Pathway of Friends

Friends, those people one considers equals and with whom he or she has regular face-to-face contact, are links in another pathway through the city. Each person has a unique friendship network with himself or herself as the **ego** or center. These networks, like all systems, have their own characteristics and their own role in city life.

One way to think about networks is to examine the level of connectedness among its members. Networks can be close-knit or loose-knit (Bott, 1957). In a **close-knit network,** all of the ego's friends are also friends of each other; in a **loose-knit network,** the ego has friendships with people who do not necessarily know each other. The two kinds of networks create different social environments for their members.

For example, members of a close-knit network where everyone is in close contact with everyone else have a very strong sense of community, of personal support. The support can be emotional, providing a sense of security and an easily accessible group of friends to share in victory or disappointment. But the support can also be more tangible as members of the network share material resources, information, practical assistance with projects, and help with the daily tasks of living in the city. The reality of closely connected friendships is that everyone in the network knows in a detailed and intimate way about the concerns and thoughts of all the others. This powerful support can amplify limited resources or it can stifle movement or even thinking outside the range acceptable to the group.

By contrast, members of a more loosely knit network do not necessarily even know of the existence of other members of the ego's network. Friendships develop in different contexts such as school, work, the neighborhood, or a sports team. Each individual friendship can have the intensity of emotional connection, sharing and mutual support, but the network lacks the overall sense of strong mutual support. Such networks can be both large and geographically dispersed. They enable their members to move easily from one context to another, facilitating social and economic mobility, but they do not provide a secure support system.

All networks, regardless of their level of connectedness, are sustained by repeated reciprocal exchanges. Reciprocity is the sustained pattern of exchange between partners in a relationship. Friendships endure through the long-term approximate balance of giving and receiving between friends. In important ways, the capacity to participate in reciprocal relationships is a measure of individual maturity. A person completely focused on taking from others lacks maturity. So does the person who insists on paying directly for each service another gives.

Social networks, like extended families, create pathways through the city, linking people from all parts of the city and all racial and ethnic groups to one another. Information about jobs, potential layoffs, sources of special food, location of the good party, safe places for children to play, sports teams, and musicians travel along the pathways of friendship. Each party, child's playground, food stand or pick-up band becomes a hub along the path, a point of intersection of many networks and the place to enter into new ones (Hannerz, 1980).

The pathway of kinship links a person with a family of origin, with the ancestors and homeland. It is a link through time as well as a link through space. The pathway of friendship can have an immediacy to it. Some relationships endure for a lifetime, sustained by a well-used pattern of reciprocity. Other relationships, friendships, emerge in a particular context, meeting specific needs, then fading as the context or the need changes. Family ties are permanent, they endure even when there is active desire to break the connection and little or no contact. But friendships demand a quality of engagement and focus on the present.

The social network, like the family system, connects individuals to the structures of the city. Individual lives are experienced in the context of family and friends. The network, by its very nature, is a creation of its key member, its ego. It is unique to that person and represents the choices that person has made about his or her life. It is the cumulative effect of many, many seemingly minor choices about friends that gives shape to a person's life. This is what is meant by the social construction of ethnicity and race. Ethnicity and race rise from family—the basic elements are present at birth. Yet ethnicity and race also rise from friends and are sustained by active participation in a network of reciprocal relationships.

The Pathway of the Patron-Client Bond

Bonds between people of unequal social or economic status create a different sort of pathway through the city. The patron is the person called to help a son get a summer job or a daughter a reference for college. The patron knows who to call to get a pothole fixed, a traffic ticket "taken care of," a loan to pay off a persistent creditor, or a lawyer to defend a relative in a criminal case. Some patrons hold political office and extend their services to many of their constituents. But other patrons operate on a smaller scale, working out of a barber shop or restaurant rather than a government office.

Clients exchange loyalty to their patron for the protection and assistance the patron provides. The loyalty can be explicit and direct such as a vote for the patron in a critical election. Or the loyalty can be more indirect, expressed in small tokens of support perhaps as simple as delivering a basket of fresh tomatoes to the back door.

The patron-client pathway through the city can be visualized as a system of tiny footpaths feeding into larger trails which in turn merge into paved roads. A patron in a local neighborhood context becomes a client to a more powerful patron with a wider network of connections. The system of interlocking patronage systems thus links the patron in the local barbershop with a powerful state senator or even the governor.

In some cities, machine politics define the political sphere in a highly visible and public manner. Power in the system accrues to the patrons in their ethnic and racial communities who can deliver the votes. Client votes depend on many small acts of protection as well as the more visible payoffs to the neighborhood such as paved streets, repaired street lights and refurbished recreation centers. Less visible returns, such as construction contracts, job security, or "fact-finding trips" go to those local patrons who are clients of more powerful patrons.

The patron-client system often articulates the ethnic and racial boundaries of the city. The pathways of kinship and friendship often cross ethnic and racial identities, creating and expressing a fluid set of relationships grounded in a particular context. In some ways, the patron-client system reflects this reality. The patron-client relationship is, like friendship, a reciprocal relationship dependent on the mutual exchange of favors over a long period of time (Wilson, 1987). But the patron, unlike the friend, leverages his or her connection with his client to gain the favor of a yet more powerful patron. The relationship is not one between equals, but rather explicitly one between persons of unequal power and status.

Paradoxically, it is to the interest of the midlevel patron with an ethnically or racially defined set of clients to keep them in a subordinate, client position while at the same time fighting vigorously for the rights of that ethnic or racial group in the public arena. The patron seeks to deliver the vote and get the favors for the ethnic or racial group without losing control over the process. It is critical for the clients to believe that there is no other avenue for economic (or social or political) mobility or even for the delivery of basic services without the intervention of the patron. Direct, unmediated access to governmental services poses a fundamental challenge to any patronage system and is frequently opposed by racial or ethnic "leaders."

The pathway of the patron-client relationship is not always as visible as machine or ethnic politics. In some contexts, the relationships between protector and client can be a subtle one, rarely discussed or activated. There may be no particular need on the part of the client or the client's loyalty may be so firm as to remain unchallenged. These latent systems only emerge in times of crisis. When the need is critical, all the favors are recalled and clients must demonstrate their loyalty to their patron with a vote, participation in a demonstration, or some other public act of support. Tight elections, legal action against the patron, risk of losing major funding for the patron's projects, and similar events are good times to explore the patron-client pathway.

It is important to distinguish patron-client relationships from two other types of links between unequals. The connection between employer and worker is not a patron-client relationship in most cases, although it is common for patron-client connections to flourish in work settings. The distinction is that the employer-worker relationship is a formal one protected by a range of administrative and legal rights. The patron-client tie, on the other hand, is informal, based on the exchange of loyalty for protection. A patron in a work environment can demand a loyalty from the worker that is stronger than that given the boss. In some work systems, the patronage system dominates all of the formal work relationships.

Mentoring or role-model projects that link successful members of racial or ethnic groups with "at-risk" youth from that group occupy a fuzzy area between employer and patron. That is, the relationships established by service organizations are formal, with the organization providing some safeguards for both the mentor and the protégé should the relationship get in difficulty. Some mentoring relationships explicitly involve the mentor in the school or work life of the protégé as an advocate. This is similar to the role of a patron. The difference is that most mentors do not use their relationships with those they work with to advance their own interests. Strong, mutual loyalty may develop and may last for many years, but the relationship at its core is an individual one.

Conceptually, patron-client ties can be seen as the informal, vertical linkages in the urban system. In some ways it is possible for a family system to blend into a patron-client system, especially in those families which cross economic and social divisions and in which the more powerful and economically secure members give advice and even direct financial assistance to their relatives. It is also possible for some friendship networks to evolve into modified patron-client systems as differences in social or political power among a group of peers emerge over time. It frequently takes a sudden crisis for the core aspect of the relationships to emerge into sharp relief. Death, sudden financial collapse, election to major office (or loss of an election to major office), winning big in the lottery, a child in trouble with the law, or an unwanted move out of town can send a jolt through the system, illuminating even those connections which routine obscures.

The Pathway of Language

Language, spoken and written, wanders along all of the pathways through the city. As it moves through the system, language acquires the coloration of its context. The intimate language of the family gives way to the rougher language of the street, and both fall before the formal demands of the school and the workplace. Simple linear thinking about language—English is spoken in the United States so the task of the immigrant is to learn this language—clearly assumes that there is only one acceptable English for immigrants to learn. A more multicausal approach to language acknowledges that there are many languages in the country, affirming the potential of bilingual education, government documents, and public signs. In the imagery of pathways, these approaches are like bridges on the interstate: mostly one-way, sometimes two-way, but always the dominant way to get from one side to the other. All the swimmers, ferries, canoes, rowboats, powerboats, and rafts that also make it to the other side are oddities, only to be stared at from a fast-moving window.

Systems thinking opens up the issue of language in the city by emphasizing the defining core of all language: relationship. Language exists in the context of a relationship between the one speaking (or signing or writing) and the one spoken (or signed or written) to. Just as there are many kinds of relationships in the city, so there are many potential languages. Three clusters of such language-based relationships are: **naming, self-defining** and **cultural.**

The name given an ethnic or racial group by others has a particular power to define, to honor, and to defile. The dominant group in any context almost always exercises its power to name those they consider to be subordinate. The name can be a crude epithet intended to degrade and hurt, but never spoken in "polite company" even by the dominant group. The name can be a more neutral, but still arbitrary one intended more simply to identify and to define. The name can enter the public life of the country by becoming official. All members of the group are expected to identify with the official name, in the case of ethnic groups, a name printed on the census interview schedule, checked off on an application form, or written on an identity card.

The power of naming balances the power to create a self-definition through name and through language. Everyone who lives in urban United States is a member of a family with a particular, unique relationship with the land and with a language. This land-language connection defines self in powerful ways. With each step into a broader and more encompassing set of social relationships, the self-definition shifts. When in one's own neighborhood, one's definition comes from the block, but when at work, the individual gives neighborhood as his or her identification. If the person is an immigrant, when in the homeland, the particular village is critical; but in the United States, the same person defines self by the country or even by region of the world.

Languaculture is a term given to the unique language pattern found among specific microcultures (Agar, 1994). It is the language of the 'hood or the language of the operating room or the language of the trucker. The concept acknowledges that culture and language are inseparable, that language arises from relationships, and that the quality of these relationships is shaped by the language used. The concept offers a way to look at the pathways through the city in a fresh way. Acceptance of and capacity to use the most inclusive of the languages of the city permits mobility along many paths. The most inclusive languaculture in the United States, the one used by the legal system, the schools, and the media, is a standardized form of English.

The issue immediately becomes more complex because no one actually speaks only standardized English in all situations. The most well-intentioned immigrant, determined to follow the straight path of the "good" immigrant, can master standard English and remain totally bewildered and confused by the questions asked by a speaker of the "welfare office" languaculture. This same speaker of only standard English can deeply offend a group of young male speakers of "street" English by not knowing the highly specialized meanings given certain words in that context. Obviously, the potential for confusion and offense only escalates when neither speaker is using "English" as the point of departure in the effort to establish a relationship.

Language is the most basic of the exchanges that sustain all relationships in the city. It expands and contracts, excludes and welcomes, reassures and offends, communicates and confuses all at the same time. Language follows the pathways of kinship, of friendship and of patron-client ties. Each set of relationships develops its own language, based in large part on the standard language of the dominant group in a particular context, but not limited to that language at all. The most powerful in the city are those who can move in many languacultures, whose fluency enables them to choose which of several paths to follow and to maintain contact with those they met on the way.

A Story

The pathways of the urban systems have been described above in generalities, but the generalities embrace the real lives of real people as they encounter one another on the pathways. One example of this reality is as follows: Students in an urban studies seminar on race, class, and ethnicity, all of them born or raised in Washington, D.C., asked their parents about migration to the city. One set of parents, engaged by the question, agreed to come to class to tell their story.

Their son beamed with pride as he introduced his mother and father to the class. The couple had come by subway from a suburb in Maryland. She wore a pale blue, tailored pants outfit, he wore slacks and a plaid sports shirt. She spoke with the eloquent cadence of the church; he with the rough vitality of work on the land. This is the story they told. The two had known each other from their childhood days in rural North Carolina. Both were from sharecropping families who owned "nothing but their families" and gave one-third of their crop to the "boss" who owned the farm. She graduated from the only African-American high school in the area; his schooling stopped at the seventh grade with World War II.

After high school, she came to Washington to stay with a cousin to earn some money before going to college. She never went back to experience her mother's powerlessness in the face of the slurs of the boss. Later, he came to Washington to court her. She worked as a domestic and he worked construction, eventually ending up working on the grounds of the University of Maryland. After their six children began to be born, she remained home to care for them.

One of the seminar members asked how they had stayed married for so long. Was it his following her to DC to court her? Both gave firm answers. She said it was too much work to raise six children as a single mother; prayer helped; and the two learned how to give and how to take. He said he was determined to support his wife and his family, even if it meant not spending time with some of his friends. At times it was difficult; he worked hard at two jobs, and would come home cross and unable to listen to her tales of the day or discipline the children.

The family moved into the African-American core of Washington in the 1950s. They lived in several apartments until marijuana surfaced in their neighborhood. The family moved in 1969 to a predominately African-American subdivision in a suburb with houses for low- and moderate-income residents. On Sundays after church, they joined other African-American families, all dressed in their best, to "stroll" up the avenue at the heart of African-American Washington, stopping at a theater or club from time to time.

Another student in the seminar interrupted to tell us about her father. He played the cornet with groups in the same clubs. Perhaps they even heard him play, or saw him and her mother.

He did not like to be supervised or watched while he worked. He taught himself everything he knew, including how to work big earth-moving machines in mixed black and white road crews in the south. He knew how to bide his time at the university until they allowed him to work the "white" machines; how to establish his ability to stand up for himself in his new African-American community; and how to wait until he was alone to count the cash payment from his second job as yardman.

For the mother, coming to Washington had meant the hope of moving into white-collar work, but eventually she found it was a hope she could not fulfill. She, like some of her cousins and in-laws, took secretarial courses at a local community college and were among the first African-American women with clerical jobs at the University of Maryland. Finally, though, the mental stress of being overworked and socially isolated became intolerable, and they quit. She responded to the call in church to go to the March on Washington in August 1963. Tears streamed down the face of one of the seminar members as she heard the story of the march again. The story of the black and white leaders holding hands across Constitution Avenue, of Mahalia Jackson singing before Martin Luther King's speech, of the crowd swaying and singing in the glow, like a halo, that came over everyone standing near the Monument. And another student remembered her mother's story of the march and another remembered sitting on her father's shoulders through the speeches.

By now they were hungry, willing to continue the conversation with the students in the elevator, but ready for their dinner.

Where Pathways Intersect: The Organs of the City

To understand race and ethnicity in the city requires analyzing the changing structure of the global economy as it affects a particular city and, at the same time, the many individual actions that occur as an individual person moves through the city. Systems thinking provides an ordered way of participating in this seemingly contradictory approach. A system is composed on interconnected parts, all of which respond to even subtle changes in the environment or field within which they operate. When one focuses on position within the system—whether the economic system or the relational system—as the primary source of behavior, one's gaze must shift outward. Instead of looking at the characteristics of racial or ethnic groups independently, assuming that knowledge of their "culture" will assist in understanding their behavior, one turns to the position of that group and those persons in the relationship and economic systems of which they are a part.

The cleared spaces where many pathways intersect are the institutional exchange centers of an urban system. A city's institutions fall along a continuum of size, formality, and durability. At one end of the continuum might be the club scene where a constantly shifting number of small, informal spots sustain the musicians who hear about where to go from others seeking to listen to or make music. The clubs, taken as a whole, are an institution in the sense of having a life and organization that persists over time (Finnegan, 1989). At the other end of the continuum might be the city council, a highly formal, rule-bound institution that has a power in the city greater than that of any of its specific members. Neighborhood associations, schools, churches, factories, offices, stores, and restaurants can fall at any place along this continuum. All of the institutions have a crucial role in the city. They are the hubs at which many paths converge. In important ways they mediate the connections between people whose pathways may differ widely. All mediating institutions (Lamphere, 1992), including the one in which this text is being used, are systems in their own terms. That is, the institution itself is a system concerned with its own preservation and the maintenance of its own ways of doing things. And, at the same time, it occupies a position in a broader system of interconnected institutions participating in the same general activity—education, making widgets, or selling food. The mediating institution, with its own internal system and part of the broader system which forms the structure of the city, must respond to those on the many smaller pathways which intersect at its door.

Leadership Amid Contradictions

Institutions in which several ethnic and racial groups meet and engage each other help to shape the quality of life for the city. Strong institutions create open space where people

can develop new relationships, expand the scope of their friendship networks, be introduced to a potentially helpful patron, or develop a new languaculture that diversifies the
potential arenas for action.

The earlier discussion of the global economic system suggested a continuum of ways
in which members of different racial and ethnic groups are connected with the system.
The informal economy enables those with limited resources to survive through a complex
set of exchanges of goods and services. The high-tech manufacturing and professional
jobs provide employment for those with advanced education and sophisticated skills. The
range of manufacturing and service jobs between the two extremes vary in terms of the
level of skill required as well as the stability they provide. Many urban structures—
schooling, religion, housing, provision of social support, transportation—are arrayed
along a continuum; informal, *ad-hoc* arrangements stand at one end, highly organized
and formal institutions at the other.

This array of structures creates the **social field** within which ethnic and racial
groups operate in the city. The social field is dynamic, energized by the movement of
many actors through its uncountable pathways. A complex, urban social field generates
multiple pressures on families and, at times, the number and intensity of pressures can
overwhelm them. This capacity of the city and its institutions to subject some of its
residents to pain and suffering dominates much current thinking about urban life. As
the sense of urban decay and failure spreads, a pervasive anxiety has come to dominate
many people's response to the challenges of living in the city. The increased anxiety has
stirred two contradictory responses: to seek togetherness and to seek separation.

The pull toward togetherness can be powerful in all ethnic and racial groups, not to mention families, friendship networks, and patron-client relationships. Togetherness expresses
solidarity, and with solidarity, a kind of security. The system as a whole develops a power-
fully held perspective to which all members adhere. Rapid flow of information through the
system, facilitated by rapid and widespread forms of communication, reinforces the collective perspective of the group. Information that challenges the sense of togetherness in the
system is disregarded, dismissed as wrong, or challenged.

In its most intense form, the countervailing pull toward separation emphasizes individual uniqueness and argues for a life apart from that of the wider society. Individuals
or groups who define themselves as separate from and not responsible to a broader social
system often maintain rigid positions of emotional or ideological clarity. Frequently, the
thinking in these closed systems is absolutist—things are either right or wrong. Isolation
and expulsion are used as threats or sanctions against those members of the system who
deviate from its position.

The presence of the two pulls sets in motion a set of contradictions for newcomers and
established residents alike. The pull toward togetherness strengthens the contention of established residents that newcomers should assimilate, should become "like us." That is, they
should speak English, behave with proper decorum, vote for established candidates, and get
a job. The opposite pull emerges when newcomers are too successful at assimilating for the
comfort of the established residents. In this case, it is argued that the newcomers should
maintain their native ways (especially for cultural events), not try to behave "above themselves," never vote as part of an ethnic or racial bloc, and wait their turn for the good jobs.

A capacity to live with these contradictions can be seen as one mark of personal maturity. Natural leaders of families, social networks, and institutions at all levels of formality

combine this kind of maturity with a powerful presence despite the intense anxiety of the wider society. The person who keeps thinking about the future when all around are reacting to the disaster of the moment attracts followers and creates pockets of effective action in the midst of even the most intense family or community crisis.

The need for mature, effective leadership is acute in today's cities. Leaders are needed to point to the horizon, thus lifting the vision of the group beyond the immediate pressures of the social field within which it operates. Leaders also work to define the boundary between the family or group and the social field, a boundary permeable enough for new information to enter, but selective enough to screen out demands to act or consume or behave in ways that are destructive. The best leaders continuously encourage members to develop their own goals and to move toward them. In the broadest terms, effective leaders direct their members toward a human society that enhances the physical, mental, and social well-being of all its members.

Racial and ethnic identity develop through a lifetime of exchanges with family, friends, and neighbors. In the city, newcomers and established residents create new pathways and shape new identities over time. For many city dwellers, the social identity at work, often at a job where acquaintances and co-workers come from many different backgrounds, is more expansive than the identity of home and neighborhood. Children in schools with many different racial and ethnic groups represented learn at an early age how to define an appropriate school identity while maintaining loyalty to family. During the course of a day or a week, aspects of racial or ethnic background move to a position of dominance or recede into insignificance. This ebb and flow over time and space gives vitality to city life through the constantly shifting constellations of racially and ethnically defined groups. This perspective on ethnicity and race stands in sharp contrast to the image of ethnic and racial identity being from birth, unchanging and primary (Goode & Schneider, 1994).

This interplay between identity and circumstance, between individual behavior and structure, broadens the analysis of ethnicity and race in the city. If circumstance and structure can be visualized as one axis on a graph and if identity and individual behavior can become the second axis, then a new way to map the city is formed. (See Figure 16.1.) The two axes, each representing a continuum of possibilities, can be used to plot an individual's or family's space in the city. A person then becomes defined, not in a linear, static sense by a single defining characteristic, but rather in terms of position within a set of relationships (Friedman, 1991).

The circumstance axis, for example, could be seen to represent conditions along a continuum with a benign and relatively crisis-free situation at one end and an intensely stress- and crisis-ridden environment at the other. The central point could be considered an environment with sufficient stimulation to provide challenge and with sufficient resources to provide for basic needs. And the individual axis might be seen as a continuum, with institutionalized adults totally dependent on others for their basic needs at one end and at the other end those leaders with the capacity to remain connected with their people while remaining calmly focused on the future.

If the city were remapped, placing men and women along the double axes of response and circumstance, rather than the single line of race or ethnicity, new vistas would be opened up. On this map, established residents and newcomers, the well-educated and the illiterate, and the wealthy and the poor, differ both in terms of their life circumstances and in terms of their ability to take effective action. An illiterate immigrant with no money can

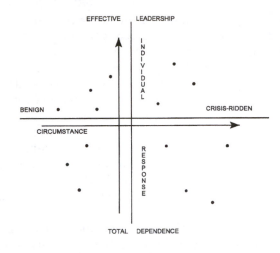

Figure 16.1
Towards a Fresh Map of the City.

be an effective leader, setting the course for those he or she leads in what may to him or her be a benign and calm environment of a city in the United States. Conversely, a person with many generations of ancestors in the United States and a college education may prove totally incapable of handling a series of life crises.

Systems thinking leads to a fresh way of mapping the city. But the map, like all maps, is not the territory. That is, the lived complexity of the city cannot be reduced to a grid in a textbook. Nonetheless, if it is a good map, it can serve as a guide to the city—a way of placing the known of one's own experience in an ordered relationship with the unknown life of the new immigrant or the fellow student from a different racial or ethnic heritage. And the process of locating the new in the grid of the familiar in itself grounds city residents in the reality of the life they share in the city.

Name _____

The City Encounters Diversity (Anthropology)

16-1. Identify, by number, the census tract in which you live and describe its characteristics including population, average age, family size, and household income for the years 1990 and 2000.

16-2. Describe the ethnic residential patterns in your central city.

16-3. Rank order (in your opinion) the five greatest pressures on families which are generated by the urban social field.

The City Evolves into Megacities

(Global Demography)

Ashok K. Dutt, Anindita Parai and Rajiv R. Thakur

While the nineteenth century was noted for the remarkable urban transformation and accompanying industrial and economic growth of Europe and America, the twentieth century was marked by the phenomenal growth of megacities in developing countries. If it is asserted that "the nineteenth century was the century of Europe and the twentieth century that of the America, then it is probable that the twenty-first century will be of Asia" (Dutt & Noble, 2003 p. 17). The developing countries, particularly Asia and Africa, present high growth rates of urbanization and population. According to United Nations estimates: a) 85.7% of the world's population growth between 1970 and 2000 was absorbed by the four developing areas of Latin America, Africa, East Asia and South Asia; b) developing countries in 2000 had about four times more population compared to that of the developed regions; and c) by 2030 the former will contain over five times more population than that of the latter (World Development Report 1984; United Nations, 2004). (See Figures 17.1 and 17.2.) The global **process of urbanization** has been very rapid since the end of the World War II, particularly in the developing regions. This rapid process has posed challenges to government, politicians, planners, and not least the communities, families, and individuals involved. Figure 16.1 portrays that: a) in 1950, a lesser number of people lived in urban areas of developing regions compared to that of the developed ones; b) an almost equal number of people lived in urban areas of both the developed and developing countries of the world by the mid 1960s; c) by 2030, about four times more people will live in urban areas of developing regions compared to that of the developed regions; and d) the number of people living in urban areas of the developed countries is increasing very slowly.

After the Second World War, as a result of population explosion, both rural and urban population increased considerably in the developing countries. Such natural growth made a significant impact on the slow growing rural economy, which was unable to absorb new labor in its working pool. The superfluous labor created an accelerated growth of rural-to-urban migration and thus a significant "push factor" was in operation. On the other hand, higher life expectancy also made a significant impact on both the urban and the rural population increase. This caused an increase in the dependency ratio, requiring the economy to support larger number of older people and younger people, both in the rural and urban areas. Urban population started to show signs of aging; subsequently numbers in the 60-plus age group increased. The

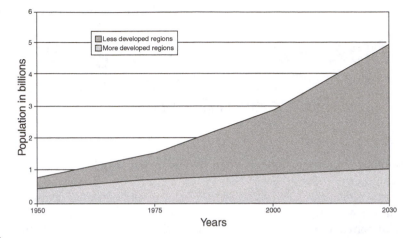

Figure 17.1
Urban Population by More Developed and Less Developed Regions of the World.
(Source: World Urbanization Prospects: The 2003 Revision.)

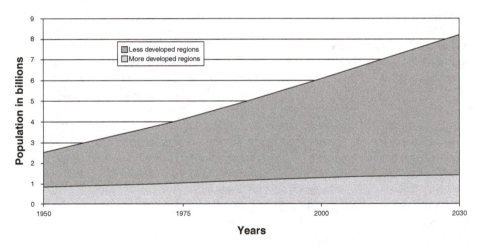

Figure 17.2
World Population by More Developed and Less Developed Regions.
(Source: World Urbanization Prospects: The 2003 Revision.)

result was that the urban population started to grow rapidly, both as a result of "rural-push" and natural urban growth (Dutt, 2001, pp. 2–3). Figure 17.2 also indicates that developing regions' population is persistently increasing while it has stabilized in the developed countries. Such a pattern closely relates to urbanization changes discussed earlier.

Asian, African, and Latin American nations have the oldest urban history. The form of cities before the twentieth century in these continents was essentially traditional/ preindustrial or colonial, though Latin America had mostly become free of colonial domination by the early 1800s. Asian and African colonies were freed from colonial domination after World War II. Religious, trading, transshipment, and administrative places turned into growth centers with subsequent urban expansion. The pattern of colonial-based urban development dates back to the sixteenth century with the advent of the European colonial domination, which generated a port-based, export oriented, urban economy existing largely for the benefit of the manufacturing and mercantile needs of the mother country (Dutt & Pomeroy, 2003). Most of the countries had one megacity, invariably along a river or coast for ease of communications and transportation, to perform the main urban functions: export of raw materials to the "mother" country and import of manufactured goods from there, along with housing the military and administrators of European origin. A large number of these cities have grown to be **primate cities,** the pivotal role of which can be gauged by the proportion of urban populations they contain (McGee, 1971). The primate cities, which are evident in countries like the Philippines (Manila), Thailand (Bangkok) South Korea (Seoul), Argentina (Buenos Aires), and Egypt (Cairo), have two or more times larger population than that of the second largest city of their countries. Other examples of primate cities in developing countries are Caracas (Venezuela), Bogotá (Columbia), Dhaka (Bangladesh), Istanbul (Turkey), Jakarta (Indonesia), Lagos (Nigeria), Mexico City (Mexico), and Teheran (Iran). India and China, being large countries with large populations that are distributed in different areas, present multiple primacies. In China, three cities—Shanghai, Beijing and Guangzhou—provide regional primacies in the east, because no city can be called primate for the country as a whole. Similarly in India, Mumbai (Bombay), Kolkata (Calcutta), and Delhi provide regional primacy in the north while Chennai (Madras), Bangalore, and Hyderabad provide a triangular primacy in the south in absence of a national primate city.

Metro Manila, with a population of 9.6 million in 2000, attracts the largest number of migrants from different parts of the country, "adding about 1 million persons to its population every five years" (United Nations, Metro Manila, 1986, p. 50) and Bangkok, with a population of 6.3 million in 2000 and "one of the world's most extreme examples of metropolitan primacy," is "larger than the combined populations of the next 12 largest cities in Thailand" (United Nations, Bangkok, 1987, p. 47). Seoul, "the premier city in Korea for nearly six centuries" and with a population of 9.9 million in 2000, is not only the nation's capital and the most important industrial and financial center, but it has also become the "development engine of the national economy, increasing its share of the gross national product (GNP) from 17.3 to 30.5 percent between 1963 and 1977" (United Nations, Seoul, 1986, p. 56).

As the colonial people came from Europe after Columbus's landing in America in 1492, they were anchored in coastal locations of the colonies where settlements, development, and urbanization accelerated, causing a general trend of economic upsurge, whereas the interior areas remained neglected. Examples are the eastern seaboard of the United States in the eighteenth and early nineteenth centuries, South American coasts, and India. In South America, large urban concentrations are coastal, whereas the interior regions are less developed. In India during the colonial time, development focused on the three major port locations—Calcutta, Bombay and Madras—and their immediate hinterland regions. Only after independence in 1947 was interior development encouraged in order to balance regional development. During the colonial time, it was in the coastal areas that the capital, primate cities, and the main focus of urbanization were lodged.

Five-story pagoda of Asakusa in Tokyo is visited by many. (Photo by Sunii Dutt.)

Thus, the dichotomy created during the colonial occupation with **coastal development** and **interior backwardness** persists even today in India and South America.

Another important feature inherited from the colonial background of the cities is the presence of two types of economy: a **modern manufacturing sector** coexisting alongside a **traditional bazaar type sector** with very little interaction between them. The bazaar type sector consists of low paying and low productive jobs such as the drivers and manual workers in the transportation sector, household workers, servants, and construction workers. These jobs are **labor intensive** and thus contribute much to the employment opportunities for the growing urban population (McGee, 1969). In Calcutta, the **informal sector** accounted for nearly eighty percent of the city's commercial units (59,220) and provided more than fifty percent of the total employment in the commercial sector (United Nations, Calcutta, 1986 p. 38). In Dhaka it was estimated that in 1980, sixty-five percent of the employment was in the informal sector; mainly in transport, street peddling and day labor (United Nations, Dhaka, 1987, p. 38).

The modern sector, on the other hand, consists of factories using machines, power, and large numbers of workers. These factories initially had products that needed to be processed near the raw materials, such as sugar and rice mills and later more cost effective sub-sectors such as cotton and jute textiles. After World War II, Asian cities began to manufacture machines, chemicals, and "high-tech" items. Japan, especially in its cities, led the way followed by Seoul, Hong Kong, Taipei, and Singapore. All five cities now reflect the characteristics of developed economies.

Worldwide population increase also had a concomitant increase in rural population. At the beginning of the twenty-first century, the rural population in the developing countries stabilized and, beginning in approximately 2015, it will start to decline. This decline will result in diminishing levels of rural to urban migration in the developing countries. Figure 17.3 also indicates that there is a constant decline in rural population in the developed countries as agriculture becomes more mechanized and farm sizes are increased in order for farmers to remain economically viable, thus indicating cessation of intra country rural/urban migration.

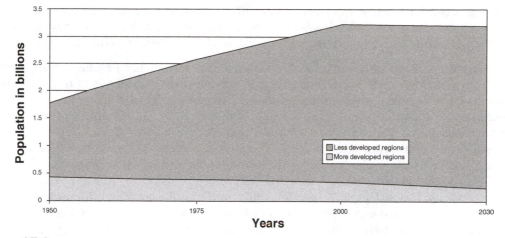

Figure 17.3
Total Rural Population by More Developed and Less Developed Regions of the World
(1960–2030). (*Source: World Urbanization Prospects: The 2003 Revision.*)

Since over half a century the number of megacities over ten million population has increased dramatically, from only two urban agglomerations (New York and Tokyo) in 1950 to four in 1975 and to 20 in 2003; fifteen of the twenty were in developing countries. Massive improvement in infrastructure and the related technology have made living in such huge agglomerations possible, though there is always a possibility of breakdown in the system with infrastructure development unable to keep pace with the fast growing population.

The Nature of Urbanization in Asia

Asia, consisting of 47.7% of the world's urban population in 2000, is a vast continent containing an immense diversity of nations. The unique heterogeneity of race, religions, languages, and ethnic backgrounds in Asian countries is unmatched by any other continent. Asian cities are ethnically diverse, with varying proportions of alien Asians, mostly Chinese and Indians who were recruited by the Europeans to help pioneer developments not only in Asia, but also in Africa, the Caribbean, and the islands of the Pacific and Indian Oceans. Since the 1970s, the oil-rich Saudi-Arabia, Kuwait, Iraq, Bahrain, and United Arab Emirates attracted a large number of temporary migrants from India, Pakistan, Indonesia, Bangladesh, Sri Lanka and Philippines to staff their growing service and technical sectors. The result was an infusion of a multi-ethnic character in selected Middle Eastern cities. Multi-ethnicity, on the one hand, poses constraints in the development programs of the cities, but if handled rationally, as in Singapore, it can be turned into an asset. In the case of Singapore, ethnic, religious, and racial harmony has been strongly encouraged and enforced by state action.

Overall the Singaporean people have a high degree of social and racial harmony. This is the result of two main factors. The Singaporean economy is growing, growing extremely quickly by Western standards. In a booming economy, everybody in society benefits. No single group of the Singaporean population is suffering. No single group is being victimized for the country's ills, as is often the case in societies where the economy is not so sound, where recent immigrants can become scapegoats on which to blame the country's maladies (Dutt & Parai, 1996, pp. 310–12).

Moreover, it is not only the oil-rich countries that attract both skilled and unskilled labor from less developed Asian countries, but the developed countries of the world have migrants from less developed countries. Most of the new migrants settle in urban areas. For example, the Vietnamese during the Cold War worked in East Germany, though many also migrated to the United States, Canada, and Australia after the United States military withdrew from the country in 1975. The United States was home to 1.5 million ethnic Vietnamese by 2004. Several more thousands work and live in France and Germany. The Vietnamese-French connection emanates from pre-1954 times, when Vietnam was a French colony. It is estimated that these migrants remit about $4 billion every year to their relatives in Vietnam, which not only reduces pressure on the Vietnamese *dong,* but which also stimulates private investment and reduces poverty.

Population Growth and Push/Pull Factors

Despite the immense diversity of the Asian cities, one factor remains common: the immense population expansion and corollary urban growth (Costa et al., 1988). In 1950, only 16.4% of Asia's total population lived in urban places and it accounted for 30.8% of the world's urban population; it is projected to increase to 59.5 and 53.2% in 2025, respectively (United Nations, 1991). Despite the fact that Asia is one of the least urbanized continents (second only to Africa), its vast area and population have created the largest number of major urban agglomerations among the continents.

A comparative analysis of the top thirty urban agglomerations of the world from 1950 to 2010 indicates specific characteristics (Figure 17.4). First, the size of the largest cities has grown considerably. New York, the topmost city in 1950, had a population of 12.3 million in contrast to Tokyo's 38.66 million in 2010. Second, out of the thirty largest urban agglomerations in 1950, twenty were in developed countries. This number was reduced to five in 2010; showing the reduction in pace of growth of large metropolitan centers in developed countries. Third, in 1950 only ten out of thirty largest cities of the world were in the developing countries. This number increased to twenty-five in the year 2010. Thus, the comparative share of the largest cities is rapidly increasing in developing countries, reflecting a much larger growth rate of population in general and accentuated rural-urban migration. Fourth, the number of African cities among the top thirty world cities is almost static. There was one in 1950 and two in 2010, indicating much lower economic growth in Africa compared to other continents. Fifth, Asian large urban agglomeration growth had been spectacular: from seven top thirty cities of the world in 1950 to 14 in 2010. This was primarily a result of accentuated rural-urban migration. Sixth, Tokyo for the first time became the largest city of the world in 1970 and is holding onto that position because its railroad-based communication network spreads into a wide and very densely populated plain lands of the metropolis. Seventh, New York was the largest world city in 1950 but it was relegated to the fourth position in 2010. This reflects the slow growth of the country's population and diminished migration from Europe and other countries to this metropolis. Eighth, Mumbai has shown a spectacular growth as it rose from eighteenth in 1950 to the seventh position in 2010. By 2015, its population is projected to rise

Table: Ranked urban agglomerations by population, 1950–2010.

1950	1960	1970	1980	1990	2000	2010
New York-Newark	Tokyo	Tokyo	Tokyo	Tokyo	Tokyo	Tokyo
Tokyo	New York-Newark	New York-Newark	New York-Newark	New York-Newark	Mexico City	Delhi
London	London	Osaka-Kobe	Mexico City	Mexico City	New York-Newark	(Mexico City
Paris	Paris	Mexico City	São Paulo	São Paulo	São Paulo	New York-Newark
Moscow	Shanghai	Los Angeles	Osaka-Kobe	Mumbai	Mumbai	Shanghai
Buenos Aires	Buenos Aires	Paris	Los Angeles	Osaka-Kobe	Delhi	São Paulo
Chicago	Los Angeles	Buenos Aires	Buenos Aires	Calcutta	Shanghai	Mumbai
Calcutta	Osaka-Kobe	São Paulo	Calcutta	Los Angeles	Calcutta	Beijing
Shanghai	Chicago	London	Paris	Seoul	Buenos Aires	Dhaka
Osaka-Kobe	Moscow	Moscow	Mumbai	Buenos Aires	Los Angeles	Calcutta
Los Angeles	Calcutta	Chicago	Rio de Janeiro	Delhi	Osaka-Kobe	Karachi
Berlin	Mexico City	Calcutta	Seoul	Rio de Janeiro	Rio de Janeiro	Buenos Aires
Philadelphia	Rio de Janeiro	Rio de Janeiro	Moscow	Paris	Dhaka	Los Angeles
Rio de Janeiro	Mumbai	Shanghai	London	Cairo	Cairo	Rio de Janeiro
Saint Petersburg	São Paulo	Mumbai	Cairo	Moscow	Beijing	Manila
Mexico City	Philadelphia	Cairo	Chicago	Jakarta	Karachi	Moscow
Mumbai	Beijing	Seoul	Jakarta	Manila	Moscow	Osaka-Kobe
Detroit	Cairo	Beijing	Shanghai	Shanghai	Manila	Istanbul
Cairo	Saint Petersburg	Saint Petersburg	Delhi	Chicago	Paris	Cairo
Tianjin	Berlin	Detroit	Beijing	Karachi	Istanbul	Guangdong
Manchester	Tianjin	Jakarta	Tehran	Beijing	Jakarta	Shenzhen
São Paulo	Boston	Manila	Karachi	Dhaka	Chicago	Paris
Birmingham	Shenyang	Delhi	Bangkok	Istanbul	London	Chongqing
Shenyang	Jakarta	Madrid	Saint Petersburg	Tehran	Chongqing	Jakarta
Rome	Hong Kong	Barcelona	Hong Kong	Bangkok	Guangdong	Seoul
Milan	Barcelona	Hong Kong	Philadelphia	Lima	Lima	Chicago
San Francisco-Oakland	Rome	Tianjin	Lima	Hong Kong	Lagos	Wuhan
Barcelona	Manchester	Tehran	Istanbul	Madras	Tehran	Lima
Glasgow	Milan Berlin	Madrid	Saint Petersburg	London		
			Hong Kong			

Figure 17.4

World Urbanization Prospects: The 30 largest Urban Agglomerations Ranked by Populations 1950–2010.
(*Source:* United States. Department of Economic and social Affairs, Population Division (2012). World Urbanization Prospects, The 2011 Revision.)

to 22.6 million, possibly surpassing Tokyo in the near future and becoming the world's largest city. The metropolis of Mumbai is dynamic and it has a very strong economic base. It is India's financial capital and is a foremost information technology center. It is also the place where *Bollywood* is located, producing the largest number of motion pictures annually compared to any other city in the world (Dutt, 2001, pp. 14–16).

The rapid rate of urbanization that currently characterizes the Asian world is one of the principle sources of problems, such as those encountered in the West during the nineteenth century (Parai & Dutt, 1994). Asian countries experienced a sharp and almost immediate urbanization trend after the Second World War. Very high rates of **natural increase** are a characteristic feature of the urban areas. As health and social welfare facilities generally tend to be much better in the cities than in the rural areas, Asian cities "exemplify the combination of **pre-industrial fertility** with **post-industrial mortality**." (Davis, 1972) In fact, very often natural increase and **in-migration** contribute in broadly equal proportions to the total growth of urban populations.

Besides natural increase, relative **rural-to-urban shifts/migration** in population are occurring also. Rural to urban migration in the Asian countries can be explained by a combination of "push" and "pull" factors. The "pull" factors toward the city are a result of comparatively better **economic growth,** prosperity, and the availability of job opportunities and health care facilities. Asian cities offer the hopes of employment and high wages to the rural population; they provide the essential sets of perceived opportunities to the rural poor. Asian rural districts contain the world's largest reservoir of potential urban migrants. Unlike the United States, the "push" factor in Asia was not caused by technological advances in agriculture but rather by high rates of natural increase leading to **rural unemployment** and **under-employment.** Surplus agricultural laborers and others in search of employment crowd the cities, which offer comparatively better opportunities. Poverty, which frequently exists in rural areas, also causes rural-to-urban migration (Berry, 1981). The application of **Green Revolution techniques** (hybrid seed, irrigation, insecticides, and fertilizers) since 1966 augmented farm jobs resulting in higher agricultural productivity.

In the case of Punjab, India, where the Green Revolution has attained its greatest success, a rural labor shortage has arisen, causing in-migration of landless laborers from the poor adjacent states like Uttar Pradesh and Bihar. In this case, agricultural modernization generated by green-revolution techniques did not cause any rural-urban migration.

Housing Problems and the Proliferation of Slums

The rapid growth of Asian cities has created new and special problems in practically all facets of human life. The most conspicuous and tragic issue is evident in the field of housing. The urban majority lives in accommodations viewed from a western perspective as shabby and lacking in the most rudimentary of facilities. Provision of proper housing facilities, particularly for low-income groups, is a constant problem for growing Asian cities.

Asian cities and their urban poor cannot afford houses that are properly surveyed, built, and serviced; therefore, the poor end up living in slums or sub-standard housing. The number of slum/squatter settlements in Bangkok increased dramatically over the past thirty years. In Calcutta as many as 55,000 people live on pavements on a regular basis and one-third of its population is housed in slums.

Developments of squatter and spontaneous settlements are commonplace. There are three distinct types of settlements a) **the homeless or pavement dweller areas,** b) **the slum and tenement dweller areas,** particularly in the primate cities, and c) **the squatter communities and shantytowns.** Squatter housing, the most common type, is usually constructed on land that has not been designated for building purposes. Typical sites for settlements are marginal lands and small vacant lots (Manila), steep hillsides (Hong Kong), land adjacent to railway lines (Kuala Lumpur and Dhaka), flood plains (Delhi) and sometimes-swampy unused land or land subject to flooding (Calcutta and Bombay).

Squatter communities and spontaneous settlements present heterogeneity in their physical fabric, location, incomes, and residents. They have their own economic and social character and are bound by their own normative standards of social and functional relations (Potter, 1985). Once the land is occupied it is difficult, if not impossible, to displace the settlers, although they do not have a legal claim to the land because it is embarrassing and politically unpopular to evict families.

Squatter settlements reflect the failure of the private and public housing sectors to provide adequate low-income housing. Where even semi-decent rental property is available, either in private tenements or in housing provided by the government, rents are high and are beyond the reach of the poor. Parallel with the housing problems, Asian cities also lack a sufficient level of public services, which cannot keep up with the rapid rates of population growth. Thus, large Asian cities are characterized by economic and social dualism. Some areas are supplied with necessary services and have decent environments, while others have worse living conditions than rural areas.

A dual approach also exists in solving the housing problem of the poor. Brick and mortar apartments with modern plumbing and a potable water supply are built by public agencies in countries such as China. In China, socialist values for equity reduce the amount of return or rent, which would be expected in a capitalist country and in relatively high-income places like Hong Kong and Singapore. In **market-economy-based** developing countries such as India, slums have been upgraded with improved sanitary and infrastructure facilities without disturbing the existing shabby housing structures. The city of Calcutta discarded the "Slum Clearance" or "Slum Redevelopment" models because of their economic and social costs, and adopted an innovative "Slum Improvement" model beginning in the early 1970s:

> *It was ultimately decided to go for limited slum improvements. This was effectively a "Sanitation Model" aimed at providing basic infrastructure facilities to slum dwellers without attempting to provide conventional housing to the target groups. The ingredients of the action program included conversion of service latrines, providing potable water supply connections, surface drainage facilities, construction of paved roads and path-ways, arranging street lighting and providing garbage vats and dustbins in adequate numbers in slum areas. This model of improvement of living conditions of slum dwellers recognized slums as a part of the city housing stock occupied by people who had been priced out of all conventional forms of housing. This model did not involve interference with the rights and interests of the landowners and thika [contract-based] tenants and physical shifting of slum dwellers further from the place of their employment. The fact that this model of development was comparatively less expensive and improvements in living conditions could be done in stages were considered to be its strengths (Chakrabarti & Halder, 1991, pp. 8–9).*

Beginning in 1992, the government of India adopted a "total sanitation" program for its urban slums in order to provide basic human needs such as primary health care, filtered water, immunization, sanitation, and women's welfare.

Urban Unemployment

Rapid population growth, along with sluggish economic development because of an insufficient industrial base results in a lack of employment opportunities for Asian cities. As early as 1956, Hauser designated Asia as "over-urbanized in relation to its degree of economic development" because "the pace of urbanization, especially in the last decade [1945–1955], has far exceeded the growth rate of economies of Asia" (Hauser, 1957, p. 286). The adoption of **capital-intensive** products and production methods from the west has had deleterious effects on the employment scene.

Countries such as Japan, South Korea, Taiwan, Singapore, and Hong Kong, which took steps in the 1960s (in the case of Japan in the 1950s) to build their basic economic structure, were able to jump start their urban economies in order to become more industrialized. Their cities in the early twenty-first century have a much better appearance and infrastructure compared to most of the other cities in Asia. Also, the oil-rich countries of the Middle East and Brunei used their oil money to avoid the need for initial labor-intensive urban economies, and they changed their cities into modern settlements with amenities comparable to those found in many Western countries.

Income distribution in developing Asian countries, particularly in the primate cities, is highly skewed, with only a fraction of the workforce able to sustain a relatively high standard of living. This low level of per capita income does not allow the people to save, either for productive enterprises or for the development of proper urban infrastructures.

Environmental Pollution

A relatively recent phenomenon, environmental deterioration and pollution is rapidly becoming among the worst ailments of urban societies in the Asian countries. The city, with its growing industries and demographic explosion, often plays a decisive role in its promotion. With a sizeable number of people living in slums, their concern is less with the quality of environment than with the struggle for the necessities of life.

One of the primary factors leading to degraded urban environments is the increase in the number of automobiles and trucks. Most Asian cities are not prepared for such an increase in motorized vehicles. Leaded gas emissions, combined with industrial smoke in cities, is so acute that the Asian cities are among the most environmentally polluted cities in the world. Delhi and Calcutta and several other large urban agglomerations have banned the use of leaded gasoline. Industrial pollution also adds to the deterioration of rivers and underground water, used for drinking. As the streets are not paved in many parts of the cities, dust causes additional problems.

In Dhaka, the old city's small-scale manufacturing units produce harmful residues that are often dumped into the river along with effluent from tanneries, sugar and jute mills and two thermal power stations (United Nations, Dhaka, 1987).

Asian cities are undergoing a large increase in improvements for their transportation systems. Besides private automobiles used by the rich, public transportation systems use trams, buses, and rails. Non-polluting metro rail systems are in operation in Tokyo, Seoul, Beijing, Hong Kong, Taipei Singapore, Bombay, Calcutta, Madras and Delhi. As over a third of the people live below the poverty line, they either walk or take public transportation. The roads of Calcutta still have hand-pulled rickshaws and carts. The common people use heavily subsidized public transportation not only for daily commuting, but also for shopping and other purposes; however, the overuse of public transportation, coupled with a limited supply of vehicles, often causes overboarding, delays, and uncomfortable rides.

Deviant Behavior

Cities, where a large percentage of adult males are unemployed, where a third or more of the people are without water service, where as many as four out of five families live in a single room, and where environmental hazards loom large, are bound to have social tensions and serious political unrest. The traditional social supports, such as the extended family and organizations representing the migrants' rural background, are no longer operative in cities. The weakness of urban centers in providing substitutes for these supports creates problems of mental stress, personal disorientation, and social disorganization, which in turn result in heightened incidences of crime, delinquency, and other related negative phenomena.

Urban migrants generally find themselves forced to live in the squatter communities, shantytowns, or slums in the older parts of large cities. They soon adopt a way of life reflected in various deviant behavior patterns such as alcoholism, prostitution, delinquency, and crime. Most of the reported urban crime is committed by slum area dwellers and in slum areas.

Crime rates have reached their peak in large cities such as Bombay, Calcutta, Karachi, and Manila. These cities have a much higher share of crime and delinquency than their population would warrant. The new migrants not only become involved directly in criminal activities, but are also victimized by them. Currently the problems of drug addiction, international level crimes, drug dealings, trafficking in women, and more violent forms of crimes, such as the increased use of guns and bombs, have begun to affect Asian cities. Cities must, as a result, divert scarce resources in order to control the rapidly increasing rates and types of crimes. Crime control measures—equipment and buildings needed by police, courts, prisons, and improved road and street lighting for greater security purposes—add to cities' financial burdens.

An age-old form of social deviation, prostitution, is becoming a special feature in some cities of developed Asia. The Tokyo Metropolitan Government, for example, "opened a big commercial complex this year next to a warren of peep shows, strip clubs and massage parlors known as Kabukicho." (Sterngold, 1993, p. A4) A developing country city, Bangkok, in the early twenty-first century attained a reputation of becoming the sex capital of the world as customers came from different parts of the world to find young innocent girls, even from Cambodia and Myanmar, who were deceptively allured to the sex shops.

New Global Urbanization Trends: Impact on Urbanization

The recent economic globalization activities have restructured the labor/capital relationship between the cities of the developed and the developing world. In the new economic framework, less skilled jobs related to the making of garments, shoes, handbags, luggage, and toys are being created in the developing countries. Outsourcing also has occurred in the form of the production of parts of machines, engines, automobiles, electronics, and computer-related hardware elements in the developing countries while cities in the developed world lose manufacturing jobs. It is cheaper and much more profitable for capitalists to manufacture the above-mentioned commodities in the developing countries and bring them to the markets of the developed countries. In addition upscale jobs, such as engineering, basic research, financial data analysis, innovative research and development and designing of chips, are also being sent by the multinational corporations to the developing countries where labor costs are much cheaper. Thus, the semi-skilled and skilled jobs are being created increasingly in selected urban areas of the developing countries. China and India are two leaders (Dutt & Noble, 2003).

Two examples from India are:

In dazzling new technology parks rising on the dusty outskirts of the major cities [of India], no one's talking about job-losses. Inside Infosys Technologies Ltd.'s impeccably landscaped 55-acre campus in Bangalore, 250 engineers develop IT applications for Bank of America. Elsewhere, Infosys staffers process home loans for Greenpoint Mortgage of Novato, California. Near Bangalore's airport at the offices of Wipro Limited, five radiologists interpret 30 CT scans a day for Massachusetts General Hospital. Not far away, 26-year-old engineer Dharin Shah talks excitedly about his $10,000 a-year job designing third-generation mobile phone chips, as sun pours through a skylight at the Texas Instrument Inc. research center. Five years ago an engineer like Shah would have made a beeline for Silicon Valley. Now he says "the sky is the limit here."

Even Wall Street jobs paying $80,000 and up are getting easier to transfer. Brokerages like Lehman brothers Inc. and Bear, Steams & Co., for example, are starting to use Indian financial analysts for number crunching work. "A basic business tenet is that things go to the areas where there is the best cost of production," says Ann Livemore, head of services at Hewlett-Packard Co, which has 3,300 software engineers in India. "Now you are going to see the same trends in services that happened in manufacturing" (Engardio, Bernstein & Kriplani, 2003, pp. 50–51, 53).

China, a developing country, poses the greatest challenge to the developed countries. This country's garment, shoe, household appliance, electronic equipment, and plastic products industries are greatly affecting manufacturing in both Western Europe and the United States. China can manufacture products thirty to fifty percent less than the United States. The result is that between 2000 and 2004, 2.7 million manufacturing jobs were lost in the United States. The result is many United States companies are not investing at home. They, as well as the Europeans and the Japanese, find it more profitable to invest in China. In China itself, private companies and foreign ventures generate seventy percent of exports. For example, bedroom furniture manufacturing is rapidly moving to China. This means a loss of jobs in the Galax (Virginia) Factory of the Vaughan-Bassett Company. In China, mega plants have been created for furniture making. Troy, Michigan, a maker of steel components for plastic injection machines suffers as Chinese products replace these components. The town of Doumen in the Pearl River delta of China makes cell phones, x-box game consoles, personal computers, and other hardware. 3Com Corporation in Marlborough, Massachusetts, has moved its engineering component to China by joining the Huawei Technologies Company. Outside of Beijing, the Semi Conductors Manufacturing Corporation has opened a chip plant, fabricating 12-inch silicon wafers. This could pull capital, people, research and development and design functions from the United States to China. The most spectacular is a three-mile-long site in Nanjing where Chinese and German entrepreneurs are in the process of making the world's largest and most modern production complex for ethylene, which is an essential ingredient for plastics. The auto parts makers in Hangzhou manufacture parts for General Motors, Ford, and Volkswagen. The Chinese way is not only to manufacture low-level products such as garments and shoes, but also to manufacture higher end products such as computer hardware, machines, electronics, and automobiles. Workers' training and their education run parallel in importance to innovation. Chinese low prices and competitive quality are difficult to match (Bremner, 2004).

Future Outlook

The urbanization process has sharpened in the developing countries, particularly in Asia, and with it most of the social and economic problems have also accelerated. There is also no sign of slowing down of urbanization levels in the near future. United Nations projections point out that world urban population will reach 4.9 billion in 2030, up from 2.9 billion in 2000; seventy percent of the urban population of the world will reside in developing countries in 2030. The rapid process of world urbanization with its attendant problems is a significant challenge for government leaders, planning officials, and city residents. The creativity and cooperation of many academic disciplines will be required to address these urban challenges and to improve the quality of urban life across the globe.

Name _____

The City Evolves into Megacities (Global Demography)

17-1. Locate and identify the major cities of South America on the map below. What do most of them have in common geographically?

17-2. Locate and identify the major cities of Africa on the map below.

17-3. Locate and identify the major cities of Monsoon Asia on the map below.

17-4. Why are the cities of the Third World called primate cities?

PART IV
Urban Prospects

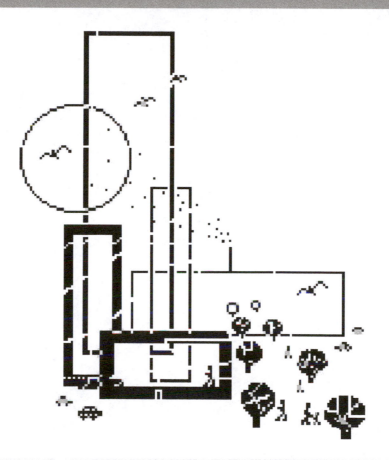

CHAPTER 18

The City Faces Its Future: Technology and the Future of the City

(Future Studies)

Jun Koo

Throughout the history of urban development, technology has played a significant role in shaping the physical and economic systems of the city. The development of water, sewer, power, transit, industrial, and most recently, information technologies have changed the way we live, travel, produce, and communicate.

During the early industrial era, firms located in the city looking for easy access to transportation networks and talents, and people lived near their jobs. The rapid growth of port and industrial cities in the 1800s, such as New York, Philadelphia, Boston, Chicago, and Cleveland, is a case in point. In the new information era, however, where firms can move goods easier than ever from one place to another and find talents easily in any place on the planet, location may not be as important as it used to be.

The advent of the automobile, computer, and the Internet changed everything. Individuals as well as businesses have less incentive to stay in the city. Thanks to dramatic technological advancements in the last century, many suburban or rural areas can offer conveniences and amenities close to those of major cities. With Internet access and credit cards, people in rural Iowa can shop at Amazon and ebay as easily as anyone living in New York or Boston. The proliferation of online shopping offers even fancy department stores, such as Bloomingdale's and Saks Fifth Avenue, to those in remote areas. In fact, over the last several years, online retail has seen a twenty to thirty percent annual growth whereas brick and mortar retail has experienced only a modest growth or none at all. Because of such a dramatic shift, some people argue that geographic location is no longer a valid concept in individual and business decisions (Gordon & Richardson, 1997). A renowned tech-guru, George Gilder (Gilder & Peters, 1995), even states that "we are headed for the death of cities. . . . cities are leftover baggage from the industrial era."

Then what does this trend mean to the future of the city? Given such changes, how might cities fare in the future? Will the city survive dramatic technological advances and maintain its stature in the next century, or will it lose its status as people pay less and less attention to location? This section critically reviews two schools of thought about technology and the future of the city and discusses a plausible scenario for the future that the city is likely to face.

Why City?

To answer this question and to understand where the current path of technological development will lead us in the future, one needs to start by discussing the costs and benefits for people living (or firms locating) in major cities. Individuals living in cities like New York, San Francisco, and Washington D.C. encounter higher rent, traffic congestion, and air pollution. At the same time, however, they also get to know people with diverse backgrounds, have access to better employment opportunities and greater cultural amenities, and learn from one another.

Many previous studies have particularly emphasized the learning opportunity that cities provide. Originally, Marshall (1890) argued that urban agglomeration facilitates interactions among people and thereby helps individuals learn from one another. Recent studies have found an increasing amount of evidence that confirms his argument. For instance, Jaffe et al (1993) found that knowledge flows only to certain geographic limits, and the benefits of knowledge flows are often strongly concentrated in urban areas. Rauch (1993) and Glaeser (1999) found a significant urban wage premium, which indicates the importance of learning effects in cities (i.e., workers in urban areas are more productive than those in non-urban areas because the increased opportunity for interaction accelerates learning). Therefore, the future of the city hinges on centrifugal and centripetal forces of urban life. If the benefits outweigh the costs, people will move into the city. If the opposite is true, people will move out of the city.

What about firms? Firms located in major cities often face similar negative as well as positive forces. They have to endure the higher cost of doing business; everything is more expensive in the city. In addition, there are significant intangible costs incurred from traffic congestion and pollution. For instance, consider the time wasted in commuting. At the same time, however, firms in large cities can more easily access a larger pool of parts suppliers, business service providers, and labor force. Also, firms located in proximity often learn from one another through competition as well as collaboration.

In the new economy where knowledge is considered a critical factor for economic success, geographic proximity among individuals and firms that facilitates the exchange of information and ideas is particularly important. Many recent studies showed that geographic concentration of economic activities is positively associated with the productivity levels of local firms (Beeson, 1987; Feser, 2001; Henderson, 1999; Moomaw, 1988). Perhaps the best-known example of such phenomenon is Silicon Valley. The informal, open, and flexible business environment of Silicon Valley provides scientists and engineers with a place for socializing and exchanging information. Workers easily move from semiconductor to disk drive firms or computer to software makers with their knowledge and experience intact. Such flows of knowledge workers among related firms stimulate the development of new ideas (Saxenian, 1994).

In sum, for both individuals and firms, there are costs and benefits involved in being located in the city. In the industrial society in the last century, the benefits usually outweighed the costs. In the information society where everything is connected, however, this may not necessarily be the case. If the relative locational benefits of the city in comparison with those of other non-urban areas are diluted because of the development of new technological innovations, particularly in information and communication technologies (ICT), the geographic distribution of social and economic activities are likely to change dramatically in the future. That is, the future of the city is largely dependent upon how much technology can affect the dynamics of costs and benefits of living and doing business in cities.

The following sections present opposing views for the future of the city. A negative view predicts that new information and communication technologies will lead to continuous decline of the city. On the other hand, a positive view predicts that the tacit nature of new knowledge will still require face-to-face human interactions and, therefore, even strengthen the status of the city in the future knowledge economy.

Demise of the City

The development of transportation and information technologies and subsequent globalization has revolutionized the way individuals and businesses behave. Technological revolutions such as the development of dust-free road surfaces based on asphalt and the mass production of automobile by Ford as well as socio-economic revolutions such as increased household income (eg., $5 minimum wage scheme by Ford) led to the advent of an automobile society. Thanks to a well-developed road system and reliable automobiles that average workers could afford, many city residents moved to suburban areas for a better, family-oriented environment, leaving central cities virtually empty at night. Such a suburbanization process has continued until today.

The dramatic advancement of information technology (IT) has expedited this trend even further. Many futurists argue that a virtually connected "electronic cottage" will eventually eliminate the need for downtown offices in the central city (Castells, 1989; Negroponte, 1995). Some suburban areas, in fact, have started developing their own employment centers, becoming more like self-reliant, independent cities. People in the suburbs go to nearby shopping malls, movie theaters, and office parks for shopping, entertainment, and work, which means less and less travel to the central city. Such a phenomenon, which is labeled as "the edge city" by Garreau (1988), reflects how transportation and information technologies have affected the spatial structure of the city. Recently, people have started moving even further out to places often called the exurb. What this phenomenon does to urban spatial structure is intriguing. If this trend continues, we will find a more and more dispersed geographic distribution of people and economic activities. Therefore, the development patterns will be dominated by dispersed clumps of small to medium cities rather than mega cities.

Consider the case of businesses. Firms no longer have to locate near parts suppliers or consumers. They can go anyplace where the production cost is the lowest. According to this view, the city will lose its dominant position as a center for employment, innovation, and new ideas. Thanks to the diffusion of information technology, more and more people living in remote areas can now access cutting-edge information in various fields. For instance, providing access to many professional and academic books and journals does not mean a multi-million dollar world-class library any longer. A virtual library and Internet access can offer the same level of richness in service as the Library of Congress.

In addition, information technology helps innovations occur anywhere. India, China, and many eastern European countries are becoming hotbeds for new IT ventures. Linux, a formidable foe of Windows, was developed by a small group of programmers in Finland. Remember the "I love you" virus that shocked the entire planet (the wired portion, of course)? The bug was created and spread by a student in Manila, Philippines. In other words, innovations are becoming more and more democratized.

A recent trend of manufacturing job shifts epitomizes the implications of information technology for firm locations. Several decades ago, the design of a new product and its production needed to be done in close geographic proximity. Designers and engineers constantly interacted to exchange ideas and improve the quality of products. Under such environment, a major city was a reasonable location choice. Today, thanks to a sophisticated IT environment, product design can be done in Italy while actual production lines are located in China. The production activities are now being moved to any location wherever labor costs are low. In other words, the development of information technology has substantially reduced the comparative advantage of locating in major cities.

If firms can get the same information benefit in rural areas or even in the Third World countries as they have in New York or Boston, why would they want to locate in major U.S. cities where they have to a pay higher price for doing business? In sum, technology serves as a strong centrifugal force that drives people and businesses out of the city. If this trend continues, that can mean the end of the modern concept of the city.

City Reloaded

On the other hand, the future of the city could unfold in an opposite direction. To understand the issue from another perspective, we first need to distinguish two different types of knowledge: codified versus tacit. Codified knowledge refers to standardized information that becomes almost like a commodity. Therefore, it can be easily understood and communicated over a distance via information and communication technologies (eg., telephone, fax, e-mail, and the Internet). Well-defined production processes of standard consumer electronics (eg., TV, VCR) are examples of codified knowledge. Therefore, the production of such goods can occur anyplace. A firm in the U.S. can now operate ten production facilities in ten different countries.

On the other hand, tacit knowledge is poorly defined and therefore is not easily transferable. It is close to heuristics based on experience. Polanyi (1967) encapsulates the essence of tacit knowledge as "we know more than we can tell." For instance, the knowledge and experience of a star scientist is not something that can be easily transferred. What he or she knows is difficult to put into words to transfer to other people. Therefore, research activities that draw heavily on tacit expert knowledge mostly occur in places where the smartest and the brightest minds are concentrated. The transfer of tacit knowledge usually requires close relationships among individuals based on face-to-face interactions.

Patent statistics published by the U.S. Patent and Trade Office (USPTO) offers circumstantial evidence for this. Over ninety percent of all U.S. patents originate in metropolitan areas, which suggests knowledge intensive innovation activities (note that this is likely to rely on tacit knowledge) are geographically concentrated in cities. In addition, corporate headquarters, whose primary function is learning and disseminating new information and knowledge, are increasingly concentrated in major metropolitan areas where such learning can take place more easily (Horst & Koropeckyi, 2000). In 2000, the top twenty percent of all metropolitan areas contain over 92.1 percent of all publicly-traded company headquarters (Census Bureau, 2000).

The discussion thus far indicates that what type of knowledge dominates the new economy in the future has important implications for the city. Since codified knowledge can be easily transferred over a distance, economic activities based on codified knowledge can locate anywhere. For instance, low-skilled manufacturing, call centers, backdoor offices, which rely on routine and standardized knowledge, are often located in rural areas or even in overseas where the cost of doing business can be minimized. On the other hand, economic activities based on tacit knowledge, such as research and development, strategic planning, and the management of global corporations, need to locate in proximity to other important factors since the proximity and face-to-face interactions can create irreplaceable value.

The characteristics of the new economy that is based on sophisticated knowledge and knowledge creation activities imply that tacit knowledge will play an increasingly important role in the future. Glaeser (1998) presents circumstantial evidence for this hypothesis. He found that despite the dramatic advancement of information and communication technology, the number of business travelers has been increasing significantly. He also found that people tend to utilize technology (eg., telephone, fax, e-mail) for initial contacts and meeting arrangements. More important and meaningful interactions occur at face-to-face meetings.

Of course, tacit knowledge only cannot explain such a phenomenon. Human psychology and sociology also play a significant role (i.e., the interconnectivity that chatting rooms in cyberspace provides does not fulfill social and psychological needs of human beings in the same way a Starbucks on every single corner of downtown does). However, the complex and therefore tacit nature of cutting-edge modern knowledge is an undeniably important explanatory factor for the need for face-to-face interactions in our modern economy.

In sum, the tacit nature of modern knowledge serves as a strong centripetal force that attracts people and businesses to the city. If our future relies on such knowledge, then the city, which is an ideal environment for interpersonal contact that generates new ideas and cutting-edge knowledge, will flourish no matter how advanced technology becomes.

Bifurcation of the Future

The discussion thus far presents two very different scenarios for the future of the city. Which scenario, then, is more likely to occur? The future of the city can unfold in either way. It depends on how cities will respond to the development of information technology and the new economy. Therefore, some cities will face the gloomy scenario and continuously decline whereas some cities will survive the new economy and continuously prosper.

To understand how the future of the city can unfold in opposite directions, one needs to understand interactions between information technology and the tacitness of knowledge. The tacitness of knowledge is not a dichotomous concept (i.e., there is no clear-cut threshold that divides tacit versus codified knowledge). Therefore, codified versus tacit concepts need to be understood as a continuum. Information technology can affect the tacit nature of knowledge and therefore play a crucial role in determining the future of the city. In particular, the development of information technology has affected the degree of tacitness of knowledge.

The tacitness of knowledge may decrease as the means of communication via information technology improves. Highly sophisticated information and communication technology helps communications of complicated knowledge and expedites the rate at which new knowledge is standardized. Although still far from perfect, modern technology can create an environment that resembles face-to-face interactions (eg., video conference). Such a technological trend has made possible the communication of some tacit knowledge over a distance, which would have been out of the question a decade ago.

The rising trend of offshore production is evidence of information technology's influence on the characteristics of knowledge, economic activities, and subsequent changes in urban spatial structure. If a city is on the frontier of producing new knowledge that is tacit and requires face-to-face interactions for transfer, firms as well as many talented minds will be attracted to the city to learn more about new knowledge and to take advantage of potential market opportunities. As long as a city continues generating new ideas and knowledge, it will remain a vibrant and attractive place for many young talents, where significant learning can take place. We have observed such phenomena in innovative cities such as Boston, San Jose, and San Francisco. New knowledge created in these cities (eg., transistor, recombinant DNA technique) has served as fuel for further growth based on information and biomedical technologies.

But what if a city somehow loses its momentum and stops producing new knowledge? Knowledge created yesterday becomes standardized as people understand more and more about it. In other words, the tacitness of new knowledge decreases significantly over time, and such knowledge eventually becomes a standard commodity that can be easily transferred and implemented over a distance. This process only accelerates because of advanced information and communication technology. Therefore, a city living on yesterday's knowledge can face serious challenges in the future.

As knowledge becomes routinized, more and more economic activities will move to places where the cost can be minimized. Firms do not have any incentive to maintain production facilities in large cities in the U.S. or Europe when the same products can be produced in China and India at a fraction of the cost. Many cities in the Midwest are examples of troubled cities living on yesterday's knowledge. A few of them, biomedical technology in Cleveland and high performance building technology in Pittsburgh in particular, show some signs of rebound based on emerging disruptive new technologies. However, most of them failed to transform their old knowledge structure and, therefore, have experienced significant declines. Without continuous production of new knowledge, a negative feedback mechanism of decline will occur, and a gloomy future scenario is likely to come true.

In sum, the future of the city could unfold in either way. Some cities that continuously reinvent themselves and create new knowledge will maintain their status and grow. On the other hand, cities that fail to keep up with such a trend in the new economy will face a significant centrifugal pressure as they lose their momentum and more and more economic activities move to areas of lower costs. In the end, the future of the city is in the hands of people who constantly seek and create new ideas and innovations. As Richard Florida (2002) elegantly put it, the creative class is the focal point of the city that will determine its fate in the future. In the new economy, therefore, the collaboration among industry, government, and civic leaders to create environment that attracts the creative class and develops as well as nurtures new ideas/knowledge is more important than ever before.

Name _____

The City Faces Its Future (Future Studies)

18-1. Describe the impact of technology on your central city and its surrounding suburbs.

18-2. Summarize the two schools of thought about technology and the future of the central city.

18-3. Which direction do you believe your city is taking and how will your city look in the future?

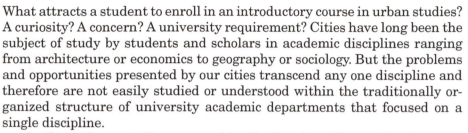

EPILOGUE

What attracts a student to enroll in an introductory course in urban studies? A curiosity? A concern? A university requirement? Cities have long been the subject of study by students and scholars in academic disciplines ranging from architecture or economics to geography or sociology. But the problems and opportunities presented by our cities transcend any one discipline and therefore are not easily studied or understood within the traditionally organized structure of university academic departments that focused on a single discipline.

In the mid-twentieth century, John Bodine, President of the Academy of Natural Sciences, told an academic audience: "Urban problems are so interwoven, so interdependent, that scholars can only consider them together; in other words, it has been found necessary to consider the urban situation as a system in its own right, inescapably transcending the traditional disciplines" (Bodine, 1965).

Scholars interested in cities recognized early in the 1960s that an interdisciplinary approach was necessary for a comprehensive study of urban areas. In the 1970s colleges and universities began to bring together faculty from many disciplines to explore the spatial and functional interrelationships characterizing urban society. These programs joined together nationally to form what is now the Urban Affairs Association (UAA).

The UAA is a forum for scholars interested in urban studies and provides leadership in fostering urban affairs as a professional and academic field.

During this same period of the 1960s, a new group of institutions emerged nationwide with a special mission to serve the urban communities where they were located. A major goal for these new urban universities was providing access to higher education for a large number of students who were place-bound. Frequently, the non-traditional urban studies programs developed within these universities. Students of such programs, then and now, gain hands-on experience applying what they learn in the classroom to serving the community through class projects and internships with community organizations. The city, then, becomes a *laboratory* for weaving together and applying what the student has learned in the classroom.

Since the inception of urban studies programs, thousands of students have graduated with either a degree or a specialization in urban studies at the undergraduate and graduate levels. These graduates are now working in a wide variety of occupations in the public, private, and non-profit sectors. Whether working for a local government, a neighborhood organization, or a bank, alumni of urban studies programs bring to their task an ability to integrate concepts, theories, and understandings gained from a variety of disciplines and perspectives, such as those reflected in this text. As a result they are uniquely prepared to bring about change and improvement of the urban condition. Therefore whatever your motivation in reading this text, for those of you interested in pursuing this fascinating field of urban studies and potentially developing a related career, many opportunities exist for addressing the challenges confronting cities in our country and throughout the world.

David C. Sweet
President Emeritus
Youngstown State University

REFERENCES

Agar, M. (1994). *Language shock.* New York: William Morrow.

Alderfer, C. P. (1972). *Existence, relatedness, and growth.* New York: The Free Press.

Alexander, E. R. (1992). *Approaches to planning: Introducing current planning theories, concepts, and issues.* (2nd ed). Langhorne, PA: Gordon and Breach.

Allott, R. W. (1992). Behavior of urban dust contaminated by Chernobyl fallout: Environmental half-lives and transfer coefficients. *Environment and Technology, 26* (11), 2142–2147.

American Economic Development Council (AEDC) (1984). *Economic development today.* Chicago: AEDC.

American Public Works Association (1990). *Public works today: A profile of local service organizations and managers.* Chicago: American Public Works Association.

Anderson, C. A., Berkowitz, L., Donnerstein, E., Huesman, I. R., Johnson, J. D., Linz, D., Malamuch, M. N., & Wartella, E. (2003). The influence of media violence on youth, *Psychological Science in the Public Interest, 4,* 81–110.

Anderson, E. (1978). *A place on the corner: A study of black street corner men.* Chicago: University of Chicago Press.

Anderson, E. (1999). *The code of the street: Decency, violence, and the moral life of the inner city.* New York: W.W. Norton.

Anderson, E. (2004). *Streetwise: Race, class, and change in an urban community.* Chicago: University of Chicago Press.

Anderson, Wayne F., David S. Arnold & (Eds.) (1983). *The Effective Local Government Manager.* Washington, DC: International City/County Management Association.

Arrandale, T. (1992). Environmentalism and racism. *Governing, 6,* (2), 222–233.

Asch, S. E. (1957). An experimental investigation of group influence. In *Symposium on preventive and social psychiatry,* pp. 15–17. Walter Reed Army Institute of Research, Washington, D.C.: U.S. Government Printing Office.

Asch, S. E. (1956). Studies of independence and conformity: I. A minority of one against a unanimous majority. *Psychological Monographs, 70* (9), 70.

Azrin, N. H., Holz, W. C., & Hake, D. F. (1963). Fixed-ratio punishment. *Journal of the Experimental Analysis of Behavior, 6* (2), 141–148.

Azrin, N. H. (1960). Effects of punishment intensity during variable-interval reinforcement. *Journal of the Experimental Analysis of Behavior, 3,* 123–142.

Bandura, A., Ross, D. M., & Ross, S. A. (1963). Imitation of film-mediated aggressive models. *Journal of Abnormal and Social Psychology, 66* (1), 3–11.

Baron, A. (1965). Delayed punishment of a runaway response. *Journal of Comparative and Physiological Psychology, 60* (1), 131–134.

Bartik, T. J. (1991). *Who benefits from state and local economic development policies?* Kalamazoo, MI: W.E. Upjohn Institute for Employment Research.

Baum, A. S. (1994). Crowding. In R. J. Corsini (Ed.), *Encyclopedia of Psychology, 1,* 365.

Beeson, P. (1987). Total factor productivity growth and agglomeration economies in manufacturing, 1959–73. *Journal of Regional Science, 27,* 183–199.

Bendavid-Val, A. (1991). *Regional and local economic analysis for practitioners.* (4th ed.) New York: Praeger.

Berry, B. J. L. (1981). *Comparative urbanization: Divergent paths in the twentieth century.* New York: St. Martin's Press.

Berry, B. J. L. (Ed.). (1976). Urbanization and counter-urbanization, *Urban Affairs Annual Reviews Vol. 11.* Beverly Hills: Sage Publications.

Berry, B. J. (1967). *Geography of market centers and retail distribution.* Englewood, NJ: Prentice-Hall.

Berry, B. J. L, & Garrison, W. (1958). The functional bases of the central place hierarchy. *Economic Geographer,* 34.

Beyers, W. B. (1983). The interregional structure of the U. S. economy. *International Regional Science Review,* 8, 213–231.

Bier, T. E. (1991). Public policy against itself: Investments that help bring Cleveland (and eventually suburbs) down. In A. Schorr (Ed.), *Cleveland development: A dissenting view.* Cleveland: David Press.

Bierhoff, H. W., Klein, R., & Kramp, S. J. (1991). Evidence for the altruistic personality from data on accident research. *Journal of Personality,* 59 (2), 263–280.

Billingsley, A. (1968). *Black families in white America.* Englewood Cliffs, NJ: Prentice-Hall.

Bindoff, S. T. (1958). *Tudor England.* Harmsworth, England: Penguin.

Bingham, R.D., & Kimble, D. (1994). *Industrial composition of edge cities and downtown: The new urban reality.* Paper presented at the annual meeting of the Urban Affairs Association. New Orleans, La.

Bingham, R. D., & Mier, R. (1993). Preface. In R. D. Bingham & R. Mier, (Eds.), *Theories of local economic development: Perspectives from across the disciplines.* Newbury Park: Sage.

Birch, D. L. (1987). *Job creation In America.* New York: The Free Press.

Birch, D. L. (1978). *The job generation process.* Unpublished manuscript. Cambridge, MA: Massachusetts Institute of Technology.

Black, S. L., & Bevan, S. (1992). At the movies with Buss and Durkee: A natural experiment on film violence. *Aggressive Behavior,* 18 (1), 37–45.

Blackwell, J. (1991). *The black community: Diversity and unity.* (3rd ed). New York: Harper-Collins.

Blair, J. P., & Premus, R. (1993). Location theory. In R. D. Bingham, & R. Mier, (Eds.). *Theories of local economic development: Perspectives from across the disciplines.* Newbury Park: Sage.

Bluestone, B., & Harrison, B. (1982). *The deindustrialization of America.* New York: Basic Books.

Bluestone, Barry, Mary Huff Stevenson & Russell Williams (2008). *The Urban Experience: Economics, Society, and Public Policy.* New York: Oxford University Press.

Bonanno, G. A. (2004). Loss, trauma,and human resilience: Have we underestimated the human capacity to thrive after extremely aversive events? *American Psychologist, 59,* 20–28.

Bonnes, M. (1991). Crowding and residential satisfaction in the urban environment: A contextual approach. *Environment and Behavior,* 23 (5), 531–552.

Boorstin, D. (1965). *The American: The national experience.* New York: Random House.

Bott, E. (1957). *Family and social network: Roles, norms, and external relationships in ordinary families.* New York: The Free Press.

Bowen, B. L. (2006). Land Use Regulation of Religious Uses: Constitutional Protections, RLUIPA, and the Zoning Power. Institute of Continuing Legal Education in Georgia, *2006 Zoning Seminar.* Athens: Institute of Continuing Legal Education in Georgia.

Brenke, S. (1992). City networking for CO_2 reduction and institution building: New partners for the earth summit? *Ekistics: The Problems and Science of Human Settlements,* 59, (352–353), 86–92.

Brenner, M. H. (1973). *Mental illness and the economy.* Cambridge, MA: Harvard University Press.

Briscoe, J. (1993). When the cup is half full. *Environment,* 35, (4), 6–15.

Broadbent, G. (1975). Function and symbolism in architecture. In B. Honkman (Ed.), *Responding to social change.* Stroudsburg PA; Dowden, Hutchison & Ross, Inc.

Bodine, J. (1965). *Liberal education for urban responsibility.* Paper presented at the Danforth Foundation Workshop.

Brown, D., Scheflin, A.W., & Whitfield, C. L. (1999). Recovered memories: The current weight of the evidence in science and in the courts. *Journal of Psychiatry and Law, 27,* 5–156.

Brown, L. R. (1994). *State of the world: A Worldwatch Institute Report on progress toward a sustainable society.* New York: W. W. Norton.

Browning, R. P., Marshall, D. R. & Tabb, D. H. (1984). *Protest is not enough.* Berkeley: University of California Press.

Bruestle, A. (1993). East Asia's urban environment. *Environmental Science and Technology,* 27, (12), 2280–2284.

Bruning, N. (1991a). Urban ecology. *Buzzworm: The Environmental Journal,* 3, (1), 18–19.

Bruning, N. (1991b). Urban recycling. *Buzzworm: The Environmental Journal,* 3, (2), 18–19.

Burger, J. M. (1987). Desire for control and conformity to a perceived norm. *Journal of Personality and Social Psychology,* 53 (2), 355–360.

Calhoun, J. B. (1962). Population density and social pathology. *Scientific American,* 2, 139–150.

Calthorpe, Peter (1993). *The Next American Metropolis: Ecology, Community, and the American Dream.* New York: Princeton Architectural Press.

Campbell, T. F. (1966). *Daniel E. Morgan: The good citizen in politics 1879–1949.* Cleveland: Case Western University Press.

Canty, D. (1993). Curitiba mayor describes innovative urban solutions. *Progressive Architecture,* 74 (11), 25–29.

Carmichael, S., & Hamilton, C. (1967). *Black power.* New York: Vintage Books.

Castells, M. (1989). *Informational city.* Williston, VT: Blackwell.

Catlin, R. A. (1993). *Racial politics and urban planning: Gary, Indiana 1980-1989.* Lexington: University Press of Kentucky.

Castle Rock v. Gonzales, 54 5U.S. ___ (2005) (slip op.).

Center for the Study of Social Policy. (1986). In R. Staples (Ed.), *The black family: Essays and studies,* (3rd ed.). Belmont, CA: Wadsworth.

Chakrabarti, A. M., & Halder, A. (1991). *Slum dwellers of Calcutta socio economic profile–1989–1990.* Calcutta: Calcutta Metropolitan Development Authority.

Chandler, Mittie Olion (2006). The City Governs Itself (Political Science). In Roberta Steinbacher and Virginia O. Benson (Eds.), *Introduction to Urban Studies,* (3rd ed.). Dubuque, IA: Kendall/Hunt Publishing Company. 175–192.

Chaves, M. (2000). *The national congregations study.* Database on-line. Available from Hartford Institute for Religious Research.

Chaves, M. (2004). *Congregations in America.* Cambridge: Harvard University Press.

Choate, P. & Walter, S. (1983). *America in ruins: The decaying infrastructure.* Durham, NC: Duke University Press Paperbacks.

Christaller, W. (1966). *Central places in southern Germany.* (Trans). by C. W. Baskin. Englewood Cliffs, NJ: Prentice-Hall, Inc.

Church, R. M. (1969). Response suppression. In B. A. Campbell, & R. M. Church (Eds.), *Punishment and aversive behavior.* New York: Appleton-Century-Crofts.

City of Clinton v. Cedar Rapids and Missouri Railroad Company, 24, Iowa 455,1868.

Claiborne, W. (1994). Cities join rain forests as to world concern. *Plain Dealer,* October 9, 5–J.

Clymer, A. (1986). Poll finds most Americans cling to ideals of farm life. *The New York Times,* February 25.

Cohen, T. (1993). Mega-cities. *Buzzworm: The Environmental Journal,* 5 (4), 20.

Commoner, B. (1990). *Making peace with the planet.* New York: Pantheon Books.

Concrete Works of Colo. v. City and County of Denver, 540 U.S. 1027 (2003).

Costa, F. J., et. al. (1988). *Asian urbanization problems and processes.* Berlin: Gebruder Borntraeger.

Cox, Raymond W. III (2004). The Profession of Local Government Manager: Evolution and Leader Style. In Charldean Newell (Ed.), *The Effective Local Government Manager,* (3rd ed.) Washington, DC: International City/County Management Association. 1–19.

Currier v. Doran, 534 U.S. 1019 (2001).

Darley, J., & Latane, B. (1968). Bystander intervention in emergencies: Diffusion of responsibility. *Journal of Personality and Social Psychology,* 8 (4), 377–383.

Davis, K. (1972). *World urbanization 1950–1970. Vol. II: Analysis of trends, relationships, and development.* Berkeley: Institute for International Studies, University of California.

Demos, E. (1994). Sustainable programs and practices: The continuing Denver commitment. *Nation's Cities Weekly,* 17, (10), 12.

DeShaney v Winnebago County Department of Social Serv. (1989). 489 U.S. 189.

di Leonardo, M. (1984). *The varieties of ethnic experience: Kinship, class, and gender among California Italian Americans.* Ithaca: Cornell University Press.

Dietsch, D. K. (1993). Brown into green. *Architecture: The AIA Journal,* 82, (8), 15.

District of Columbia v. *Heller.* (2008) 554 U.S. 570.

Dombrowski, C. (1987). EPA's next target. *American City and County,* 102, (2), 10.

Dominguez, M. M., & Carton, J. S. (1997). The relationship between self-actualization and parenting style. *Journal of Social Behavior and Personality,* 12, 1093–1100.

Doob, C. B. (2004). *Race, ethnicity, and the American urban mainstream.* New York: Pearson Education, Inc.

Dutt, A. K. (2001). *Global urbanization: Trends, form and density gradients,* Allahabad: Professor R. N. Dubey Foundation, Allahabad University.

Dutt. A. K. & Noble, A. G. (2003). Challenges to Asian urbanization in the 21st century: An introduction. In A. K. Dutt *et. al* (Eds.), *Challenges to Asian urbanization in the 21st century* (pp. 1–18). Dordrecht: Kluwer Academic Publisher.

Dutt, A., & Parai, A. (1996). Singapore: A multi-ethnic city-state. In A. Dutt (Ed.). *Southeast Asia: A ten nation region.* Boston: Kluwer Academic Publishers.

Dutt, A. K. & Pomeroy, G. (2003). Cities of South Asia. In S.D. Brunn, J. F. Williams & D.J. Zeigler (Eds.), *Cities of the world: World regional urban development.* (pp. 331–372). Lanham/NewYork/London: Rowman & Littlefield Publishers.

Dye, Thomas R. (2008). *Understanding Public Policy,* (12th ed.). Upper Saddle River, NJ: Pearson Prentice Hall.

Dye, Thomas R., & Sparrow, Bartholomew H. (2009). *Politics in America,* (8th ed.). New York: Longman.

Dziegielewski, B. (1992). Tapping alternatives: The benefit of managing urban water demands. *Environment,* 34, (9), 6–11.

England, Robert B. (2003). City Managers and Urban Bureaucracy. In John P. Pelissero (Ed.), *Cities, Politics and Policy: A Comparative Analysis.* Washington, DC: Congressional Quarterly Press. 197–216.

Eisinger, P. (1983). Black mayors and the politics of racial economic advancement. In W. C. McReady (Ed.), *Culture, ethnicity, and identity.* New York: Academic.

Engardio, P., Bernstein A., & Kriplani M. (2003). Is your job next, *Business Week,* February 3, 50–60.

Engelbrekt, K. (1992). A Bulgarian city struggles with pollution. *RFE / RL Research Report,* 20, 48–54.

Eron, L. D. (1987). The development of aggressive behavior from the perspective of a developing behaviorism. *American Psychologist,* 42 (5), 435–442.

Farr, Douglas (2012). *Sustainable Urbanism: Urban Design with Nature.* Hoboken, NJ: John Wiley & Sons.

Felbinger, Claire E. (2010). "The City Maintains Itself: Public Works." In Harvey K. Newman (Ed.), *Citizenship, the Community, and Public Service.* Dubuque, IA: Kendall Hunt Publishing Company. 19–31.

Feldman, G. (1994). When women know too much. *New York Times,* October 12.

Feser, E. (2001). A flexible test for agglomeration economies in two US manufacturing industries. *Regional Science and Urban Economics, 31,* 1–19.

Finnegan, R. H. (1989). *The hidden musicians: Music-making in an English town.* Cambridge: Cambridge University Press.

Fischer, C. (1984). *The urban experience.* New York: Harcourt Brace Jovanovich.

Fisher, J. S. (1981). Structural adjustments in the Southern manufacturing sector. *Professional Geographer,* 33, 466–479.

Flanagan, W. G. (1990). *Urban sociology: Images and structure.* Boston: Allyn and Bacon.

Florida, R. (2002). *The rise of the creative class: And how it's transforming work, leisure, community and everyday life*: Basic Books.

Former Cincinnati Ordinance 229–1996 § 1(A), (D).

Former Cleveland Ordinance No. 415–89 (1989)

42 United States Code § 1973 (1970)

Foust, J. B., & DeSouza, A. R. (1978). *The economic landscape: A theoretical introduction.* Columbus, Ohio: Charles E. Merrill Publishing Co.

Fredrickson, H. G. & Johnson, G. A. (2001). The adapted American city: A study of institutional dynamics, *Urban Affairs Review,* 36 (6), 872–884.

Freedman, J. (1979). Theoretical note reconciling apparent differences between the responses of humans and other animals to crowding. *Psychological Review,* 86 (1), 80–85.

Friedman, E. (1991). Bowen theory and therapy. In A.S. Gurman & Kniskern, D. P., (Eds.), *Handbook of family therapy.* (pp. 134–170) New York: Brunner/Mazel.

Friedmann, J. (1973*). Retracking America: A theory of transactive planning.* Garden City, NY: Anchor Press/Doubleday.

Friesema, P. H. (1969). Black control of central cities: The hollow prize. *American Institute of Planners Journal,* 35, 75–79.

Gause, John (1981). Quoted in Fred A. Kramer, *Dynamics of Public Bureaucracy: An Introduction to Public Management,* (2nd ed.). Cambridge, MA.: Winthrop Publishers.

Gallo, I. C., & Matthews, K. A. (2003). Understanding the association between socioeconomic status and physical health: Do negative emotions play a role? *Psychological Bulletin, 129,* 10–31.

Gans, H. (1962). *The urban villagers: Group and class in the life of Italian Americans.* New York: The Free Press.

Gappert, G. (1993). The future of urban environments: Implications for the business community. *Business Horizons,* 36 (6), 70–74.

Garibaldi, A. (1991). Blacks in college. In C. V. Willie, A. M. Garibaldi, & W. L. Reed, *The education of African Americans.* Westport: Auburn.

Garreau, J. (1988). *Edge city: Life on the new frontier.* New York: Doubleday.

Georgia v. Ashcroft, 539 U.S. 461 (2003).

Gilder, G., & Peters, T. (1995). City vs. country. *Forbes ASAP, Feb 27,* 56–61.

Gilleo v. Ladue. (1994). 774 F.Supp. 1564 (E.D. Mo. 1991), *aff'd,* 986 F.2d 1180 (8th Cir. 1993), *aff'd,* 114 S. Ct. 2038.

Gilligan, C. (1982). *In a different voice.* Cambridge, MA: Harvard University Press.

Glaesar, E. L. (1998). Are cities dying, *Journal of Economic Perspectives, 12,* 139–160.

Glaesar, E. L. (1999). Learning in cities, *Journal of Urban Economics, 46,* 254–277.

Glick, P. (1986). Demographic pictures of black families. In H. P. McAdoo (Ed.), *Black families.* Newbury Park, CA: Sage Publications.

Goldfarb, W. (1945). Effects of psychological deprivation in infancy and subsequent stimulation. *American Journal of Psychiatry,* 102, 18–33.

Gomez v. Watsonville. (1988). 863 F.2d 1407 (9th Cir.), *cert. denied,* 489 U.S. 1080 (1989).

Gomillion v. Lightfoot, 364 U.S. 339 (1960)

Goode, J., & Schneider, J.A. (1994). *Reshaping ethnic and racial relations in Philadelphia: Immigration in a divided city.* Philadelphia: Temple University Press.

Gordon, P., & Richardson, H. W. (1997). Are compact cities a desirable planning goal?, *Journal of the American Planning Association, 63,* 95–106.

Graham, F. Jr. (1992). Gambling on water. *Audubon,* 94 (4), 64 -69.

Greater New Orleans Broadcast Ass'n. v. United States, 527 U.S. 173 (1999).

Grove, N. (1987). Air: An atmosphere of uncertainty. *National Geographic,* 17 (1), 502–537.

Gutis, P. S. (1987) The end begins for trash no one wanted. *New York Times,* Sept. 2, B1.

Haider, D. (1989). Economic development: Changing practices in a changing U.S. economy. *Environment and Planning,* 7, 451–469.

Hannerz, U. (1980). *Exploring the city: Inquiries toward an urban anthropology.* New York: Columbia University Press.

Hansell, William H. (2004). Leading a Manager's Life. In Charldean Newell (Ed.), *The Effective Government Manager,* (3rd ed.). Washington, DC: International City/County Management Association. 209–230.

Hansen, N. (1979). The new international division of labor and manufacturing decentralization in the United States. *Review of Regional Studies,* 9, 1–11.

Hardin, G. (1968). The tragedy of the commons. *Science* 162, 1243

Harlow, H. F. (1958). The nature of love. *American Psychologist,* 13, 673–685.

Harrigan, J. (1991). *Politics and policy in states and communities.* New York: Harper Collins.

Harrigan, J. (1993). *Political change in the metropolis.* Glenview: Scott, Foresman.

Harrigan, J. & Vogel, R. (2000). *Political change in the metropolis.* New York: Longman.

Harrison, B. (1994). The myth of small firms as job generators. *Economic Development Quarterly,* 8 (7), 3–18.

Hartman, C. (1974). *Yerba Buena: Land grab and community resistance in San Francisco.* Berkeley: Earl Warren Legal Institute, University of California at Berkeley.

Harvey, L. D. (1993). Tackling urban CO_2 emissions in Toronto. *Environment,* 35 (7), 16–20.

Hasen, A. D. (1994). The quest for an advanced regional air quality model. *Environmental Science and Technology,* 28 (2), 70A–77A.

Haurwitz, R. K. M. (1992). Soothing the city soul. *Buzzworm: The Environmental Journal,* 4 (5), 18–19.

Hauser, P. M., (Ed.). (1957). *Urbanization in Asia and the far east.* Calcutta: UNESCO.

Healy, P. (1993). European planning systems: Diversity and convergence. *Urban Studies,* 30, 701–720.

Henderson, V. (1999). The effects of urban concentration of economic growth. *NBER Working Paper 7503.*

Heneggeler, J. (1993). Turf battles. *Agricultural Engineering,* 74 (2), 12–14.

Herbst, K. (1992). Brazil's model city: Is Curitiba too good to be true? *Planning,* September, 24–27.

Hellman, L. (1988*). Architecture for beginners.* New York: Writers and Readers Publishing.

Hill, R. (1993). *Research on the African-American family: A holistic perspective.* Westport, Conn: Auburn.

Hiss, T. (1992). On the sunny side of the street. *Amicus Journal,* 14 (2), 12–17.

Hoover, E. M., & Vernon, R. (1959). *Anatomy of a metropolis.* Cambridge: Harvard University Press.

Horner, L. L. (1994). *Black Americans: A statistical sourcebook.* Palo Alto, CA: Information Publications.

Horner, L. L. (2002). *Black Americans: A Statistical Sourcebook.* Palo Alto, CA: Information Publications.

Horst, T., & Koropeckyi, S. (2000). Headquarters effect. *Regional Financial Review, Feb,* 16–29.

Horton, C. P., & Smith, J. C. (Eds.). (1990). *Statistical record of black America.* Detroit: Gale Research, Inc.

Hoyt, H. (1939). *The Structure and growth of residential neighborhoods.* Washington, D.C.: Federal Housing Administration.

Huesmann, L. R., & Eron, L. D. (1986). The development of aggression in American children as a consequence of television viewing. In L. R. Huesmann, & L. D. Eron (Eds.), *Television and the aggressive child: A cross-national comparison.* Hillsdale, NJ: Erlbaum.

Iacobucci, D., & McGill, A. L. (1990). Analysis of attribution data: Theory testing and effects estimation. *Journal of Personality and Social Psychology, 59,* 426–441.

International City Management Association. (1988). *The municipal year book 1988.* Washington, D.C.

International City Management Association. (1993). *The municipal year book 1993.* Washington, D. C.

International City/County Management Association. (2005). *The municipal year book 2005* Washington, D. C.

International City Management Association. (2003). *The Municipal Year Book 2003.* Washington, DC.

International City Management Association. (2010). *The Municipal Year Book 2010.* Washington, DC.

Jacobs, Allen B. (2011). *The Good City: Reflections and Imaginations.* New York: Routledge and Co. Publishers.

Jacobs, Allen B., & Appleyard, Donald. (1987). Towards an Urban Design Manifesto. In Allan Jacobs and Donald Appleyard (Eds.), *The City Reader.* New York: Routledge and Co. Publishers.

Jacobs, J. (1961). *The death and life of great American cities.* New York: Vintage.

Jaffe, A., & Trajtenberg, M. (1993). Geographic localization of knowledge spillovers as evidenced by patent citations. *Quarterly Journal of Economics, 108,* 557–598.

Jencks, C. (1971). *Architecture 2000.* New York: Praeger.

Johnson, W. C. (1989). *The politics of urban planning.* New York: Paragon House.

Johnson v. City of Cincinnati, (2000) U.S. Dist. LEXIS 19708 (S.D. Ohio 2000), *aff'd* 310 F.3d 484 (2002), *cert. denied,* 539 U.S. 915 (2003).

Johnson v. State. (1988). 755 S.W.2d 92 (Tex. Cr. App.*), aff'd sub nom Texas v. Johnson,* 491 U.S. 397 (1989).

Jones, B. (1990). *Neighborhood planning: A guide for citizens and planners.* Chicago: APA Planners Press.

Jones, J. M. (1997). *Prejudice and racism* (2nd ed.). New York: McGraw-Hill.

Jones, T. E. (2003). *The metropolitan chase: Politics and policies in urban America.* Englewood Cliffs: Prentice Hall.

Jorgenson, I. (1992). Urban planning and environmental policy in the context of political and economic changes in Central Europe. *International Journal of Urban and Regional Research,* 16 (4), 648 -650.

Josephson, W. D. (1987). Television violence and children's aggression: Testing the priming, social script, and disinhibition predictions. *Journal of Personality and Social Psychology,* 53 (5), 882–890.

Judge, P. G., & De Waal, F. B. M. (1997). Rhesus monkey behaviour under diverse population densities: Coping with long-term crowding. *Animal Behaviour.* Vol 54(3), 643–662.

Kahneman, D., & Tversky, A. (1973). On the psychology of prediction. *Psychological Review,* 80 (4), 237–251.

Kahneman, D., & Tversky, A. (1972). Subjective probability: A judgment of representativeness. *Cognitive Psychology,* 3 (3), 430–454.

Karnig, A. K. & Welch, S. (1980). *Black representation and urban policy.* Chicago: University of Chicago Press.

Kaufman, S. (1991). Decision making and conflict management processes in local government (1991). In R. Bingham (Ed.), *Managing local government.* New York: Sage.

Kaufman, S., & Smith, J. (1993*). Implementing change in existing locally unwanted land uses (ELULUs): A case study.* Presented at the Conference of the American Collegiate Schools of Planning, October.

Keane, D. (1990). London crawling. *Punch,* 299 (7808), 19

Keller, L. F. (1989). Public administration, city management and the American enlightenment. *International Journal of Public Administration.* 12 (3) 213–249.

Kelley, H. H. (1967). Attribution theory in social psychology. In D. Levine (Ed.), *Nebraska symposium on motivation* (pp. 192–238). Lincoln: University of Nebraska Press.

Kelley, T. M. (2005). Natural resilience and innate mental health. *American Psychologist,* 60, 265.

Kelo v. New London, 545 U.S. ___ (2005) (slip op.).

Kennedy, D. (1991). Permaculture and the sustainable city. *Ekistics: The Problems and Science of Human Settlements,* 58 (348 -349), 210–215.

King, L. J. (1984). *Central place theory.* Newbury Park: Sage.

Kingdon, John W. (1995). *Agendas, Alternatives and Public Policy,* (2nd ed.). New York: Harper Collins Publishers.

Knight, R. V. (1993). Sustainable development—sustainable cities. *International Social Science Journal,* 45 (1), 35–54.

Kobasa, S. C. (1979). Stressful life events, personality, and health: An inquiry into hardiness. *Journal of Personality and Social Psychology,* 37, 1–31.

Kocheisen, C. (1992). EPA says more cities are meeting air quality standards. *Nation's Cities Weekly,* 15 (44), 9.

Kohlberg, L. (1976). Moral stages and moralization: The cognitive-developmental approach. In T. Lickona (Ed.), *Moral development and behavior: Theory, research and social issues.* New York: Holt, Rinehart, Winston.

Koines, A. (1988). A scorecard on the urban environment. *EPA Journal,* 14 (4), 8–10.

Kramer, Fred A. (1981). *Dynamics of Public Bureaucracy: An Introduction* to Public Management, (2nd ed.). Cambridge, MA: Winthrop Publishers.

Kroll, L. (1999). Creative Curitiba—the urban design of Curitiba, Brazil. *Architectural Review.* 205 (1227) 92–95.

Krumholz, N., & Clavel, P. (1994). *Reinventing cities: Equity planners tell their stories.* Philadelphia: Temple University Press.

Krumholz, N., & Forester, J. (1990). *Making equity planning work: Leadership in the public sector.* Philadelphia: Temple University Press.

Kunstler, James Howard (1993). *The Geography of Nowhere.* New York: Simon and Shuster. A Touchstone Book.

Lamphere, L., (Ed.). (1992). *Structuring diversity: ethnographic perspectives on the new immigration.* Chicago: University of Chicago Press.

Laswell, Harold (2011). Quoted in Thomas R. Dye (2008), *Understanding Public Policy,* (12th ed.). Upper Saddle River, NJ: Pearson Prentice Hall.

Lazarus, R.S. (1993). From psychological stress to the emotions: A history of changing outlooks. *Annual Review of Psychology,* 44, 1–21.

Le Corbusier. (1946). *Towards a new architecture.* Fredrick Etchells (trans). London: Architecture Press.

Le Corbusier. (1973). (Trans). *The Athens charter.* New York: Grossman Publishers.

Lee, E. S. (1966). A theory of migration, *Demography,* 3.

Levi-Strauss, C. (1963) *Structural anthropology.* C. Jacobsen & B. Schoepf (trans). New York: Basic Books.

Levy, J. (2000). *Urban American: Processes and problems*: Englewood Cliffs: Prentice Hall

Liebow, E. (1967). *Talley's corner: A study of Negro street corner men.* Boston: Little Brown.

Lincoln, C. & L. Mamiya. (1990). *The black church in the African American experience.* Durham, Duke University Press.

Livezey, L. (2000). *Public religion and urban transformation: Faith in the city.* New York: New York University Press.

Loftus, E. F. (1997). Repressed memory accusations: Devastated families and devastated patients. *Applied Cognitive Psychology, 11,* 25–30.

Loftus, E. F., Klinger, M. R., Smith, K. D., & Fielder, J. (1990). A tale of two questions: Benefits of asking more than one question. *Public Opinion Quarterly,* 54 (3), 330–345.

Loftus, E. F., & Palmer, J. C. (1974). Reconstruction of automobile destruction: An example of the interaction between language and memory. *Journal of Verbal Learning and Verbal Behavior,* 13 (5), 585–589.

Logan, J. & H. Molotch. (1987). *Urban fortunes: The political economy of place.* Berkeley: University of California Press.

Logan, John R., & Molotch, Harvey L. (2008). Quoted in Barry Bluestone, Mary Huff Stevenson, and Russell Williams, *The Urban Experience: Economics, Society, and Public Policy*. New York: Oxford University Press.

London, S. (1991). The person-sensitive environment. *Journal of Environmental Health,* 53 (5), 62.

Long, N. (1958). The local community as an ecology of games. *The American Journal of Sociology.* 64 (3), 251–261.

Lopez, R. S. (1966). The crossroads within the wall. In O. Handlin & J. Burchard (Eds.), *The historians and the city.* Cambridge: Cambridge University Press.

Lore, R. K., & Schultz, L. A. (1993). Control of human aggression. *American Psychologist,* 48 (1), 16–25.

Lynch, K. (1960). *The image of the city.* Boston: MIT Press.

Markusen, A., Hall, P., & Glasmier, A. (1986). *High tech America: The what, how, where, and why of the sunrise industries.* Boston: Allen & Unwin.

Markusen, A. (1985). *Profit cycles, oligopoly and regional development.* Cambridge, MA: The Massachusetts Institute of Technology Press.

Marshall, A. (1890). *Principles of economics.* London: Macmillan.

Marx, K. (1959). Toward the Critique of Hegel's Philosophy of Right. In L. Feuer (Ed.), *Marx and Engels: Basic writings on politics and philosophy.* Garden City, N. Y.: Anchor Books.

Maslow, A. H. (1970). *Motivation and personality* (2nd ed.). New York: Harper & Row.

Mazzoni, G. & Memon, A. (2003). Imagination can create false autobiographical memories. *Psychological Science, 14.* 186–188.

McCarthy, J. (1997). Revitalization of the core city: The case of Detroit. *Cities.* 14, (1) 1–11.

McDonald v. *Chicago.* (2010) 561 U.S. 3025, 3020.

McElroy, J. C. (1991). Attribution theory applied to leadership: Lessons from presidential politics. *Journal of Managerial Issues,* 3 (1), 90–106.

McGee, T. G. (1971). *The urbanization process in the third world: Explorations in search of a theory.* London: Bell and Sons Ltd.

McGee, T. G. (1969). *The southeast Asian city: A social geography of the primate cities of southeast Asia.* New York: Frederick A. Praeger Publishers.

McHarg, Ian L. (1969). *Design with Nature.* Hoboken, NJ: John Wiley & Sons.

McNally, E.J., (2003). *Remembering trauma.* Cambridge: Harvard University Press

Mead, M. (1935). *Sex and temperament in three primitive societies.* New York: William Morrow.

Merriam-Webster collegiate dictionary, Tenth Edition (1996). Springfield, MA: Merriam-Webster, Inc.

Meyers, S. L., & Simms, M. C. (1988). *The economics of race and crime.* New Brunswick, NJ: Transaction Books.

Michigan Constitution (1835).

Milgram, S. (1974). *Obedience to authority.* New York: Harper & Row.

Milgram, S. (1970). The experience of living in cities: A psychological analysis. In F. F. Korten, S. W. Cook, & J. I. Lacey (Eds.), *Psychology and the problems of society.* Washington, D.C.: American Psychological Association. p. 153.

Miller, M. (1993). Can Mexico City clean its air? *International Wildlife,* 23 (2), 12–17.

Miller, N. E. (1960). Learning resistance to pain and fear: Effects of overlearning, exposure, and rewarded exposure in context. *Journal of Experimental Psychology,* 60, 137–145.

Mitchell, W. J. (1995). City of bits. Boston: MIT Press

Moomaw, R. L. (1988). Agglomeration economies: localization or urbanization? *Urban Studies, 25,* 150–161.

Morgan, David R., & England, Robert E. (1999). *Managing Urban America,* (5th ed.). New York: Chatham House.

Moriarty, B. M. (1986). Regional industrial change, industrial restructuring and U.S. industrial policy, *Review of Regional Studies,* 16, 1–10.

Morrison, (1986). The town ecology built. *Maclean's,* 99 (16), 8–10.

Morrison, A. R. (1986). *High tech America: The what, how, where and why of the sunrise industries.* Boston: Allen and Unwin.

Mumford, L. (1961). *The City in history: Its origins,its transformations, and its prospects.* New York: Harcourt Brace Jovanovich.

Nash, J., & Fernandez-Kelly, M., (Eds). (1983). *Women, men and the international division of labor.* Albany: State University of New York.

National Commission for Employment Policy. (1978). *Trade and employment.* Report No. 30, November.

National Council on Public Works Improvement (1988). *Fragile foundations: A report on America's public works.* Washington, D. C.: U. S. Government Printing Office.

Negroponte, N. (1995). *Being digital.* New York: Alfred A. Knopf.

Nelson, A. C. (1993). Theories of regional development. In R. D. Bingham, & R. Mier, (Eds.). *Theories of local economic development: Perspectives from across the disciplines.* Newbury Park: Sage.

Neumark, Gerald M. "Public Administration and Politics: A Culture Clash." (Retrieved June 23, 2011). http://digitalarchive.gsu.edu/pmap_facpubs/1/.

Neumark, Gerald M. (2010). Citizenship in the Federal System. In Harvey K. Newman (Ed.), *Citizenship, the Community, and Public Service.* Dubuque, IA: Kendall Hunt Publishing Company. 9–18.

Newman, H. (1994). Black clergy and urban regimes: The role of Atlanta's concerned black clergy. *Journal of Urban Affairs,* 16 (1), 23–33.

Newman, H. (1991). God and the growth machine. *Review of Religious Research.* 32 (3), 237–243.

Newman, H. (1977). *The vision of order: White protestant Christianity in Atlanta, 1865–1906.* PhD dissertation. Emory University.

Newman, Harvey K. (2010). Citizenship in the Local Community. In Harvey K. Newman (Ed.), *Citizenship, the Community, and Public Service.* Dubuque, IA: Kendall Hunt Publishing Company. 1–7.

NJ Stat. Ann. § 13:1I-10 (West Supp. 1978)

Norberg-Shultz, C. (1975). *Meaning in western architecture.* New York: Rizzoli.

Northouse, Peter G. (2007). *Leadership: Theory and Practice,* (4th ed.). Thousand Oaks, CA: Sage Publications.

Norton, R. D., & Rees, J. (1979). The product cycle and the spatial decentralization of American manufacturing, *Regional Studies,* 13, 141–151.

Ohio Constitution (1802)

Olpadwala, (1992). The sustainability of privilege: Reflections on the environment, the third world city, and poverty. *World Development,* 20 (4), 627–640.

Opheim, T. (1993). Fire on the Cuyahoga. *EPA Journal,* 19 (2), 44.

Ostrom, V. & Ostrom, E. (1977). Public goods and public choices. In E. S. Savas (Ed.), *Alternatives for providing public services* (pp 7–14). Boulder, CO: Westview Press.

Palen, J. J. (1992). *The urban world.* New York: McGraw-Hill.

Parai, A. & Dutt A. K. (1994). Perspectives on Asian urbanization: An east-west comparison. In A. K. Dutt *et. al* (Eds.), *The Asian city: Processes of development, characteristics and planning.* (pp. 369–92). Dordrecht: Kluwer Academic Publishers.

Park, R. E., Burgess, E., & McKenzie, R. D., (Eds.). (1925). *The city,* Chicago: University of Chicago Press.

Pearce, F. (1992). Back to the days of deadly smog. *New Scientist,* 136, (1850), 24–28.

Pelissero, John. (2003). The Political Environment of Cities in the Twenty-First Century. In John P. Pelissero (Ed.), *Cities, Politics, and Policy: A Comparative Analysis.* Washington, DC: Congressional Quarterly Press. 1–34.

Penn Central Transp. Co. v. New York. (1975). 377 N.Y.S.2d 20 (N.Y.A.D.), *aff'd,* 366 N.E.2d 1271 (N.Y. 1977), *aff'd,* 438 U.S. 104 (1978).

Perry, Clarence Arthur (1929). "The Neighborhood Unit," Monograph One. Vol. 7, Regional Survey of New York and Its Environs, Neighborhood and Community Planning. New York: New York Regional Plan, 1929.

Peterson, D. J. (1993). Chelyabinsk: Environmental affairs in a Russian city. *Environmental Science and Technology,* 27 (4), 596 -600.

Pevsner, N. (1968) The sources of modern architecture and design. New York: F.A. Praeger.

Philadelphia v. New Jersey. (1978). 437 U.S. 617.

Phillips, E. B. & LeGates, R. T. (1981). *City lights.* New York: Oxford University Press.

Phillips, E. Barbara (2010). *City Lights: Urban-Suburban Life in the Global Society,* (3rd ed.). New York: Oxford University Press.

Pirenne, Henri. (1937). Trans. by I. E. Clegg. *Economic and social history of Medieval Europe.* New York: Harcourt Brace.

Polanyi, M. (1967). *The tacit dimension.* New York: Doubleday.

Pollitt, K. (1994). *Personable creatures.* New York: Knopf

Porter, M. E. (1990). *The competitve advantage of nations.* New York: The Free Press.

Portes, A., & Rumbaut, R. (1990). *Immigrant America: A portrait.* Berkeley: University of California Press.

Potter, R. B. (1985). *Urbanization and planning in the third world.* New York: St. Martin's Press.

Press, C. & VerBurg, K. (1991). *State and local governments in a dynamic federal system.* New York: Harper Collins.

Price, W. F., & Crapo, R. H. (2002). *Cross-cultural perspectives.* Belmont: Wadsworth

Raboteau, A J. (1978). *Slave religion: The "invisible institution" in the antebellum south.* New York: Oxford University Press.

Rapoport, A. (1979). Cultural origins of architecture. In J. C. Synder & A. J. Catanese (Eds), *Introduction to architecture.* New York: McGraw-Hill.

Rapoport, A. (1969). *House form and culture.* Englewood Cliffs, NJ: Prentice Hall

Rauch, J. (1993). Productivity gains from geographic concentration of human capital: Evidence from the cities, *Journal of Urban Economics, 34,* 3–33.

Reed, A., Jr. (1986). *The Jessie Jackson phenomenon: The crisis of purpose in Afro-American politics.* New Haven: Yale University Press.

Reed, W. (1993), (Ed.) *African-Americans: Essential perspectives.* New York: Auburn.

Rees, J. (1979). Technological change and regional shifts in American manufacturing, *Professional Geographer,* 53, 45–59.

Richmond v Croson Co. (1989). 488 U.S. 469.

Robbins, Stephen P. (1980). *The Administrative Process,* (2nd ed.). Englewood Cliffs, NJ: Prentice-Hall.

Rosenbloom, D. (1998). *Public administration: Understanding management, politics and law in the public sector.* (4th ed). New York: McGraw-Hill

Rosenfeld, S. A., Bergman, E. M., & Rubin, S. (1985). *After the factories: Changing employment patterns in the rural south.* Research Triangle Park: Southern Growth Policies Board.

Ross, B.H., Levine, M. A. & Stedman, M. S. (1991). Urban politics. Itasca, IL: F.E. Peacock.

Rossi, P. (1955). *Why families move.* Glencoe, IL: The Free Press.

Rusk, D. (1993). *Cities without suburbs.* Washington, D.C.: Woodrow Wilson Center Press

Roth, L. (1993). *Understanding architecture.* New York: Haper Collins.

Rutman, D. B. (1982). Boston: A citty upon a hill. In A. B. Callow (Ed.), *American urban history: An interpretive reader with commentaries.* (3rd edition). New York: Oxford University Press.

Sandburg, C. (1916). *Chicago poems 1916.* New York: Holt.

Sanders, I. T. (1958). *The community: An introduction to a social system.* New York: Ronald Press Co.

Savas, E. S. (1987). *Privatization: The key to better government.* Chatham, NJ: Chatham House.

Savas, E. S. (1982). *Privatizing the public sector: How to shrink government.* Chatham, NJ: Chatham House.

Saxenian, A. (1994). *Regional advantage: Culture and competition in Silicon Valley and Route 128.* Cambridge, MA: Harvard University Press.

Seitz, J. (1991). Urban air quality: The strategy. *EPA Journal,* 17 (1), 27 -29.

Selye, H. (1974). *Stress without distress.* Philadelphia: Lippincott.

Sepulveda, L. (1993). High hopes for help from Clinton. *Environmental Action,* 25 (1), 33–35.

Sharp, E. B. (1990). *Urban politics and administration: From service delivery to economic development.* New York: Longman.

Simmel, G. (1950). The metropolis and mental life. In Wolff, K. (trans.). *The sociology of Georg Simmel.* New York: Free Press.

Sjoberg, G. (1960). *The preindustrial city: Past and present.* New York: The Free Press.

Skinner, B. F. (1938). *The behavior of organisms.* New York: Appleton-Century-Crofts.

Smith, J. (1996). Arresting the homeless for sleeping in public: A paradigm for expanding the Robinson Doctrine. *Columbia Journal of Law and Social Problems, Inc.* 29, 293

Sommers, C. H. (2001). *The war against boys.* New York: Simon & Schuster.

Sorauf, F. J. & Beck, P. A. (1988). *Party politics in America.* Glenview, IL: Scott, Foresman.

Spitz, R. A. (1946). Anaclitic depression. *Psychoanalytic Study of the Child,* 2, 313–342.

Staples, R. (1986). The political economy of families. In R. Staples (Ed.), *The black family: Essays and studies.* Belmont, CA: Wadsworth Publishing Co.

Sterngold, J. (1993). Dark days for those who live for night. *The New York Times.* Friday, October 22.

Stivers, Camilla. (2000). *Bureau men, settlement women: Constructing public administration in the progressive era.* Lawrence: Kansas University Press.

Stone, C. (1989). *Regime politics: Governing Atlanta, 1946–1988.* Lawrence: University Press of Kansas.

Stone, Clarence N., Whelan, Robert K. & Murin, William J. (1986). *Urban Policy and Politics in a Bureaucratic Age,* (2nd ed.). Englewood Cliffs, NJ: Prentice Hall.

Stone, D. C. (1974). *Professional education in public works/environmental engineering and administration.* Chicago: American Public Works Association.

Susskind, L. & Cruikshank, J. (1987). *Breaking the impasse.* New York: Basic Books.

Suttles, G. (1968). *The social order of the slum: Ethnicity and territory in the inner city.* Chicago: The University of Chicago Press.

Svarah, James H. (1998, Jan.–Feb.). The Politics-Administration Dichotomy Model as Aberration. *Public Administration Review, 58.* 51–58.

Svarah, James H. (2004). Achieving Effective Community Leadership. In Charldean Newell (Ed.), *The Effective Government Manager,* (3rd ed.). Washington, DC: International City/County Management Association. 21–56.

Swinton, D. (1988). The economic status of blacks: 1987. In J. Dewart (Ed.), *The state of black America.* New York: National Urban League, Inc.

Terminiello v. Chicago. (1949). 337 U.S. 1.

Terry, L. (2003) *Leadership of public bureaucracies: The administrator as conservator.* Armonk: M.E. Sharpe.

Tevesz, M.J. & Savin, S. M. (1987). Lake shores in retreat. *Gamut,* 21, 21–35.

The Declaration of Independence (U.S. 1776).

Thigpen, D. (1993). The playground that became a battleground. *National Wildlife,* 31 (2), 14–17.

Thorndike, E. L. (1932). *The fundamentals of learning.* New York: Teachers College, Columbia University.

Tiger, L. (1999). *The decline of males.* New York: St. Martin's Griffen.

Trank, A. (1991). The healthy city. *Buzzworm: The Environmental Journal,* 3 (5), 18–19.

Tversky, A., & Kahneman, C. (1973). Availability: A heuristic for judging frequency and probability. *Cognitive Psychology,* 5 (2), 207–232.

Ullmann, E. L. (1941). A theory of location for cities. *American Journal of Sociology,* 46,853–864.

Umoren, J. A. (1992). Maslow hierarchy of needs and OMBRA 1987: Toward need satisfaction by nursing home residents. *Educational Gerontology,* 18 (6) p. 657–670.

United Nations. (1986). *Population growth and policies in mega-cities: Seoul.* Population Policy Paper No. 4, Department of International Economic and Social Affairs.

United Nations. (1986). *Population growth and policies in mega-cities: Metro Manila.* Population Policy Paper No. 5, Department of International Economic and Social Affairs.

United Nations. (1987). *Population growth and policies in mega-cities: Dhaka.* Population Policy Paper No. 8, Department of International Economic and Social Affairs.

United Nations. (1986). *Population growth and policies in developing nations. Mega-cities: Calcutta.* Population Policy Paper No. 1, Department of International Economic and Social Affairs.

United Nations. (1986). *Population growth and policies in mega-cities: Bombay.* Population Policy Paper No. 6, Department of International Economic and Social Affairs.

United Nations. (1987). *Population growth and policies in mega-cities: Bangkok.* Population Policy Paper No. 10, Department of International Economic and Social Affairs.

United Nations. (1991). *World urbanization prospects 1990. Estimates and projections of urban and rural populations and of urban agglomerations.* New York: United Nations Publication.

United Nations. (2004) *World urbanization prospects 2003,* New York: United Nations.

U.S. Census Bureau. (2000) *Statistical abstract of the United States: 2000,* Table 1, p. 7

U.S. Environmental Protection Agency (1988*). Report to Congress: Solid waste disposal in the United States.* II, EPA/530–SW-88–011B, October.

United States Constitution (1787)

Vanacour, Martin (2004). Promoting the Community's Future. In Charldean Newell (Ed.), *The Effective Government Manager,* (3rd ed.). Washington, DC: ICMA. 83–112.

Vinter, A. (1986). The role of movement in eliciting early imitations. *Child Development,* 57 (1), 66–71.

Von Hoffman, A. (2003). *House by house, block by block: The rebirth of America's urban neighborhoods.* New York: Oxford University Press.

Von Thunen, J. H. (1978). The isolated state, 1826. In Foust & DeSouza, *The economic landscape: A theoretical introduction.* Columbus, Ohio: Charles E. Merrill Publishing Co.

Wachs, M., & Crawford, M. (1993). *The car and the city: The automobile, the built environment and daily life.* Ann Arbor: University of Michigan Press.

Wade, R. (1964). *Slavery in the cities: The South, 1820–1860.* New York: Oxford University Press.

Waldheim, Charles (Ed.) (2006). *The Landscape Urbanism Reader.* New York: Princeton Architectural Press.

Walker, R. (1941). *The planning function in local government.* Chicago: University of Chicago Press.

Ward v. Rock Against Racism, 491 U.S. 781 (1989).

Ward, J. (1993). Happy unfunded mandate day. *American City & County,* 108 (10), 6.

Warren, R. L. (1972). *The community in action.* Chicago: Rand McNally.

Watson, J. B., & Rayner, R. (1920). Conditional emotional reactions. *Journal of Experimental Psychology, 3*, 1–14.

Weber, A. (1929). *Theory of location of industries.* Trans. by C. J. Friedrich. Chicago: University of Chicago Press.

Weiner, J. (1990). *The next one hundred years: Shaping the fate of our living earth.* New York: Bantam Books.

West, Jonathan P. (2011). The Impact of Management Work Habits on Public Sector Performance: A Study of Local Government Managers. *Public Personnel Management. 40*(1), 63–87.

West Virginia State Bd. of Ed. v. Barnette. (1943). 319 U.S. 624.

Wheat, L. F. (1986). The determinants of 1963–77 regional manufacturing growth: Why the south and west grow, *Journal of Regional Science, 26*, 635–659.

Wheeland, Craig M. (2004). Enhancing the Governing Body's Effectiveness. In Charldean Newell (Ed.), *The Effective Government Manager.* (3rd ed.). Washington, DC: ICMA. 57–82.

White, S. B., & Osterman, J. D. (1991). Is employment growth really coming from small establishments? *Economic Development Quarterly, 5* (3), 241–257.

Whyte, W. F. (1943). *Street corner society.* Chicago: University of Chicago Press.

Whyte, William Hollingsworth (1980). *The Social Life of Small Urban* Spaces, (1st ed.). Naperville, IL: Conservation Foundation.

Wildavsky, Aaron (1964). *The Politics of the Budgetary Process.* Boston: Little, Brown and Company.

Williams, B. (1988). *Upscaling downtown: Stalled gentrification in Washington, D.C.* Ithaca: Cornell University Press.

Williams, F. (1993). River ways. *Buzzworm: The Environmental Journal, 5* (3), 20.

Wilson, S. P. (1910). *Chicago and its cesspools of infamy.* Chicago: Privately printed.

Wilson, W. (1887). The study of administration. *Political Science Quarterly* 2. 197–222.

Wilson, W. J. (1987). *The truly disadvantaged.* Chicago: University of Chicago Press.

Wilson, R. A., & Schulz, D. A. (1978). *Urban sociology.* Englewood Cliffs, NJ.

Winthrop, J. (1960). A modell of Christian charitie. In H. Smith, R. Handy, and L. Loetscher (Eds.), *American Christianity: An historical interpretation with representative documents.* Vol. 1. New York: Charles Scribner's Sons.

Wirth, L. (1938). Urbanism as a way of life. *American Journal of Sociology, 44*, (July).

Wirth, L. (1964). Urbanism as a Way of Life. In A. Reiss, Jr. (Ed.). *Louis Wirth on Cities and Social Life.* Chicago: University of Chicago Press.

Wolfinger, R. E. (1984). Why political machines have not withered away and other revisionist thoughts. In Hahn, H. & Levine, C. H. (Eds). *Readings in urban politics: Past, present and future.* New York: Longman.

Wolf, K. H. (1950). *The sociology of Georg Simmel.* New York: The Free Press.

World Development Report. (1984). Published for The World Bank. Oxford University Press.

Yadav, C. S. (1989). Migration and urbanization in India: A case study of Delhi. In F. J. Costa, et. al., (Eds.), *Urbanization in Asia: Spatial dimensions and policy issues.* Honolulu: University of Hawaii Press.

Zelov, C. (1995). Jaime Lerner: toward a rechargeable city—mayor of Curitiba, Brazil. *Whole Earth Review.* 85. 60.

Zimmerman, H. (1990). To the bitter end. *New Perspectives Quarterly, 7* (3), 56–57.Glenview, IL: Scott, Foresman.

INDEX